Effective Methods of Teaching Business Education

National Business Education Association Yearbook, No. 51

2013

Editor
Beryl C. McEwen
North Carolina A&T State University
Greensboro, NC

Published by

NBEA

National Business Education Association
1914 Association Drive
Reston, VA 20191-1596
(703) 860-8300 • Fax: (703) 620-4483
www.nbea.org

Effective Methods of Teaching Business Education

Copyright © 2013 by the National Business Education Association

National Business Education Association
1914 Association Drive
Reston, VA 20191-1596

ISBN 0-933964-78-1

Any views or recommendations expressed in this book do not necessarily constitute official policy of the National Business Education Association.

The web addresses listed were accurate when this book was written but may have changed since publication.

TABLE OF CONTENTS

PREFACE

Producing an NBEA yearbook is a true labor of love and hope—love for the discipline, love for fellow business educators, and hope for the future of the profession. In addition to the work of the chapter authors and this editor, this 2013 NBEA yearbook is a gift of love from other business educators, who wrote many of the chapters in previous editions of this yearbook. This, of course, is the third edition of the "Methods of Teaching Business Education" first published in 2003, with the second edition in 2008. To acknowledge the contributions of past authors, each chapter that was updated by a new author in 2013 begins with a statement acknowledging the contributions of the previous author. The business education community thanks all authors, both former and current.

This and the previous two yearbooks in the series respond to the constant evolution of the business education discipline. Beginning with the first edition in 2003, they have become a critical part of business teacher education programs throughout the country and are required reading in many business teacher education classrooms. All 20 chapters in the yearbook have been updated and now share the latest research, instructional strategies and tools, as well as current resources to support learning in business education.

Part I, Business Education Perspectives, has two chapters: Chapter 1, The Foundations of Business Education, and Chapter 2, The Business Education Curriculum in the Education System. Chapter 1 traces the history of business education from its origin in the 17th century to the present day, focusing on the research and major legislation that have impacted the discipline. Chapter 2 discusses the foundation of the discipline and highlights the vision and purpose of business education at various educational levels.

Part II, Instructional Concepts for Business Education, has six chapters: Chapter 3, Planning for Instruction; Chapter 4, Evaluating and Assessing Student Performance; Chapter 5, Providing Differentiated Instruction for Diverse Student Needs; Chapter 6, Classroom Management; Chapter 7, Teaching in the Online Classroom; and Chapter 8, Integrating Business Education with Core Academics. These six chapters will take the reader through critical processes related to planning units of instruction and daily lessons; designing the most authentic assessment; considering the diverse needs of students with special needs, including gifted students; designing and managing classrooms for instructional effectiveness and mutual respect; designing instruction that maximizes the uniqueness of the online classroom; and presenting strategies for integrating the teaching academics into business education courses, thereby helping students better understand and value academic content that often seems irrelevant to students' professional and personal goals.

Part III, The Business Education Curriculum: Methods and Resources, has 10 chapters: Chapter 9, Information Technology; Chapter 10, Business Communication; Chapter 11, Accounting; Chapter 12, Business Foundations and Management; Chapter 13, Economics and Personal Finance; Chapter 14, Business Law; Chapter 15, Entrepreneurship; Chapter 16, International Business; Chapter 17, Marketing; and Chapter 18, Work-Based Learning. These chapters present content relevant to specific courses at various levels of the education system, from secondary through graduate education. Many instructional strategies and tools are presented, as are a variety of traditional and technology-based resources.

Part IV, Organizational and Professional Responsibilities, has two chapters: Chapter 19, Sponsoring Student Organizations, and Chapter 20, Investing in Professional Growth. Chapter 19 presents a wealth of information on student organizations and how they serve and develop students in many ways. Chapter 20 ends the 2013 yearbook with a discussion of the benefits of active participation in one or more of the many business education associations.

A total of 35 business educators wrote the 20 chapters of the 2013 NBEA yearbook, giving many hours of time and tremendous talent to the process. The chapters, no doubt, will contribute greatly to preparing the next generation of business educators, while also supporting current new and experienced business teachers at all levels. I am personally grateful to all the chapter authors for their willingness to serve business education and for their commitment to generativity in our discipline.

Special thanks are extended to the group of 25 business educators who served as members of the review board and provided blind review to the authors of each of the chapters. The conscientious work of the reviewers, coupled with the authors' openness to constructive feedback, has resulted in chapters that maintain the very high standards set for the NBEA yearbooks.

I am also indebted to the NBEA Publications Committee, led by Peter Meggison; editor Pamela S. Cubberly; and NBEA Executive Director Janet Treichel, for their advice and assistance along the way. To my two job supervisors during this project, Dean Quiester Craig and Provost Winser Alexander, whose willingness to count this project among my job responsibilities made it possible for me to carve out time to complete it, I offer my thanks. In addition, to my husband Thaddeus, who is always in my corner encouraging and supporting me, you have my continuing love and gratitude for your support during this project.

Beryl C. McEwen, Editor
North Carolina A&T State University
Greensboro, NC

BOARD OF REVIEWERS

Special thanks to the members of the review board, for their time and talent graciously given to review the 20 chapters of the 2013 NBEA Yearbook, *Effective Methods of Teaching Business Education.*

The Foundations of Business Education

Mary Margaret Hosler
University of Wisconsin–Whitewater
Whitewater, WI

Peter Meggison
Massasoit Community College
Brockton, MA

Business education has an interesting story of transformation since the early 1600s when the purpose of the discipline was little more than to teach penmanship and bookkeeping. Through the centuries, business education has expanded its focus, broadened its curriculum offerings, and widened its appeal to a larger population of students. In the 21st century, the business education program prepares students to function as a consumer—the *about* business mission—and to work in a global economy—the *for* business mission. This chapter reviews the evolution of business education from its inception to the present, with emphasis on its chronological development, federal funding and laws, curriculum, and mission.

ELEMENTS OF BUSINESS EDUCATION

Business education is often referred to in the context of vocational education, or career and technical education. A definition of each of these terms will provide an explanation of each concept and how the three are related.

Business Education

Business education or *commercial education* (an earlier term for business education) is a term dating back hundreds of years. Some form of education for commercial endeavors can be found throughout the history of education. Even though a type of shorthand was used in ancient Greece, it was not until the rise of the Roman Empire that it became widespread. Cicero's secretary, Marcus Tullius Tiro, was the author of a shorthand system that lasted until the Middle Ages and was a forerunner of today's cursive systems (Glatte, 1959).

Bookkeeping, too, has an equally long history. Today's double-entry method can be traced back to the Middle Ages. Fra Luca Pacioli, considered the father of accountancy, was the first to present this method, commonly referred to as the Italian method, in 1494 (Andruss, 1943).

In several statements in the past, the Policies Commission for Business and Economic Education (PCBEE) has defined business education. Statement No. 71 (PCBEE, 2002) states that business education is "education *for* and *about* business." Education *about* business means preparing all learners for the various roles they will play as economically literate citizens. Education *for* business means building on these general understandings about business in a way that prepares learners to be employed in a variety of careers.

The National Business Education Association's (NBEA's) *National Standards for Business Education* (NBEA, 2007) defines business education in the following statement: "...education for and about business offers students the opportunity to master the fundamental knowledge and skills needed to succeed in business—wherever in the world it is conducted—and more importantly, an equal opportunity to succeed in life" (p. x).

Vocational Education

The term *vocational education* historically has meant instruction designed to prepare individuals for the world of work. Early vocational education served to provide workers with agricultural, industrial, and homemaking skills. As business education and marketing education were added to the curriculum, they were included in the term "vocational" education because the courses prepared students for the world of work. The 1968 amendments to the Vocational Education Act of 1963 specifically excluded preparation for professional-level jobs (generally requiring a baccalaureate degree) from the definition of federally aided vocational education, except for the training of students and teachers preparing to become teachers in a vocational education program (Roberts, 1971).

Career and Technical Education

After many years of discussion about the word "vocational," the American Vocational Association at its December 1998 convention voted to change its name to the Association for Career and Technical Education or ACTE (Roberts, 1999). ACTE answers the question "What is career and technical education?" as follows: "Today's cutting-edge, rigorous, and relevant career and technical education (CTE) prepares youth and adults for a wide range of high-wage, high-skill, high-demand careers" (ACTE, 2013). Following the adoption of the new name, state associations and student organizations began changing to the new terminology (Roberts, 1999).

Relationship between Business/Vocational/Career and Technical Education, and General Education

Is business education a part of the general education provided to students in school? This question has been debated since the early 20th century with no clearly defined answer. When comprehensive high schools formed in the early 1900s, business education and other vocational offerings became a part of the curriculum. It was assumed that by offering vocational as well as academic subjects under one roof, all students would have access to both types of programs and be able to transfer readily from one to the other as interests or aspirations changed (Shimberg, 1971). When the Cardinal Principles of Education were published in 1918, vocational efficiency was included as one of the priority goals (Barlow, 1974). This would provide the impression that business education had a definite place within the general education program of the student. When general business courses were added to the business education program in the 1930s, the mission of business education took on the "how" of business giving a broader definition to the field.

However, with the advent of Sputnik in 1957, educators began a campaign to fill the high school curriculum with "solid subjects," such as mathematics, science, and foreign languages, so graduates could compete with their Russian counterparts. Vocational educators reported a high degree of separation between academic and vocational subjects (Shimberg, 1971). Business education was viewed as nonacademic, nonessential for graduation and college entrance, based on a narrow view of the field as specific job training (Sapre, 1989).

In an apparent effort to bridge the divide that was occurring between those studies perceived as academic and those as vocational, the newly formed PCBEE spoke to the role of business education in the curriculum. Statement No. 1 (PCBEE, 1961) reads "Business education in American secondary schools consists of both general education and vocational preparation for store and office occupations. These two elements of business education are essential parts of secondary education in America." The commission reiterated its position in Statement No. 47 (PCBEE, 1989) when stating that business education is a critical component in the general education of all students. Even with these commission statements, business education still did not enjoy equal standing with college preparatory subjects (Hall, 1990).

Toward the end of the 20th century and upon entering the 21st century, a trend toward recognizing the importance of business education / career and technical education as an integral part of the general education of students began to unfold. The Carl D. Perkins Vocational and Applied Technology Act of 1990 departed from previous acts in separating career and technical education from the rest of the school by now emphasizing the integration of career and technical education with academic instruction (Hosler, 2003). Daggett and Jaffarian (1990) commented that business education is a broad and diverse discipline that should be a part of the general education of all students. The PCBEE (2005) issued Statement No. 76 to again emphasize the importance of business education in the total school curriculum: "Learning for and about business is inherently academic. Business education provides a rigorous and relevant contextual learning opportunity for core content (English, math, science, and social studies)" (p. 1). Technological advances will require even more connection between academics and career and technical education creating some form of career and technical education to be imbedded in all of education (Reese, 2009).

Business education is forming a closer partnership with academics in the general education of all students, as the educational system works to define the appropriate curriculum for the 21st century. The reality of this partnership is evidenced when, in an interview, U.S. Education Secretary Arne Duncan stressed that K–12 educators have the responsibility to prepare all students to be college- and career-ready, not either/or (Kidwai, 2011).

THE EVOLUTION OF BUSINESS EDUCATION

The following paragraphs detail the history of business education in the United States from colonial times to the present, with an emphasis on federal legislation that provides money to support career and technical education programs.

17th and 18th Centuries

A dual and differentiated system of education existed in the 1600s. The provisions of the English Poor Law of 1601 that were adopted by the colonists encouraged an apprenticeship system by requiring parishes to place the children of poor families with masters to teach them a trade.

From 1620 to 1640, 20,000 persons known as Puritans arrived in New England. These included college educated men. A need was recognized, therefore, to establish a formal system of education for youth. This resulted in the establishment of the Latin grammar schools.

To serve the children of the elite, Boston Latin Grammar School, a college preparatory school for boys, opened in 1635; Harvard, the first college, opened in 1636 (Thompson, 1973). Vocational education became the preparation for learning a trade, whereas students entering the Latin Grammar School went on to a profession (Thompson). It was during this period, however, that a need was seen to provide some structured education for persons involved with rudimentary commercial activities. One of the earliest records of formal training in this area indicates that James Morton taught children to "read, write, and cast accounts" in Plymouth in 1635 (Monroe, 1917). "Casting" was not bookkeeping but more a form of arithmetic with commercial applications. Casting seemed to be a popular course offering in the organized schools that developed in ensuing years.

Private schools operating on a tuition basis offered a curriculum of handwriting, arithmetic, bookkeeping, and English. Governing boards, usually appointed by the churches, dominated public schools. These schools offered commercial courses such as handwriting, arithmetic, and bookkeeping. Only a few admitted girls (Bartholome, 1997).

Even though formal business education was observable during these colonial days, it was through the apprenticeship system that most boys who desired to pursue business careers received their training. As a forerunner of today's cooperative programs, boys were allowed to leave school early and work in stores and offices to gain practical experience in bookkeeping and business practices.

Discussions continued in the 1700s about control over public versus privately run schools. In 1779 Thomas Jefferson stated that, for the public schools to serve the entire population, they must be free from religious or private control; this concept eventually became accepted. In the public schools, which would be established and maintained by the states, vocational education could develop as the states saw fit (Thompson, 1973).

English grammar schools started to develop during the 18th century to cater to the needs of young men who did not wish to enter the professions. Bookkeeping was included in the curriculum of these schools. John Green taught the subject in Boston in 1709; George Brownell in New York City in 1731; and Andrew Lamb in Philadelphia in 1733 (Haynes & Jackson, 1935). Records show that bookkeeping also appeared in Maryland and South Carolina schools shortly after this time. Evening schools that were also established during these years included bookkeeping as a course offering. Penmanship was also offered as it was felt that good handwriting should be demonstrated by those involved with commercial pursuits.

A different type of education was established with the founding of Franklin's Academy in Philadelphia in 1749. The trustees listed four aims of the academy:

(1) To educate boys at home in America
(2) To fit bright youths for government positions
(3) To prepare the poorer type to become teachers
(4) To attract students from the neighboring colonies for the commercial advantage resulting from their patronage of local businesses (Haynes & Jackson, 1935, p. 10).

In the last quarter of the 18th century, a number of commercial textbooks were written, particularly in the area of bookkeeping. They had a significant impact on the development of business education, as they were written by teachers for use in their own classes and later came to be used in other schools as well (Knepper, 1941).

19th Century

Three events in the early 1800s—the Embargo Act, the Non-Intercourse Act, and the War of 1812—closed American markets to foreign manufactured goods. These events led to the promotion of vocational education or training as a national economic policy because a large labor force was needed to produce goods (Thompson, 1973).

Private business schools. The rapid growth of industry in the United States in the early to mid-19th century necessitated the development of an educational enterprise that would more readily meet the needs of businesses than was possible in other forms of education that existed at that time. Private business schools, commonly referred to as "commercial colleges," were established as business ventures to meet this need. Through the rest of the 19th century, they remained as one of the chief, if not the major, agencies for teaching business subjects and the preparation of clerical workers (Meggison, 1989).

The first business college was established in 1824 with instruction in reading, penmanship, arithmetic, algebra, astronomy, history, geography, commercial law, and political economy (Bartholome, 1997).

James A. Bennett was an early leader in the development of private business schools. An author of bookkeeping textbooks, he developed teaching materials that were the forerunners of today's "practice sets" and "simulations." He used facsimile business papers for recording transactions and thought the schools should replicate procedures found in counting houses in student practice work. Two distinguishing features of Bennett's schools were the practice of unlimited attendance and the short-term course, which became very popular as these early schools were composed mostly of adults (Haynes & Jackson, 1935). Bennett also advocated the general education values of business training, a precursor of the consumer education movement a century later.

The first "commercial college" is said to have been opened in Philadelphia in 1834 by R. Montgomery Bartlett, a bookkeeper who saw the need for education in the field. This pioneer of business education was associated with the business college movement for more than half a century. Following his Philadelphia venture, he subsequently opened colleges in Pittsburgh in 1835 and Cincinnati in 1838. At that time, "Bartlett's Commercial College" emphasized bookkeeping and penmanship. Following his death, his son continued to manage the college until 1909 (Reigner, n.d.).

The U.S. Commissioner of Education credited Dolber's Commercial College, which was organized in New York City in 1835, as the first institution in America devoted solely to commercial education. During this period, private business schools grew rapidly; schools were located in other major cities such as Boston, St. Louis, New Orleans, and Providence (Haynes & Jackson, 1935).

These schools filled a very specific need—providing clerical training to young men in order to obtain employment. The establishment of these schools showed that this type of training could more appropriately be accomplished through formal school training rather than through the unstructured apprenticeship system. A common criticism of these schools was that the training was very narrow and that broad business concepts were not being developed. Because the schools were organized around the profit motive, another criticism was that the owners sometimes exploited students by allowing students to enroll who did not have the ability or the background to be successful academically.

Tonne and Nanassy (1970) describe the formation of the first chain of business colleges:

According to R. C. Spencer, writing in 1888, the earliest step toward formal organization was taken about 1850 by R. C. Bacon who founded Bacon's Mercantile Colleges in Cincinnati, Cleveland, and Madison. This unified management lasted only a short time. The Bryant & Stratton chain was started in Cleveland in 1852. By 1865 this chain was composed of 44 schools in 44 cities, all under the same general management. (p. 376)

Among the more notable individual schools of this period were the Eastman Schools, which opened in Rochester, New York, in 1853, and Packard Business College, which opened in New York City in 1858. Shorthand was introduced in the Packard Business College in 1872, followed by typewriting in 1873. Many of the business college chains failed because of the Civil War and subsequent economic depression during the 1860s. However, this trend was reversed in the period immediately following the Civil War, as Tonne and Nanassy (1970) explain:

A great opportunity for the private business school to flourish came during the period of reconstruction following the Civil War. Thousands of young men, mustered out of the armies where they had tasted various experiences, did not care to go back to the farms. They wanted speedy and efficient preparation for some kind of employment in the cities. The opportunities on the farm, moreover, had declined somewhat because of the increased farm efficiency resulting from Civil War manpower shortages. The best opportunities were apparently to be found in bookkeeping and related clerical occupations. This desire for rehabilitation resulted in a rapid growth of private business schools. (p. 377)

First federal aid: the Morrill Act. In the first half of the 1800s, the agricultural sector of the economy demanded vocational and practical education, leading Congress to pass the Morrill Act in 1862 (Gordon, 1999). This act, the first legislation passed by the federal government to support collegiate-level vocational education, established land-grant colleges that offered programs in agriculture, mechanical arts (engineering), and military science.

High schools. The first public high school in the United States was founded in Boston in 1821. Known as the English Classical High School for Boys, it included bookkeeping in the curriculum (Daughtrey, 1965). In 1827 a law was passed in Massachusetts that mandated that every community of 500 or more families establish a high school and include bookkeeping as a subject (Wanous, 1957). During these early years of the development of public high schools, however, only the subjects of bookkeeping, penmanship, grammar, and arithmetic were available for persons preparing for business (Knepper, 1941).

Shorthand, then known as phonography, was offered in the high schools of St. Louis and Philadelphia in 1863 (Lyon, 1922). Isaac Pitman published his shorthand system in 1837, and most of the shorthand systems taught in the 19th century were a derivative of this system. John Robert Gregg brought his shorthand system, first published in England in 1888, to Boston in 1893. Nearly all schools teaching shorthand in the 20th century used the Gregg system (Douglas, Blanford, & Anderson, 1973).

The first practical typewriter was invented by Christopher Latham Sholes and patented in 1868 (Clem, 1955). Combined with shorthand, this provided an impetus for schools to provide training for office occupations and eventually opened the doors to women in securing office positions (Bliven, 1954). Typewriting eventually became the most popular business subject offered in the curriculum and became a graduation requirement in some school systems. Touch typewriting was developed by Frank McGurrin in 1878 (Russon & Wanous, 1973) and within a few years several textbooks employing his method were being marketed (Knepper, 1941).

Other business subjects, including commercial law and business correspondence, were also introduced in various schools during the years following the Civil War.

20th Century

At the turn of the 20th century, private business schools taught typewriting and shorthand, along with the traditional business subjects of the past. As comprehensive high schools began to form at the beginning of the century, "commercial" courses moved into the secondary curriculum. In a survey completed by Lyon, the number of students enrolled in business courses in the public high schools increased from 15,220 in 1893 to 278,275 in 1918—an increase of 1,728.35% (Lyon, 1922). By the 1920s, business education began to experience significant enrollment at the high school level (Hosler, 1971). Much of the training that was formerly available only through private business schools was now being carried on in the high schools and, therefore, resulted in a markedly decreased number of private business schools.

Data show that in terms of actual student enrollment, typewriting, shorthand, and bookkeeping—which had come to be known as "the big three" (Knepper, 1947)—commanded the largest percentage of student enrollment, a trend that would continue for most of the 20th century. Other business courses such as elementary business training, commercial law, economic geography, and office practice started to find their way into high school business programs (Nolan, Hayden, & Malsbary, 1967). Larger high schools were able to develop complete programs of business training with courses sequenced during a three- or four-year period.

A leading business educator of the late 19th century was Edmund J. James of the Wharton School of Commerce of the University of Pennsylvania. As a result of an investigation he conducted of European commercial schools, his influence began to be felt in the development of improved programs and courses (Knepper, 1941). James advocated a four-year commercial curriculum at the high school level. The National Education Association Committee of 1915 advocated two different tracks in the commercial program—one in bookkeeping and the other in stenography (Graham, 1933).

Graham analyzed the evolution of business education in the United States. As a result of her study of early aims and curricula, she identified the following, in rank order, as the 10 major purposes of business education as expressed in 47 published statements from 1825 to 1918:

1. To prepare pupils for specific office positions (as clerks, bookkeepers, stenographers, etc.)
2. To give that form of general education which will prepare young people to enter business pursuits (related knowledge)
3. To adapt business education to social and civic life
4. To prepare pupils for later promotion
5. To provide opportunity for mental discipline
6. To fulfill the general objectives of all secondary education
7. To give business information and skills useful to all pupils in personal, social, and civic life
8. To give practical training to boys and girls who cannot meet the examination requirements of other courses
9. To prepare for university work in commerce
10. To help the United States win commercial supremacy (Graham, 1933, pp. 42–43).

Commercial high schools. The first commercial high school was opened in Washington, DC, in 1890 (Nichols, 1933). Shortly thereafter, others were established in other large cities, and by 1925 there were 20 such schools in the United States. The chief aim of these schools, obviously, was to prepare students for careers in business, even though their programs were not too different from those found in the comprehensive high schools. Sequential programs, covering a three- or four-year period, were found in most of the schools. Specialized options included bookkeeping, secretarial, and merchandising sequences.

Although these high schools did flourish for a short time, they were eventually discontinued in most cities. Critics felt that their objective was too narrow and that youth could be better served by affiliating with a comprehensive high school. The few high schools of commerce that continue to exist today are more comprehensive than was their original intent.

Marketing education. At one time, the concept of training workers for jobs in retail sales did not exist. Lucinda Wyman Prince, a member of the Women's Educational and Industrial Union in Boston, conducted the first comprehensive investigation of retail occupations in 1905. At that time sales clerks' wages were low; the job was looked down on and lacked social approval. As a result of her findings, she concluded that sales clerks could be trained to sell. She proposed to the management of W. A. Filene's ready-to-wear store that a few clerks be sent to her at the union for training in how to sell merchandise. A condition imposed was that the company would increase the wages of each trainee; the lowest increase was 50 cents and the largest was $14 a week (Nichols, 1979). Thus, retail store training was begun.

The first cooperative education program was established in 1914 by a business teacher—the head of the commercial education department at the Fitchburg (Massachusetts) High School arranged with local employers to take his seniors for a few hours a week because he believed that his students would benefit from real office experience (Nichols, 1979).

For some educational leaders, the next move was to get high schools to include retail store training in their business education programs. Boston's superintendent of schools became convinced of the need for retail training and attempted to lead the effort, but the heads of business departments and business teachers were opposed. In their view, stenographic jobs were more attractive than store jobs, for the latter had traditionally been considered unskilled labor. Besides, they reasoned, the retail courses would "drain from the enrollment in the shorthand courses" (Nichols, 1979).

Business teacher education. Little, if any, formal training was available to teachers of business subjects until the beginning of the 20th century. Before that time, teachers of business secured their training through practical office work experience on the job, through private business schools, or through self-instruction. The first collegiate institution to offer a program of preparation for business teachers was Drexel Institute in Philadelphia in 1898 (Graham, 1933). Ten years later, the Salem (Massachusetts) Normal School was credited with becoming the "first public state institution to provide for the professional as well as the technical training of business teachers in an integrated approach" ("Timeline," 2004, p. 34). The school awarded 36 bachelor's degrees in commercial education in 1925 ("Timeline," 2004).

Business teacher education experienced a slow growth during the first 20 years of the 20th century. By 1923 only 37 schools had started courses for training commercial teachers. Some of the outstanding programs were found at the state normal schools at Salem, Massachusetts; Whitewater, Wisconsin; Plattsburg, New York; Trenton, New Jersey; Albany, New York; and Willimantic, Connecticut (Haynes & Jackson, 1935).

During this period, business teacher education programs were also being established in private universities. One of the first to offer such a program was New York

University, which shortly thereafter started to offer graduate course work in business teacher education (Sapre & Gillespie, 1981). As programs started to become somewhat standardized, attempts were made to develop curricula with a balance of requirements in general education, business content, education, and specialized business education methods courses. Most business teacher education programs offered, and continue to offer, various options to prospective business teachers. These options included concentrations in accounting, secretarial skills, computer information systems, basic business, or a combination thereof.

By the mid-1960s more than 400 collegiate institutions were offering programs of business teacher education. During the past 25 years; however, many of these programs have been eliminated due to declining enrollment, lack of administrative support, and pressures from outside accrediting agencies. Currently, 62 programs in colleges and universities throughout the United States offer business teacher education preparation that are affiliated with the National Association for Business Teacher Education or NABTE ("Business education," 2011). However, a number of smaller programs offer similar preparation but are not affiliated with NABTE.

Smith-Hughes Act. An advocacy group called The National Society for Vocational Education formed in 1906 to work for several years to obtain support for vocational education as Congress considered different bills. On February 23, 1917, President Wilson signed into law the Smith-Hughes Act (PL 64-347), which provided federal funding for vocational education in secondary schools. The act specified that, before a state could receive funds, it must establish a responsible state vocational board to develop a state plan on how the federal funds would be used (Thompson, 1973). The boards fostered the notion of vocational education as separate from academic education (Gordon, 1999).

Although the Smith-Hughes Act did not appropriate funds for business education programs, it did provide assistance to states to conduct studies, investigations, and reports. The act created a seven-member Federal Board for Vocational Education with one spot on the board for business education. Because of the work he had done on behalf of business education, Frederick G. Nichols, an administrator for the New York City Schools who later became a professor at Harvard University, was appointed to the board to represent business education. In October 1933, the administrative functions of vocational education were transferred to the U.S. Office of Education, and the federal board continued in an advisory capacity until President Truman abolished it in 1946 (Nichols, 1979). Nichols is considered "the father of business education" because of his pioneering and all-encompassing efforts to raise the status of business education in the American educational system.

Nichols believed that retail selling education should be placed in the business department and that it should be regarded as a type of business education. *Bulletin No. 22* issued by the Federal Board for Vocational Education and written by Nichols, carried this statement: "This Board has decided, after careful investigation, to consider training for retail selling as belonging in the commercial department of vocational training" (Nichols, 1979, p. 141).

Economic education. Economic education in the public schools in the United States started with the Junior Business Training course developed by Nichols in the early 1920s. The emphasis in economic education shifted during the depression years of the 1930s from the junior business model, which enabled those who did not complete the high school program to get a job, to an emphasis on consumer behavior such as budgeting and thrift and then to the study of economic principles in later years (Bahr & Wegforth, 1976).

After writing a series of books on junior business training, in 1936 Nichols authored *Junior Business Training for Economic Living*, designed for the eighth and ninth grades. His memoirs (Nichols, 1979) mention that the text was an attempt to move away from the vocational emphasis of the curriculum toward economics—an introduction to the fundamentals of thrifty living, or making the most of one's resources. As more and more people completed high school, however, the focus of the course changed into a general business course for economic understanding. The course received renewed interest as a result of the consumer movement of the 1960s and, more recently, has been spurred on by the need to educate youth in personal finance concepts. Some states have mandated that such a course be taught as a required course for high school graduation.

International business education. Business education has historically incorporated international business in the curriculum since the late nineteenth century. Economic geography, originally known as commercial geography, was offered in the private business schools and later found its way into both high school and college business curricula. In many schools, economic geography was a required course for students pursuing a business sequence.

Objectives for the courses varied with its grade placement, and a frequent criticism of the course—often due to lack of teacher preparation in the subject matter—was that it was just a presentation of disparate factual information without any relationship to the global economic scene. Weersing reported that teachers of the subject believed its chief objective was for students to gain "a better understanding of the factors controlling commerce and industry" (Weersing, 1929). Nearly half a century later, Daughtrey (1974) found "the development of an understanding of the influence of geographic factors on the economic development of a country and its people and their trade and commerce with other countries" as the key objective of the course (p. 560).

Nationwide, more than 178,000 high school students were enrolled in the course in 1934 (Strong, 1944); the number diminished to 80,000 by 1960 (Tonne, 1961). With the advent of information technology in the latter part of the 20th century, the course lost the prestige it once held and, by default, was eradicated from the curriculum.

During more recent years, however, with the impact of globalization on all aspects of American business endeavors, business educators have found the need for their students to understand how the countries of the world are interconnected, not only economically but also socially and politically. Specific courses in international business are now required in nearly all collegiate-level business programs; bachelor's and master's programs allow for a concentration in this specific area. In addition, most business textbooks (marketing, management, ethics, human resources, communication, information technology, and other areas) contain chapters devoted to globalization and its relationship to these various facets of business activities.

Vocational education legislation, 1929–1946. Following the trend of federal support for business education, the next half century would see the passage of a series of laws that expanded the field even further. The federal government continued to support those vocational areas funded by the Smith-Hughes Law by passing the George-Reed Act of 1929 (PL 70-702), which provided funding for vocational home economics education and vocational agricultural education. The George-Ellzey Act of 1934 (PL 72-245) provided additional funding for vocational education in agriculture, trades and industry, and home economics. The George-Deen Act of 1936 (PL 74-673) authorized about $14 million a year for vocational education to agriculture, home economics, and trade and industrial education (Gordon, 1999). This act was particularly significant because *distributive* (marketing) occupations were recognized for the first time with an authorization of $1.3 million (Thompson, 1973). The law was passed in the middle of the Depression, when much had been written about the inefficiency of the distribution system. In this economic atmosphere, the George-Deen Act was designed as an in-service program for employed individuals, as the act stipulated that students in a supported program must be employed 15 hours a week. Subsequently, some states and schools began requiring their vocational education students to work 15 hours a week to meet the stipulation of the law. The 1963 Vocational Education Act removed this requirement.

The George-Barden Act (PL 79-586) of 1946 doubled the money authorized for annual appropriations for marketing education. Funding was limited to supporting only cooperative education (part-time) programs and evening courses for employed workers (Gordon, 1999).

Vocational Education Act and Amendments. The 1960s and 1970s saw a round of federal legislation that infused new life into business education. In the early 1960s unemployment was high, and vocational education was criticized for failing to respond to manpower trends. At the same time, a concern for persons with special needs began to emerge. In 1961 President Kennedy appointed a panel of consultants to study vocational education. The report resulting from this panel set the stage for the passage of the Vocational Education Act of 1963 and the 1968 amendments.

After the report of the panel of consultants in 1962, President Kennedy sent an education bill to Congress that included one section dealing with vocational education. This bill eventually became the Vocational Education Act of 1963 (PL 88-210).

The bill, signed into law by President Johnson in December 1963, originally read that the act was to maintain, extend, and improve existing programs of vocational education. The original wording specified continued funding for agriculture, home economics, marketing education, and trade and industrial education, but *not* business education.

A committee consisting of Hamden L. Forkner, Russell J. Hosler, and Paul S. Lomax was appointed to attempt to have business education included in the 1963 act. The committee had the support of the U.S. Office of Education, the executive director of the American Vocational Association (now ACTE) and the National Education Association. Business education had not been supported by previous acts mainly because of lobbying by private business schools that did not want their competitors supported by public funds. However, by 1963 private business schools had diminished in numbers. The committee members met with legislators in Washington, DC, including Representative Carl D. Perkins. According to Russell Hosler (1971), they were able to convince Representative Perkins to include the term "business education" within the bill. The act now read: "...those programs which were previously supported and business education for the office."

For a period of time after the passage of the act, a separation developed among those who would define the objectives of business education. Russell Hosler wrote:

There appears to be a tendency on the part of some to identify the objectives of business education with the source of financial support. Some would suggest that "vocational business education" is that which is reimbursed, and if it is not reimbursed it is then "general business education" (1969, p. 243).

The Vocational Education Amendments of 1968 (PL 90-576) helped to address that split by setting forth a list of rigid specifications necessary to qualify for the monies allocated. Consequently, both state and federal governments exerted more direct control over local programs of vocational education than ever before. The first priority of the act was to support vocational education programs designed to assist the "hard to reach and the hard to teach" (Thompson, 1973, p. 79). The 1968 amendments discontinued categorical aids that had started with the Smith-Hughes Act; all areas of vocational education had to compete for the appropriated funds. However, the amendments did insert new categories for funding that included special needs, cooperative education, and innovative programs (Thompson, 1973).

The Vocational Education Amendments of 1976 (PL 94-482) extended and increased funding of the Vocational Education Act of 1963 and the 1968 amendments.

In addition, states were given assistance in overcoming sex discrimination and sex stereotyping in their vocational programs (Gordon, 1999).

In 1983 when the National Commission on Excellence in Education published *A Nation at Risk*, it observed the United States was losing ground in international economic competition and attributed the decline to low standards and poor performance of the American educational system. Perhaps in reaction to the commission's report, the Carl D. Perkins Vocational Education Act of 1984 (PL 98-524) was passed. This act amended the 1963 act and replaced the amendments of 1968 and 1976. It changed the emphasis of federal funding in vocational education from primarily expansion to program improvement, including support for at-risk populations. The Perkins Act emphasized equity in vocational education by providing relevant training for the disadvantaged, reducing sex stereotypes by enrolling students in nontraditional programs, and serving special populations more effectively (National Commission on Secondary Vocational Education, n.d.).

Changes in the business curriculum. The changes fostered by this era of federal educational support were significant. By 1970 the principal subjects taught in the business program continued to be typewriting, bookkeeping, and shorthand, but now general business and business arithmetic would occupy the most popular category alongside these subjects. The enrollment in typewriting and distributive (marketing) training had increased tremendously (Tonne & Nanassy, 1970). The Vocational Education Act and its amendments had successfully fostered increased interest and greater enrollments in business education, particularly in programs preparing students for office occupations.

In the late 1970s and early 1980s, because of technological developments, new terms were coming into the vocabulary of business educators and questions were raised about curriculum design. The business education curriculum changed rapidly, and debates were taking place about typewriters versus computers in the classroom. Questions were being raised about the value of shorthand in the curriculum; bookkeeping had taken on the label of accounting, and typewriting was soon to become keyboarding. A chapter on data processing in the 1980 NBEA Yearbook recommended "…all business students should take at least an introduction to data processing course" (Drum, 1980, p. 53). Topics to include in that introductory course included data processing and the punch card. In the same yearbook, Anderson (1980, p. 60) wrote "considering the demand for secretaries who can take dictation, it is evident that business is still a long way from the total concept of word processing…" Just a few years later, however, Wood wrote, "The microcomputer, with its wide availability and use in the home, business, industry, government, and education, has launched us into the new century…Every discipline and level within education must deal with the advent of the small computer and the power, problems, and promise that it brings to education" (Wood, 1985, p. 72).

The term "office of the future" came into widespread use in the last quarter of the 20th century (Robles, 2009), and business educators responded to this multifaceted concept in a variety of ways. Curriculum offerings were totally revamped at all levels of instruction that included business courses to reflect this "future," which was so rapidly approaching. Professional associations and publishing companies, as well as computer software/hardware vendors and manufacturers, responded to changing needs by offering workshops and programs that prepared teachers with the methods and materials to embrace the "future" that was just around the corner.

Carl D. Perkins Vocational and Applied Technology Act. This act of Congress, signed by President George Bush in 1990 (PL 101-392), amended and extended the Perkins Act of 1984. The new name given to the act indicated Congressional interest in both academic and career and technical skills to prepare for work in a global society. The act carried appropriations of $1.6 billion a year through 1995 for state and local programs that taught the skill competencies necessary to work in a technologically advanced society (Reese & Thompson, 2002). In addition, the legislation initiated support for the concept known as *TechPrep,* the cooperative arrangement that combines academic and technical courses at the secondary and postsecondary levels.

The Secretary's Commission on Achieving Necessary Skills reports. In the 1990s Congress sought additional ways to match the needs of the workforce with the preparation given in the nation's schools. Two reports written by the Secretary's Commission on Achieving Necessary Skills (SCANS) in 1991 and 1992 indicated that an improved match needed to be made between what work requires and what students are taught by changing how instruction is delivered and how students learn.

These reports perhaps led to three pieces of legislation passed by Congress in 1994: (1) The School-to-Work Opportunities Act, (2) Goals 2000: Educate America Act, and (3) the National Skill Standards Act. The connection among all three acts was the development of standards (Kaufmann & Wills, 1999).

The School-to-Work Opportunities Act. The School-to-Work Opportunities Act was intended to address the national skills shortage (Gordon, 1999). It gave grants of more than $1.6 billion to support programs that included internships, career academies, apprenticeships, and job shadowing. The act expired in October 2001.

Goals 2000: Educate America Act. The Goals 2000: Educate America Act established voluntary national education goals to promote coherent, systematic education reform. The objective was to establish standards for student achievement upon completion of grades 4, 8, and 12 (Kaufmann & Wills, 1999).

The National Skill Standards Act. The National Skill Standards Act was Title V of Goals 2000. Standards were to be used for developing curricula and instructional materials at the various educational levels (Kaufmann & Wills, 1999).

Workforce Investment Act. The Workforce Investment Act (PL 105-220) passed in 1998 made one-stop career centers the key vehicles for employment and training programs funded by the Labor Department (Hosler, 2000).

Carl Perkins Amendments. President Clinton signed the 1998 Carl D. Perkins Vocational-Technical Education Act Amendments (PL 105-332), which required states to report student achievement more extensively than in the past and called for career and technical students to meet challenging academic standards. However, the amendments did not define the term "challenging" (Hosler, 2000). This legislation supported improvement of programs to increase both the career and academic preparation of students (Lynch, 2000).

The technology curriculum. By the1990s the curriculum for business education had changed, reflecting the use of computers at all levels of education, advancements in technology, and legislation enacted by Congress. Keyboarding was now offered at the elementary level, thus taking the keyboard out of the exclusive control of the business educator. Terms such as database, desktop publishing, globalization, spreadsheet, telecommunications, and the Internet became part of the curriculum, while online and hybrid courses became new modes of delivery. Business educators had the opportunity to integrate technology with subject matter to provide students with greater breadth and depth of information. Standards for business education were developed by states in reaction to the accountability measures required by various federal laws (Rader, 2005).

Policies Commission for Business and Economic Education. Business education relies on its policy makers to speak as one voice for the profession in defining the mission, objectives, and philosophy of the discipline. The PCBEE is the body that issues statements for business educators to use in defining the role of business education within the total education environment. A brief history of the commission is presented here.

In 1958 the executive board of the United Business Education Association (later, the National Business Education Association) authorized President Dorothy Travis to issue an invitation to the Delta Pi Epsilon president to meet in Washington, DC, to discuss the possible formation of a committee that would issue statements of suggested policies for business education. As a result of their meeting, the Commission for the Advancement of Business and Economic Education was established under the joint sponsorship of the United Business Education Association and Delta Pi Epsilon, with financial responsibility divided equally (Hosler & Hosler, 1992).

When the commission was established in 1959, it became the PCBEE. It later expanded its membership to include representation from the Business Education Division of the Association for Career and Technical Education, formerly known as the American Vocational Association. The purpose of the commission was to identify and define both existing and emerging issues in business and economic education.

Since its inception through 2013, the commission has issued 93 statements. These are often referred to as the "This We Believe" statements, as most begin with those words. When the commission started, it appeared to place business education at the secondary and postsecondary levels, as reflected in statements issued in the early years. Not until 1977 did the commission include elementary schools in describing the mission of business education. Many of the statements speak to the present and future direction of business education; however, the commission takes a position on a diversity of topics; such as curriculum development, career education, professionalism, computer literacy, and the virtual environment. These statements "serve as yardsticks against which legislative leaders, business people, parents, as well as professional educators are able to assess the effectiveness of the components of business education and the total discipline" (PCBEE, 1997, p. vi).

The purposes and goals of business education as promulgated by the PCBEE are endorsed by business educators throughout the country and by many professional groups of business educators meeting to consider specific issues confronting the field (Brower, 1989).

21st Century
Congress exhibited its support of career and technical education programs early in the 21st century through its reauthorization of the Carl D. Perkins Vocational and Technical Education Act of 1998.

Career and Technical Education Improvement Act of 2006. On August 12, 2006, President Bush signed the Carl D. Perkins Career and Technical Education Improvement Act of 2006 (PL 109-270). The new act provided increased focus on the academic achievement of career and technical education students, strengthened the connections between secondary and postsecondary education, and improved state and local accountability (U.S. Department of Education, 2007).

The most notable provisions of the 2006 act were that it used the term "career and technical education," instead of "vocational education," throughout and maintained the TechPrep program as a separate federal funding stream within the legislation. The act authorized the legislation through fiscal year 2012, for a total of six instead of five years (ACTE, 2007); however, it was not included in the 2011 budget, thus eliminating TechPrep a year earlier than was originally planned.

Impact of federal legislation. Although federal legislation has provided funding for career and technical education and specifically business education for many years, the legislation has drawn both criticism and support. Federal funds were intended to stimulate the development of new programs, and gradually state and local funds were to be allocated to support these programs (Thompson, 1973). For example, the 1994 School-to-Work Opportunities Act that ended in 2001 forced states to find ways to continue programs that were started with federal seed money after the federal funding was discontinued.

Without federal support and monies, business education would not have been able to develop the excellent programs that are now available to students at all levels of education.

SUMMARY

The early business education curriculum that provided instruction in shorthand, typewriting, and bookkeeping has evolved into a program that offers a wide range of courses beginning at the elementary level. Business education has become a multilevel discipline that embraces technology and provides preparation for students to work in a global marketplace and to function as intelligent consumers. With the support of federal dollars provided through numerous laws and, in particular, the landmark 1963 Vocational Education Act, business educators have been able to expand the subject matter in the curriculum, resulting in programs that are responsive to current needs. Because of the broad array of offerings, business education can make important contributions to the general education of all students.

Even though further transformations will occur in course content and delivery methods, the dual objectives of providing education for occupational competence and for economic efficiency have always been and will continue to define the parameters of business education.

REFERENCES

Anderson, R. I. (1980). Word processing. In M. H. Johnson (Ed.), *The changing office environment: NBEA 1980 yearbook* (Vol. 18, pp. 55–65). Reston, VA: National Business Education Association.

Andruss, H. A. (1943). *Ways to teach bookkeeping and accounting* (2nd ed.). Cincinnati, OH: South-Western Publishing Company.

Association for Career and Technical Education. (2007). Welcome to ACTE online! What's new. Perkins reauthorization resources & webcast. Retrieved from http://www.acteonline.org

Association for Career and Technical Education. (2013). What is CTE? Retrieved from https://www.acteonline.org/cte/#.UWwMZqKNqE4

Bahr, G., & Wegforth, R. P. (1976). A historical development of an economic emphasis in business education. In R. B. Woolschlager & E. E. Harris (Eds.), *Business education yesterday, today, and tomorrow: NBEA 1976 yearbook* (Vol. 13, pp. 20–40). Reston, VA: National Business Education Association.

Barlow, M. L. (Ed.). (1974). Prologue. In M. L. Barlow (Ed.). *The philosophy for quality vocational education programs* (pp. 13–34). Washington, DC: American Vocational Association.

Bartholome, L. W. (1997). Historical perspectives: Basis for change in business education. In C. P. Brantley & B. J. Davis (Eds.), *The changing dimensions of business education: NBEA 1997 yearbook* (Vol. 35, pp. 1–16). Reston, VA: National Business Education Association.

Bliven, B., Jr. (1954). *The wonderful writing machine.* New York, NY: Random House.

Brower, W. A. (1989). The philosophy of business education. In B. S. Kaliski (Ed.). *Asserting and reasserting the role of business education: NBEA 1989 yearbook* (No. 27, pp. 1–8). Reston, VA: National Business Education Association.

Business education professional development roster: NABTE member schools and universities. (2011). *Business Education Forum. 66*(2), 54–55.

Clem, J. E. (1955). *Techniques of teaching typewriting* (2nd ed.). New York, NY: Gregg Publishing Division, McGraw-Hill Book Company, Inc.

Daggett, W. R., & Jaffarian, R. A. (1990). Business education in the 1990's—A window of opportunity. In S. L. O'Neil (Ed.), *Strategic planning for the 1990's: NBEA yearbook* (No. 28, pp. 168–171). Reston, VA: National Business Education Association.

Daughtrey, A. S. (1965). *Methods of basic business and economic education.* Cincinnati, OH: South-Western Publishing Company.

Daughtrey, A. S. (1974). *Methods of basic business and economic education* (2nd ed.). Cincinnati, OH: South-Western Publishing Company.

Douglas, L. V., Blanford, J. T., & Anderson, R. I. (1973). *Teaching business subjects* (3rd ed.). Englewood Cliffs, NJ: Prentice-Hall, Inc.

Drum, W. O. (1980). Data processing. In M. H. Johnson (Ed.), *The changing office environment: NBEA 1980 yearbook* (Vol. 18, pp. 45–54). Reston, VA: National Business Education Association.

Glatte, H. (1959). *Shorthand systems of the world.* New York, NY: Philosophical Library.

Gordon, H. R. D. (1999). *The history and growth of vocational education in America.* Boston, MA: Allyn and Bacon.

Graham, J. (1933). *The evolution of business education in the United States and its implications for business-teacher education.* Southern California Educational Monographs 1933–34, Series Number 2. Los Angeles, CA: University of Southern California.

Hall, J. C. (1990). A business education perspective: Past…present…future. In S. L. O'Neil (Ed.), *Strategic planning for the 1990's: NBEA yearbook* (No. 28, pp. 1–11). Reston, VA: National Business Education Association.

Haynes, B. R., & Jackson, H. P. (1935). *A history of business education in the United States.* Monograph 25. Cincinnati, OH: South-Western Publishing Company.

Hosler, M. M. (2000). *A chronology of business education in the United States 1635–2000.* Reston, VA: National Business Education Association.

Hosler, M. M. (2003). The foundations of business education. In M. H. Rader (Ed.), *Effective methods of teaching business education in the 21st century: NBEA 2003 yearbook* (No. 41, pp. 1–16). Reston, VA: National Business Education Association.

Hosler, R. J. (1969). Objectives of business education. *Balance Sheet, 50*(6), 243.

Hosler, R. J. (1971). *Discussion on the history and development of business education.* Seminar presentation at the University of Wisconsin-Madison.

Hosler, R. J., & Hosler, M. M. (1992). *The history of the National Business Education Association.* Reston, VA: National Business Education Association.

Kaufmann, B. A., & Wills, J. L. (1999). *User's guide to The Workforce Investment Act of 1998* (E. Ries, Ed.). Alexandria, VA: Association for Career and Technical Education.

Kidwai, S. (2011). Changing the image of CTE. *Techniques, 86*(4), 17–19.

Knepper, E. G. (1941). *History of business education in the United States.* Ann Arbor, MI: Edwards Brothers, Inc.

Knepper, E. G. (1947). Historical development of the business curriculum. In *The changing business education curriculum.* (Yearbook, Vol. IV, p. 25). New York, NY: Eastern Commercial Teachers Association and National Business Teachers Association.

Lynch, R. L. (2000). *New directions for high school career and technical education in the 21st century* (Information Series No. 384). Columbus, OH: ERIC Clearinghouse on Adult, Career, and Vocational Education, Ohio State University.

Lyon, L. S. (1922). *Education for business* (2nd ed.). Chicago, IL: University of Chicago Press.

Meggison, P. F. (1989). Business education in years gone by. In B. S. Kaliski (Ed.), *Asserting and reasserting the role of business education: NBEA 1989 yearbook* (Vol. 27, pp. 9–19). Reston, VA: National Business Education Association.

Monroe, W. S. (1917). *Development of arithmetic as a school subject.* Bulletin No. 10. Washington, DC: U.S. Department of Interior, Bureau of Education.

National Business Education Association. (2007). *National standards for business education: What America's students should know and be able to do in business* (3rd ed.). Reston, VA: Author.

National Commission on Secondary Vocational Education. (n.d.). *The unfinished agenda: The role of vocational education in the high school.* Columbus, OH: The National Center for Research in Vocational Education.

Nichols, F. G. (1933). *Commercial education in the high school.* New York, NY: D. Appleton-Century Company.

Nichols, F. G. (1936). *Junior business training for economic living.* New York, NY: American Book Company.

Nichols, F. G. (1979). *Frederick G. Nichols' memoirs, 1878–1954: The early view of business education.* St. Peter, MN: Delta Pi Epsilon.

Nolan, C. A., Hayden, C. K., & Malsbary, D. R. (1967) *Principles and problems of business education.* (3rd ed.). Cincinnati, OH: South-Western Publishing Company.

Policies Commission for Business and Economic Education. (1961). *A proposal for business-economic education for American secondary schools.* Reston, VA: National Business Education Association.

Policies Commission for Business and Economic Education. (1989). *This we believe about the role of business education as a component of general education* (Statement No. 47). Reston, VA: National Business Education Association.

Policies Commission for Business and Economic Education. (1997). *The Policies Commission for Business and Economic Education.* Reston, VA: National Business Education Association.

Policies Commission for Business and Economic Education. (2002). *This we believe about the need for business education* (Statement No. 71). Reston, VA: National Business Education Association.

Policies Commission for Business and Economic Education. (2005). *This we believe about business education as core academic content* (Statement No. 76). Reston, VA: National Business Education Association.

Rader, M. H. (2005). A comparison of state and national standards for business education. *NABTE Review, 32,* 10–15.

Reese, S. (2009). Gazing into the future. *Techniques, 84*(5), 14–19.

Reese, S., & Thompson, J. (2002). A new age of technology. *Techniques, 77*(2), 38–43.

Reigner, C. G. (n.d.). *Beginnings of the business school.* Baltimore, MD: The H. M. Rowe Company.

Roberts, M. (1999). The making of a leader. *Techniques, 74*(8), 20–22.

Roberts, R. W. (1971). *Vocational and practical arts education* (3rd ed.). New York, NY: Harper and Row.

Robles, M. (2009). An analysis of business education recruitment strategies over the past 25 years: then and now. *The Delta Pi Epsilon Journal, 51*(1), 1–14.

Russon, A. R., & Wanous, S. J. (1973). *Philosophy and psychology of teaching typewriting* (2nd ed.). Cincinnati, OH: South-Western Publishing Company.

Sapre, P. M. (1989). Toward a redefinition of business education. In D. S. Marrone (Ed.), *Alpha Chapter Delta Pi Epsilon 13th annual Peter L. Agnew memorial lecture.* New York, NY: New York University.

Sapre, P. M., & Gillespie, K. R. (1981). History of business education at New York University, 1913–1980. In P. M. Sapre (Ed.), *Early leaders in business education at New York University.* Reston, VA: National Business Education Association.

Secretary's Commission on Achieving Necessary Skills. (1991). *What work requires of schools.* A SCANS report for America 2000. Washington, DC: U.S. Department of Labor.

Secretary's Commission on Achieving Necessary Skills. (1992). *Learning a living: A blueprint for high performance.* A SCANS report for America 2000. Washington, DC: U.S. Department of Labor.

Shimberg, B. (1971). How, when, and where of vocational instruction. In G. F. Law (Ed.), *Contemporary concepts in vocational education* (pp. 184–190). Washington, D.C.: American Vocational Association.

Strong, E. P. (1944). *The organization, administration, and supervision of business education.* New York, NY: The Gregg Publishing Company.

Timeline: Commemorating 150 years. (2004, Fall). *Sextant: The Journal of Salem State College, 13*(1), 34.

Thompson, J. F. (1973). *Foundations of vocational education.* Englewood Cliffs, NJ: Prentice-Hall, Inc.

Tonne, H. A. (1961). *Principles of business education* (3rd ed.). New York, NY: McGraw-Hill Book Company.

Tonne, H. A., & Nanassy, L. C. (1970). *Principles of business education* (4th ed.). New York, NY: McGraw-Hill Book Company.

U.S. Department of Education. (2007). Vocational education: Carl D. Perkins Career and Technical Education Act of 2006. Retrieved from http://www.ed.gov/policy/sectech/leg/perkins/index.html

Wanous, S. J. (1957). A chronology of business education in the United States. *UBEA Forum XI*(8), 55.

Weersing, F. J. (1929). *Reorganization of commercial education in public high schools.* Cincinnati, OH: South-Western Publishing Company.

Wood, M. (1985). Implementing an information processing program. In J. A. Hibler & B. C. Fry (Eds.), *Information processing in the business education curriculum: NBEA 1985 yearbook* (Reston, VA: National Business Education Association [Yearbook appears as journal entry in *Business Education Forum 39*(8), April–May, pp. 72–78)].

The Business Education Curriculum in the Education System

Marcia A. Anderson
Southern Illinois University
Carbondale, IL

As a segment of the entire U.S. educational system, the business curriculum encompasses the educational experiences of business students at all levels. Business education curricula include a variety of programs, courses, units, course objectives, student competencies, assessments, and extracurricular activities that have evolved over the years (Rader & Meggison, 2007). This chapter addresses traditional and nontraditional structures for the delivery of business instruction at all levels, from elementary school through college and into the workplace. The topics presented in the chapter include an overview of the business curriculum at the various levels of instruction; factors that impact the business curriculum, business teacher education, and accreditation; and trends and issues impacting business education.

THE BUSINESS CURRICULUM

Business education is an area of study appropriate for every educational level and delivery system, both traditional and nontraditional. Because of its mission to prepare individuals *for*, *about*, and *in* business, numerous opportunities exist for developing awareness of and practical application of business content (Stitt-Gohdes, 2011).

Traditional Settings

The purpose of education or training is to provide a series of organized instructional experiences for the learner. These experiences include programs and courses taught at all levels of education, including elementary schools, secondary schools, higher education institutions, and training programs in business settings. *Curriculum* refers to the subject content and skills that make up a structured educational program (Morrison, Ross, & Kemp, 2004).

Business education curriculum development. The business education curriculum has traditionally been part of the larger education system, comprising a variety of teaching and learning contexts. The business education curriculum includes the business subjects to be taught at various educational levels and the communication processes, both human and technical, to ensure that the subjects are learned. Delivery of business education at all levels of instruction begins with the curriculum development process.

The business curriculum likewise encompasses content *for*, *about*, and *in* business. When developing the business curriculum, a teacher must consider whether the experiences are intended for personal business use, use in a business career, or both. The first step in planning is the task analysis phase, in which a teacher determines objectives and decides how to "deliver" the material to the students. During the planning process, the teacher must also consider the unique nature of each individual, needs of the local community, the subject matter content, and other factors that impact the business curriculum (Mager, 1997).

Teachers must be aware of their objectives and then clearly communicate desired outcomes to learners. Broad goals and specific objectives should be determined through (a) consideration of the demands of society and the job, (b) characteristics of the students, and (c) potential contributions from related fields that can enrich the learning experience (Mager, 1997). State and national standards also influence the nature of instructional goals and objectives. Planning is of prime importance in the curriculum development process; adequate planning is essential for programs to be successful.

National Business Education Association: its curriculum vision. In 1983 the National Business Education Association (NBEA) appointed a task force on concepts and strategies to guide how business education should relate at various levels of instruction (NBEA Task Force on New Concepts and Strategies, 1983). This NBEA task force developed a list of curriculum standards for teaching business content, first published in 1988: *National Standards for Business Education* (NBEA, 2007). Its third edition is based on a comprehensive curriculum model that integrates 11 business content areas: accounting, business law, career development, communication, computation, economics and personal finance, entrepreneurship, information technology, international business, management, and marketing. In addition, each content area emphasizes the two critical threads of "information technology and human relations—technology because it is the problem-solving and decision-making tool that supports every discipline, and human relations because no business, not even a technology-based business, can succeed if it ignores the human factor" (p. xi). These NBEA standards further address four traditional levels of business education curriculum delivery—elementary, middle / junior high, secondary, and postsecondary—with the corresponding standards at each level.

The elementary school curriculum. The *National Standards for Business Education* (NBEA, 2007) defines the role of business educators in the elementary school (grades K–6) curriculum as follows:

> Business educators at this level begin with the assumption that learning is lifelong. They serve as resource persons: technology coordinators, peer coaches, media specialists, or team teachers. By partnering with elementary teachers, business educators are able to integrate technology and career awareness into the curriculum. (p. xii)

The *National Standards for Business Education* (NBEA, 2007) indicate that business content such as career development, communication, computation, economics and personal finance, and especially information technology is delivered at this level. However, at the elementary school level, computer keyboarding is probably the business subject that has had the greatest effect on the curriculum. Keyboarding is essential because it enhances instruction as students are learning to read, write, and spell. As early as the first typewriting study, conducted in 1929, researchers concluded that typewriting (keyboarding) enhances the learning process in language arts. Evidence showed that (a) elementary school children can learn to key correctly and well, (b) keyboarding experiences accelerate language arts skills and competencies, (c) creative composition expression can be stimulated by work at the computer keyboard, (d) elementary school children submit neater papers and make more projects and displays when their materials are typed, and (e) added use of the computer and the typewriter improved attitudes toward schoolwork (Anderson & Baker, 1994; Bartholome & Long, 1986).

Keyboarding in elementary schools is often taught or led by business educators. In many schools, computer laboratory instructors teach keyboarding with assistance from business teachers, or business teachers act as advisors to computer laboratory instructors or classroom teachers. The goal for keyboarding students in elementary schools is to be able to key 25–30 words a minute in the third grade, with gradual improvement through the sixth grade (Bartholome, 2003). Early keyboarding skills are generally at the beginning level, and later employment-level skills using the computer keyboard require a considerably higher level of expertise. Highly skilled people in industry are able to key at 70–100 words a minute (Bartholome, 2003).

Keyboarding is the foundational information technology skill developed at the elementary level; students also learn introductory applications (word processing, spreadsheets, databases, presentations, and graphics) and other computer literacy concepts. Information technology skills must be reinforced in the middle / junior high school and high school levels to ensure progressive skill development.

The middle / junior high school curriculum. Middle schools usually consist of grades 6–8, and junior high schools of grades 7–9. However, other combinations may occur in the public middle / junior high schools. The *National Standards for Business*

Education (NBEA, 2007) addresses the role of business educators in the middle / junior high school curriculum as follows:

> In middle/junior high school, business educators teach students to use technology effectively in the learning process, regardless of subject matter. Students are introduced to key concepts in basic business, entrepreneurship, and personal finance and how these concepts are integrated in a business venture. (p. xii)

The middle / junior high school curriculum primarily includes exploratory and career awareness experiences and continues to build basic skills of reading, spelling, writing, and computing. Various information technology applications, especially word processing, are continued in the middle / junior high school. Typical business-oriented classes include the following:

- Information literacy, which teaches students how to use the Internet to research information and write reports

- Career awareness and technology careers classes, which introduce students to the world of work

- Basic business and personal finance, which provide students with basic business and personal money management principles

The secondary school curriculum. The secondary school curriculum usually consists of grades 9–12 or 10–12. At the secondary level, students refine their basic skills and become involved in career preparation. The *National Standards for Business Education* (NBEA, 2007) addresses the role of business in the secondary school curriculum as follows:

> Business educators at the secondary level facilitate learning in a student-centered environment, guiding learners as they develop the skills needed to be effective consumers, citizens, workers, and business leaders...Learners continue to explore careers, apply work-based skills, gain business experience, and participate in student organizations. (p. xii)

In many states, the 9th grade is included in high schools, and students at that level begin to learn foundation skills for business and industry. Emphasis is on the use of technology as a tool for facilitating business functions, including the use of the Internet, multimedia, and the computer for communication and computation.

Typical business courses offered at the secondary level include accounting, business communication, business math, computer applications (word processing, spreadsheets, databases, presentations, and graphics), business law, business management, business technology, e-commerce, economics, entrepreneurship, interactive media and web design, information technology, international business, introduction to business, input technology, keyboarding applications, marketing, network systems, personal finance, and business computer programming (Nebraska Department of Education, 2011). Specialized marketing courses such as fashion merchandising and sports marketing are also popular. Most programs are now organized according to career clusters, which will be discussed in a later section.

Students in the 11th and 12th grades may take advanced courses in computing/ programming, telecommunications, multimedia, web page design, and other business topics. Industry-sponsored technology certification is frequently available at these grade levels. Courses such as the Microsoft Certified Professional, Cisco Certified Networking Associate, Novell Certified Network Administrator, and other industry certifications are offered in the business education curriculum. Courses leading to these certifications begin in secondary programs and continue at the postsecondary level of instruction. Business and marketing teachers also provide work-based learning through cooperative education programs and business internships.

Postsecondary schools. Business education programs are found in a wide variety of postsecondary schools, including community/junior colleges, technical colleges and institutes, and career colleges. The *National Standards for Business Education* (NBEA, 2007) describes the business curriculum at the postsecondary level, as follows:

> Two-year postsecondary/community colleges or technical colleges are ideal places for providing education and training to people who want to broaden their educational experiences, change careers, expand employability options, and/or upgrade technological skills. Certificate and degree programs, when combined with practical work experiences, can smooth the transition from high school to two- and four-year colleges or to the business world. (p. xii)

Community/junior colleges. Community colleges, sometimes referred to as junior colleges, fulfill complex roles. One role is to provide the first two years of college to those who intend to transfer to a four-year institution, another role is to provide employability skills for those who need only two years of college, and a third role is to provide ongoing education for people who have already been to college and are retraining or are working and want to improve their job skills. Many classes are taught in the evening or online for students who are unable to attend during the day. Some states have community colleges that are part of the higher education system.

Community college business programs build on the skills learned in high school and in some cases may even duplicate some of those skills. Classes taught at the community college may include a variety of information technology courses and industry certification classes, such as Novell, Cisco, and Microsoft, that are typically taught by business instructors. Community college students who plan to transfer to business programs at four-year colleges typically take some of their prerequisites at the community college. Transfer courses taught may include accounting, business law, business communication, business statistics, marketing, economics, and management.

The associate of arts and/or science degree program is a degree program of primarily general education for students who wish to transfer to a four-year school. Although some career preparation may be involved, at least one-third or more of the program usually relates to general education. Besides providing short-term certificate programs, such as industry-sponsored technology certifications, community colleges typically offer the associate of applied science degree. This degree prepares students for employment in a variety of fields, including business. Students generally work toward an associate of applied science degree in business fields, such as office systems, accounting, marketing, and information technology ("Community college," n.d.).

Technical colleges and institutes. These institutions are postsecondary schools that award no higher than a two-year degree or diploma in a vocational, technical, or career field. Technical colleges often offer degrees in applied sciences and in adult and continuing education ("Community college," n.d.). Business courses offered in these institutions tend to be more specialized and aligned with the needs of a specific business occupation.

Career colleges. A career college is a for-profit postsecondary institution providing professional, career-specific programs. Other terms used to describe a career college are private business college, proprietary school, or independent college. Career colleges offer programs ranging from short-term certificates and diplomas to bachelor's, master's, and doctoral degrees. Business-related programs prevalent in career colleges include accounting, allied medical, business administration, hospitality management, information technology, and legal administration. Students should be advised that career college credits may not be transferable to colleges and universities (U.S. Department of Education, 2008).

College and university curriculum. The *National Standards for Business Education* (NBEA, 2007) do not address the business curriculum at the college and university level because that area is very broad. To teach at a four-year college or university, a faculty member generally must possess a doctoral degree. The Association to Advance Collegiate Schools of Business (AACSB) international accreditation assures quality and promotes excellence and continuous improvement in undergraduate and graduate education for business administration and accounting. This accreditation process requires that the curriculum include such general knowledge and skill areas as communication abilities, ethical understanding and reasoning abilities, analytical skills, use of information technology, multicultural and diversity understanding, and reflective thinking skills. The suggested management-specific knowledge and skills areas include financial theories, group and individual dynamics, statistical data analysis, domestic and global economic environments, human resource management and development, and creation of value through integrated production and distribution of goods (AACSB, n.d.).

Workforce training and development. Instruction delivered through educational institutions prepares individuals to enter the workforce. After entering the workforce, individuals must frequently update and upgrade their knowledge and skills. Instructional approaches in educational settings are fairly standard, with set routines and predetermined curricula. In contrast, workplace instruction is sponsored, planned, designed, conducted, and evaluated at either the organization's site or another location such as a college campus. The purpose is to provide immediate upgrading and/or retraining to employees for specific competencies that enhance job performance. Rapid technological change drives the demand for continuous educational growth of employees whose performance impacts organizational productivity. Business educators are among the trainers, instructors, and human resource specialists that organizations use to facilitate instruction designed as part of the organization's human resource mission (Miller & Miller, 2009).

Nontraditional Settings

The greatest change in recent years has been in the different settings now available for individuals to acquire business education content knowledge. Most of the changes can be attributed to advancements in and access to technology.

Web-based courses/programs. Business educators believe that the profession of teaching business is emerging from classroom to cyberspace, work sites, and other nontraditional settings because of innovations in technology. These technology-driven learning opportunities are modeling the delivery systems (Policies Commission for Business and Economic Education [PCBEE], 2001). Web-based courses and programs are discussed in chapter 7 of this yearbook on online teaching in the classroom.

Alternative scheduling. In contrast with the traditional daily six-, seven-, or eight-period schedule, a block schedule consists of three or four longer periods of daily instruction. With the increased span of teaching time, longer cooperative learning activities can be completed in one class period; however, if a student misses a day under the modular schedule, that student is actually missing two or sometimes even more days (National Education Association, n.d.).

At the postsecondary level, strategies such as departing from traditional semester- or quarter-length courses and developing weekend programs have been implemented to encourage college attendance among new segments of the local population. The advent of online learning has revolutionized the delivery of education. The scheduling of online courses generally aligns with the university calendar; however, some courses allow students to enroll in and complete the course at almost any point in time (Fekula, 2010). Continuing education options, such as providing seminars and lectures for business professionals have become popular in postsecondary venues (Tulane University, 2013).

Industry-based certification programs. The increase in the number of credentialing programs sponsored by industry is one of the most significant trends related to education for information technology (IT) careers. A number of business teachers have been quick to take advantage of certification in order to develop expertise in the computer technology that they have the opportunity to teach.

These industry-sponsored certificates were developed to provide well-trained workers and, in some cases, to address the shortage of qualified employees within the IT field. Credentialing programs (such as CompTIA A+, Microsoft Certified Systems Engineer, Cisco Certified Internetwork Expert, Certified Novell Network Engineer, and Sun Certified Programmer for the Java Platform) have the advantage of enabling people to learn a clearly defined set of competencies quickly. With successful completion of the program, students may find multiple hiring opportunities, depending on the current demand in the job market (Randall & Zirkle, 2005).

Certification is usually offered as an educational benefit to workers and costs paid by employers. More companies are offering certification, and even high schools and community/technical colleges now offer courses leading to certification. After students complete the appropriate coursework and pass the industry-sponsored test, they receive a certificate indicating the software and hardware skills in which they have become certified. Concern exists that, for example, IT instructors and administrators may be making curriculum programming decisions that are based more on marketing and convenience than on specific program information, such as passage rates on examinations, preparation for postsecondary studies, and job placement opportunities. Making informed curriculum decisions also requires an understanding of the current IT workforce and future employment projections to ensure the marketability of students and their prolonged success in the IT workforce (Randall & Zirkle, 2005).

Dual enrollment/credit. Dual enrollment programs allow high school students to earn credit simultaneously toward a high school diploma and a postsecondary degree or certificate. According to the U.S. Department of Education (2007), all but three states have enacted dual enrollment policies. These state-level policies shape the dual enrollment programs and, in turn, the services that students receive. Twenty-one states have comprehensive policies with few course restrictions, liberal credit-granting policies, and minimal (or no) student fees. Twenty-six states have "limited policies," which do not provide funding for student tuition and have more restrictions on credit and student access. Variation also exists in how programs are financed, who can participate, where the courses are offered, who teaches the course, what the student mix is, and how many courses are offered through the program. Many states restrict the number of credits that students can earn, whereas others offer multiple credits in a sequenced program of study (U.S. Department of Education, 2007).

Career and Technical Education

Career and technical education (CTE) offers programs for students, workers, and lifelong learners of all ages to fulfill their working potential. Business education and other career fields such as agriculture, family and consumer science, health science, and engineering and technology education provide career-related courses and programs that are constantly evolving due to the changing global economy. According to U. S. Department of Education (2003) data, business education teachers represent the largest instructional category within CTE.

CTE has a long and rich history in the United States. Today's CTE has evolved from a limited number of vocational programs available at the turn of the 20th century into a broad system that encompasses a variety of challenging fields in diverse subject areas that are constantly developing due to the changing global economy.

Today's CTE provides the following to students:

- Academic subject matter taught with relevance to the real world
- Employability skills, from job-related skills to workplace ethics
- Career pathways that link secondary and postsecondary education
- Second-chance education and training
- Education for additional training and degrees, especially related to workplace training, skills upgrades, and career advancement (Association for Career and Technical Education, 2011b)

Features of career and technical education programs that play a major role in the business education curriculum include career clusters, curriculum integration, and business student organizations.

Career clusters. Education pathways allowing students to explore and prepare for careers are organized into *career clusters,* which are groupings of occupations and broad industries based on commonalities. The 16 career clusters representing more than 79 career pathways help students navigate their way to greater success in college and career. These career clusters identified by the U.S. Department of Education provide an organizing tool for curriculum development. The clusters relating to business programs include business management and administration, education and training, finance, information technology, and marketing, sales, and services. Career clusters identify pathways from secondary school to two- and four-year colleges, graduate school, and the workplace to help students learn how the academic and technical skills they are learning in school will transfer to jobs and careers in their futures (National Association of State Directors of Career Technical Education Consortium, 2012).

Curriculum integration. Considerable emphasis has been placed on the development of common academic standards that emphasize international benchmarking in terms of curriculum content (Barton & Coley, 2011). One recommendation from the Association for Career and Technical Education's (ACTE's) 2006 high school reform position statement was to create incentives for students to pursue the core curriculum in an interest-based context. Connecting rigorous academic expectations with the relevance of an interest-based curriculum can help connect students to learning in meaningful ways. Many of the nation's leading high school reform models highlight the value of using an interest-based context or real-world applications, such as school-based enterprises. Business education has long been a leader in ensuring relevant, integrated curricular opportunities for students (Hyslop, 2007).

Business student organizations. All CTE areas support the cocurricular opportunities provided through student organizations such as Business Professionals of America, DECA, Future Business Leaders of America, and Phi Beta Lambda as a vital component of the curriculum (Association for Career and Technical Education, 2011a). In 2011 NBEA announced a new division—the National Business Honor Society—designed to honor and bring national recognition to outstanding students in business education programs at the secondary level. Any high school junior or senior who has completed or is currently enrolled in his/her third business course and has a 3.0 (overall) and 3.5 (business course) grade point average is eligible for membership. Any public or independent secondary school offering a business curriculum that reflects the National Standards for Business Education is eligible to apply for a local chapter charter (NBEA, n.d.). A 2006 research study revealed a statistically significant positive relationship between business program enrollment trends and the presence of an active business student organization (Stapleton & Anderson, 2006).

FACTORS IMPACTING BUSINESS EDUCATION INSTRUCTION

Several factors influence the delivery of instruction for, about, and in business. The business curriculum and instructional methods are shaped by major factors such as technology, national standards, funding legislation, teacher credentialing, and program accreditation.

Technology

Technology has affected business since 500 B.C. when the abacus was invented in the Middle East. Two inventions in the 1800s, the telephone and the typewriter, probably influenced business more than any other technology up to that time. The computer undoubtedly has affected the business world even more than the telephone and the typewriter. Computers are the foundation for IT, which is recognized as the most important enabling technology for businesses around the world. Information technology is responsible for creating and revitalizing products, services, companies, and industries. Allowing for better management of information and innovations, IT has improved productivity, quality of life, and the standard of living (Courter & Marquis, 1997).

Technology is moving at the speed of light and also improving the speed at which students can be taught how to use computers. Students are getting cell phones and mobile computers at an early age and texting is now a common form of social communication. When technology is integrated in a meaningful way in classrooms, it can have a positive effect on the rate at which students learn and provides an additional aspect for students to gain a more interactive, rich and robust experience while learning.

Although the percentage of students currently using digital textbooks is relatively small, according to Glenn (2010), some educators believe that within the next 10 years, most U.S. college students and many high school students will be reading course content on an electronic device, instead of a paper-based book. Business teachers worldwide provide the instruction for productive use of current technologies and will be the leaders for future technology integration.

National Standards and Funding Legislation

Alarming data concerning education in the United States continue to be cited in news sources: deficiencies in reading and math scores, students with disabilities and English-language learners scoring below proficiency, students academically ill prepared to compete with international peers, and increasing high school dropout rates. These trends are some of the educational challenges addressed by current legislation (Commission on No Child Left Behind, 2007).

No Child Left Behind Act. Since 2003 the No Child Left Behind Act of 2001 (NCLB) has been working to close the achievement gaps and improve public schools. Lawmakers, when enacting the legislation, agreed that standards, accountability, teacher quality, and options for students were vital for improving student achievement and that collaboration among the federal government, states, and school districts—based on results rather than simple compliance—could bring about improvements.

"More than any other federal education law in history, NCLB has affected families, classrooms, and school districts across the nation" (Commission on No Child Left Behind, 2007, p. 12). Virtually every facet of school practice has been affected by this law, including what is taught in elementary, middle, and high school classes; how students are assessed; how teachers are hired; and how money is allocated. Teaching and learning have changed because of NCLB. Administrators and teachers have made a concerted effort to align curriculum and instruction with state academic standards and assessments; they are also making better use of test data to adjust their teaching to address students' individual and group needs. Many districts have become more prescriptive about what and how teachers are supposed to teach (Commission on No Child Left Behind, 2007).

Common Core State Standards. The Common Core State Standards Initiative is a state-led effort coordinated by the National Governors Association Center for Best Practices and the Council of Chief State School Officers. The standards were developed in collaboration with teachers, school administrators, and experts to define the knowledge and skills students should have within their K–12 education careers so that they will graduate from high school able to succeed in entry-level, credit-bearing academic college courses and in workforce training programs (Common Core State Standards Initiative, 2011). Consistent standards will provide appropriate benchmarks for all students, regardless of where they live.

State leaders and the National Association of State Directors of Career Technical Education Consortium collaborated in developing *Common Core State Standards and Career and Technical Education: Bridging the Divide between College and Career Readiness* (Meeder & Suddreth, 2012). The standards are designed to reflect the broad program-level expectations for each of the 16 career clusters and related pathways.

Career and technical education legislation. The Carl D. Perkins Career and Technical Education Improvement Act of 2006, plays a major part in shaping the business education curriculum. This 2006 legislation placed increased focus on the academic achievement of CTE students, strengthened the connections between secondary and postsecondary education, and improved state and local accountability. The legislation takes an important step toward aligning the Perkins Act's academic measures with those in the NCLB legislation of 2001 (Turner, 2006). This current Perkins legislation is slated for reauthorization in 2013.

The impact of NCLB on business and other CTE programs at the high school level has been significant. Students' opportunities to take business education courses has tended to decrease because of increased graduation requirements in core academic areas such as mathematics and science, despite businesses' need for employees with competencies associated with the business education curriculum. As business education enrollments have declined, the demand for business employees possessing basic workplace skills, computer technology skills, and international business skills continues to increase (Brumley, Pollard, & Yopp, 1993).

A nationwide research study of more than 700 high school principals indicated overwhelming support for business education courses as critical electives in secondary education curriculum; however, other school requirements such as meeting NCLB goals may hinder schools from fully implementing such support (Russell-Drage, 2004). Administrators and educators responsible for secondary school curricula need to recognize the contribution of business education to students' overall academic achievement (PCBEE, 2005).

The PCBEE (2005) further stated that business courses meeting substantial academic content standards should fulfill academic graduation requirements. For several years, schools in various states have offered students the opportunity to gain academic credit through interdisciplinary courses that integrate academic and business content. These courses include business economics, consumer economics, and math for business and industry (Hyslop, 2007). The PCBEE (2005) emphasized that business teachers must be leaders in curriculum efforts to integrate academic and business content. In addition, business teachers should keep their principals apprised of student academic success to ensure their continued support for the business education curriculum.

Teacher Certification/Licensure and CTE Credentialing

Teacher education programs delivered by institutions in the various states are approved by state departments of education. In many instances, reciprocal certification agreements are available among states to enable teachers who have completed an accredited program in one state to be eligible for certification in another state. In some states, the NBEA standards (2007) and the National Association for Business Teacher Education standards (2010) are used as guidelines for subject matter content of the standards.

To be certified/licensed as business teachers, most states require teachers to complete a business teacher education program that includes student teaching experience. Most states also require business teachers to pass basic skills, teaching proficiency, and/or content area proficiency tests. Additional courses may be required for a middle school teaching endorsement. The certification structure in many states provides CTE certification or endorsement in addition to secondary education certification/licensure. Career and technical certification requires specific courses, generally one year of work experience in business and industry, and specific endorsements such as work-based learning or cooperative education program coordination.

Many states have enacted legislation allowing alternate routes for individuals to attain teaching certification. With both high retirement and high attrition rates among K–12 teachers and an increasing student population nationwide, more teachers are needed. Instead of drawing primarily from the traditional pool of teacher preparation candidates primarily comprising college students and recent graduates, alternative certification programs can attract older, nontraditional candidates who have bachelor's or master's degrees in business and a wealth of business experiences. Nontraditional teacher education programs can help meet the needs of a specific local setting by training people close to home, where they are likely to stay (U.S. Department of Education, 2004).

Teacher Education and Business Education Program Accreditation

Accreditation is the hallmark of quality business education programs. Several professional organizations are involved in the accreditation of business teacher education or business programs. Accrediting agencies include the National Council for Accreditation of Teacher Education (NCATE), which together with the Teacher Education Accreditation Council (TEAC) consolidated educator accreditation under a new agency, the Council for the Accreditation of Educator Preparation (CAEP); the National Board for Professional Teaching Standards (NBPTS); the Association to Advance Collegiate Schools of Business International (AACSB); and the Accrediting Council for Independent Colleges and Schools (ACICS).

Accreditation of teacher education. Most higher education institutions with quality teacher education programs belong to NCATE/CAEP. The NBEA and NABTE, as well as state-sponsored standards for business education, are incorporated as part of ongoing NCATE reviews of teacher education institutions (NCATE, 2012).

National board teacher certification. National board certification is offered to teachers on a voluntary basis through the National Board for Professional Teaching Standards, with the goal of establishing high and rigorous standards for what accomplished teachers should know and be able to do. Applicants develop a portfolio based on their experiences in the classroom, including their student teaching experiences. National board certification demonstrates that a teacher's practice measured against high and rigorous standards is above and beyond the requirements for state certification (National Board for Professional Teaching Standards, 2012).

Accreditation of college-level business programs. AACSB International is the accrediting agency for bachelor's, master's, and doctoral degree programs in business and accounting. More than 650 member institutions hold AACSB business accreditation, of which more than 178 have additional specialized accreditation for accounting programs (AACSB, n.d.).

Accreditation of independent colleges and schools. The Accrediting Council of Independent Colleges and Schools (ACICS) accredits professional, technical, and occupational programs in private postsecondary institutions offering certificates, diplomas, and degrees from the associate's through the master's designed to train and educate persons for careers in which business concepts, management techniques, or business-related disciplines support/constitute the career activity. ACICS-accredited institutions are required to meet and maintain high standards of faculty qualifications, student retention, and student placement (ACICS, 2012).

TRENDS AND ISSUES IMPACTING BUSINESS EDUCATION

Several trends and issues impacting business education and the business curriculum have been discussed in previous sections. Additional trends and issues affecting business education include diverse student populations, funding for education programs, globalization of the economy, and impact of social media on education.

Diverse Student Populations

Educators constantly seek information to assist them in meeting the educational needs of students from diverse cultures, ethnicities, languages, academic and social backgrounds, as well as alternative lifestyles and other diverse characteristics. Demographic projections indicate that public schools—pre-school through postsecondary—will continue to show tremendous demographic changes. Schools often face a cultural mismatch with a large percentage of students of color compared with a large percentage of Caucasian teachers. Business educators of all cultural backgrounds must be willing to provide appropriate instruction for all students and to expect no less than the best from all students.

Funding for Education Programs

The current fiscal crisis that most states face can be expected to have a large impact on the ability of U.S. school districts to provide a quality education in upcoming years.

As Finegold, Schardin, and Steinbach (as cited by Hungerford & Wassmer, 2004) discussed, this crisis is attributable to the recent recession, subsequent weak recovery, and the unwillingness of politicians in previous fiscal years to take the necessary steps of raising taxes and/or cutting expenditures. Although some states have responded by raising taxes, most states plan to address their fiscal crises by cutting spending, including their expenditures for locally provided elementary and secondary education. It is anticipated that school districts in the weakest fiscal condition to deliver a quality public education will be hurt the most (Hungerford & Wassmer, 2004).

Globalization of the Economy

According to the PCBEE (2004), global issues have affected many aspects of business education. Global issues, which are a major concern of government and industry, present a challenge to business educators, who are preparing students to thrive and compete successfully in a global economy. Global business should emphasize economic systems, business practices, political and legal structures, and multicultural contexts of the world, and their interdependence. A solid foundation for success in the global business world demands a curriculum in which knowledge of the traditional areas of business is integrated with knowledge and understanding of global issues.

Impact of Social Media on Education

Social networking communities are here to stay. Little or no doubt exists that students are actively engaged in online communities, but the long-term effect of social networking on education is generally unknown. According to Dunn (2011), many students rely on the accessibility of information on social media specifically and the web in general to provide answers, which may mean a reduced focus on learning and retaining information.

Social networking has both positive and negative impacts on business education. Students who attempt to multitask by checking social media sites while studying show reduced academic performance. Their ability to concentrate on the task at hand is significantly reduced by the media distractions. Students who spend a great deal of time on social networking are less able to communicate effectively in person. However, social networking has increased the rate and quality of collaboration for students. They are better able to share information quickly, which can increase productivity and help them learn how to work well in groups. Social networking teaches students skills they will need to survive in their future careers. By spending so much time working with new technologies, students develop more familiarity with computers and other electronic devices. With the increased focus on technology in education and business, this familiarity will help students build skills that will aid them throughout their lives (Dunn, 2011).

SUMMARY

Instruction *for*, *about*, and *in* business affects all levels of education, including elementary schools, middle / junior high schools, secondary schools, community/junior colleges, technical colleges, career colleges, universities, and workforce training and development. Business instruction enhances basic skills at the elementary level. At other levels of instruction, the business curriculum broadens to include personal and occupational business skills. Business educators must constantly develop curricula to keep offerings up to date with changes in technology and other factors that affect the curriculum, including national education standards, funding legislation, teacher education standards, accreditation, diversity, and globalization. Federal legislation and various school reform initiatives have profoundly affected the delivery of business education in secondary education. Organizations that accredit business and business teacher-education programs ensure that standards are maintained and that quality instruction is delivered to business students. Business educators are encouraged to continue the profession's mission, as stated by the PCBEE (1997) in its statement:

We believe that business educators will continue to focus their efforts on the learner by developing a rigorous curriculum based on relevant standards, adopting flexible schedules in a creative environment, and using teaching strategies and advanced technologies to support the delivery of business education. Business educators will continually modify business education to meet the changing needs of the learner, workplace, and society. (p. 16–17)

REFERENCES

Accrediting Council of Independent Colleges and Schools (ACICS). (2012). About ACICS. Retrieved from http://www.acics.org

Anderson, M. A., & Baker, C. M. (1994). English skill development in keyboarding. *The Delta Pi Epsilon Journal, 36*(3), 176–188.

Association for Career and Technical Education. (2011a). Career and technical student organizations. Retrieved from https://www.acteonline.org/general.aspx?id=762#. UTnw3aKjPSw

Association for Career and Technical Education. (2011b). What is career and technical education? Retrieved from https://www.acteonline.org/WorkArea/DownloadAsset. aspx?id=1918

Association to Advance Collegiate Schools of Business International (AACSB). (n.d.). Accreditation. Retrieved from http://www.aacsb.edu/accreditation/Accredited Members.asp

Bartholome, L. (2003). Delivery systems for business education. In M. H. Rader & L. A. Kurth (Eds.), *Effective methods of teaching business education in the 21st century: NBEA 2003 yearbook* (Vol. 41, pp. 17–34). Reston, VA: NBEA.

Bartholome, L., & Long, I. (1986). Teach keyboarding to elementary school students. *National Association of Laboratory Schools, 1*(4), 22–28.

Barton, P. E., & Coley, R. J. (2011). *The mission of the high school: A new consensus of the purposes of public education?* Princeton, NJ: Educational Testing Service.

Brumley, D., Pollard, C., & Yopp, M. C. (1993, Winter). Views, beliefs, and opinions of secondary business education by state employment service managers and secondary principals in the Pacific Northwest. *The Delta Pi Epsilon Journal, 35*, 39–50.

Carl D. Perkins Career and Technical Education Improvement Act of 2006. S. 250, 109th Cong. 20U.S.C. 2301 (2006) (enacted).

Commission on No Child Left Behind. (2007). *Beyond NCLB: Fulfilling the promise to our nation's children.* Washington, DC: The Aspen Institute.

Common Core State Standards Initiative. (2010). Implementing the Common Core State Standards. Retrieved from http://www.corestandards.org

Community college. (n.d.). In *Gale Encyclopedia of Education.* Retrieved from http://www.answers.com/topic/community-college

Courter, G., & Marquis, A. (1997). *The learning guide to computers.* Alameda, CA: SYBEX.

Dunn, J. (2011, July 11). The 10 best and worst ways social media impacts education. Retrieved from http://edudemic.com/2011/07/social-media-education

Fekula, M. J. (2010). Perpetual enrollment online courses: Advantages, administration, and caveats. *Online Journal of Distance Learning Administration, 13*(1), 3. Retrieved from http://www.westga.edu/~distance/ojdla/spring131/fekula131.html

Glenn, J. M. L. (2010, December). The advance of digital textbooks. *Business Education Forum, 65*(2), 6–12.

Hungerford, T. L., & Wassmer, R. W. (2004, April). *K–12 education in the U.S. economy: Its impact on economic development, earnings, and housing values.* Washington, DC: National Education Association. Retrieved from http://www.nea.org/assets/docs/HE/economy.pdf

Hyslop, A. (2007). Create incentives for students to pursue the core curriculum in an interest-based context. *Techniques, 82*(2), 28–29.

Mager, R. F. (1997). *Preparing instructional objectives.* Atlanta, GA: The Center for Effective Performance.

Meeder H., & Suddreth. T. (Meeder Consulting Group). (2012, May 24). *Common core state standards and career and technical education: Bridging the divide between college and career readiness.* Prepared with the ACTE and the National Association of State Directors of Career Technical Education Consortium. Retrieved from http://www.achieve.org/CCSS-CTE-BridgingtheDivide

Miller, W. R., & Miller, M. F. (2009). *Instructors and their jobs.* Homewood, IL: American Technical Publishers.

Morrison, G. R., Ross, S. M., & Kemp, J. E. (2004). *Designing effective instruction.* New York, NY: John Wiley.

National Association for Business Teacher Education. (2010). *Business teacher education curriculum guide & program standards* (3rd ed.). Reston, VA: NBEA.

National Association of State Directors of Career Technical Education Consortium. (2012). *Career clusters at-a-glance.* Retrieved from http://www.careertech.org/career-clusters/glance/at-a-glance.html

National Board for Professional Teaching Standards. (2012). *What teachers should know and be able to do.* Retrieved from http://www.nbpts.org/standards/stds.cfm

National Business Education Association. (2007). *National standards for business education: What America's students should know and be able to do in business* (3rd. ed.). Reston, VA: Author.

National Business Education Association. (n.d.). National Business Honor Society. Retrieved from http://nbea.org/newsite/about/NBHS.html

National Council for Accreditation of Teacher Education (NCATE). (2012). About NCATE. Retrieved from http://ncate.org/Public/AboutNCATE/tabid/179/Default.aspx

National Education Association. (n.d.). Research spotlight on block scheduling: NEA reviews of the research on best practices in education. Retrieved from http://www.nea.org/tools/16816.htm

NBEA Task Force on New Concepts and Strategies. (1983). Future direction and re-commended actions for business education. *Business Education Forum, 38*(2), 3–11.

Nebraska Department of Education. (2011). Curriculum. *Business, marketing and management career field.* Retrieved from http://www.education.ne.gov/BMIT/curriculum.html

No Child Left Behind Act of 2001. H.R. 1, 107th Cong. Pub. L. No. 107–110, 115 Stat. 1426 (2002) (enacted).

Policies Commission for Business and Economic Education. (1997). This we believe about the delivery of business education. *Business Education Forum, 52*(1), 16–17.

Policies Commission for Business and Economic Education. (2001). This we believe about the emerging roles of the business educator. *Business Education Forum, 56*(1), 14–15.

Policies Commission for Business and Economic Education. (2004). This we believe about business education in a global environment. *Business Education Forum, 59*(1), 16–17.

Policies Commission for Business and Economic Education. (2005). This we believe about business education as core academic content. *Business Education Forum, 60*(1), 17–18.

Rader, M. H., & Meggison, P. (2007). The business education curriculum. *The Delta Pi Epsilon Journal, XLIX*(1), 26–31.

Randall, M. H., & Zirkle, C. J. (2005). Information technology student-based certifi-cation in formal education settings: Who benefits and what is needed. *Journal of Information Technology Education, (4),* 287–306. Retrieved from http://informing science.org/jite/documents/Vol4/v4p287-306Randall78.pdf

Russell-Drage, K. (2004). *Perceptions of secondary school principals regarding the role of business education in secondary education curriculum* (Unpublished doctoral dissertation). Southern Illinois University–Carbondale.

Stapleton, J. L., & Anderson, M. A. (2006). Searching for effective promotion: Current recruiting and promotion strategies in business education. *NABTE Review, 33,* 10–21.

Stitt-Gohdes, W. (2011). *The business education profession: Principles and practices* (2nd ed.). Little Rock, AR: Delta Pi Epsilon.

Tulane University. (2013). Economics seminar series and related events. Retrieved from http://econ.tulane.edu/seminars.shtml

Turner, S. (2006). Accountability measures: Create collaboration incentive. *Techniques, 81*(8), 12.

U.S. Department of Education. (2003, August). Public secondary school teachers, by subject taught: Selected years, spring 1966 through spring 2001. National Center for

Education Statistics. Retrieved from http://nces.ed.gov/programs/digest/d05/tables/dt05_069.asp

U.S. Department of Education. (2004, November). Innovations in education: Alternative routes to teacher certification. Retrieved from http://www.ed.gov/admins/tchrqual/recruit/altroutes/index.html

U.S. Department of Education. (2007). The role of state policies in shaping dual enrollment programs. Retrieved from http://www2.ed.gov/about/offices/list/ovae/pi/cclo/dual.html

U.S. Department of Education. (2008). Career colleges and technical schools: Thinking about going to a career college or technical school? Retrieved from http://www2.ed.gov/students/prep/college/consumerinfo/index.html

Planning For Instruction

Stephen D. Lewis
Robert B. Blair
Vincent W. Smith
Middle Tennessee State University
Murfreesboro, TN

The authors, editor, and publisher acknowledge and express appreciation for the work done by Cheryl Wiedmaier, Kelly Wilkinson, and Herbert F. Brown, authors of this chapter in the previous edition. Thank you for your contribution to this yearbook and to business education.

The most important component of any student's education is often what occurs in the classroom. Interactions between students and the teacher, as well as among students, play a critical role in students' educational achievement. Diverse student populations found in many schools today require varied approaches to content delivery. To ensure that each student receives maximum benefit from instruction, teachers must place significant emphasis on planning.

This chapter provides the basis for successful planning. The discussion includes a brief summation of business education standards at national, state, and local levels as well as industry standards. The chapter then focuses on instructional planning, from general unit plans through specific lesson plans and including developing a course syllabus, and briefly touches on assessment.

PLANNING OVERVIEW

Experienced teachers know that proper planning is requisite and critical to all teaching and learning activities. Furthermore, effective instructional planning demonstrates a teacher's commitment to professionalism and the education of students.

Appropriate planning makes the teacher's task easier; but more important, it ensures a better learning environment for students. Teachers who plan successfully have more time for instruction because they spend less time with routine noninstructional tasks such as record keeping (Meador, n.d.).

Effective planning for instruction encompasses several essential skills. These skills include identifying appropriate standards, developing a comprehensive course syllabus, determining course content, designing a suitable learning environment, creating flexible unit and lesson plans, and formulating relevant assessments.

STANDARDS

Educators determine core and content standards as the first step in instructional planning. Core standards involve rigorous skills and knowledge in English Language Arts and Mathematics that need to be effectively taught and learned" (Common Core State Standards Initiative, n.d., para. 2). "Content standards describe what students should know and be able to do in any given content area" (Cox, 2000, p. 9).

Rader (2005) concluded, "Standards are necessary to ensure equal access to education programs for every child, establish benchmarks for assessment, and provide the basis for the delivery of instruction" (p. 14). National, state, and local standards, where available, provide excellent resources for planning business course content. Standards for specific industries are accessible at various government and corporate websites.

National Standards

Business teachers may find the *National Standards for Business Education: What America's Students Should Know and Be Able to Do in Business* (National Business Education Association, 2007), a particularly helpful resource in planning courses. This publication, which is updated periodically, includes achievement standards and student performance expectations for 11 content areas and is available for purchase at NBEA's website (http://www.nbea.org). Additional standards specific to economics and personal finance are available through the Council for Economic Education (http://www.councilforeconed.org) and the Jump$tart Coalition (http://jumpstart.org).

State Standards

In addition to national standards, most states have standards designed specifically for use by their schools. State standards typically provide specific competencies, as well as student performance indicators, which teachers may use as evidence that a standard has been met. The Commission on Information and Communications Technology (n.d.) defines competency as "a desirable quality or behavior" (p. 1). A performance indicator will "identify the actions an individual would normally take to perform the area of competence" (p. 2). If the local school system does not provide state standards, teachers should check the Internet for standards developed for their state. Keying "business education standards for [state name]" into an Internet search engine will likely yield the desired results. The following sites provide links to some state standards.

- Business, Management & Administration Curriculum Standards and Competencies 2013–2014, Tennessee (http://www.tn.gov/education/cte/standardsnew/Bus StandardsandCompetencies.shtml)

- Pennsylvania Academic Standards Cross-Referenced with National Business Education Standards (http://www.portal.state.pa.us/portal/server.pt/community/ career_technical_education/7692/pennsylvania_academic_standards_cross-referenced_with_national_business_education_standards/507829)

- 2013–2014 Business Management & Administration Career Cluster Curriculum Frameworks, Florida Department of Education (http://www.fldoe.org/workforce/ programs/business.asp)

- Career and Technical Education–Texas Essential Knowledge and Skills and Coherent Sequences (http://www.tea.state.tx.us/index2.aspx?id=5415 #Subchapter_D)

Local Standards

Local school districts generally implement the content standards that are provided by the state. An advisory board may be consulted to provide input for setting additional standards appropriate for the local area. With the advent of the No Child Left Behind (NCLB) Act of 2001 and Race to the Top Initiative (2009) and their concurrent account-ability requirements, some schools now post state standards in classrooms as an infor-mation source for students, parents, and other classroom visitors. These postings also serve as a reminder to teachers of what students are expected to learn. Because business is such a dynamic discipline, standards at all levels should be reviewed regularly for relevance. Although some states have received waivers from specific requirements of NCLB, local school systems can require standards that exceed national and state expectations.

Industry Standards

Business disciplines vary extensively; as a result, industry standards for these diverse disciplines may differ dramatically. Where established industry standards exist, they may be used to determine appropriate standards for business programs. Business as well as government sources provide practical information for educators. In many instances, certification programs offer minimum standards needed for specific entry-level employment. The following sources can be very helpful in developing program standards:

- The Florida Department of Education provides an extensive list of websites (http://www.fldoe.org/workforce/programs/IndustryCert), each offering information related to industry certifications.

- Microsoft certification information for various MS Office applications is available online at http://www.microsoft.com/learning/en/us/mos-certification.aspx#fbid =E3AtJ_BJMZO.

- The International Association of Administrative Professionals offers two certifications: Certified Administrative Professional and Organizational Management. Information is available at http://www.iaap-hq.org/certification.

- Career and Technical Education Consortium of States has developed standards and assessment systems for career and technical education that have been validated by business, industry, and labor. Information is available at http://ctecs.org/assessment.htm.

- General information about specific industry requirements can be found in the *Dictionary of Occupational Titles, Occupational Outlook Handbook*, or *O*NET OnLine*. Each is easily accessible online by entering the title into an Internet search engine.

COURSE PLANNING

Once appropriate standards have been identified, teachers must begin planning for specific courses. Planning obviously varies from one course to another, particularly when lecture, laboratory, or technology courses are involved. Certain elements, however, are fundamental for planning any course. Course content, a syllabus, and the learning environment are essential ingredients for all course plans.

Course Content

Business educators must serve in a variety of roles to plan effectively for instruction: facilitator, educational designer, collaborator, mentor, political advocate, and continual learner, according to the Policies Commission on Business and Economic Education (n.d.) in its Policy Statement No. 68. National, state, local, and industry standards guide the selection of course content. These standards represent minimum expectations of learning, and teachers are encouraged not just to meet but to exceed these standards in planning a successful course.

Providing a course syllabus is commonplace in higher education. Business educators at the secondary level as well should consider developing a syllabus for each course. A syllabus serves as an informational guide to outline a number of essential course elements. The faculty at Garfield High School (n.d.) in Seattle, Washington, emphasize that such a document is a "tool for communicating high expectations to students and parents" (para. 1). They also indicate that such syllabi may ensure common sequences of content and requirements across multiple sections of the same course.

A syllabus should be customized for individual courses and reflect the teacher's style and personality. A syllabus may include the following common elements:

- **Identification.** This section identifies the official course title, number, credit value, and all information necessary to describe the course.

- **Teacher contact information.** Faculty provide information for parents and students to use in contacting the teacher during the course, including phone number, e-mail address, website, and hours of availability.

- **Description.** The course description should contain a brief but comprehensive statement describing the overall nature of the course and its contribution to the student. This statement should be consistent with any statements published in a school handbook, website, brochure, or other source.

- **Objectives.** Course objectives reflect statements of expected student learning as a result of the completion of the course as outlined.

- **Assignments.** This section itemizes assignments within the course. Often broken into categories, teachers may group these into homework, classwork, quizzes, tests, projects, or other groupings. The number and frequency of assignments for each grading period should be outlined.

- **Grading plan.** The grading plan reflects how students will be graded during the administration of the course. Grading systems (such as percentage or point systems) should be clearly explained. A grading scale used to define any course letter grade should be included and referenced to eliminate any confusion.

- **Policies.** Course policies that impact the course should be documented in this section. These may include policies regarding attendance, late work, behavioral issues, acceptable use policies, etiquette, and common housekeeping tasks.

- **Prerequisites/requirements.** Course requirements involve any special items that students may need to have available for the course that the teacher may not provide. These may include special media, prerequisite skills, supplies, or other items.

- **Content.** A description of major topics should be provided to orient students to the nature of the course.

- **Schedule.** A calendar displaying the major course assignments and due dates assists students and parents in planning throughout the term.

- **Resources.** Any resources that may be used to help students succeed in the course should be listed. These may vary from labs provided by the institution to websites, reference manuals, and tutorials.

- **Acknowledgements.** The teacher may choose to add a signature section to ask students and/or parents to acknowledge receipt, understanding, and acceptance of the requirements. This may be shown at the end of the document and a copy retained by the teacher (Garfield High School, n.d.; Wiedmaier, Wilkinson, & Brown, 2008).

Learning Environment

The learning environment must be carefully designed and implemented when planning an effective business course to ensure optimal learning results. The learning environment sets the stage on which all learning occurs. An appropriate learning environment involves all influences that impact the learning process, including physical, emotional, cultural, technological, and political elements.

The physical environment includes color, lighting, sound, equipment, furniture, and temperature. Organizational planning by customizing spaces for comfort and work-flow support the learning process. The teacher should devise procedures for the most efficient collection and distribution of supplies and documents. Seating arrangements impact visual as well as social activities within the classroom (Douglas, Blanford, & Anderson, 1973).

Emotional elements include the tone and mood at any given time of all participants in the learning process: students, teachers, and visitors. Familiarity with all stakeholders is critical for developing a positive emotional climate. Teachers should quickly learn students' names and communicate classroom rules and discipline practices (Douglas, Blanford, & Anderson, 1973).

Cultural elements emphasize norms and common practices for students in that environment. These are often learned behaviors over time and are not easily changed. Cultural aspects of the learning environment are complicated by the diversity of students in many classrooms. The inclusion of English-language learners or other special needs students pose major challenges for effective planning.

Technological elements include resources that teachers use during the unit or lesson. These should be listed as shown on the sample lesson plan. Accommodations should be made in case website access is not available before or during the lesson.

Political elements describe the degree of control held by the teacher and expected levels of student participation. This may describe the willingness of the teacher to use a participatory or nonparticipatory classroom management style.

UNIT PLANNING

Once course standards have been determined, the course planned, and the syllabus constructed, unit planning becomes an important strategy to organize effective instruction. Unit planning involves making informed decisions on the organization of content into manageable and logical components as a means to plan assessment measures.

Unit Content

Far too often new teachers ask, "How many lessons or how much content is needed to create a unit?" Unfortunately, no easy answer is available. Frequently teachers decide by looking at the table of contents of their textbook and use the author's outline. An outline should reflect a logical cluster of sequential learning in a manageable portion so that students may be evaluated using fair and measured assessments. Unit size may be determined by course standards and should not necessarily reflect a textbook unit.

Unit Plans

Unit plans are compilations of related lessons designed to set forth unit objectives and to provide structure to the instruction. O'Bannon (2006) states that such a plan is a "long range plan…It contains multiple lessons that are related" (para. 1). Unit plans take on similar structures to lesson plans but reflect a longer vision for the achievement of objectives. Lesson plans achieve learning objectives in one or two days; unit plans may take several days or weeks to accomplish stated objectives. A unit plan, such as shown in Table 1, may include the following elements:

- **Objectives.** Provide performance statements of expected student achievement resulting from unit completion.

- **Prerequisites.** State all required previous learning.

- **Curriculum standards alignment.** Identify national, state, local, and industry standards that relate to the unit content.

- **Topical outlines.** List lesson or chapter topics that will be included.

- **Pre-assessment.** Describe how students' knowledge will be measured before instruction.

- **Instructional strategies.** Identify any specific strategies that will be used to introduce or reinforce learning.

- **Strategies to meet diverse student needs.** Describe any specific means that will be used to meet the needs of diverse students in the learning environment.

- **Instructional procedures.** Outline in detail each lesson strategy that is included in the unit.

- **Post-assessment.** Assess student learning in comparison to unit objectives. Compare pre-assessment results to determine net learning gains.

- **Resources.** List resources necessary for the teacher to deliver the unit (Douglas, Blanford, & Anderson, 1973; Wiedmaier, Wilkinson, & Brown, 2008).

LESSON PLANNING

Effective lesson planning is the foundation for successful teaching. According to Dettmer (2006): "Purposes of teaching are to expand thinking, enhance feeling, cultivate senses and movements, and enrich relationships for students and their teachers, coaches, and counselors in order to optimize potential" (p. 72). At a minimum, consideration must be given to learning domains, taxonomy of learning, learning objectives, and lesson plans.

Learning Domains

Learning domains force teachers to consider different learning styles to address the needs of diverse students. "A domain is a sphere or range of influence or activity" (Dettmer, 2006, p. 71). Students learn through four different domains:

- **Cognitive** (thinking) is the primary mode of acquiring information, such as learning facts, ideas, and concepts. For example, learning in personal finance that "APR" represents the annual percentage rate of interest charged on a loan.

Table 1. Partial Unit Plan

UNIT PLAN (Partial)

Unit Title: Using Credit   **Estimated Time:** Fourteen, 90-minute class periods
Prerequisite(s): Unit 3: Spending and Credit and access to calculator or Excel functions

Curriculum Standards Alignment:
- NBEA: Personal Finance Standard VII: Using credit. Achievement standard: Analyze factors that affect the choice of credit, cost of credit, and the legal aspects of using credit.
- TCS: Standard 2.0: Evaluate practices for successful money management. Standard 3.0: Analyze the risks, costs, and benefits of financial management.

Resources:
- Mandura, J., Casey, M., & Roberts, S. J. (2010). *Personal financial literacy.* Boston, MA: Prentice Hall.
- Calculators or calculator accessory on computers; Excel or other spreadsheet software.

Topical Outline: (Lessons, number of days)

Chapter	Topic	Length (periods)
9	Obtaining and Protecting Your Credit	4
10	Personal Loans and Purchasing Decisions	5
11	Credit Cards and Other Forms of Credit	5

Unit Objectives:
(Unit objectives should include higher-order thinking, as reflected in Bloom's Revised Taxonomy.)
Upon successful completion of this unit and its associated lessons, students will be prepared to do the following:

- Identify three advantages and three disadvantages of using credit
- Explain the value of understanding one's credit history
- Describe the personal loan process
- Differentiate between secured and unsecured loans
- Calculate the interest on an auto installment loan
- Evaluate buy versus lease options
- Explain the advantages and disadvantages of student loans

Unit Pre-Assessment:
Students will be asked to complete a written pretest before the start of this unit. Analysis of results will indicate if students have prerequisite knowledge or advanced knowledge of topics that may be skipped.

Instructional Strategies:
Strategies to be used in this unit may include lecture, group discussion, case study, software application of loan calculation, Internet Web Quests, and guest speakers from local financial institutions and university financial aid offices.

Instructional Procedures:
Instructional procedures are outlined in each lesson plan contained in this unit.

Unit Post-Assessment:
A written test covering objectives and competencies of this unit will be administered at the conclusion of the unit. Results will be compared with pre-assessment instruments to determine the extent of knowledge gain for each student.

Reflection of Unit:
In this section, the teacher will record comments during the presentation of this unit and at its conclusion regarding the success of the learning event. This information is to be used in consideration of future uses of this unit.

- **Affective** (feeling) deals with behaviors, attitudes, and values. The student's attitude toward a particular brand of automobile illustrates the affective domain.

- **Sensorimotor** (sensing and moving) involves learning by doing. Using Internet computer skills to investigate the cost of car ownership would show sensorimotor skills.

- **Social** (interacting) is learning through interacting with others. A team project or presentation on students' rationale for choosing a particular car might illustrate social learning awareness.

Taxonomy of Learning

Bloom's Taxonomy of Learning has long been used as a means to categorize learning levels from lower order thinking to higher order thinking. Table 2 illustrates the Revised Bloom's Taxonomy of Learning ("Bloom's Revised," n.d.).

Learning typically occurs from the lowest to the highest order classification.

- **Remembering**, the lowest order classification, refers to the ability to recall facts or concepts from memory (e.g., a formula such as *interest = principal x rate x time*).

- **Understanding** indicates an ability to interpret meanings. An example would be explaining why automobile owners must purchase insurance.

- **Applying** is using knowledge and understanding in a new or different context. Using a decision-making model to select an automobile within a personal budget demonstrates this concept.

- **Analyzing** involves separating information into its component parts. Comparing and contrasting selected features of three different vehicles illustrates this idea.

- **Evaluating** encompasses measuring ideas against established criteria, such as critiquing safety features of a selected automobile.

- **Creating** includes taking ideas or elements and designing or constructing a new outcome or product. For example, students might demonstrate this domain level of learning by designing an advertisement for the selected automobile using the data discovered, such as price, safety features, fuel economy, or other features (Krathwohl, 2002).

Learning Objectives

Learning objectives are foundational elements to a successful lesson plan. Objectives are used as standards by which student learning outcomes are measured. Manton, Turner, and English (2004) suggested using Bloom's Taxonomy as a framework for developing educational objectives. Teachers should strive to include learning objectives that incorporate higher levels of Bloom's Taxonomy, where appropriate.

Effective learning objectives should focus on the learner, not the instructor. Although objectives often begin with a stem such as "The student will…," objectives should be

Table 2. Bloom's Revised Taxonomy Planning Worksheet

		Actions	Products	Learning Activities
Higher-Order Thinking	**Creating:** Putting together ideas or elements to develop an original idea or engage in creative thinking	Designing Constructing Planning Producing Inventing Devising Making	Film story, project, plan, new game, song, media project, advertisement, painting	
	Evaluating: Judging the value of ideas, materials, and methods by developing and applying standards and criteria	Checking Hypothesizing Critiquing Experimenting Judging Testing Detecting Monitoring	Debate, panel, report, evaluation, investigation, verdict, conclusion, persuasive speech	
	Analyzing: Breaking information down into its component elements	Comparing Organizing Deconstructing Attributing Outlining Structuring Integrating	Survey, database, mobile, abstract, report, graph, spreadsheet, checklist, chart, outline	
Lower-Order Thinking	**Applying:** Using strategies, concepts, principles, and theories in new situations	Implementing Carrying out Using Executing	Illustration, simulation, sculpture, demonstration, presentation, interview, performance, diary, journal	
	Understanding: Understanding of given information	Interpreting Exemplifying Summarizing Inferring Paraphrasing Classifying Comparing Explaining	Recitation, summary, collection, explanation, show and tell, example, quiz, list, label, outline	
	Remembering: Recall or recognition of specific information	Recognizing Listing Describing Identifying Retrieving Naming Locating Finding	Quiz, definition, fact, worksheet, test, label, list, workbook, reproduction	

Source: http://img.docstoccdn.com/thumb/orig/129927384.png

specific, observable, and measurable. Nadler and Nadler (1994) recommended that objectives should contain three major components: performance, condition, and criterion. The performance element states what the student will be able to do after completing the lesson. The condition element specifies the "limitations or constraints under which the performance is expected to take place" (p. 116). The criterion element indicates the performance expectation. A sample learning objective incorporating these elements might read: "Upon completion of this lesson, the student will calculate percentage markup on 10 grocery items (*performance*) in 10 minutes (*condition*) with 100% accuracy (*criterion*).

Lesson Plans

Once the unit plan is developed, the teacher then divides the unit plan content into daily lessons that can usually be accomplished during one or two class periods (Table 3). The daily lesson plans represent the most detailed aspects of the planning process. However, a simple way for the teacher to remember an effective lesson outline is to keep in mind that the teacher needs to (a) get the students' attention and tell them what they are going to do in class, (b) complete the instruction, (c) review what they have done, and (d) provide feedback.

Although the lesson plan format is not standardized across the United States, some common components should be included to ensure a well-developed lesson. The following nine elements are recommended for daily lesson plans:

- Descriptive lesson information including the course name, time, location, instructor name, lesson topic, grade level(s) or ages, time allotment, materials and media, and classroom arrangement.

- Lesson objective(s) describing the specific learning outcomes achieved by successful completion of the lesson. The lesson objective(s) should be written in measurable terms that indicate both "how" and "to what extent" student achievement will be measured. Essential questions should also focus learning. These should be visible to the students through an objectives slide or written on a whiteboard.

- Curriculum standard alignment clearly stated on the daily lesson plan.

- An anticipatory set (sometimes called a "bell ringer") that piques student interest in the lesson topic. The set may include a video clip; cartoon; song; game; bold, controversial, or intriguing statement/fact; lively review of the previous day's lesson; series of questions related to that day's topic; or any number of activities that encourage active involvement of all students in the classroom. Teachers should strive to help students make real-life connections with the lesson topic to deepen learning.

- Instructional procedures detailing the introduction of the lesson objectives, learning strategies and activities, managing transitions, monitoring, guided practice, independent practice, re-teaching, and enrichment. Instructional procedures should also contain a time element to prompt the teacher to maximize instructional time.

Table 3. Completed Lesson Plan

PERSONAL FINANCE
Time and Location
Instructor's Name

Lesson Topic
Purchasing an automobile

Grade Level(s) (or Ages)
9–12

Time Allotment
1 day/block schedule (90 minutes)

Materials and Media
- *Managing Your Personal Finances,* 6th Edition, by J. S. Ryan, (2010), (Mason, OH: Cengage Learning)
- Microcomputers and peripherals
- Digital projector
- Internet
- Microsoft Word 2010
- Microsoft Excel 2010
- Assignment sheet with grading rubrics
- Data storage media
- Printer paper

Classroom Arrangement
No special classroom arrangement will be required for this lesson. All students will have access to a computer.

Lesson Objectives
By the end of the lesson the student will have done the following:
- Prepared an Excel spreadsheet to compare a minimum of 10 features, the prices, and the purchasing, financing, and leasing options for the three automobiles selected, using guidelines provided on the assignment sheet.
- Written a one-page report to justify the automobile purchasing decision using the information obtained by applying the six-step decision-making model.

Curriculum Standards Alignment
- NSPF I.1-2.3: Apply the steps in a rational decision-making process to a situation involving an economic decision by an individual
- NSPF V.2.3: Use reliable consumer resources to collect information for making buying decisions about durable and nondurable goods
- NSPF V.3-4.1: Compare the costs and benefits of purchasing, leasing, and renting
- TSPF 2.1: Apply a decision-making process to personal financial choices
- TSPF 2.5: Analyze personal risk management (automobile insurance)
- TSPF 3-1: Demonstrate knowledge of basic principles of consumer finance
- TSPF 3.3: Analyze consumer debt management
- TSPF 3.4: Examine various forms of credit payment
- TSPF 3.5: Compare and contrast various types of loans

(Note: NSPF = NBEA National Standards for Business Education, Personal Finance; and TSPF = Tennessee Department of Education Standards for Personal Finance. Business standards not included in national or state standards should be identified separately on the lesson plan.)

Anticipatory Set/Bellringer (10 minutes)
Engage students in a brief discussion about the three models of automobiles (new or used) that they researched in yesterday's lesson. What are some of the desired features they found for their choices? Have students show photographs of the selected automobiles. In addition to the purchase price, what other expenses are associated with purchasing and maintaining an automobile? What purchasing, financing, or leasing options are available for your selected automobiles? Why do you think it is important to explore the purchase of an automobile while

Table 3. Completed Lesson Plan (cont.)

you are still in school? Can you think of other "big" purchasing decisions that you will make throughout your life?

Provide an overview of the lesson and clearly state the lesson objectives and expected outcomes (objectives also appear on the assignment sheet and on the whiteboard).

Review the decision-making steps covered in a previous lesson and ensure that students have completed the first two steps before continuing the lesson:

- **Step 1: Define the problem**
  - o Purchasing an automobile
    - Search for available vehicles (new and used)
    - Determine a fair price
    - Negotiate the price
    - Research insurance rates
    - Investigate finance or lease options
    - Research consumer protection (warranties, laws, etc.)
    - Explore the cost of operating an automobile (gas, oil, depreciation, insurance, registration and title, maintenance, repairs, accessories.

- **Step 2: Obtain accurate information**
  - o Manufacturer websites
  - o Dealership websites
  - o ConsumerReports.org
  - o Automobile Association of America
  - o Edmunds.com
  - o CarBuyingTips.com
  - o *Kelly Blue Book*
  - o *Money Magazine*
  - o IndianaConsumer.com
  - o About.com
- **Step 3: Compare choices**
- **Step 4: Make a decision**
- **Step 5: Take action**
- **Step 6: Evaluate decision**

Instruction (70 minutes)
The following teaching strategies will be used in this lesson:
- **Group instruction** (15 minutes) to discuss details of the spreadsheet assignment and one-page report. The instructor will review the grading rubric for the project with students, frequently checking for understanding.
- **Demonstration and guided practice** (15 minutes) to show students how to build the spreadsheet according to instructions on the assignment sheet. The instructor will guide students through the correct insertion and formatting of the document titles and column headings to ensure uniformity.
- **Independent practice** (40 minutes). Once the spreadsheet shell has been completed and saved, students will work independently by inserting the collected data into the spreadsheet. During the independent practice, the instructor will move about the classroom, monitoring student progress and frequently checking for understanding. While students are working independently, the instructor will provide oral feedback as needed.
- **Questioning** (5 minutes) will be used throughout the independent practice as students work to complete the spreadsheet and one-page report. Students will be questioned about checking the document format, proofreading for accuracy, saving the document occasionally, and other questions as needed.

Closure (5 minutes)
The following strategies will be used to bring closure to this lesson:
- Students will volunteer to verbalize learning by sharing what was learned in this lesson and how it can be applied in the future. Were the learning outcomes achieved?
- Ask a student to summarize the lesson in her or his own words.
- The instructor will preview the next lesson by informing students about sharing their automobile purchasing decision at the beginning of the next class. Students will discuss how they arrived at their decision.

Table 3. Completed Lesson Plan (cont.)

Assessment
The following assessments will be used in this lesson:
- The Excel spreadsheet and one-page report will be submitted for grading at the end of the lesson.
- A brief, informal, oral report from the one-page written report will be presented by each student at the beginning of the next lesson to inform the class about the purchasing decision.
- A unit test will be administered at the end of the unit.

(Some teachers may find including a table listing objectives, assessments, and accommodations/adaptations helpful.)

Diverse Student Populations Plan
(State how to adapt instruction to accommodate the needs of students with IEPs, special needs, etc.)

Reflection
(In this section the teacher will record comments during the presentation of the lesson and at its conclusion regarding the success of the learning event. This information is used to improve future lessons.)

- Lesson closure ensures that students reflect on what was accomplished in the lesson. This is an opportunity for students to verbalize the learning by sharing the lesson outcomes in their own words. Instructors may incorporate additional independent practice, re-teaching (when necessary), and enrichment activities to reinforce learning objectives. Lesson closure is an appropriate time to preview the next lesson, which helps students understand how learning outcomes for each lesson are connected.

- Evaluation of student learning through multiple assessment strategies.

- Plan for dealing with diverse student populations (individual educational plans, English-language learners, etc.).

- Reflections on the lesson delivery and student learning outcome attainment force critical thinking about all aspects of the lesson and making necessary adjustments for improvement. After presenting the lesson, teachers should determine which method of delivery worked best. Instructions should be refined and notes made for the next time the lesson is taught. Students' ability to follow oral and written instructions to produce a desired result should be noted. In addition, teachers should determine areas when students asked the most questions and where they needed the most assistance. Furthermore, these questions should be incorporated into a list of frequently asked questions to be used for future classes.

ASSESSMENT

Legislation enacted in recent years, including The No Child Left Behind Act of 2001 and Race to the Top Initiative (2009), has compelled states to adopt "high-stakes" formal assessment procedures or risk losing federal education funds. Likewise, accrediting bodies have increased emphasis on assessment when evaluating local school systems for accreditation. The Policies Commission for Business and Economic Education (2007) in its Policy Statement No. 80 espoused the necessity for rigorous assessment and suggested that "...assessments should be aligned with curriculum standards" (para. 9).

Effective assessment procedures are indispensable to teachers in the planning processes. Assessment data on student learning outcomes provide teachers with invaluable knowledge for adapting course content and classroom activities for future instruction. Garrison and Ehringhaus (n.d.) define formative assessment as obtaining "information needed to adjust teaching and learning while they are happening" (p. 1). Examples include observations, practice presentations, questioning, and peer/self-assessment. Summative assessment is "a means to gauge, at a particular point in time, student learning relative to content standards" (p. 1). Examples include chapter tests, semester exams, and state assessments. In addition, state and local systems are increasingly placing more emphasis on student learning outcomes when evaluating teacher effectiveness, so it is imperative that teachers consider assessment in their planning processes. Assessment of learning is addressed more fully in Chapter 4.

SUMMARY
Effective planning is critical to successful instruction and learning. Committed teachers diligently plan each aspect of their instruction. Appropriate planning allows teachers to deliver high-quality instruction and to model professional behavior for all stakeholders.

Course content that includes national, state, local, and industry standards should be incorporated into the planning process. A responsive learning environment, which must consider diverse learning styles, is vital to successful planning. Comprehensive, flexible unit and lesson plans with clearly stated learning objectives ensure student learning. Furthermore, effectiveness of instructional planning is determined through use of appropriate assessment techniques.

REFERENCES
Bloom's revised taxonomy planning worksheet (n.d.). Retrieved from http://img. docstoccdn.com/thumb/orig/129927384.png

Commission on Information and Communications Technology. (n.d.). National ICT competency standard (NICS) for teachers. Retrieved from http://www.slideshare.net/ischoolwebboard/national-ict-competency-standards-for-teachers

Common Core State Standards Initiative. (n.d.). Common core state standards initiative: Standards-setting criteria. Retrieved from http://www.corestandards.org/assets/Criteria.pdf

Cox, J. (2000). Are standards worth it? *Thrust for Educational Leadership, 29*(5), 8–11.

Dettmer, P. (2006). New blooms in established fields: Four domains of learning and doing. *Roeper Review, 28*(2), 70–78. Retrieved from Academic Search Premier database.

Douglas, L. V., Blanford, J. T., & Anderson, R. I. (1973). *Teaching business subjects.* Englewood Cliffs, NJ: Prentice Hall, Inc.

Garfield High School. (n.d.). Setting high expectations through a course syllabus. Retrieved from http://ghs.seattleschools.org/index.cfm?fuseaction=page&sectionid=96

Garrison, C., & Ehringhaus, M. (n.d.). Formative and summative assessments in the classroom. Retrieved from http://www.amle.org/Publications/WebExclusive/Assessment/tabid/ 1120/Default.aspx

Krathwohl, D. R. (2002). A revision of Bloom's taxonomy: An overview. *Theory into Practice, 41*(4), 212–218. Retrieved from Academic Search Premier database. doi: 10.1080/00461520903433562

Mandura, J., Casey, M., & Roberts, S. J. (2010). *Personal financial literacy.* Boston, MA: Prentice Hall.

Manton, E., Turner, C., & English, D. (2004). Testing the level of student knowledge. *Education, 124*(4), 682–687.

Meador, D. (n.d.). Qualities of an effective teacher. *Teaching.* About.com. Retrieved from http://teaching.about.com/od/pd/a/Qualities-Of-An-Effective-Teacher.htm

Nadler, L., & Nadler, Z. (1994). *Designing training programs.* Houston, TX: Gulf Publishing Company.

National Business Education Association. (2007). *National standards for business education: What America's students should know and be able to do in business.* Reston, VA: Author.

O'Bannon, B. (2006, November 2). Planning for instruction: Unit plan. Retrieved from http://edtech2.tennessee.edu/projects/bobannon/unit_plans.html

Policies Commission for Business and Economic Education. (2007). This we believe about rigor in business education (Statement No. 80). Retrieved from http://www.nbea.org/newsite/curriculum/policy/no_80.pdf

Policies Commission for Business and Economic Education. (n.d.). This we believe about the emerging roles of the business educator (Statement No. 68). Retrieved from http://www.nbea.org/newsite/curriculum/policy/no_68.pdf

Rader, M. (2005). A comparison of state and national standards for business education. *NABTE Review,* (32), 10–15.

Ryan, J. S. (2010). *Managing your personal finances.* Mason, OH: Cengage Learning.

Wiedmaier, C., Wilkinson, K., & Brown, H. F. (2008). Planning for instruction. In M. H. Rader (Ed.). *Effective methods of teaching business education in the 21st century* (Yearbook No. 46, pp. 37–52). Reston, VA: National Business Education Association.

Evaluating and Assessing Student Performance

Nancy Zeliff
Northwest Missouri State University
Maryville, MO

The author, editor, and publisher acknowledge and express appreciation for the work done by Marcia Bush and Judith J. Lambrecht, authors of this chapter in the previous edition. Thank you for your contribution to this yearbook and to business education.

Evaluating and assessing student performance is an integral part of teaching. Novice teachers and those outside of education may perceive assessment to be the last step in the learning process. However, evaluating and assessing student performance must be identified and planned for in advance by the teacher in an assessment plan. This chapter explores definitions and examples of evaluation and assessment, discusses validity and reliability, and provides guidelines for developing and using varied assessments such as portfolios, rubrics, selected response test questions, and constructed response questions. How to develop an assessment plan; differentiate assessments for students with special needs, English-language learners (ELLs), and gifted learners; and use assessment data in decision making are also discussed.

PROCESS OF EVALUATION ASSESSMENT

Defining the varied terms used in evaluation and assessment is important, as many are used synonymously. Evaluation and assessment are "multidimensional, active processes focused on student learning and instructional improvement" (Musial, Nieminen, Thomas, & Burke, 2009, p. xvii).

Definitions

Although often used interchangeably, evaluation and assessment are different. Bush and Lambrecht (2008) stated that assessment is a more comprehensive term that includes judging, quantifying, and giving feedback. Evaluation is the judgment—or placing of a value or score—on a performance, product, or response. Musial et al. (2009) defined assessment as clarifying what a learner knows and can do. Testing and measurement, too, are often used synonymously with assessment. Linn and Gronlund (2000) and Musial et al. defined testing as the process of assessing student skills and knowledge through an instrument administered at a fixed time under certain conditions and measurement as a process that assigns a numerical value to a test or assessment.

Purposes of Assessment

Musial et al. (2009) outlined five purposes of assessment, which include providing feedback to learners, finding out what other knowledge the learner needs to learn, diagnosing learner difficulties or misconceptions, identifying what learners know when compared with other learners, and improving programs or educational units. Other purposes of assessment include motivation of students, placement of students in appropriate learning environments, evaluation of programs, assignment of grades, and teacher evaluation (Gronlund, 2006).

Validity and Reliability

Two very important elements of assessment are validity and reliability. Validity can be increased by sound construction and administration of assessment methods. Increased reliability can be achieved by the use of assessment instruments, such as rubrics and checklists.

Validity. Validity refers to the appropriateness with which an assessment measures what is intended to be measured (Gronlund, 2006). If an accounting teacher wishes to assess an accounting student on the preparation of a balance sheet, the most valid assessment is for the student to prepare a balance sheet. Musial et al. (2009) defined two types of validity: content and criterion. Content validity is the degree to which the assessment measures what was intended to measure. If the accounting student completed a selected response exam of 20 true-false questions about the balance sheet, this exam would be of low validity. A true-false exam may just measure the student's ability to guess the correct answer to these 20 questions and not the student's knowledge on preparing a balance sheet. Criterion validity measures how an assessment aligns with another assessment. For example, the accounting exam that measures a student's ability to complete a balance sheet may correlate with the advanced placement accounting exam.

Reliability. Reliability is the degree to which an assessment is stable or consistent. Test-retest reliability determines an assessment's reliability when the assessment is administered to the same students at two different times. Time between administrations can negatively affect the assessment's reliability. Too short a time may mean that the students simply recall the same assessment questions. If new information has been presented to students, the reliability of the assessment can also be adversely affected (Musial et al., 2009).

Equivalent form reliability is necessary in standardized assessments, so that multiple users taking the assessments on different dates and at different locations are assessed on the same objectives. Internal consistency reliability ensures that the assessment includes only the intended concepts and content. Herman and Baker (2005) stated that inter-rater reliability is the most recognized type of reliability and refers to the consistency of scoring students by more than one evaluator. Assessments with selected response questions are scored objectively and maintain higher inter-rater reliability, whereas assessments with constructed response questions require subjective grading and can have lower reliability (Musial et al., 2009).

Musial et al. (2009) discussed how to increase validity and reliability in assessments. Evaluators should consider the following:

- Use longer tests: the more test questions, the more opportunities students have to showcase what they know and can do.

- Write and use sound test questions, ensuring that the test questions match what was taught

- Remove unrelated questions from the test.

- Include clear and concise directions for all sections of the test.

- Use objective scoring over subjective grading to increase reliability, so evaluators have definitive right and wrong answers to use as a basis in scoring the test.

Discerning the differences among key assessment terms is important. Assessment is a more comprehensive term that includes objective and subjective assessment measures. Evaluation assigns a value or judgment on student work. Testing encompasses the use of an instrument at a fixed time, and measurement yields a numerical value assigned to an assessment.

TYPES OF ASSESSMENT

Teachers should use a variety of assessment measures to determine more accurately what a student knows and can do. Varied assessments include formal and informal; formative, interim, and summative; traditional versus alternative; authentic; performance; and norm versus criterion referenced.

Formal Assessment

Formal assessments are planned and prepared for and formalized in delivery, time, and structure. A unit exam on four chapters and topics in a personal finance class is a formal assessment. A three-minute timing in a keyboarding class is a formal assessment. Outside of the classroom, high-stakes testing such as the ACT, PRAXIS, CPA, or a state-board exam for health professionals are all formal assessments.

Informal Assessment

Informal assessments can also be planned and prepared for but are less formal in delivery, time, and structure. A teacher can plan to spot-check student proficiency with formulas in an Excel spreadsheet by asking students to "show formulas" on students' monitors. The teacher then walks around the computer lab and sees that the correct formulas were entered or uses computer lab monitoring software to see all students' screens from the teacher's workstation. Another informal assessment can be the observation of keyboarding technique among keyboarding students, ensuring their hand and arm placement and posture are correct for keyboarding. Informal assessments can also be "on the fly." At the end of a business law class, the teacher may ask students to complete a "three-minute write" and pose questions to the teacher that were unanswered or still remain from class discussion. This informal assessment is helpful on assessing student comprehension and can lead to the next class presentation.

Formative Assessment

Formative assessment is ongoing assessment as students are learning concepts and skills. Pinchok and Brandt (2009) identified that "formative assessment is a process in which teachers use various tools and strategies to determine what students know, identify gaps in understanding, and plan future instruction to improve learning" (p. 2). Gronlund (2006) stated that formative assessments measure learning outcomes from a segment of instruction, such as a textbook chapter or instructional unit. Any form of assessment can be used in formative assessment, but the assessment should align with objectives and classroom activities. Timely feedback from these assessments is essential to help the student achieve.

Summative Assessment

Summative assessments occur at the end and are a summary or assessment of the end result. The most common instructional summative assessment is a comprehensive final exam at the end of a course or term. Lambrecht (2000) identified that high-stakes testing often occurs at the end of courses and programs. If the results of summative assessments are positive, certification, graduation, admittance, or licensure often results. If the results of summative assessments are negative, then remediation may be the result. Students are the most common recipient of summative assessments; however, school districts and colleges and universities undergo accreditation, which is also a summative assessment. If accreditation is not achieved as a result of the summative assessments, the programs or organizations must enact change and improvements.

Traditional Assessment

Traditional assessment is identified by assessment measures that are commonplace and have been used perhaps for generations within particular curriculum areas. Objective tests consisting of multiple choice or true-false questions are common assessments for assessing the lower levels of the cognitive domain or a learner's knowledge about a particular subject matter. Spelling exams are common assessments to assess a learner's language arts skills. Speed typing tests are traditional assessments for a keyboarding student. Traditional assessment is appropriate because of its high validity; however, alternative assessments should also be used.

Alternative Assessment

Alternative assessments are often used to assess a learner's affective domain and the higher levels of the cognitive domain. For example, it is better to assess the soft skills or human relations skills through observations by supervisors or teachers, rather than by students taking a paper/pencil exam. A student's behavior and attitude can be assessed by anecdotal records and observations. Peer and self-assessment measures are helpful in identifying skills that need improvement or those at which a student excels. Another type of alternative assessment is performance assessment, which more readily measures multiple domains of learning. Tasks are performed in order to measure the student's skills and competence. Musial et al. (2009) stated that performance assessments give teachers "the opportunity to evaluate a cognitive skill while it is being performed" (p. 205). Mock job interviews are an excellent means to measure a student's interviewing skills and communication skills when the student is "performing" a simulated job interview. Although objective or essay exam questions could address job interview skills on a paper/pencil exam, observing and using a checklist to assess job interview skills is more valid and more reliable. Exam questions that require written or essay responses are considered performance assessments, as well as essays, compositions, and written work.

Authentic Assessment

Authentic assessments require students to complete real-world tasks and activities, rather than contrived projects from workbooks and textbooks. Musial et al. (2009) defined authentic tasks as those similar to what professionals in a discipline perform daily.

Norm-Referenced Assessment

Norm-referenced assessments interpret student performance and provide a relative ranking of students (Gronlund, 2006). Standardized examinations that are summative in nature provide norm-referenced results and include the PRAXIS, GRE, ACT, and MFAT. Administrators use the rankings of students from one school district compared with other students as an indicator of achievement and progress by both the student and the program or institution. Norm-referenced assessment is typically used in districtwide or state-level assessments (Lambrecht, 2000).

Criterion-Referenced Assessment

In contrast to norm-referenced assessment, Gronlund (2006) stated that criterion-referenced assessment interprets assessment results or what an individual student can do without reference to the performance of other students. Lambrecht (2000) stated that with criterion-referenced assessments, students' results are compared with standards and learning outcomes. Criterion-referenced assessments are typically used for mastery exams.

METHODS OF ASSESSMENT

This section discusses construction suggestions and the advantages and disadvantages of two methods of assessment: traditional paper/pencil exams and performance-based assessments. Also discussed are tools for evaluation, including checklists and rubrics, which add reliability to the assessment process; developing an assessment plan; and assigning course grades.

Traditional Paper/Pencil Exams

Traditional paper/pencil exams are those that include selected and constructed response questions. Objective types of exams, also called selected response questions, fall into this category.

Selected response questions. Selected response questions are objective types of questions that include multiple choice, true-false, and matching. Students "select" their response from given options of answers. The advantages of selected response questions include the ease and speed in providing formative feedback to the student, parents, and other stakeholders; ease in grading; and ability to compare scores among students, classes, and schools taking the same assessment. Disadvantages of selected response questions include the lack of insight into students' reasoning and learning and the chances that students are guessing the correct answers (Musial et al., 2009).

Multiple-choice questions. Multiple-choice questions can measure the lower levels through the higher levels of the cognitive domain and are the most commonly used type of exam question, especially on standardized tests. These questions are not as easy to construct as other types of questions but are easy to score. Students are less prone to "guessing" with multiple-choice than true-false questions. Good multiple-choice questions should include (a) a stem, which presents an incomplete statement or question, (b) a single correct answer, (c) alternatives to the correct answer, and (d) distracters. Developing the question (stem) and the right answer are relatively easy; the difficult part is writing the alternatives and meaningful distracters so the question is valid and measures what it intends to measure. When writing the alternative answers, one should be clear on the relationship between the alternatives and the question within the stem. When composing distracters, it is important to ensure they are sufficiently incorrect so prepared students can identify which answer is wrong. Well-written distracters should be plausible to students who did not prepare adequately for the exam (Musial et al., 2009).

Apply caution in using "all of the above" and "none of the above." When used only because not enough choices of answers were provided, students will recognize this overuse and discount these options as a correct answer. Some students may find the correct answer among the first alternatives and not read further to select these options. When using "all of the above," be sure that all answers are indeed correct. Furthermore, avoid indirect clues when writing multiple-choice questions. Students will readily identify the correct answer as the most lengthy answer, so use parallel format and length of all choices (Musial et al., 2009).

True-false questions. True-false questions also measure varied levels of the cognitive domain. They are easy to construct and easy to score. When writing sound true-false questions, educators should use important concepts and facts, rather than trivial information. Correct answers must be distinctly true or false and should not include obvious clues. Furthermore, verbatim textbook phrases should not be used in true-false questions but rather more global and factual information (Musial et al., 2009).

Matching questions. Matching items require the learner to identify common characteristics between two or more sets of items, usually vocabulary. Advantages of using matching questions include the ease of creation and scoring and the ability to assess a broad conceptual base. Disadvantages of matching questions stem from the chance of guessing correct answers by the test taker and that these questions can only assess recall of information, not higher-order thinking. When constructing sound matching items, "offering an unequal number of items in [your] two columns is an effective way to reduce the possibility of answering correctly through the process of elimination" (Musial et al, 2009, p. 131).

Constructed response questions. Constructed response questions include questions on exams in which the learner must construct a response. Common examples are short answer and essay.

Short-answer questions. Short-answer questions require the learner to supply the answer, unlike true-false and multiple-choice questions, for which students select an answer from those provided. Short-answer questions should be clear and unambiguous, because students are expected to recall information and remember the context in which the information was presented, read, or studied. Advantages of short-answer questions are that they adequately measure vocabulary and the language of a discipline and are a quick formative type of assessment. A disadvantage is that these questions primarily measure recall and can be time consuming to grade, because of the wide range of potential answers (Musial et al., 2009).

Essay questions. Essay questions allow the student more choices in constructing their answers. Essay questions assess higher-order cognitive domains and enhance a student's exam preparation and study skills. Essay questions are also fairly easy to construct. Two disadvantages to the use of essay questions include the amount of time needed to score the responses and the potential bias or lack of objectivity in grading essay exams (Musial et al., 2009).

Two types of essay questions are the restricted-response essay and the extended-response essay. The restricted essay exam restricts or limits the student response. Recollection of facts and the ability to summarize and defend one's response is often necessary. The extended-response essay question may not have a definitive right or wrong answer but relies on "evaluation, organization, analytical reasoning, or originality" (Musial et al., 2009, p. 145).

Publisher test banks. Publishing companies provide ancillary materials, which include test banks to accompany textbooks. Advantages in using publisher test banks are the large number of questions from which to choose and the ease of use, especially for electronic test banks. The disadvantage of using publisher test banks is often the lack of alignment with standards and objectives of the course (Bush & Lambrecht, 2008).

Teacher-prepared test questions. Teacher-developed exams and test questions are advantageous because they are written with specific standards and objectives of the course in mind. Using teacher-prepared test questions can, however, reduce the validity of an assessment if the items are poorly constructed. The use of publishers' test banks can increase the validity of the assessment, if the teacher wisely selects exam questions from those provided in the test bank (Bush & Lambrecht, 2008).

Item analysis. Item analysis enhances the likelihood of better teacher-made tests. In item analysis, teachers use procedures to evaluate the quality of questions used on an assessment. Individual questions are reviewed on item difficulty: the "ratio or percentage of individuals who answered an item correctly" (Musial et al., 2009, p. 322). Computing an item analysis is time consuming; however, online assessments and computerized testing software can compute the analysis automatically, and this analysis can lead to more valid and reliable assessments.

Performance-Based Assessments

Performance-based assessments include those assessments for which the student performs a task, completes a project or written work, or gives an oral performance. To clarify the expectations of these varied assessments to the student and to ensure higher reliability, checklists or rubrics should be used in scoring these performance-based assessments.

Presentations. Presentations by students are an excellent way to assess content-specific knowledge, as well as technology skills and oral communication skills. Presentations can be an extension of case studies, projects, and portfolios. Students not only prepare these performance-based assessments but present information about their work to their peers and teacher (Bush & Lambrecht, 2008).

Written work. Students complete written work through varied assessments. Case studies, research papers, article reviews, blogs, and journals are examples of written assessments. Written work can assess communication skills, personal reflections, and content knowledge. Use of rubrics can minimize bias and subjectivity and increase reliability in the use of written assessments.

Portfolios. Portfolios show student learning to a degree that not many assessments can. Musial et al. (2009) stated that portfolios can reveal a great deal about students and allow students to assume ownership in their assessment. Fernsten and Fernsten (2005) stressed that the key components of portfolios are the reflections written by the students. Students analyze their achievement of the course objectives and evaluate their work and growth through these written reflections.

Portfolios also provide a means for students to showcase their creativity and organizational skills. Portfolios can be time intensive for the student; however, they have a direct carryover to the workplace as the portfolio can be used in the job search process and shared with prospective employers (Bush & Lambrecht, 2008).

Tools for Assessment
Use of checklists and rubrics can increase the inter-rater reliability of assessments. These tools of assessment clearly define the criteria that will be assessed for both the student and teacher.

Checklists. A checklist includes a list of criteria to be met or applied in completing an exercise or learning activity. Bush and Timms (2000) stated that checklists are an excellent organizer for the student, who can check that all components of the assignment are completed. Whether the checklist is a simple list or a more complex matrix of components of a presentation or project, the teacher can check off components that are present. Figure 1 provides an example of checklist for a Windows Movie Maker project in a digital media class.

Figure 1. Digital Media: Windows Movie Maker Project

Project component	Criteria present (check if present)
Introductory title at beginning of movie	
Video clip present	
5–8 digital pictures in .jpg format	
Transitions and effects as appropriate	
Title for each picture: on or before/after picture	
Voice recording: good quality and volume	
Music clip present	
Credits at end	
Sufficient timing to view/read/hear	
Color scheme appropriate	
Copyright laws followed	
Effective and entertaining	
Comments:	

Rubrics. A rubric or scoring guide takes the criteria from the checklist even further. Musial et al. (2009) described a rubric as a scoring guide with specific performance levels used to assess a research paper, project, or performance. Two specific types of rubrics are useful in assessing student performance: analytic and holistic.

Analytic rubrics identify specific knowledge and skills that are expected in a performance or product. The criteria are assigned performance levels and weighted separately. Specific feedback on each of the criteria provides the learner very specific information. A final score is the total of all the criteria. Analytic rubrics are very effective with formative assessments (Bush & Timms, 2000).

Holistic rubrics are used to assess the performance or product as a "whole" and judge the overall quality of that performance or product. Rather than list separate criteria and expected performance levels, three to four written statements are made to describe "exceptional" to "inadequate" performances or products (Musial et al., 2009). Bush and Lambrecht (2008) indicated that holistic rubrics are useful as summative assessments.

The first step in developing a rubric is writing the descriptive criteria. The second step is to determine how many performance levels are needed: three or four performance levels work best. If more than four levels are used, differentiating among the criteria is more difficult. The third step in rubric development is describing the criteria for the various performance levels. Begin with the highest performance level, and use action verbs to describe the performance or appearance. Avoid using nonspecific adverbs (i.e., nearly or occasionally) and differentiating performance levels by quantity (i.e., four of five components are present). The final step is the assignment of a value or points for each performance level and criterion. Points assigned can be equal or weighted, depending on the importance of the criteria in the overall performance or product (Zeliff & Schultz, 1998). Many online interactive tools are also available. An example of an analytic rubric for creating a logo in Photoshop can be found online at http://rubistar.4teachers.org/index.php?screen=PrintRubricDownloadFile&rubric_id=2206693& (Zeliff, 2012). Figure 2 provides an example of rubric for a portfolio made with Adobe Acrobat Professional in a multimedia class.

Advantages of using rubrics are many. Communication of expectations is clear between teachers and students, and the rubrics provide specific feedback to students. Reliability and objectivity in grading are increased because the teacher clearly sees both the criteria and the varied performance levels to be met. Time spent by the teacher in grading is also reduced because the rubric is an organizer of what is to be graded and already includes printed feedback for the student (Bush & Timms, 2000).

Developing an Assessment Plan

An assessment plan includes the types of assessments and the grading system that will be used. The plan covers course objectives; a crosswalk of those objectives to national, state, or industry standards; and the specific assessment that will measure

Figure 2. Digital Media Electronic Portfolio

	Commendable	Acceptable	Not acceptable
Presentation and content	Designed professionally. Layout design used represents portfolio well. No misspelled words. Content of portfolio should be helpful to owner in job search and helpful to prospective employer to see skills of applicants. (5 points)	Layout and design acceptable. No misspelled words. Portfolio could be used in job search. (2–4 points)	Poor layout and design. One or more misspelled words. Do not recommend using this portfolio in the job search. (0–1 points)
Required items • **Introduction** • **Reflection** • **Audio folder with audio file** • **Video folder with video file**	Purpose of portfolio evident. Text-based introduction present. Two required folders are present. All other required items present. (8–10 points)	Purpose of portfolio clear. Text-based introduction present but not strong. One required folder missing. One other required item missing. (4–7 points)	Required items missing. Not clear that portfolio would be used in future by owner. No introduction. (0–3 points)
Video and audio files	Audio recording in mp3 and video in .swf format present. Audio recording clear, inviting, with good volume and voice. (5 points)	Audio and/or video formats not correct. Audio recording not of best quality for voice, volume, clarity, and message. (2–4 points)	Either video or audio file are not present. Audio recording of poor quality and distracts from portfolio. (0–1 points)
Overall effect	Pride in work evident; exhibits technical skill in Adobe Acrobat. Color scheme, fonts, and layout effectively present portfolio in professional manner. (5 points)	Pride in work is evident; Adobe Acrobat skills apparent. Color scheme, fonts, and layout are appropriate. (2–4 points)	Evidence of little pride in work completed. Color scheme, fonts, and layout used are not appropriate for professional portfolio and may make "reading" portfolio difficult. (0–1 points)
Comments:			
			+ _____ /25 points for Portfolio

each objective. The plan should also include an example of each assessment used, which can include tests, portfolios, projects, modules, performances, case studies, interviews, observations, student self-assessment, and peer assessment. Specific checklists or rubrics used to score the varied assessments are also included in the assessment plan. The grading system used must also be discussed in an assessment plan. The responsibility belongs to the teacher to communicate clearly the grading policy to students.

ASSESSMENTS FOR EXCEPTIONAL STUDENTS

Students with exceptionalities include students with special needs, English language learner (ELL) students, and gifted students; these students may require accommodations to assessments in the location, time, format, and type of assessment given them. Public and private school districts and colleges and universities vary in their policies regarding the modification of assessments for students with exceptionalities. State and federal laws and regulations influence the accommodations that must be granted.

Special Needs Students

Special needs students who require assessment accommodations may have an individualized education plan or assessment accommodation plan. Elliott, Thurlow, Ysseldyke, and Erickson (1997) described several recommendations for assessment accommodations that may be necessary:

- Modify the *setting* in which the student takes the assessment to create an environment free from noise and other distractions.

- Alter the *presentation* of the assessment to a manner that fits the needs of the student.

- Read the assessment to the student or translate it into another language.

- Make *time* adjustments to an assessment as needed.

- Modify the *response* that the student provides to an assessment.

- Computerize the assessment so that a pencil/pen does not have to be used or vice versa.

Furthermore, the *scheduling* of the assessment is a factor. For students with documented test anxiety, accommodations are made to reduce that anxiety. Students who have medications given at a particular time of day may be scheduled to take exams at certain times of day that are better for them due to their medication schedule.

English-Language Learners

ELL students are not disabled but have limited language proficiency and have different cultural backgrounds and educational experiences that may affect their performance on assessments. The following instructional elements addressing the needs of ELL students should be considered:

- Incorporate diversity into classroom instruction by recognizing and validating cultural perspectives.

- Ensure all students, including ELL students, understand the assessment directions.

- Enact structured rules for the classroom and assessments so all students know the teacher's expectations during assessments (Elliott, et al., 1997).

Gifted Students

Unlike students with special needs, students with exceptional gifts and talents (the gifted) are not included in federal legislation for special education. Not all states and school districts include gifted students in their accommodations. However, teachers need to assess gifted students fairly. Modifications in assessments for gifted students should not include more of the same problems or assignments that nongifted students receive. Rather, Lidz and Elliott (2006) encouraged the use of dynamic assessment, authentic assessment, and problem-based assessment for gifted students. An example of a dynamic assessment in personal finance would include a unit exam of selected and constructed response questions about savings and investments. Following the initial exam, additional instruction would be provided to the gifted student in areas that need improvement, and a follow-up assessment would then take place. Authentic and problem-based assessments should be offered to all students but are best suited for gifted students.

USING ASSESSMENT DATA FOR IMPROVEMENT

Teachers are largely held accountable for the learning of their students and should strive to help them to continually improve. One way to demonstrate this accountability is through the use of assessment data to improve instruction and programs. Teachers should carefully review student assessment data and make decisions about the improvements to be made. They should implement, monitor, and continually adjust the improvements to ensure continued learning gains.

Data from criterion-referenced exams and teacher-constructed assessments provide those teachers valuable information about the specific knowledge and skills students have obtained through instruction. The use of pre-tests and post-tests in units of instruction can reveal to teachers that specific objectives have or have not been met (White, 2007).

Assessments provide feedback to students on their progress toward meeting specific learning objectives of a course or program and provide teachers with feedback on their teaching effectiveness. Data from the varied assessments are useful to educational stakeholders as evidence of effective instruction in courses and programs. In addition, these data are critical to the continued improvement of program effectiveness and student learning.

SUMMARY

Evaluating and assessing student performance is not the end result of teaching but a major component that must be planned for and organized. Teachers should plan for multiple assessments, including a variety of types, methods, and tools for each business education course. Alternative, authentic, and soundly constructed performance assessments that are both valid and reliable are necessary to determine if students meet the course or program objectives. Checklists and rubrics used in assessing performances and products help improve the reliability of those assessments. Formative and summative assessments, both formal and informal, given during and after instruction provide valuable feedback to not only students, but also teachers and administrators. Teachers can use data from these assessments for instructional improvements and other decision making.

REFERENCES

Bush, M., & Lambrecht, J. (2008). Evaluating and assessing student performance. In M. Rader, G. A. Bailey, and L. A. Kurth (Eds.), *Effective methods of teaching business education: NBEA 2008 yearbook* (Vol. 46, pp. 80–93). Reston, VA: National Business Education Association.

Bush, M., & Timms, M. (2000). Rubric- and portfolio-based assessment: Focusing on student progress. In J. Rucker (Ed.), *Assessment in business education: NBEA 2000 yearbook* (Vol. 38, pp. 103–120). Reston, VA: National Business Education Association

Elliott, J., Thurlow, M., Ysseldyke, J., Erickson, R., & National Center on Educational Outcomes. (1997). *Providing assessment accommodations for students with disabilities in state and district assessments.* NCEO policy directions. Retrieved from ERIC Document Database (ED416628).

Fernsten, L., & Fernsten, J. (2005). Portfolio assessment and reflection: Enhancing learning through effective practice. *Reflective Practice, 6*(2), 303–309. doi:10.1080/14623940500106542

Gronlund, N. E. (2006). *Assessment of student achievement* (8th ed.). Boston, MA: Pearson Education Inc.

Herman, J. L., & Baker, E. L. (2005, November). Making benchmark testing work. *Educational Leadership 63,* 48–54. Retrieved from http://www.kckps.org/teach_learn/pdf/group3/t_l12_making.pdf

Lambrecht, J. J. (2000). Characteristics of good assessment. In J. Rucker (Ed.), *Assessment in business education: NBEA 2000 yearbook* (Vol. 38, pp. 25–38). Reston, VA: National Business Education Association.

Lidz, C. S., & Elliott, J. G. (2006). Use of dynamic assessment with gifted students. *Gifted Education International, 6*(2–3), 151–161. doi:10.1177/026142940602100307

Linn, R. E., & Gronlund, N. E. (2000). *Measurement and assessment in teaching* (8th ed.). Upper Saddle River, NJ: Prentice-Hall, Inc.

Musial, D., Nieminen, G., Thomas, J., & Burke, K. (2009) *Foundations of meaningful educational assessment.* New York, NY: McGraw-Hill.

Pinchok, N., & Brandt, W. (Learning Point Associates). (2009). Connecting formative assessment research to practice: An introductory guide for educators. Retrieved from ERIC Database (ED509943).

White, R. (2007). Data-driven instruction. In M. Bush and K. Schultz (Eds.), *Assessment for an evolving business education curriculum: NBEA 2007 yearbook* (Vol. 45, pp. 117–129). Reston, VA: National Business Education Association.

Zeliff, N. (2012). 44-626 Photoshop Logo. Retrieved from http://rubistar.4teachers.org/index.php?screen=PrintRubricDownloadFile&rubric_id=2206693&.

Zeliff, N., & Schultz, K. (1998). *Authentic assessment in action: Preparing for the business workplace.* Little Rock, AR: Delta Pi Epsilon.

Providing Differentiated Instruction for Diverse Student Needs

Barbara Washington
Pam Matlock
Murray State University
Murray, KY

The authors, editor, and publisher acknowledge and express appreciation for the work done by Beryl C. McEwen, author of this chapter in the previous edition. Thank you for your contribution to this yearbook and to business education.

What is clear is that our society is moving toward increased diversity, and children come to the classroom with almost as many different experiences and expectations as there are children. (Aronson & Patnoe, 2011, p. 1)

With increasing diversity in today's society, a typical business education classroom is a challenging and exciting heterogeneous environment. The student population in most schools reflects this diversity in gender, culture, ethnicity, age, socioeconomic status, language, and exceptionalities, such as physical, cognitive, emotional, behavioral, and gifted/talented. Within these diversities, individual students also vary widely in experiential backgrounds, learning preferences, motivation, interests, and readiness levels. Today's business educators have the opportunity to accommodate this diversity by embracing highly effective teaching philosophies and applying effective teaching/learning strategies. Once teachers accept the inclusion of these diversities in their classrooms, the focus rightfully and responsibly transitions to a plethora of opportunities and challenges. Categorizing students into diverse labels, such as learning disabilities, at-risk, English learner, or gifted, is prevalent in our schools; however, most educators would agree that their focus should be on labels such as exceeds expectations, meets expectations, or making progress toward expectations. The spotlight then shines on teaching and learning and the differentiation required.

DIVERSITY

The definition of diversity in the schools is as reflective of today's dynamic society. In schools, diversity includes the 13 categories of special education. Teaching students with disabilities requires mandated efforts to close the widening gaps in achievement, while including them into the general education curriculum "to the maximum extent appropriate" (Individuals with Disabilities Education Improvement Act of 2004 or IDEIA). Conversely, diversity also includes the students with gifted and talented abilities. These students deserve opportunities to have their achievement gap widen and outdistance that of their peers. In addition, diversity reflects the cultures, languages, and expectations for all persons representing the entire spectrum of socioeconomic levels; appropriately, diversity encompasses the individual differences in learning interests, motivational levels, and readiness of each student therein.

The 2004 Individuals with Disabilities Education Improvement Act (P.L. 108-446), accountability and high stakes testing currently in our schools, and professional research and literature reviewed all indicate overwhelming support for differentiation as the appropriate educational response to diversity. In addition, according to Duncan (2012), there is now discussion about reauthorization of the Elementary and Secondary Education Act of 2001 (commonly referred to as "No Child Left Behind"). Considering these factors, now more than ever, business education teachers are required to work in collaboration with special educators, English-learner educators, and a host of other service providers, in order to provide accommodations and research-based strategies to students with diverse needs.

Collaboration with special educators could require the business educator to attend the individualized education program (IEP) meetings to assist in the design of an IEP for students with disabilities, as defined by IDEIA and the Part B amendment (IDEIA, 2008). Business educators are expected to implement the IEP's accommodations and modifications to the student's program of studies. Secondary students will have a transition plan, which outlines postsecondary and career readiness goals. The business educators' expertise will be instrumental in designing and implementing a program to meet these transition goals.

Diverse Learners

A working knowledge of the major characteristics reflective of diverse learners will assist educators in making informed decisions concerning their needs. To adjust instruction and expectations, a clearer understanding of the different categories is necessary.

Learners with preferred learning styles. Learning style theory addresses how students learn, the personal characteristics they bring to learning tasks, and the means by which they accommodate and assimilate new information (Raymond, 2012). This includes visual, auditory and kinesthetic learners. Learning style proponents believe teachers should select methods of instruction that match their students' learning style strengths, increasing the likelihood that instruction will be successful (Carbo, 2009).

Gifted and talented learners. Gifted learners are defined as individuals who give evidence of high achievement capability in areas such as intelligence, creativity, arts, leadership, or in specific academic fields and who need services or activities not ordinarily provided by the school in order to fully develop those capabilities (No Child Left Behind Act, 2001).

Unmotivated learners. Motivation encourages students to persist in doing something they are already capable of doing. Diverse learners may present significant motivation concerns in the classroom. These learners tend to develop an expectation of failure and do not believe that they can control their own destiny. They also tend to attribute success or failure to forces outside their control or they see no relationship between task outcomes and their own efforts (Raymond, 2012).

English learners. Our schools are a microcosm of today's world. Second language acquisition is a process that is influenced by several cognitive and environmental factors. These include (a) the age the student began the process of learning English, (b) acculturation, (c) attitude and motivation to achieve proficiency in a second language, and (d) learning style that may be different from the teacher's preferred styles (Cummins, 2000).

Learners with disabilities. The federal government, through the IDEIA (2004) describes 13 disability categories that qualify learners to receive special education services. They are: autism spectrum disorders, deaf-blindness, deafness, emotional disturbance, hearing impairment, intellectual disabilities, multiple disabilities, orthopedic impairment, other health impairment, specific learning disabilities, speech or language development, traumatic brain injury, and visual impairment including blindness. Within these categories are many conditions, such as stuttering, ADHD (attention deficit hyperactivity disorder), and Tourette syndrome. In 2010 the 111th Congress passed Rosa's Law (PL 111-256), which officially renamed the mental retardation category to the more respectful label, intellectual disabilities.

Differentiation Challenges

One of the challenges for business educators is to seek a variety of methods to meet the needs of the diverse learners in their classrooms. Beers (2003), the author of *When Kids Can't Read*, issues a differentiation challenge in this statement:

My chant of "These kids can't read," wasn't the wrong chant—they *couldn't* read. What was wrong was using that as an excuse for not teaching them. Once I was willing to add the question, "They can't read, so what am I to do?" the answers— not one, but many—began to emerge (p. 7).

Although difficulty in reading is only one example of the differentiation challenges facing business educators, this quotation appropriately addresses the need for teachers to accept responsibility for teaching diverse learners and challenges educators to seek a variety of strategies for accommodating the diverse needs of peoples. There is no single best method.

Fairness

It must be noted that the chorus of "It's not fair!" from faculty and other students is sometimes heard when individuals are given what is perceived to be special treatment, when the most unfair treatment would be to treat everyone the same. Fairness means giving students what they need to be successful (Lavoie, 2009). These differentiations are given to level the "playing field" and keep individuals engaged in the educational process.

In most school systems today, learners are educated within the mandated national, state, or district curricula. Without needed differentiation, many diverse learners are at risk for academic and/or social failure as they attempt to learn through the mandated curricula and "one size fits all" strategies. Making adjustments in the business education learning environment, such as implementing IEP accommodations and evidence-based interventions will result in providing the opportunities for diverse learners to access the general education curriculum successfully.

Universal Design for Learning

One way of differentiating and ensuring access to the general curriculum is through the concept of the Universal Design for Learning (UDL), which has been applied to teaching and learning through the Individuals with Disabilities Education Improvement Act (IDEIA, 2004). It encourages the development of universal design features in the planning stages to ensure more students can access the general curriculum (Smith, 2007).

UDL is part of the general delivery of learning and frequently includes technology as part of the solution. An e-book or digital version of the textbook is an example of a UDL feature. Although using this accommodation is essential for some students, it could also remove barriers for others, including English learners or unmotivated readers. UDL accommodates those who require it and incidentally supports many others. UDL provides the basis for lesson plan differentiation in content, delivery, and product from its initial design, and not as an afterthought (Colarusso & O'Rourke, 2010).

DIFFERENTIATED INSTRUCTION: CONTENT, PROCESS, AND PRODUCT

Differentiated instruction is a teaching philosophy based on the premise that instructional approaches should vary and be adapted in relation to individual and diverse students in classrooms (Tomlinson, 2003). Differentiated instruction requires educators to be flexible in their approach to teaching by adjusting their planning and delivery, as opposed to expecting students to adjust to a "one size fits all" curriculum. Differentiated instruction has the potential to impact learning positively by offering teachers a means to provide instruction to a wide range of students.

Authors of differentiated instruction cite several key elements necessary to guide differentiation in the education environment. Tomlinson and Strickland (2005) identify three elements of the curriculum that can be differentiated: *content* (what students learn), *process* (how students learn), and *product* (how students demonstrate their mastery of knowledge or skills). The following sections describe these three differentiation elements.

Content Differentiation Strategies

Content is differentiated by concentrating on the most relevant and essential concepts, processes, and skills or by increasing the complexity of learning. Although some students will need more instruction and practice, others will need less. Teachers differentiate content when they (a) pre-assess students' skills and knowledge and match learners with appropriate activities, according to their readiness, (b) give students choices about topics to explore in greater depth, and (c) provide students with basic and advanced resources that match their current levels of understanding (Heacox, 2002). Many strategies exist to help business educators differentiate the content in their curriculum.

Curriculum compacting. One instructional strategy to accommodate content is *curriculum compacting*. Compacting enables students to skip parts of the curriculum they have already mastered and move on to more challenging content and activity. When teachers compact a curriculum, they examine and identify a particular subject area for the skills or content that could be pre-assessed, accelerated, or eliminated. This practice allows a focus on the essential ideas and skills of the content area, eliminating ancillary tasks and activities. When working with classes that include advanced learners, compacting is a particularly effective strategy (Colarusso & O'Rourke, 2010).

Tiering. Another well-documented content accommodation strategy is *tiering*. Tiered instruction allows all students to focus on essential concepts and skills, yet still be challenged at the different levels at which they are individually capable of working. Teachers can tier content based on complexity. When tiered by complexity, teachers can address the needs of students who are at introductory levels as well as those who are more advanced. *Tiering* by resources allows teachers to choose materials at a variety of reading levels and complexity of content. Teachers can use Bloom's taxonomy as a guide to tier the content at various challenge levels (Tomlinson, 2003).

Scaffolding. *Scaffolding* is a highly effective content strategy in which the teacher provides temporary support structures to assist students in accomplishing new tasks and concepts. *Scaffolding* helps to maintain a challenging curriculum without the effects of "watered down" approaches. When *scaffolding*, educators support students, only as needed, through questioning and explaining, as well as implementing instruction using visual aids, graphic organizers, outlines, or other useful charts and tables (Mercer, Mercer, & Pullen, 2011).

Process Differentiation Strategies

After the content strategies for the group and/or individuals have been determined, the processes implemented by teachers in differentiating must be selected. These processes are as diverse and varied as the diversities they serve. The process in which the teacher presents the material partly reflects student achievement. This section discusses examples of explicit teaching, collaborative teaching, and motivation strategies.

I do it; we do it; you do it. Explicit teaching infers that students need a teacher. This model of teaching requires both direct teaching by the instructor and the indirect facilitating of learning by the teacher. "I do it, we do it, you do it" is simplistic wording for an effective, as well as motivational, model for explicit teaching. This model uses direct instruction from the teacher, interactive activities between the teacher and students, and the opportunity for feedback and evaluation of progress toward the objectives. It is widely used when teaching new concepts and providing structure for differentiation. The process is easily embedded in most lesson plans. Table 1 identifies three steps to explicit teaching.

Table 1. Steps to "I Do It, We Do It, You Do It" Explicit Teaching

Step 1	Step 2	Step 3
Direct "explicit" instruction	Guided practice	Independent practice / collaborative learning
I do it	We do it	You do it / you do it together
My turn	Our turn	Your turn / your turn together

Source: Adapted from Maiers (2009).

Although highly effective when teaching new content material, the design of this model of explicit teaching can also work efficiently in review lessons. For instance, the teacher shares review points and details, students partner or review material in an interactive manner, and students independently demonstrate their knowledge. After assessment, the teacher will determine whether the class moves to new content by those who mastered the content that was taught or whether further differentiation through explicit teaching is necessary for those who did not meet expectations.

Collaborative learning/peer assistance. Learning the traditional "3 Rs" can be enhanced through *collaborative learning* and *peer assistance* learning. The Partnership for 21st Century Skills proposed fusing "the 3Rs" with the "4 Cs" (critical thinking, communication, collaboration, and creativity) as a way of blending content with 21st century skills (Kay, 2011). Incorporating *collaborative learning* activities into the learning environment of the classroom has merit both as a 21st century skill and as a preferred learning strategy for many students.

Much research points to the benefits of heterogeneous or mixed grouping. Kagan and Kagan (2009) believed that collaborative learning is the most powerful tool in developing higher-order thinking. By varying groups, the teacher can ensure that all students will learn how to work collaboratively and cooperatively. By assigning different roles within groups, students will also learn how to work independently and with responsibility in a group of their peers. Some activities are maximized by occasionally grouping students based on similar interests, gender, or ability. Groups can vary from pairs, triads, groups of four, or even larger groups for instructional purposes. In most cases, students should be assigned to groups before the activity and not allowed to self-select to ensure proper group dynamics. The teacher can ensure that all students have opportunities to work with others who are both similar and dissimilar to themselves in interests, learning styles, and readiness (McEwen, 2008). Business teachers may find that flexible use of student groups is the heart of differentiated instruction.

Jigsaw variations. A popular cooperative learning strategy dating from the 1970s has been the *jigsaw method*, which has opportunities for both independent and interdependent learning. Students are divided into basic work or home groups and given an assignment. Students become experts on their assigned piece of the topic and then contribute their expertise to their home group. Aronson and Patnoe (2011) point to the positive changes in both academic performance and morale through the use of this technique, which enables students to cooperate with one another while developing important interpersonal skills.

Reciprocal grouping. Applying the classic comprehension research of Palincsar and Brown (1984) on the importance of summarizing, predicting, questioning, and clarifying, *reciprocal grouping* is a collaborative learning activity that can be effectively implemented in the business classroom. This is an engaging strategy to assist with comprehension of the reading material. Part of the success of this strategy is that students are assigned and taught specific roles.

When using *reciprocal grouping* with oral reading from the textbook, the class is divided into groups of four students. Each pupil is assigned a job as summarizer, predictor, questioner, or clarifier. At designated times during the oral reading; the teacher will pause and direct the students to "go to work." Students will then individually "do their jobs." *Reciprocal grouping* is an example of collaborative learning that can be easily differentiated when specific jobs are assigned based on the competencies or interests of the students.

Cooperative learning. An extension of collaborative learning is *cooperative learning*, which incorporates collaboration and social skill building, while addressing the 3 Rs and 4 Cs. It emphasizes the importance of social skill building during the collaborative activities. When *cooperative learning* is used, research supports gains in achievement at all grade levels, a decrease in achievement gaps for minority and low-achieving students, improvement in mixed-race interaction, and improvement in the development of personal and social skills (Kagan & Kagan, 2009).

This method also addresses a variety of learning issues for gifted students, including social skills and motivation. Because many gifted students excel academically but struggle socially, *cooperative learning* enhances their skills in leadership, problem solving, and conflict resolution. Improvement in their understanding of the skills, talents, and perspectives of others is cited. "When we turn the chairs around in our classrooms and have students work together on a regular basis, we radically transform classroom dynamics. Students who otherwise would not be motivated become engaged. Students have the opportunity to do what most students want to do—which is to interact in positive ways with their peers" (Kagan & Kagan, 2009, p. 4.1).

Motivation. One of the frustrations in teaching unmotivated learners is their lack of effort, which is often the reason for failure, rather than inadequate skills or abilities. Basketball coaches practice free throws because practice/effort will result in improvement in free throw percentages and will win games. Unfortunately, this concept of practicing to improve does not readily generalize to unmotivated students. Although intrinsic motivation is the ultimate goal, extrinsic motivation becomes the responsibility of the teacher. Motivation to take the first step is often necessary to encourage those students who procrastinate or are slow to get started.

Teachers might apply the respected research of Brody (1987) who determined three essential preconditions for improvement in motivation: the importance of a well-managed and well-structured classroom, the teacher's support of diversity in the classroom, and the monitoring of meaningfulness and difficulty level of the instructional content. Much research, especially the work of Sprick (2006, 2009), has focused on these three variables.

Student motivation to engage in any behavior is related to the degree to which they value the rewards of engaging in that behavior or task and their expectations of being successful with it (Sprick, 2006). Students who believe they have the skills and understand the reasons for performing the skills are more motivated. Teachers who make assignments based on student abilities and provide the rationale for completing the assignments will improve the probability of motivating students to complete the task.

PRODUCT/ASSESSMENT DIFFERENTATION STRATEGIES
Product/assessment differentiation strategies are the third way of differentiating instruction. An effective way of motivating students to engage in assignments and assessments is to provide students with choices. Educators should provide multiple options for students to express what they know. Culminating activities provided at the end of instruction and chosen by students let them apply and extend what they have learned. Teachers should be open minded about how each student shows content understanding and mastery. Students should be given the opportunity to produce work individually or in groups based on their productivity levels, talents, and interests (Tomlinson & Strickland 2005). NBEA publications such as the quarterly newsletter *Keying In* are a valuable resource in current and creative options.

Project-based learning. *Project-based learning* could be a differentiation strategy that engages students in learning knowledge and skills through an extended inquiry process structured around complex, authentic questions and carefully designed products and tasks. Recognizing that students have different styles, students learn through projects that allow them to inquire into the content in a more direct and meaningful way. Project-based tasks are inherently differentiated and range from smaller projects, lasting one or two weeks in length, to semester-long projects. *Project-based learning* allows for multiple assessment opportunities for teachers and students. Projects can include conducting experiments, building models, developing posters, delivering multimedia presentations, writing journal entries, collecting pictures, creating a timeline, making a recording, and many other options using technology (Colarusso & O'Rourke, 2010).

Problem-based learning. Another approach to differentiate products and assess student knowledge is *problem-based learning*. Once a teacher is familiar with students' backgrounds, learning styles, interests, and readiness levels, questions can be adapted to fit individual needs. Questions can be used to stimulate thinking about a concept and challenge students to higher levels of thinking appropriate to the content and learning outcomes. Teachers can also allow more wait time for student responses or provide opportunities to pair with a partner for more meaningful learning. Essential thought-provoking questions can connect a new concept with previously learned content to drive the success level upward for students by creating important connections (Campbell, 2008).

Anchor activity. An *anchor activity* is a product differentiation strategy that allows the student to work on an ongoing assignment directly related to class content. *Anchoring activities* can be worked on independently throughout a unit or a semester. They are tied to the content and are a logical extension of learning during a unit. Activities should expand the goals and outcomes for which each student is held accountable. Examples may include keeping a process log, working on a portfolio, working on a learning packet, or working at a learning or interest center (Campbell, 2008).

WebQuest. WebQuest (http://www.webquest.org) is an inquiry-based activity that allows students to use Internet resources to complete a task. WebQuests offer an interactive learning environment that a teacher can use to stimulate creativity and encourage critical thinking among students in their "quest" for knowledge. They may be used to foster collaborative work and solve real-world problems to conclude a unit of instruction (McEwen, 2008).

Technology. Technology and digital media can help make differentiation practical and achievable in a diverse classroom. Digital materials make it possible for the same material to be presented, accessed, and even adapted on a student-to-student basis. Use of the Internet is an inexpensive option for providing digital materials to the classroom. Handhelds provide an array of applications. Students can use them for organizing, writing, reading, collecting data, visualizing, calculating, assessing, and concept mapping. These devices are effective in active learning situations in which students ask questions, gather and analyze information, and share results. Students are able to share documents to upload or download both to and from the web. Teachers can also supplement their materials with innovative products such as multimedia tools, graphic organizer software, text-to-speech and text-to-image programs, CD-ROM books, and learning software. O'Connor, Kieser, and Olivo (2011), in their article "Engaging the Millennial Generation in Business Education Classes" presented many creative assignments that combine product differentiation, assessment, and technology.

Assessment. Excellent examples of differentiated assessment can be found in the O'Connor et al. (2011) article and in Chapter 4 "Evaluating and Assessing Student Performance" in this yearbook. In a differentiated environment, assessment is diagnostic and informative. Assessment is ongoing, varied, and embedded in the curriculum. Assessment should be designed on a continuum that begins with what is to be taught and ends with frequent opportunities to show learning has taken place. Pre-assessment, checks for understanding along the way, teacher observation and questions, ongoing assignments, peer and self-assessment, quizzes, tests, and performance and alternative assessments are all types of differentiated assessments that can be used to demonstrate student understanding of the material.

SUMMARY

Diverse learners pose challenges for educators. Differentiation is a philosophy that can provide teachers with the theory and practice to challenge appropriately the broad scope of students in classrooms today. Business educators must believe their students' learning and productivity will increase when their methods of instruction align with their students' diversities. Educators must be committed to developing learning environments in which students are increasingly self-regulated, independent, and efficient learners (Wery & Nietfield, 2010). Business educators should address the uniqueness of students by differentiating the content, process, and product of their lessons. Differentiation will change the effectiveness of teachers' lessons by increasing the probability of student success. By incorporating differentiation on a consistent basis, the business teacher is taking responsibility for seeking effective strategies to motivate, engage, and prepare today's diverse students with 21st century skills. Table 2 lists resources teachers can use to support differentiation in their classrooms.

REFERENCES

Aronson, E., & Patnoe, S. (2011). *Cooperation in the classroom: The jigsaw method* (3rd ed.). London: Pinter & Martin, Ltd.

Beers, K. (2003). *When kids can't read: What teachers can do.* Portsmouth, NH: Heinemann.

Brody, J. (1987). Synthesis of research and strategies for motivating students to learn. *Educational Leadership*, 40–48.

Campbell, B. (2008). *Handbook of differentiated instruction using the multiple intelligences: Lesson plans and more.* Boston, MA: Pearson Publishing Inc.

Table 2. Resources to Support Differentiated Instruction

Resource	Web Address
The Access Center	http://www.k8accesscenter.org
Association for Supervision and Curriculum Development	http://www.ascd.org
Center for Applied Special Technology UDL Toolkits	http://www.cast.org/teachingeverystudent/toolkits
Center for Implementing Technology in Education	http://www.cited.org
Dare to Differentiate	http://daretodifferentiate.wikispaces.com
Differentiation Central	http://www.diffcentral.com/videos2.html#categories
Teachers Network	http://teachnet.org/ntol/howto/adjust
Teachnology: How to Differentiate Instruction	http://www.teach-nology.com/tutorials/teaching/differentiate
Teach with Technology	http://www.4teachers.org
Tech for Learning	http://www.tech4learning.com
WebQuests	http://www.webquest.org
What Works Clearinghouse	http://ies.ed.gov/ncee/wwc

Carbo, M. (2009). Match the style of instruction to the style of reading. *Phi Delta Kappan, 90*(5), 373–378.

Colarusso, R. D., & O'Rourke, C. M. (2010). *Special education for all teachers* (5th ed.). Dubuque, IA: Kendall Hunt Publishing Co.

Cummins, J. (2000). *Language, poverty, and pedagogy: Bilingual children in the crossfire.* Clevedon, England: Multilingual Matters Ltd.

Duncan, A. (2012). After ten years, it's time for a new NCLB [No Child Left Behind]. U.S. Department of Education Homeroom. Retrieved from http://www.ed.gov/esea

Heacox, D. (2002). *Differentiating instruction in the regular classroom: How to reach and teach all learners, grades 3–12.* Minneapolis, MN: Free Spirit Publishing, Inc.

Individuals with Disabilities Education Act of 1990, Pub. L. No. 101-476. Stat. 104 Stat. 1142.

Individuals with Disabilities Education Improvement Act of 2004, Part B Supplemental Regulations. (2008). Retrieved from http://idea.ed.gov

Individuals with Disabilities Education Improvement Act of 2004, Pub. L. No. 108-446, Senate Bill 1248.

Kagan, S., & Kagan, M. (2009). *Kagan cooperative learning.* San Clemente, CA: Kagan Publishing.

Kay, K. (2011). The seven steps to becoming a 21st century school or district. Retrieved from http://www.edutopia.org

Lavoie, R. (2009). *Beyond F.A.T. City: A look back, a look ah*ead [DVD]. Alexandria, VA: PBS Video.

Maiers, A. (2009). Recipe for learning success: I do, you do, we do. Retrieved from http://www.angelamaiers.com/2009/09/recipe-for-learning-success-i-do-you-do-we-do.html

McEwen, B. C. (2008). Providing differentiated instruction for diverse student needs. In M. H. Rader (Ed.), *Effective methods of teaching business education: NBEA 2008 yearbook* (Vol. 46, pp. 53–65). Reston, VA: National Business Education Association.

Mercer, C. D., Mercer, A. R., & Pullen, P. C. (2011). *Teaching students with learning problems* (8th ed.). Upper Saddle River, NJ: Pearson Publishing Inc.

No Child Left Behind Act of 2001. PL. 107-110.

O'Connor, M. A., Kieser, A. L., & Olivo, J. J. (2011). Engaging the millennial generation in business education classes. *Business Education Forum, 66*(2), 36–39.

Palincsar, A. S., & Brown, A. L. (1984). Reciprocal teaching of comprehension-fostering and comprehension-monitoring activities. *Cognition and Instruction, 2,* 117–175.

Raymond, E. B. (2012). *Learners with mild disabilities: A characteristics approach* (4th ed.). Upper Saddle River, NJ.: Pearson.

Rosa's Law, 156, U.S.C. § 2781 (2010).

Smith, D. (2007). *Introduction to special education: Making a difference.* Boston, MA: Pearson.

Sprick, R. (2006). *Discipline in the secondary classroom: A positive approach to behavior management.* San Francisco, CA: Jossey-Bass.

Sprick, R. (2009). *CHAMPS: A proactive and positive approach to classroom management.* Eugene, OR: Pacific Northwest Publishing, Inc.

Tomlinson, C. A. (2003). *Fulfilling the promise of the differentiated classroom.* Alexandria, VA: Association for Supervision and Curriculum Development.

Tomlinson, C. A., & Strickland, C. A. (2005). *Differentiation in practice: A resource guide for differentiating curriculum, grades 9–12.* Alexandria, VA: Association for Supervision and Curriculum Development.

Wery, J. J., & Nietfield, J. L. (2010). Supporting self-regulated learning with exceptional children. *Teaching Exceptional Children, 42*(4), 70–78.

Classroom Management

Diane J. Fisher

Sharon Rouse

University of Southern Mississippi

Hattiesburg, MS

The authors, editor, and publisher acknowledge and express appreciation for the work done by Tena B. Crews and Wanda L. Stitt-Gohdes, authors of this chapter in the previous edition. Thank you for your contribution to this yearbook and to business education.

By providing a positive classroom environment, effective teachers set the stage for all students to learn. The role that classroom management plays in helping students reach their academic goals is vital to teaching and learning. Although teachers may know their subject matter, how students learn, and various teaching methods, the ability to manage the learning environment can be a factor in reducing teacher burnout and retaining them in the teaching profession. This chapter discusses the definition of classroom management, its role in effective teaching, and related classroom management research, theories, and strategies that can be used in business education classes as well as others. To further promote an environment conducive to learning, the chapter provides computer lab rules, which covers ethics for the virtual environment and digital citizenship guidelines and suggestions.

CLASSROOM MANAGEMENT

Classroom management includes the way a teacher organizes, disciplines, and facilitates a class to ensure learning occurs (Orlich, Harder, Callahan, Trevisan, & Brown, 2007). Levin and Nolan (1991) stated, "Teachers who manage their classrooms effectively enjoy teaching more, and have greater confidence in their ability to affect student achievement" (p. 9). The definition indicates that the main element of learning is a teacher's control in the classroom.

Definition of Classroom Management

Classroom management describes the process used to maintain an organized and smoothly running learning environment. Classroom management is more than preserving order and control; it includes implementing educational goals that maintain an environment conducive to learning. Many factors affect the learning environment, including the organization of physical space, storage of classroom materials, and establishment of classroom rules and procedures (Moore, 2009). According to Evertson and Weinstein (2006), classroom management has two distinct purposes: to maintain an orderly environment for academic learning and to enhance student social and moral growth. In an effectively managed classroom, students know what is expected of them, wasted time is limited, confusion is clarified, disruption is restricted, and the climate is work oriented, pleasant, and relaxed (Wong & Wong, 2009). A teacher's ability to establish an effective classroom is important to students.

Role of Classroom Management in an Effective Learning Environment

One of a teacher's most important jobs is classroom management. Effective classroom management increases student engagement and decreases disruptive behaviors. In an analysis of 50 years of research about what helps students learn, the results revealed that, of 228 variables, classroom management had the largest effect on student achievement (Wang, Haertel, & Walberg, 1993). Although maintaining an effective classroom is difficult, inspired teachers carefully plan and use a management system that supports learning and keeps students involved in their lessons.

Although the dynamics of classroom management are complex, the quality of teacher-student relationships is the foundation for all phases of classroom management (Marzano, Marzano, & Pickering, 2003). In another 2003 study, Marzano and Marzano found that the most effective teacher-student relationships exist when teachers exhibit appropriate levels of dominance, cooperation, and awareness of high-needs students. Teachers must demonstrate appropriate behaviors and provide continuous feedback in order to establish student-learning goals. Teachers can demonstrate dominance by providing clear behavior expectations and learning goals, displaying assertive behavior, and including conduct rules, procedures, and consequences.

CLASSROOM MANAGEMENT RESEARCH

Classroom management research in the 21st century draws attention to the need to focus on educating the "personalized" student rather than the impersonalized student in the classroom (Freitas & de Yapp, 2010). The Interstate New Teacher Assessment and Support Consortium Standards (InTASC, 2011, p. 2) clearly indicate that student differences matter and effective teachers must build positive, healthy relationships that connect with students and promote a sense of community in the classroom.

Classroom Management Theories, Models, and Approaches

Teachers must develop classroom practices that work within the constraints of their school's policies. Teachers use four approaches to classroom management to enhance learning: behaviorist, preventative, logical consequences, and intervening.

B. F. Skinner's **behaviorist approach** focuses on the study of observable behavior. Although he did not work in classrooms, he suggested that a student's behavior could benefit from the use of scientific application of behavioral principles and classroom management research. This approach requires the teacher to develop systematic reinforcement with consequences for both positive and negative behaviors (Skinner, 1976).

Jacob Kounin, Alfie Kohn, and Barbara Coloroso offered a more **preventative approach** that integrates teaching and discipline. Labeled as "lesson movement," Kounin's management strategies have promoted active learning in not only regular education students but also in special needs students (Kounin, 1970).

From earlier work by German psychiatrist Alfred Adler (1978), the **logical consequences approach** views students' misbehavior as emerging from unmet needs. Dreikurs (Dreikurs and Grey, 1993), who was influenced by Adler's work, underscored the importance of meeting students' need for acceptance while also emphasizing the role of consequences in shaping behavior. Teachers must consider the motivation and goals of student behavior in the development of classroom management plans. Then, teachers must apply logical consequences to actions to assist students in taking responsibility for their behaviors. Dreikurs (1968) believed that encouragement, not praise, holds the potential for motivating students and building their self-esteem, self-confidence, and self-discipline. His strategies are prevalent in the education system today because they have proven to be effective ways to manage a classroom (Tauber, 2007). The importance of appropriate consequences is also underscored by Canter and Canter (2001), who also emphasized the value of catching students being good and then providing appropriate feedback and reinforcement

In recent years, classroom management research has turned to developing relationships rather than punishments in the classroom and preventing and intervening with current discipline problems, which is the **intervening approach**. It provides positive outcomes for students to achieve in managed classrooms, and when they provide students with comprehensive and supportive engagements, it promotes learning (Gordon, 1989). This type of classroom management focuses on teachers providing positive outcomes for student achievement in managed classrooms, and it provides teachers and students with comprehensive and supportive engagements (Marzano, Marzano, and Pickering, 2003). This intervening approach rejects traditional models of reward and punishment. Instead, it focuses on how student conflicts can be resolved in a way that will improve their relationships with their teacher and peers (Tauber, 2007).

Application of Theory to Practice

To add practical application in managing a classroom, the 2012 George Lucas Educational Foundation resource guide provides 10 tips on how to improve student engagement and build a positive climate for learning and discipline:

- Build community by building caring relationships—between teacher and student, student and student, and classroom and community—which is the cornerstone of good classroom management.

- Design a safe, well-managed, and friendly classroom environment.

- Include students in creating rules, norms, routines, and consequences.

- Create various communication channels—the more modes the better.

- Always be calm, fair, and consistent.

- Know the students.

- Address conflict quickly and wisely.

- Integrate positive classroom rituals.

- Keep it real! Attach learning to students' lives by discovering the things students are interested in, such as trends, music, TV shows, and games, and incorporate those into teaching.

- Partner with parents and guardians. Trying to connect home and school with a call sharing positive news is worth the extra effort and can open doors for better student-parent-teacher relationships (The George Lucas Foundation, 2012).

When teachers apply these 10 tips and engage students, they enhance the climate for building relationships.

Classroom management supports positive learning communities, which is a critically important element to the success of a teacher. When teachers create classroom communities within learning environments, they must consider using combinations of the behaviorist, preventative, logical consequences, and intervening approaches. Holliday (2005) indicated that "successful teachers have four common characteristics: passion for the subject matter and thorough preparation to teach the content, belief that what they teach makes a difference, and desire to improve students' lives" (p. 2). If the teacher creates an effective classroom climate, he or she is more likely to unleash the full potential of learners.

CLASSROOM MANAGEMENT STRATEGIES

Strategies used to manage the classroom include organizing the physical environment, communicating classroom rules, establishing and reinforcing classroom procedures, and managing student behavior. Teachers should begin by consulting the school handbook to learn the standard operating procedures and routines of the school. Often procedures may be established by the school for routines such as taking attendance, reporting tardiness, issuing hall passes, making up work after school, recording grades, using the school library, and conducting parental conferences (Moore, 2009). Once these procedures are in place, teachers must devote time to preparing the classroom and developing other classroom procedures that will maximize instruction.

Organizing the Physical Environment

Teachers should make the best use of classroom space to permit orderly movement and avoid distractions. The following tips were offered by Emmer, Evertson, and Worsham (2006):

- Use a room arrangement consistent with instructional goals and activities.

- Keep high-traffic areas free of congestion.

- Be sure students are easily seen by the teacher.

- Keep frequently used teaching materials and student supplies readily accessible.

- Be certain students can easily see instructional presentations and displays. (pp. 2–3)

Marzano (2007) offers additional elements to consider when preparing the classroom, including access to technology and equipment, room decoration, materials and supplies storage, students' desks and chairs, and the teacher's work area. Furthermore, Pedota (2007) stated that the classroom should be a showcase for student work and encouraged teachers to display student work to let them know their work is important.

Communicating Classroom Rules

To communicate expectations to students, teachers must have a planned system of rules and procedures. A rule identifies general expectations or specific standards, such as "Respect Others." Stating rules positively helps communicate appropriate behavior. Teachers should limit the list of rules to five or six, discuss the rules with students on the first day of class, explain each rule by describing the behavior it covers, post the rules in the room, and focus students' attention on them throughout the first few days of school. Emmer, Evertson, and Worsham (2006) gave the following examples of commonly used rules for the classroom:

- Bring materials to class.

- Be in assigned seat when bell rings.

- Be polite to and respectful of others.

- Listen and stay seated when someone is talking.

- Respect other people's property.

- Obey school rules.

Teachers should be familiar with school policies concerning consequences for rule violations and be consistent in applying consequences. Consequences often include extra homework, detention, or loss of privileges to participate in field trips and fun activities (Rischer, 2008).

Establishing and Reinforcing Classroom Procedures

To provide smooth transitions and reduce interruptions in the classroom, teachers should determine routines for such activities as leaving the room, returning to the room, fire and disaster drills, and a split lunch period. Establishing proper procedures for distributing, collecting, and storing papers and materials will also help keep students on task, diminish disruptions in instruction, avoid wasting time, and complete work in a smooth, organized manner.

To maintain efficient use of class time and permit groups to work independently, group work procedures should include how students will move in and out of groups, how groups are assigned leadership and other roles, how groups should relate to each other, and how groups should communicate with the teacher. Classroom procedures can also include desired behaviors of students in the group.

The best time to interact with students about classroom procedures is at the beginning of the school year or semester. Teachers who explain their procedures and discuss them with their students provide positive academic expectations that often lead to classrooms that are more effective. Wong and Wong (2009) encouraged teachers to use the three-step approach—explain, rehearse, reinforce—to teach procedures. Throughout the term, reviewing rules and procedures periodically is necessary (Marzano, 2007; Emmer, Evertson, & Worsham, 2006).

Managing Student Behavior

An important component of managing student behavior is to establish trust and mutual respect among students and teachers. Pedota (2007, p. 165) outlines 10 strategies that combine structure and fairness with clear expectations to produce a safe learning environment and positive student behavior:

- Be yourself. Do not be an imitation of someone else. Success will follow if you allow your own personality to show.

- Treat your students, as you would like to be treated.

- Always give students hope—make them feel that they can accomplish anything.

- Keep parents informed. Parental involvement will support your role as a teacher.

- Before you speak, get everyone's attention and say what you mean and mean what you say.

- Be proactive. Move around the room and keep your eyes moving.

- Remember self-esteem is as crucial for adolescents as it is for you—avoid sarcasm or actions that belittle an individual in front of classmates.

- Your actions, words, and deeds should model the behavior that you expect from your students.

- Class rules should be reasonable, fair, equitable, and used in a consistent manner.

- Develop a philosophy of "we" rather than "I" and use a personal approach in working with your students.

Teachers who establish and consistently use these procedures are likely to create a learning environment for students in which they can be motivated to succeed.

TECHNOLOGY LAB MANAGEMENT

The National Education Technology Standards (NETS) offer standards for technology labs, including the following: model and teach legal and ethical practices related to technology; apply technology resources to enable and empower learners with diverse backgrounds, characteristics, and abilities; identify and use technology resources that affirm diversity; promote safe and healthy use of technology resources; and facilitate equitable access to technology resources for all students. These five elements should connect with the guidelines to ensure students are respectful, responsible, and sensitive to the rights of others (NETS Project & Brooks-Young, 2006).

Acceptable Use Policy

The Internet can be a powerful tool in an educational setting, with positive and negative topics and information at the click of a button. Most schools have a technology use code of conduct, pledge, or behavioral standards set by the district or school board.

Having a signed agreement allows all parties to review the guidelines and expectations of technology usage. Wentzell (n.d.) defined an "acceptable use policy" (AUP):

An AUP is a written agreement signed by students, their parents or guardians, and teachers. The AUP outlines the terms, conditions, and rules of Internet use for the district or individual school. (Para. 5)

An AUP provides parents, teachers, and students with guidelines, expectations, and consequences for computer use in the classroom.

Ethics and Privacy in the Virtual Environment

In 1997 Richard Severson wrote *The Principles of Information Ethics*, providing four basic principles that still apply to the information technologies of the 21st century. They are "respect for intellectual property, respect for privacy, fair presentation, and doing no harm" (p. 39). He also gave four tests for examining ethical dilemmas: "get the facts straight, identify the moral dilemma, evaluate the moral dilemma using the principles of information ethics to decide which side has the most ethical support, and test your solution: will it stand up to public scrutiny?" (Bell, 2006, para. 4). Following these basic principles allows users to gain mutual respect for each other and entitles them to digital citizenship.

Digital Citizenship

According to Ribble, Bailey, and Ross (2004), "Digital citizenship can be defined as the norms of behavior with regard to technology use" (p. 7). Learning to use technology appropriately and respecting other users' creative rights is necessary in a world immersed in technology (Ribble, 2013). Digital citizenship encourages and promotes the ethical use of technology. *Digital Citizenship in Schools* (Ribble & Bailey, 2007) provides useful ways for enhancing digital citizenship.

SUMMARY

The role of effective teachers is to establish a professional presence in the classroom and build relationships with students to set the stage for learning. When teachers understand and promote classroom management theories and use effective models and approaches, they are able to create a positive learning environment for students. However, if classroom disruptions do occur, classroom policies or rules and knowledge of behavior management will limit the amount of time spent on re-establishing a classroom environment that is conducive to learning.

REFERENCES

Adler, A. (1978). *The education of children*. Chicago, IL: Regnery Publishing.

Bell, M. (2006, March/April). Looking to the future. *MultiMedia & Internet@Schools, 13*(2). doi:15464636

Brownsburg Community School Corporation (n.d.). Brownsburg Community School Corporation Acceptable Use Policy 2011–2012. Retrieved from http://www.browns burg.k12.in.us/documents%5CBCSC-AUP.pdf

Canter L., & Canter, M. (2001). *Assertive discipline: Positive behavior management for today's classroom*. Santa Monica, CA: Lee Canter and Associates.

Dreikurs, R. (1968). Psychology in the classroom: A manual for teachers. New York, NY: Harper & Row.

Dreikurs, R., and Grey, L. (1993). Logical consequences: A new approach to discipline. New York, NY: Plume.

Emmer, E. T., Evertson, C. M., & Worsham, M. E. (2006). *Classroom management for middle and high school teachers* (7th ed.). Boston, MA: Pearson–Allyn and Bacon.

Evertson, C. M., & Weinstein, C. S. (2006). Classroom management as a field of inquiry. In C. M. Evertson and C. S. Weinstein (Eds.), *Handbook of classroom management: Research, practice, and contemporary issues* (pp. 3–16). Mahwah, NJ: Lawrence Erlbaum Associates.

Flowers, B., & Rakes, G. (2000). Analyses of acceptable policies regarding the Internet in selected k–12 schools. *Journal of Research on Computing in Education, 32*(3), p. 353.

Freitas, S., & de Yapp, C. (2010). *Personalizing learning in the 21st century*. London, England: Continuum International Publishing.

Holliday, C. O. (2005). The human connection. *Clearing House, 79*(1), 21–23.

Interstate New Teacher Assessment and Support Consortium (InTASC). (2011, April). InTASC model core teaching standards: A resource for state dialogue. Council of Chief State School Officers. Retrieved from http://www.ccsso.org/Documents/2011/InTASC_Model_Core_Teaching_Standards_2011.pdf

Kounin, J. (1970). *Discipline and group management in classrooms*. New York, NY: Holt, Reinhardt, & Winston.

Levin. J., & Nolan, J. F. (1991). *Principles of classroom management: A hierarchical approach*. Englewood Cliffs, NJ: Prentice-Hall, Inc.

Marzano, R. J. (2001). *Designing a new taxonomy of educational objectives*. Thousand Oaks, CA: Corwin Press.

Marzano, R. J. (2007). *The art and science of teaching: A comprehensive framework for effective instruction*. Alexandria, VA: Association for Supervision and Curriculum Development.

Marzano, R. J., & Marzano, J. S. (2003). The key to classroom management. *Educational Leadership, 61*(1), 6–13.

Marzano, R. J., Marzano, J. S., & Pickering, D. J. (2003). *Classroom management that works*. Alexandria, VA: Association for Supervision and Curriculum Development.

Moore, K. D. (2009). *Effective instructional strategies: From theory to practice* (2nd ed.). Thousand Oaks, CA: SAGE Publications.

NETS Project. (2008). *National educational technology standards for students* (2nd ed.). Washington, DC: ISTE.

Orlich, D. C., Harder, R. J., Callahan, R. C., Trevisan, M. S., & Brown, A. H. (2007). *Teaching strategies: A guide to effective instruction*. Boston, MA: Houghton Mifflin Company.

Pedota, P. (2007). Strategies for effective classroom management in the secondary setting. *Clearing House, 80*(4), pp. 163–168.

Ribble, M. (2013). Digital citizenship: Using technology appropriately. Retrieved from http://www.digitalcitizenship.net/Nine_Elements.html

Ribble, M., & Bailey, G. (2007). *Digital citizenship in schools* (2nd ed.). Eugene, OR: ISTE Publications.

Ribble, M., Bailey, G., & Ross, T., (2004). Digital citizenship: Addressing appropriate technology behavior. *Learning and leading with technology, 32*(1), 6–9, 11).

Rischer, A. (2008). Management strategies help to promote student achievement. *Education Digest, 74*(3), 47–49.

Severson, R. (1997). *The principles of information ethics*. Armonk, NY: M. E. Sharpe.

Skinner, B. (1976). *About behaviorism*. New York, NY: Random House, Inc.

Tauber, R. T. (2007). *Classroom management: Sound theory and effective practice* (10th ed.). Westport, CT: Greenwood Publishing Group.

The George Lucas Education Foundation. (2012). Ten tips for classroom management. *Edutopia*. Retrieved from http://www.edutopia.org/classroom-management-resource-guide

Wang, M. C., Haertel, G. D., & Walberg, H. J. (1993). What helps students learn? *Educational Leadership, 51*(4), 74–79.

Wentzell, B. (n.d.). *Writing an acceptable use policy for your school.* Retrieved from http://catnet.adventist.ca/files/resources/res_96.pdf

Wong, H. K., & Wong, R. T. (2009). *The first days of school: How to be an effective teacher.* Mountain View, CA: Harry K. Wong Publications.

Teaching in the Online Classroom

Lisa Gueldenzoph Snyder
Sherrie Drye Cannoy
North Carolina A&T State University
Greensboro, NC

Technology provides instructors with the opportunity to engage students both with the content of the course as well as with other students in a wide variety of ways. Instructional technologies are used at all levels of education—from preschool classrooms to doctoral programs—and across all content disciplines to enhance traditional classroom experiences and to replace face-to-face settings to support online education. Although online teaching and learning dissolves educational boundaries by providing "anywhere and anytime" education, it also presents a challenge for online educators who must learn and apply new instructional paradigms to support high-quality educational experiences "that students can embrace and educators can sustain" (Dykman & Davis, 2008a, p. 11). To that end, this chapter provides a toolkit of strategies to help online instructors plan effective instructional design, select delivery options, create strong learning communities, and assess student learning.

FOUNDATIONS OF ONLINE EDUCATION

Online education is often synonymous with terms such as distance education, virtual education, or even correspondence education. No matter what term is used, the common theme is that a difference in place and time exists between the instructor and the students (Robles, 2011). Distance education began in the 1800s with correspondence courses (Robles, 2011; Valentine, 2002). Coursework was completed by hand and sent via the postal service between the student and instructor. The concept of correspondence education continues today; but rather than transferring documents by postal mail, students receive instruction—such as lecture presentations, visual demonstrations, class discussions, and assessments—and submit coursework via technology. Online education uses web-based and mobile technologies as the foundation to support effective anytime/ anywhere teaching and learning (Barbera, 2004; Rungtusanatham, Ellram, Siferd, & Salik, 2004; U.S. Department of Education, 2010). The following sections define online education and outline the status and significance of online education.

Definitions of Online Education

Technically, the concept of online education is encompassed under the broader umbrella of distance education (Irlbeck, Kays, Jones, & Sims, 2006; U. S. Department of Education, 2010). Distance education involves a separation between the instructor and students through time and place, no matter if the medium used is correspondence by mail, telephone, e-mail, or a structured learning management system (LMS). Online education, as a subset of distance education, requires some component of web-based technology. In their study of online education in the United States, Allen and Seaman (2010) defined four different levels of online education. These levels are based on the percentage of content that is delivered online. They stated the following:

- *Traditional education* involves face-to-face interaction only.

- *Web-facilitated education* includes web-based content that supplements face-to-face education with only 1 to 29 percent of the content delivered online.

- *Blended or hybrid education* combines online and traditional face-to-face education, with 30 to 79 percent of the content delivered in an online format.

- *Online education* delivers 80 percent or more of the content in an online format. (p. 4)

Choosing the appropriate format for a class requires an analysis of the advantages and disadvantages of each of these four approaches (Zeliff, 2011). The analysis should consider student and faculty needs, and institutional resources. For more information, Zeliff (2011) offers an analysis of the advantages and disadvantages of each approach. For the purposes of this chapter, online education is defined as "the application of telecommunications and electronic devices to enable students to receive resources and instruction, synchronously or asynchronously, from a separate place than that of the teacher" (Robles, 2011, pp. 3–4).

Status and Significance of Online Education

Online education increases access to education for a broader population of students at all levels of the educational system (Dykman & Davis, 2008a). In 2008, 4.6 million K–20 students (kindergarten through postsecondary) were enrolled in at least one online class, which was a 17 percent increase from 2007 enrollments (Allen & Seaman, 2010). Just two years later, the number jumped to 6.1 million students with more than 2,500 college and universities offering online courses (Lytle, 2011). Several factors contribute to the push to implement online education. For example, online courses can provide solutions for students who work full-time, are in the military, have childcare issues, are not physically able to attend classes due to health problems or impairments, want opportunities not offered at their schools, such as advanced placement courses, or seek specialized retraining for job opportunities.

Variation exists in the implementation of online education across the United States. Larger and more established educational institutions tend to teach more online students (Allen & Seaman, 2010). In the business education field, as in many other fields, online education was initially offered primarily at the secondary level (Hite, 2011). However, as school administrators at all levels perceived the Internet and availability of computers as an opportunity to serve a wider population of students, online enrollments increased at the postsecondary level as well. The Sloan Consortium reported that 65.5 percent of chief academic officers surveyed at colleges and universities indicated that online education was a crucial component of an institution's long-term strategy (Lytle, 2011). Online education allows schools to leverage existing resources and technologies while increasing enrollments. Additionally, it facilitates continued learning in cases of pandemics (such as H1N1); therefore, some school systems have incorporated online education as part of their contingency plans (Allen & Seaman, 2010).

Although online programs can offset budget cuts (Rungtusanatham et al., 2004), online classes can be more expensive to develop due to the need for additional training and staff support resources to create interactive online environments and to transform on-campus classes into an online format. Instructors may also receive stipends for developing online course content. However, an economic benefit is often experienced in the long term, as once they are developed, online classes often result in increased enrollments while reducing overhead campus costs (Program Evaluation Division, 2010).

Initially, individual courses were offered online. Today, home-schooled K-12 students can earn their diplomas completely online. College and universities—both in the public and private sectors—offer online bachelor's, master's, and doctoral degrees without any residential requirements (Rungtusanatham et al., 2004). Economic and competitive pressures combined with technological opportunities have led many institutions to view online education as a core component of their educational missions (Allen & Seaman, 2010).

The environment is conducive to the implementation of online classrooms. The question now is not *whether* educational institutions should develop online education, but *how* they should develop them (Rungtusanatham et al., 2004). Despite the demand for online education, there is still skepticism on the part of faculty in terms of its legitimacy and value for student learning (Allen & Seaman, 2010; Benton, 2009; Dykman & Davis, 2008a). Online instructors must continuously adapt to new technologies and address a wide variety of pedagogical needs; this ongoing process can be daunting, especially for new faculty. Learning to teach online places instructors in the "role of the student once again" and opens instructors to the possibility of making mistakes (Benton, 2009). Benton suggested viewing the online and face-to-face environments as two methodologies to accomplish the same goal—student learning. Embracing the virtual environment requires an understanding of how to plan effectively for online teaching and learning. The next section discusses pedagogical issues for online business educators.

PLANNING EFFECTIVE ONLINE INSTRUCTION

Several qualities of good teaching are common regardless of the learning environment. Effective instructors (a) are passionate about their content, (b) connect with their students on a personal level, (c) are flexible in meeting their students' diverse learning needs, and (d) are creative in their lesson planning. However, demonstrating excellent teaching skills in a traditional face-to-face classroom does not guarantee the same instructor will be equally successful in an online classroom. Effective online instructors are also (a) technically savvy and able to learn new technologies intuitively, (b) motivational moderators and facilitators to encourage student participation, (c) very well organized and detail oriented throughout the entire course, and (d) willing to communicate with students daily and provide quick responses to their questions and concerns. Online instructors must also be knowledgeable about online learners and their unique learning styles as well as issues related to academic integrity and ethical behavior in the online environment.

Online Learners and Learning Styles

The virtual classroom offers unique challenges for understanding how to address the learning styles of online students. In the traditional classroom, instructors have the advantage of seeing students at work. In the online classroom, fewer cues exist to assess student comprehension. Therefore, it is important for instructors to provide a variety of strategies to address different learning styles. Hemby (2011) outlined eight learning styles that should be considered when planning online courses. Table 1 identifies teaching techniques that can be varied for different types of learners. The challenge is to first determine the students' style and then deliver the content to meet their individual learning needs.

In addition to understanding learning styles, online instructors need to plan for students with disabilities. Online audio and visual technologies can be used to enhance accommodations. Effective use of web-based technology can provide a learning environment that is conducive to students with disabilities. Many schools offer information to help students and instructors work together to adapt instructional strategies. For example, Johns Hopkins University (2012) identified the following techniques for accommodating students' needs:

- Posting copies of classmates' and/or instructor's notes

- Providing extended time for exams

- Allowing breaks during exams

- Allowing calculator, spellchecker, thesaurus, reader, and/or scribe during exams

- Providing alternative forms of the exam, such as an oral test or an essay instead of multiple-choice format

Table 1. Learning Styles and Associated Teaching Techniques

Type of learner	Learner needs	Teaching technique
Sensing	Concrete, practical, factual, and procedural information	Concrete, real-world examples and learning activities; demonstrations
Intuitive	Theories and concepts	Creativity and flexibility in assignments; use of external resources
Visual	Visual representations	Pictures, flow charts, diagrams
Verbal	Spoken and written materials	Discussions, presentations, podcasts, written notes
Active	Activity and collaboration with others	Projects or new content; collaboration with other students
Reflective	Opportunities to process information alone	Individual tasks and self-assessments
Sequential	Structure and orderly progress with small incremental steps	Detailed step-by-step procedures and feedback
Global	Holistic perspective for when learning occurs in large increments	Overall structure of content and tasks and overview of each unit

Source: Adapted from Hemby (2011).

- Providing extended time to complete assignments

- Including oral instructions and descriptions of materials

- Presenting instructions or demonstrations in more than one way

- Making the syllabus available before the start of the semester

Academic Integrity and Ethical Behavior

Because the perception that the online format increases the temptation for students to cheat, instructors need to take additional steps to ensure academic integrity (Rowe, 2004). One option is to require all tests to be proctored, either on campus in a testing center or, when at a distance, at a proprietary agency, such as a Sylvan Learning Center. A second alternative is to require students to use webcams while taking a test so the instructor can monitor their physical presence. Additionally, some learning management systems include lock-down tools that prohibit students from navigating away from an assessment. Cizek (1999) and Rowe (2004) shared other features that can be used with online tests, such as showing one question at a time, limiting the time allowed, password-protecting the test, using a test bank pool to randomize questions for each student, using settings to prevent printing and copying/pasting of the test questions, and using varied test formats.

Students have been known to use spyware and sniffer software to peek electronically at other students' tests (Rowe, 2004). They also may purposely break connections to the LMS server during the test to request that they be able to retake the test. Although integrity-preserving LMS features should be considered when selecting delivery options for online courses, they will not take the place of diligence on the instructor's part to be aware of work that is out of character for students.

To encourage academic integrity, instructors should list clear policies in the syllabus about violations of integrity and include specific examples of violations and their consequences. Additionally, the procedures for taking online tests should be clearly stated. For example, guidelines should indicate what will happen if students are locked out of a test or if they have an emergency situation that prevents them from taking the test at the scheduled time. To document the students' awareness and understanding of these guidelines, the first question of a test could ask students to verify that they will follow the academic integrity code during the test.

Online classes present other challenges with regard to academic integrity and ethical behavior, such as posting inappropriate content or sharing homework files in discussion forums or collaborative group pages. Discussions that require students to respond to other student comments or questions create a sense of community and responsibility. However, students should not be allowed to provide so much assistance that they share answers to assignments. For example, in a programming class, it would not be acceptable for a student to post sections of programming code in response to another student's question about how to complete a module.

SELECTING DELIVERY OPTIONS

Creating an effective online environment is the foundation for a successful online education experience. Correspondence courses may depend solely on e-mail to deliver instruction and submit coursework. However, several well-developed applications are available to create a rich learning experience. The interface should be easy to use and well organized (Henderson & Livingston, 2011).

Because "today's classrooms are a web of students [and] instructors…who interact with families, local and global communities, and businesses and industries all through the use of the Internet," the dilemma for online instructors is "knowing who the audience is, understanding the content, and determining the best approach to delivering that content" (Hodge, 2011, p. 43). In online education, technology should be viewed as a tool—as a means to an end, not the end itself. Like any other teaching tool, such as textbooks, instructors should evaluate technologies to determine what value can be added to student learning (Hodge, 2011).

Most business education classes are conducive to online delivery (Robles, 2011). For example, online courses in business communication can be effective if they include video lectures to explain content, writing examples that demonstrate both effective and ineffective communication, and multiple opportunities to demonstrate and assess students' learning (Johnson, 2011). Additionally, computer application courses are often effectively delivered online if they are supported by interactive e-learning applications (e.g., Cengage's SAM; Pearson's MyITLab) or textbooks with detailed step-by-step directions and screen shots that students can use to double-check their progress through a chapter tutorial (Bennett, 2011). However, hands-on courses in other disciplines are not as easy to deliver online, such as chemistry labs and nursing procedures that require specific resources and equipment.

Table 2 presents a variety of technologies and tools that support online instruction. These technologies are also used to supplement face-to-face courses because they support a variety of teaching and learning techniques.

Learning management systems—also known as course management systems—are web-based tools that provide an interface for instructors and students to access the course content and interact with each other. LMS environments provide a structure for delivering course materials, such as the syllabus, calendar, assignments, quizzes, tests, links, videos, and audio material. Students can also use e-portfolio software, such as TaskStream, to create virtual collections of their work submitted throughout a course or degree program. This work can be accessed by instructors, students, employers, and administrators to gauge student success and document accreditation data. Instructors can post the same material for multiple sections, and this material can be easily transferred to other class sections.

Beyond LMS environments, various emerging technologies can be used to supplement online education. Some of these can be integrated into LMS systems; others are designed to be used separately. Examples of these tools are listed in Table 2, but many others are available to enhance the interaction of online education. Hodge (2011) identified a comprehensive list that includes presentation software, movie makers, audio tools, podcasts, simulations, mind maps, social bookmarking, document sharing, image editors, communication applications, wikis, blogs, video communication, social spaces, online assessments, and virtual brainstorming. However, before integrating any of these technologies, instructors should determine how the tool will be used enhance student learning. For example, online audio presentations, business interviews, and video cases can provide insight into new business theory or concepts (Timm, 2011). Video demonstrations and screen shots can be used to demonstrate hands-on skills such as computer programming, web development, or desktop software use (Bennett, 2011).

CREATING A STRONG LEARNING COMMUNITY THROUGH INTERACTION

A strong online learning community is based on the participation and interaction of both the students and the instructor. Online environments should provide many opportunities for participation and interaction. Instructors must "press hard to overcome the impersonal nature of the machinery that makes up the online medium" (Dykman & Davis, 2008b, p. 160). Therefore, when planning an online class, instructors should

Table 2. Learning Management Systems and Online Educational Tool

Name	Type of Tool	Web Address
ATutor	Open source LMS	http://atutor.ca
Blackboard/WebCT	Proprietary LMS	http://www.blackboard.com
Canvas	Open source LMS	http://www.instructure.com
CCNet	Open Source LMS	http://www.zumosoftware.com/index.html
Claroline	Open source LMS	http://www.claroline.net
Coggno	Corporate training	http://coggno.com
Google Moderator	Interactive presentation tool	http://www.google.com/moderator
Joomla	Open source LMS	http://www.joomla.org
LAMS	Proprietary LMS	http://www.lamsinternational.com
CodePlex	Microsoft open source learning	http://lg.codeplex.com
Lino (Online Stickies)	Virtual brain-storming	http://en.linoit.com
MIT Open Courseware	Free courseware	http://ocw.mit.edu/index.htm
Moodle	Open source LMS	http://moodle.org
Prendismo	Video archive	http://www.prendismo.com/collection
RCampus	LMS and e-portfolio	http://www.rcampus.com
Sakai	Open source LMS	http://sakaiproject.org
SpicyNodes	Node maps for visual learning	http://www.spicynodes.org
TaskStream	Learning achieve-ment tool, e-portfolio	https://www.taskstream.com/pub
Word It Out	Word clouds	http://worditout.com

consider how they will support frequent and meaningful interaction among three criteria—student-student, student-instructor, and student-content interactions (Gaytan & Cannoy, 2010).

Building rapport among students in an online environment is critical. Several teaching methods and technology tools can be used to support an interactive learning community. Just as in face-to-face classes, the use of student groups or teams facilitates interaction among students and promotes collaborative learning experiences. Groups can use wikis, blogs, and collaboration applications, such as Google Docs, to share files and work on assignments. Students can video chat through LMS features or through external tools, such as Skype, to enhance their communication experience.

Additionally, students' photos can be posted with biographies they write to reduce the sense of anonymity online. Discussion boards or online forums can simulate the class discussions that occur in traditional face-to-face classrooms. However, there are several differences. Students who are shy or lack confidence to speak up in a face-to-face class may be more participatory in an online discussion in which they do not physically become the center of attention when they contribute to the conversation. In this case, the online environment is less intimidating (Balaji & Chakrabarti, 2010). However, students who lack effective writing skills may feel less comfortable sharing their responses in writing online, and students with poor typing skills may not provide as much detail as they would in a face-to-face classroom. The instructor's facilitation and participation in discussion boards has a positive influence and encourages students to use reflective thinking (Balaji & Chakrabarti). Therefore, instructors should read all posts, comment on threads, and provide individual feedback to students that address the student's discussion content.

Although most interaction may take place through discussion boards and chat rooms, the most critical interaction occurs through instructor feedback to students regarding their performance and learning. Prompt and meaningful feedback is consistently stated as a critical component for student learning in online communities (Dittmar, 2011; Gaytan & McEwen, 2007; Robles & Braathen, 2002). Feedback can be provided through rubrics, self-assessments, peer evaluations, discussion boards, chats, quizzes, and tests. Qualitative feedback is more appropriate to improving student reflection and learning throughout the course. Studies have shown that students prefer to have variety in the types of assignments given so that they receive different types of feedback (Gaytan & McEwen, 2007). Additionally, research has long suggested that the instructor's role (both online and in face-to-face classes) has evolved from lecturer (i.e., "sage on the stage") to that of facilitator (i.e., "guide on the side") in the student's journey of discovery (Dykman & Davis, 2008a; Kingsley, 2011; Warschauer, 2011). This change in the instructor's role enhances both the quality and quantity of feedback and focuses on the process of learning, which promotes student knowledge and stimulates students' critical thinking, problem solving, and reflective analysis. Therefore, ongoing feedback throughout the course is a foundation for continued student improvement.

ASSESSING STUDENT LEARNING

Assessment is the "systematic basis for making inferences about the learning and development of students. More specifically, assessment is the process of defining, selecting, designing, collecting, analyzing, interpreting, and using information to increase students' learning and development" (Erwin, 1991, p. 14). Assessing student learning is as important in online courses as it is in face-to-face classes and should be incorporated into curriculum planning (Crews & Wilkinson, 2010; Gaytan & McEwen, 2007). Instructors must first identify learning goals for the course and determine which types of activities will reflect students' achievement of those goals. A direct link should exist between the stated learning goals and the assessment of student learning (Swan, Shen, & Hiltz, 2006). The process of assessment should be an iterative loop that includes the following steps (Wright, 2004):

- Setting goals or asking questions about student learning and development

- Gathering evidence that will show whether these goals are being met

- Interpreting the evidence to see what can be discovered about students' strengths and weaknesses

- Using those discoveries to change the learning environment so that student performance will be improved

- Checking to see whether interventions worked, and/or new questions about learning are addressed (p. 186)

Grades are a form of feedback, but the use of rubrics and descriptive responses to student work can be more meaningful and result in improved performance. Assessment should be multidimensional, and web-based technologies provide a variety of ways to measure learning (Robles & Braathen, 2002). For example, students and instructors find that "projects, portfolios, self-assessments, peer evaluations, weekly assignments, timed tests and quizzes, and discussion boards" are diverse and effective ways to measure student learning (Gaytan & McEwen, 2007, p. 129). These techniques can be used for both formative and summative assessments. Formative assessments provide continuous feedback throughout the course to "help students improve their achievement of intended instructional outcomes" (Accountability Services Division, n.d., p. 1). Formative assessments may or may not be used in formal grading schemes, but they should occur frequently to monitor student performance. Summative assessments are used to formally evaluate student learning and usually occur at the end of a learning module (Crews & Wilkinson, 2010). Summative assessments typically include exams, reports, student presentations, and portfolios.

Assessing the Quality of the Online Classroom

Educational institutions have increasingly been called upon to be more accountable for assessing student learning. For example, accrediting agencies such as the Association to Advance Collegiate Schools of Business and the National Council for Accreditation of Teacher Education require comprehensive assessment data to document student learning. Other initiatives such as standardized testing encourage educators and administrators to emphasize learning outcomes.

Online courses should be assessed using the same data-driven criteria with which face-to-face courses are assessed. However, in addition, online courses should go further to incorporate the concepts of "total quality management" (TQM) into assurance of student learning. TQM is a philosophy used in businesses to prioritize customer relationship management and focus on continuous improvement (Weaver, 1992). TQM can be applied in the educational setting to evaluate online learning experiences based on the following criteria (Chao, Saj, & Tessier, 2006; Shwalb, 2010; Young & Norgard, 2006):

- Complete course content, including overview and expectations provided on the first day

- Clear directions for completing and submitting all required coursework

- Consistent organizational structure and navigation of content

- Quality and quantity of opportunities for engaged interaction

- Effective links to both internal and external resources

- Technical support availability (for both students and instructors)

In essence, with TQM, assessment becomes part of the educational process (Swan et al., 2006). The assessment enables a focus on the process of improvement rather than on outcome statistics (Wright, 2004). Parker (2004) stated that assessment measures should reflect "integrity of the teaching and learning processes within institutions" (p. 403).

Administrative Support and Evaluation

Assurance of student learning can suffer if there is not administrative support for online education. Many instructors believe that administrators support the concept of online education but not the resources needed to implement it properly. Administrators should ensure that instructors have proper training and are rewarded for excellent online teaching (Parker, 2004). Allen & Seaman (2010) reported that nearly 20 percent of the respondents stated that their institutions did not provide any training (formal or informal) for online teaching. Only the largest institutions tended to have the resources to offer in-house training. Due to lack of resources, the informal mentoring approach was used by 59 percent of the institutions surveyed (Allen & Seaman, 2010). In the same study, administrators said, "their faculty accept the value and legitimacy of online education does not reach a majority among any class of institution [public, private, etc.]" (p. 3). The lack of formal training and allocation of resources may lead to the perception that administrators are not committed to maintaining a quality online program.

Instructors spend a large amount of time developing online course materials, monitoring online courses in progress, interacting with students, and evaluating student work. Even though there are opportunities to compensate instructors for additional development time, not all instructors receive additional pay. "Providing appropriate compensation for the faculty and staff in recognition of additional effort and gains in productivity has always been and will continue to be a challenge in terms of fairness" (Sherron & Boettcher, 1997, p. 28). Because online teaching is often very time consuming, online instructors may put less emphasis on research and service activities, thereby falling behind in tenure and promotion requirements (Sherron & Boettcher, 1997; Valentine, 2002).

SUMMARY

Distance education began with correspondence courses that supported the disseminated instructional materials and coursework through postal mail. Today, distance education supports a wide variety of online delivery options through web-based and mobile technologies. As a component of distance learning, online education supports web-facilitated instruction, blended or hybrid education, and completely online course and/or degree delivery. As advances in technology continue to reshape communication channels and social interaction, online education will continue to grow and significantly impact educational opportunities at all levels to reach a wide audience of learners.

Effective online instruction requires more than good face-to-face teaching success. Online instructors must be motivated facilitators and prompt communicators who are technically savvy, well organized, and detail oriented. They must also have knowledge of diverse learning styles and how to support those styles in an online environment. Additionally, accommodations should be considered to support students with disabilities. The challenges of academic integrity and ethical behavior should also be addressed.

When selecting online course delivery options, instructors should consider all options and critically evaluate technologies to determine what value can be added to student learning. A strong learning community can be built by ensuring both the quantity and quality of interaction, participation, and engagement of students with the content, students with other students, and students with the instructor. Instructor feedback is critical in supporting student success in an online course.

Assessment of student learning should be directly tied to the learning goals of the course. Formative assessment should be integrated throughout the course through a wide variety of measures. Summative assessments should be used only after students have received ample opportunities for practice, feedback, and reflection. Assessment should also support continuous improvement through TQM initiatives. With full administrative support, online education can increase student enrollments and help institutions deal with budget constraints. However, to maintain quality online programs, administrators must allocate resources to provide formal online training and support.

REFERENCES

Accountability Services Division. (n.d.). Learn more about formative assessment. North Carolina Department of Public Instruction. Retrieved from http://www.dpi.state.nc.us/accountability/educators/vision/formative

Allen, E., & Seaman, J. (2010). *Learning on demand: Online education in the United States.* Needham, MA: Sloan Consortium and Babson Survey Research Group. Retrieved from http://www.sloan-c.org/publications/survey/pdf/learningondemand.pdf

Balaji, M. S., & Chakrabarti, D. (2010). Student interactions in online discussion forum: Empirical research from the "Media Richness Theory" perspective. *Journal of Interactive Online Learning, 9*(1), 1–22.

Barbera, E. (2004). Quality in virtual education environments. *British Journal of Educational Technology, 35*(1), 13–20.

Bennett, C. (2011). Technology courses. In L. G. Snyder (Ed.), *Online business education: NBEA 2011 yearbook* (No. 49, pp. 137–144). Reston, VA: National Business Education Association.

Benton, T. (2009, September 18). Online learning: Reaching out to the skeptics. *The Chronicle of Higher Education.* Retrieved from http://chronicle.com/article/Online-Learning-Reaching-Out/48375

Chao, T., Saj, T., & Tessier, F. (2006). Establishing a quality review for online courses. *Educase Quarterly,* (3), 32–39.

Cizek, G. J. (1999). *Cheating on tests: how to do it, detect it, and prevent it.* Mahwah, NJ: Lawrence Erlbaum.

Crews, T., & Wilkinson, K. (2010). Assessment in online environments. In L. G. Snyder (Ed.), *Online business education: NBEA 2011 yearbook* (No. 49, pp. 111–123). Reston, VA: National Business Education Association.

Dittmar, E. (2011). Interaction in online education. In L. G. Snyder (Ed.), *Online business education: NBEA 2011 yearbook* (No. 49, pp. 98–110). Reston, VA: National Business Education Association.

Dykman, C., & Davis, C. (2008a). Online education forum: Part one–The shift toward online education. *Journal of Information Systems Education, 19*(1), 11–16.

Dykman, C., & Davis, C. (2008b). Online education forum: Part two–Teaching online versus teaching conventionally. *Journal of Information Systems Education, 19*(2), 157–164.

Erwin, T. D. (1991). *Assessing student learning and development.* San Francisco: Jossey-Bass.

Gaytan, J., & Cannoy, S. D. (2010). Using the Shannon and Weaver Communication Model to achieve effective communication in online courses. *Journal of Business and Training Education, 19,* 35–46.

Gaytan, J., & McEwen, B. C. (2007). Effective online instructional and assessment strategies. *The American Journal of Distance Education, 21*(3), 117–132.

Hemby, K. V. (2011). Online learners and students' learning styles. In L. G. Snyder (Ed.), *Online business education: NBEA 2011 yearbook* (No. 49, pp. 82–97). Reston, VA: National Business Education Association.

Henderson, R., & Livingston, B. (2011). Preparing to teach online: What you need to know. In L. G. Snyder (Ed.), *Online business education: NBEA 2011 yearbook* (No.

49, pp. 29–40). Reston, VA: National Business Education Association.

Hite, N. G. (2011). Research in online education. In L. G. Snyder (Ed.), *Online business education: NBEA 2011 yearbook* (No. 49, pp. 16–28). Reston, VA: National Business Education Association.

Hodge, E. (2011). Instructional design for online education. In L. G. Snyder (Ed.), *Online business education: NBEA 2011 yearbook* (No. 49, pp. 41–55). Reston, VA: National Business Education Association.

Irlbeck, S., Kays, E., Jones, D., & Sims, R. (2006). The phoenix rising: Emergent models of instructional design. *Distance Education, 27*(2), 171–185.

Johns Hopkins University (2012). Types of disabilities. Retrieved from http://web.jhu. edu/disabilities/ faculty/types_of_disabilities

Johnson, B. (2011). Business communication courses. In L. G. Snyder (Ed.), *Online business education: NBEA 2011 yearbook* (No. 49, pp. 155–165). Reston, VA: National Business Education Association.

Kingsley, P. (2011). The Socratic dialogue in asynchronous online discussions: Is constructivism redundant? *Campus-Wide Information Systems, 28*(5), 320–330.

Lytle, R. (2011, November 11). Study: Online education continues growth. *U. S. News and World Report.* Retrieved from http://www.usnews.com/education/online-education/articles/2011/11/11/study-online-education-continues-growth

Parker, N. (2004). The quality dilemma in online education. In T. Anderson & F. Elloumi (Eds.), *Theory and practice of online learning* (pp. 385–421). Athabasca, Canada: Athabasca University. Retrieved from http://cde.athabascau.ca/online_book/ch16.html

Program Evaluation Division. (2010). *University distance education courses cost more to develop but the same to deliver as on-campus courses.* North Carolina General Assembly Final Report to the Joint Legislative Program Evaluation Oversight Committee. Report Number 2010-03.

Robles, M. (2011). History of online education and its impact on business education. In L. G. Snyder (Ed.), *Online business education: NBEA 2011 yearbook* (No. 49, pp. 1–15). Reston, VA: National Business Education Association.

Robles, M., & Braathen, S. (2002). Online assessment techniques. *The Delta Pi Epsilon Journal, 44*(1), 39–49.

Rowe, N. (2004, Summer). Cheating in online student assessment: Beyond plagiarism. *Online Journal of Distance Learning Administration, 7*(2). Retrieved from http://www.westga.edu/~distance/ ojdla/summer72/rowe72.pdf

Rungtusanatham, M., Ellram, L. M., Siferd, S. P., & Salik, S. (2004). Toward a typology of business education in the Internet age. *Decision Sciences Journal of Innovative Education, 2*(2), 101–120.

Sherron, G. T., & Boettcher, J. V. (1997). *Distance learning: The shift to interactivity.* CAUSE Professional Paper Series, No. 17. Retrieved from http://net.educause.edu/ir/library/pdf/pub3017.pdf

Shwalb, G. (2010, November 23). Assessing the quality of online courses: Quality matters. *Educational Technology Newsletter: UMass Boston EdTech.* Retrieved from http://umbedtech.wordpress.com/2010/11/23/assessing-the-quality-of-online-courses-quality-matters

Swan, K., Shen, J., & Hiltz, S. (2006). Assessment and collaboration in online learning. *Journal of Asynchronous Learning Networks, 10*(1). Retrieved from http://www-new. kent.edu/ehhs/dl/upload/assessment-and-collaboration.pdf

Timm, J. (2011). Basic business courses. In L. G. Snyder (Ed.), *Online business education: NBEA 2011 yearbook* (No. 49, pp. 124–136). Reston, VA: National Business Education Association.

U.S. Department of Education. (2010). Evaluation of evidence-based practices in online learning: A meta-analysis and review of online learning studies. (Contract No. Ed-04-CO-0040 Task 0006). Washington, DC: SRI International.

Valentine, D. (2002). Distance learning: Promises, problems, and possibilities. *Online Journal of Distance Learning, 5*(3). Retrieved from http://www.westga.edu/~distance/ ojdla/fall53/valentine53.html

Warschauer, M. (2011). *Learning in the cloud: How (and why) to transform schools with digital media.* New York: Teachers College Press.

Weaver, T. (1992). Total quality management. *ERIC Digest.* No. 73. Eugene, OR: ERIC Clearinghouse on Educational Management. Retrieved from http://www.eric.ed.gov/ PDFS/ED347670.pdf

Wright, B. (2004). More art than science: The postsecondary assessment movement today. In J. Bourne & J. C. Moore (Eds.), *Elements of quality online education: Into the mainstream* (Vol. 5 in the Sloan-C Series, pp. 185–197). Needham, MA: Sloan-C.

Young, A., & Norgard, C. (2006). Assessing the quality of online courses form the students' perspective. *The Internet and Higher Education, 9*(2), 107–115.

Zeliff, N. (2011). Delivery options of online education. In L. G. Snyder (Ed.), *Online business education: NBEA 2011 yearbook* (No. 49, pp. 68–81). Reston, VA: National Business Education Association.

Integrating Business Education with Core Academics

Jill White
Charlotte Boling
University of West Florida
Pensacola, FL

The National Council of Teachers of English, in 1935, defined integration as the unification of all subjects and experiences (Drake & Burns, 2004). In the next few decades, three instructional approaches to integration emerged: multidisciplinary integration of concepts, interdisciplinary activities, and transdisciplinary projects. While multidisciplinary integration relates to thematic-based learning and transdisciplinary integration focuses on project-based instruction, the focus of this chapter is interdisciplinary integration. Interdisciplinary integration strives to involve core academic classes with other instructional classes. In business education classes, core academics are integrated into theory as well as applied in an authentic setting.

This chapter discusses core elements of academics as well as why integrate, how to integrate literacy in business education, how to integrate social studies into business classes, and how to integrate science, technology, engineering, and mathematics (STEM) into business education. The chapter interweaves a variety of strategies for integration and shares resources.

ELEMENTS OF CORE ACADEMICS

Although the 1990 Carl Perkins Amendment paved the way for significant emphasis on college and career readiness, more is required due to the constant changes in business and industry. In response to this need, the National Governors Association and the Council of Chief State School Officers developed Common Core State Standards (CCSSs) to prepare students for success in college and work (Common Core State Standards Initiative, 2011).

Common Core State Standards

Common Core State Standards provide a structure through which teachers may align their content standards to standards from other disciplines. The CCSSs were designed to ensure college and career readiness for a global and migratory audience. Supported by the Association for Career and Technical Education (Reese, 2011), the criteria used in developing the standards follow:

- The CCSSs must align with college and work expectations.

- The CCSSs are clear, understandable, and consistent across all states.

- The CCSSs must include rigorous content and application of knowledge through high-order skills.

- The CCSSs build on strengths and lessons of current state standards.

- The CCSSs are informed by other top-performing countries so that all students are prepared to succeed in our global economy and society.

- The CCSSs are evidence based.

The CCSSs include college and career readiness anchor standards that address English, language arts, and mathematics. These subjects were selected for two reasons: (a) annual reading and math assessments per the No Child Left Behind Act of 2001 (NCLB, 2001), which called for the assessment of reading and math annually in grades 3–8 and once in high school and (b) reading and math serve as the building blocks of other subjects.

The release of the CCSSs created a collaborative movement among state legislators and educational organizations. Resources such as the *P21 Common Core Toolkit: A Guide to Aligning the Common Core State Standards with the Framework for 21st Century Skills*, developed by the Partnership for 21st Century Skills (2011), provided impetus and instructional examples for teachers to review their curricula and lessons to better integrate core content. The "12th Grade: Sample ELA Lesson Starter 1" (Figure 1) on page 19 of the toolkit is one example that is available in the public domain.

Career Academy Models

Career academies also provide settings in which business education and core academics can merge effectively. Career academies exist in schools throughout the United States and are a primary example of how core academics and business education can be integrated into a theme-based program of study. In 1968 the first career academy was established in Philadelphia, Pennsylvania, to address the lack of a skilled workforce. The National Career Academy Coalition model is based on the Career Academy National Standards of Practice (2004). These standards incorporate core elements aligned with each career academy. One of the primary components of the National Standards of Practice is the integration of academics across disciplines.

Figure 1. 12th Grade: Sample ELA Lesson Starter 1

Sample student outcome: Students collaboratively write a proposal to help solve a community problem in innovative ways.

Example: After completing a literature unit on the American dream in which students have read *The Great Gatsby, Death of a Salesman,* and *A Raisin in the Sun,* they explore what it means to have access to an American dream. Students are asked to create nonprofit people to meet their American dream without duplicating current services offered in the community. Students conceive of organizations, formulate extensive grant proposals that help them vie for funding from the fictitious Society for the American Dream, and compete against each other for funding of up to $500,000. Students pitch their ideas and advocate for funding to the grant panel, comprising community representatives, not teachers.

Common Core Standards	P-21 Skills Represented
RL. 11-12.9. Demonstrate knowledge of eighteenth-, nineteenth-, and early-twentieth-century foundational works of American literature, including how two or more texts from the same period treat similar themes or topics. SL. 11-12.2. Integrate multiple sources of information presented in diverse formats and media (e.g., visually, quantitatively, orally) in order to make informed decisions and solve problems, evaluating the credibility and accuracy of each source and noting any discrepancies among the data. WHST. 11-12.4. Produce clear and coherent writing in which the development, organization, and style are appropriate to task, purpose, and audience. WHST. 11-12.5. Development and strengthening of writing as needed by planning, revising, editing, rewriting, or trying a new approach, focusing on addressing what is most significant for a specific purpose and audience.	• Civic literacy • Critical thinking • Collaboration • Communication • Creativity • Information literacy

Source: Partnership for 21st Century Skills (2011).

Although career academies vary from one state to another as well as from one school district to another, one of the consistent components of the career academy model is the integration of core academics across all disciplines. School performance data indicate that students enrolled in the career academy programs at Hapeville High School in Atlanta, Georgia, have higher standardized test scores, lower dropout rates, and fewer disciplinary violations.

WHY INTEGRATION?

Integration is the key to successful implementation of common core standards, curriculum frameworks, National Business Education Association (NBEA) standards, and career academy pathways. According to Education.com (n.d.) "Integrated, interdisciplinary instruction is a teaching strategy that combines curriculum and academic standards from more than one content area." Higher-order thinking skills are required of students who participate in integrative approaches to instruction. Integration not only raises the bar through higher-order thinking skills but also encompasses rigorous learning outcomes for students. In Dale Parnell's book, *Why Do I Have to Learn This?* (1995), he stated that "excellence in education will happen only as we deepen student understanding by teaching for meaning" (p. 7). Integration is the vehicle that provides the meaning and connections for students.

The *National Standards for Business Education* (NBEA, 2007), curriculum frameworks, the inclusion of core academic standards, and the career academy model provide guidelines for quality education in all areas of business education. Business education teachers provide students content related to "personal finance, decision-making strategies to become wise consumers, and the economic principles to succeed in an ever-changing international marketplace" (NBEA, 2007, para.1). NBEA standards specify the necessary competencies, skills, and content knowledge for students to become productive citizens and informed consumers. Aligned with the additional standards referenced above and the integration of career and academic education, the NBEA focus becomes multidimensional as educators prepare students for college and career readiness.

Specific examples and strategies for including core academics in the business education curriculum are presented next. Literacy skills, including social studies concepts, and STEM content areas are presented. In addition to concepts and strategies, resources are provided for business educators.

INTEGRATING LITERACY IN BUSINESS CLASSES

Literacy is the cornerstone of business education instruction. It is fundamental to all learning activities. Literacy is the overarching concept that includes all of the skills one needs to read, write, discuss, and create. According to the National Council for Teachers of English (2007), "literacy encompasses reading, writing, and a variety of social and intellectual practices that call upon the voice as well as the eye and hand. It also extends to new media—including non-digitized multimedia, digitized multimedia, and hypertext or hypermedia" (p. 1). Although there are many literacy elements (including comprehension, vocabulary, fluency, and word identification), two specific elements that deserve attention in the business education career and technical education (CTE) classroom are reading and writing instruction.

Reading in the Business Classroom

As an essential learning element of literacy, reading is monitored through the assessments required in the No Child Left Behind (NCLB) Act of 2001. Reading also serves as a foundation for Common Core State Standards and 21st Century Skills. College and career readiness depends on a student's ability to read and comprehend. *Reading Next: A Vision for Action and Research in Middle and High School Literacy* (Biancarosa & Snow, 2004) provides the framework for effective reading instruction for the CTE student. This report calls for specific attention to instruction and infrastructure. The instructional elements include direct, explicit comprehension instruction; effective instructional principles embedded in content; motivation and self-directed learning; and ongoing formative assessments of students. The infrastructure elements include such items as extended time for literacy instruction, professional development, and frequent assessments of students and programs. Although a teacher may not use all of these elements during one instructional setting, a combination of these factors may be used to enhance reading instruction.

Business education students read for different purposes. An important lesson for students is to realize that there are different types of texts (novel, historical events, or cause and effect) and different ways to read (skim, scan, extensive, or intensive). Students *skim* a chapter in a science textbook as a pre-reading activity to identify the major concepts. Next, students in business education classes may *scan* a section of the newspaper to identify specific sources of information. An example of *extensive* reading may include acquiring the overall meaning of a text and connecting the content with current world events. Last, students may experience *intensive* reading whose purpose is to focus on a specific section of a manual and study detailed information (Beare, 2012). Students may improve their reading ability when provided with strategic instruction on the types of text, the types of reading, and an opportunity to practice.

Teaching Writing in the Business Education Classroom

Writing is an essential component of literacy involving the *process* of writing and the *product*. The written composition is the *product* through which students demonstrate their literacy abilities and content knowledge. As students research, write, revise, and edit their composition, the teacher provides strategic instruction concerning the *process* of writing. *Writing Next: Effective Strategies to Improve Writing of Adolescents in Middle and High Schools* (Graham & Perin, 2007) outlines 11 effective elements of writing instruction:

- **Writing strategies:** Instructional methods used to plan, revise, and edit compositions.

- **Summarization:** Explicit and systematic instruction on summarizing texts.

- **Collaborative writing:** Students plan, draft, revise, and edit their compositions in teams or pairs.

- **Specific product goals:** Students complete specific, reachable goals for their composition.

- **Word processing:** Computers and word processors are used as instructional supports for writing assignments.

- **Sentence combining:** Students are taught to construct more complex, sophisticated sentences using combination methods.

- **Inquiry activities:** Students analyze data with the intent of developing ideas for a particular writing task.

- **Process writing approach:** A workshop environment that provides an avenue for extended writing opportunities, writing for authentic audiences, personalized instruction, and cycles of writing.

- **Study of models:** Students analyze and emulate models of good writing.

- **Writing for content learning:** Students use the writing process as a tool for learning content.

These essential elements are necessary for effective writing instruction. However, they should not be used in isolation but rather as part of a complete literacy program. Students need equal opportunities to think critically, discuss openly, read, write, and evaluate the writing process and the content. The instructor should specifically address elements of the literacy *process*, ensuring students demonstrate content knowledge through a composition *product*.

Strategies for Teaching Literacy

The October 2011 issue of *Techniques: Connecting Education and Careers* is an excellent resource for teaching reading in the business education classroom. In this issue, the extensive reading strategies suggested in "Supporting the Development of Reading in the CTE Classroom" (Wichowski, 2011) are also supported by the reading next and writing next initiatives, discussed above. Three instructional strategies recommended for the business classroom include K-W-L, Think-Pair-Share, and Reading Walk-Through.

K-W-L. The know-want-learn (K-W-L) strategy requires an interactive conversation between the teacher and the students. The questions asked during this learning process are (a) What do I know? (b) What do I want to know? and (c) What have I learned? The teacher manages the learning process while students engage in research and writing activities to increase content knowledge and comprehension.

Think-Pair-Share. This strategy is a collaborative activity in which students think about a particular topic and discuss it with a partner. Examples might include effective marketing techniques for a new photography business, or what steps need to be taken to write a marketing proposal? Students discuss the topics with their "shoulder-partner" (neighbor or the person sitting beside the student) by taking turns offering suggestions and questioning their partner's ideas.

Reading Walk-Through. The Reading Walk-Through is an instructional strategy that serves as an advanced organizer and begins the comprehension process before the student starts to read. Struggling readers often lack the literacy skills necessary to read and write effectively. The Reading Walk-Through strategy requires students to identify major elements of the chapter, sub-headings, charts, and graphs before the reading activity takes place. By completing a Reading Walk-Through the student begins to gain an understanding of the general concepts presented in this chapter. Teachers use this strategy to introduce new vocabulary words or difficult concepts.

Business teachers are not expected to be reading specialists. However, knowledge of literacy strategies is needed for effective instruction and success for business education students. Business education instructors who implement effective literacy instructional strategies help develop students who are skillful readers and writers. The reading (literacy) and writing instructional strategies presented here are effective classroom activities that will augment students' literacy skills and increase individual college and career readiness opportunities.

INTEGRATING SOCIAL STUDIES IN BUSINESS CLASSES

The social studies curriculum framework (National Council for the Social Studies, 2010) focuses on 10 themes: culture; time, continuity, and change; people, places, and environments; individual development and identity; individuals, groups, and institutions; power, authority, and governance; production, distribution, and consumption; science, technology, and society; global connections; and civic ideals and practices. Social studies content from a business education perspective consists of economics and personal finance, entrepreneurship, international business, management, and marketing concepts. As communities and school district personnel work together to establish partnerships, social studies activities come to the forefront.

The document-based question (DBQ) strategy is an inquiry approach that teachers use to teach problem-based learning and social studies concepts (The DBQ project, n.d.). This teaching strategy focuses on an essential question and primary resource documents that elaborate on the concepts associated with the essential question. This strategy emphasizes the use of communication, decision-making, and conflict management skills that students use to solve problems.

Each DBQ project includes a "hook" exercise, background knowledge development, analysis of primary resource documents, a student product, and an assessment of the product. Students are required to discern the history behind the essential question and the issues involved in solving or understanding the question. The teaching strategy provides an avenue for analyzing documents to solve a problem. Students research the topic and investigate the documents to answer a question or solve a problem.

Strategies for Teaching Social Studies

As business educators integrate social studies into their curricula, the national frameworks should be reviewed. In the National Council for the Social Studies (NCSS, 2010a) publication, *National Curriculum Standards for Social Studies: A Framework for Teaching, Learning, and Assessment*, the council developed specific instructional standards that can be used for integrated instruction or design of single-discipline lessons. The DBQ strategy can be used to integrate social studies and business education topics such as global economics, financial literacy, and technology management systems. Business education teachers and business teacher education students are encouraged to research business topics to determine how they can align the DBQ to the business education curriculum. DBQ strategies can be adapted to many instructional settings.

Resources for Teaching Social Studies

A variety of resources are available for integrating social studies into the curriculum. The NCSS website (http://www.socialstudies.org) includes a variety of teaching ideas and professional development opportunities. The NCSS (2010b) publication *Teaching with Documents* (http://www.socialstudies.org/publications/twd) is a free downloadable resource that includes national standards, lesson plans, and printed resources to support classroom instruction. Additional lesson plans and instructional resources are available at http://www.socialstudies.org/resources.

INTEGRATING STEM IN BUSINESS CLASSES

The Secretary's Commission on Achieving Necessary Skills (1991, p. 22) indicated that skills in systems and technology should be taught in science courses. The current literature supporting science, technology, engineering, and mathematics (STEM) education has been at the forefront of educational reform (Becker & Park, 2011). Becker & Park's research indicated that "75% of the fastest growing occupations in our global economy require significant science and mathematics training" (p. 23). STEM content areas are essential to the success of our educational system.

One of our goals in education is to help students become more skilled at problem solving, decision making, and analysis. As we strive to meet these goals, we also meet the needs of our business and industry partners. The STEM Education Coalition, the U.S. Department of Education, and the National Science Foundation, as well as other agencies, offer support for STEM-related curricula and programs.

Strategies for Teaching STEM Classes

As educators become more driven by technology, they must generate more student interest in the STEM content areas. Students need to be aware of the educational opportunities available to them in STEM disciplines. Goonatilake and Bachnak (2012) suggested that "career interests and interventions are needed to strengthen students' academic preparation to succeed in STEM disciplines" (p. 15).

Ford Next Generation Learning has created curricula that can be used in STEM classes. The 20 Ford Partnership for Advanced Studies (FordPAS) modules are "academically rigorous, standards-based content with realistic applications in areas such as design and product development, information systems, environmental sustainability, global economics, business planning, personal finance, and marketing" (FordPAS, 2005, para. 1). The curriculum is theme based and can be used in both academic and elective classes. Themes included in the modules cover putting math to work; getting smart about business; manufacturing for tomorrow; data, decisions, and design; living in a global economy; and foundations in 21st century skills. The curriculum content is aligned with state standards in California, Florida, Michigan, and Texas. The teachers' guides and modules can be downloaded at no cost by accessing the Ford website (http://fordpas.org). Teachers may use the modules as enrichment activities or include them in daily lesson plans.

As business educators integrate STEM content areas into their classroom instruction, special emphasis should be placed on meeting the standards for each content area. Science instruction in business classes is primarily related to the scientific process, whereas *National Standards for Business Education* (NBEA, 2007) addresses mathematics from a financial perspective. The National Education Technology Standards guide teaching and learning in the digital age (International Society for Technology in Education, 2012).

Resources for Teaching STEM

A variety of resources are available for integrating STEM content into the curriculum. The National Research Council (2011) released a framework for K–12 science, technology, and engineering. These standards incorporate the National Academy of Science, National Academy of Engineering, and National Research Council. The web page for these frameworks noted the following:

> The framework identifies the key scientific ideas and practices all students should learn by the end of high school. It will serve as the foundation for new K–12 science education standards, which will be developed by a group of states to replace standards issued more than a decade ago. The framework is also designed to be useful for curriculum and assessment designers, teacher educators, and others who work in K–12 science education. (NRC, 2011, p. 1)

In addition to the links provided above, the National Council of Teachers of Mathematics has provided a series of resources for teachers. Its series entitled "Reasoning and Sense Making" describes mathematics examples to help students analyze and graph geometric functions, solve problems that relate to real-world experiences, and compare their own reasoning abilities with their classmates. (For additional information related to these resources, see http://www.nctm.org/standards/content.aspx?id=23749). The International Society for Technology in Education also provides excellent standards and resources for teaching, learning, and leading in the digital age. See their website at http://www.iste.org/standards.aspx.

The April 2012 issue of NBEA's *Business Education Forum* provides excellent resources for the integration of STEM education into the business classroom. Maylen-Smith (2012) described opportunities for business educators to "prepare their students for a meaningful career in the STEM workplace" (p. 23). Maylen-Smith postulated that "in addition to the integration of STEM into existing business programs, new discoveries and advances in STEM provide new opportunities to build partnerships and expand programs" (p. 27). The authors of this chapter support her position and advocate the integration of core academics, as well as STEM content, as another way to strengthen existing business education courses and programs. Additionally, McEwen & McEwen (2012) outline strategies for integrating STEM into entrepreneurship education. The authors also support incorporating STEM content in the business classroom "to help students develop critical core skills" (p. 35).

SUMMARY

This chapter has focused on the integration of core academics in the business educa-tion classroom. The primary areas outlined in this chapter have been literacy (reading and writing), social studies, and STEM. The chapter has also provided a range of resources and examples for practicing teachers as well as business teacher education candidates.

As core academics are integrated into business classes, teachers must provide a rigorous and relevant curriculum to prepare students to succeed in the world of work. Integrated learning activities provide a more personal learning experience for business students. These activities combine core academics with related business technology skills and standards to accomplish relevant, real-world projects. With strong academic knowledge and professional skills integrated into the business education classroom, tomorrow's students will be well prepared to make a difference in the global workforce.

REFERENCES

Beare, K. (n.d.). Reading: Identifying skill requirements. Retrieved from http://esl. about.com/od/readinglessonplans/a/l_readtypes.htm

Becker, K., & Park, K. (2011, July–September). Effects of integrative approaches among science, technology, engineering, and mathematics (STEM) subjects on students' learning: A preliminary meta-analysis. *Journal of STEM Education, 12*(5 & 6), 23–37.

Biancarosa, G., & Snow, C. E. (2004). *Reading next: A vision for action and research in middle and high school literacy: A report to Carnegie Corporation of New York.* Washington, DC: Alliance for Excellent Education. Retrieved from http://www. all4ed.org/files/ReadingNext.pdf

Career Academy national standards of practice. (2004). Retrieved from http://www. aypf.org/publications/Career%20Academy%20National%20Standards%20of%20 Practice.pdf

Common Core State Standards Initiative. (2011). Implementing the Common Core State Standards. Retrieved from http://www.corestandards.org

Drake, S. M., & Burns, R. C. (2004). *Meeting standards through integrated curriculum.* Alexandria, VA: Association for Supervision and Curriculum Development.

Education.com. (n.d.). Glossary of education: Integrated, interdisciplinary instruction. Retrieved from http://www.education.com/definition/integrated-interdisciplinary-instruction

Ford Partnership for Advanced Studies (FordPAS). (2005). Theme descriptions. Retrieved from http://fordpas.org/theme-descriptions

Goonatilake, R., & Bachnak, R. (2012, January–March). Promoting engineering education among high school and middle school students. *Journal of STEM Education, 13*(1), 15–21.

Graham, S., & Perin, D. (2007). *Writing next: Effective strategies to improve writing of adolescents in middle and high schools, A report to Carnegie Corporation of New York.* Washington, DC: Alliance for Excellent Education. Retrieved from http://www. all4ed.org/files/WritingNext.pdf

International Society for Technology in Education (ISTE). (2012). National education technology standards. Retrieved from http://www.iste.org/standards.aspx

Maylen-Smith, J. (2012). Staking a claim in the STEM education landscape: Opportunities for business education. *Business Education Forum, 66*(4), 23–27.

McEwen, T., & McEwen, B. (2012). Integrating STEM competencies into entrepreneurship education. *Business Education Forum, 66*(4), 32–36.

National Business Education Association. (2007). *National standards for business education: What America's students should know and be able to do in business* (3rd ed.). Reston, VA: Author.

National Council for Teachers of English. (2007). *Adolescent literacy* (Policy research brief). Retrieved from http://www.ncte.org/library/NCTEFiles/Resources/Positions/Chron0907ResearchBrief.pdf

National Council for the Social Studies. (2010a). *National curriculum standards for social studies: A framework for teaching, learning, and assessment.* Silver Spring, MD: Author. Retrieved from http://www.socialstudies.org/standards

National Council for the Social Studies. (2010b). Teaching with documents. Retrieved from http://www.socialstudies.org/publications/twd

National Council of Teachers of Mathematics. (2012). Focus in high school mathematics: Reasoning and sense making. Retrieved from http://www.nctm.org/standards/content.aspx?id=23749

National Research Council. (2011, July). *A framework for K–12 science education.* Retrieved from http://www.nextgenscience.org/framework-k%E2%80%9312-science-education

No Child Left Behind (NCLB) Act of 2001, Pub. L. No. 107-110, § 115, Stat. 1425 (2002). Retrieved from http://www2.ed.gov/policy/elsec/leg/esea02/107-110.pdf

Parnell, D. (1995). *Why do I have to learn this? Teaching the way people learn best.* Waco, TX: Center for Occupational Research and Development.

Partnership for 21st Century Skills. (2011). *P-21 common core toolkit. A guide to aligning the Common Core State Standards with the Framework for 21st Century Skills.* Washington, DC: Author. Retrieved from http://www.p21.org/storage/documents/P21CommonCoreToolkit.pdf

Reese, S. (2011, October). CTE and the common core state standards. *Techniques: Connecting Education and Careers, 86*(7), 16.

Secretary's Commission on Achieving Necessary Skills, U.S. Department of Labor. (1991, June). *What work requires of schools* (ED 332 054). Washington, DC: Author.

The DBQ project. (n.d.). The DBQ project is… Retrieved from http://dbqproject.com

Wichowski, C. P. (2011, October). Supporting the development of reading in the CTE classroom. *Techniques: Connecting Education and Careers, 86*(7), 36–39.

Information Technology

Herbert F. Brown

Alicia Finnell

Appalachian State University

Boone, NC

The authors, editor, and publisher acknowledge and express appreciation for the work done by George A. Mundrake, author of this chapter in the previous edition. Thank you for your contribution to this yearbook and to business education.

Employers today expect their employees to have technological skills for the workplace (Gibbs, Steel, & Kuiper, 2011). Depending on their level of expertise and their career goals, students may choose to continue building their skills at the postsecondary level or use their skills on the job. Technical skills taught in information technology (IT) courses today provide a solid foundation of transferable technical and employability skills that will be valuable to employers (Grant, Malloy, & Murphy, 2009).

Because information technology is so important in the workplace and in the personal lives of individuals, it is important that IT courses keep pace with changing times. Employers seek and hire students who are ready and able to apply current technical skills when they enter the workplace (Gibbs et al., 2011). IT skills are so fundamental today that they are an expectation just like reading, math, and writing are; it is now an essential competency all students need. For the United States to be competitive in the global job market, business educators must strive to prepare students with the technical skills that business and industry expect.

This chapter discusses IT courses taught at the secondary and postsecondary levels, related teaching strategies for those courses, and technological trends that should be included in the business education IT curriculum, as well as skills needed by all students.

A CHANGING INFORMATION TECHNOLOGY CURRICULUM

In order to keep pace with changes in business and changes in technology, IT curricula must also change. Students today possess more advanced technical skills than those a generation before. Exposure to technology occurs very early. Students learn to use the technology before they even learn to touch type; therefore, technology is not foreign to most students and they embrace it. These are reasons for developing and implementing a more advanced curriculum. The *National Business Education Standards* from the National Business Education Association or NBEA (2007) and the National Educational Technology Standards (NETS) from the International Society for Technology in Education or ISTE (n.d.) are used as a framework for designing and enhancing the K–16 IT curriculum.

Today many students have the opportunity to start learning about information technology as early as kindergarten through the integration of computer technology in their classrooms (Computer Science Teachers Association, 2012). In junior high and middle school IT courses, students are taught to use software in application suites, such as OpenOffice (openoffice.org) and Microsoft Office. At the high school and collegiate levels, business education students enrolled in IT courses learn advanced communication and computer applications, multimedia, web page design, networking, and computer programming. Many IT programs have undergone a rigorous evaluation process, known as industry certification that assesses course content and skills taught to students in order to demonstrate that students are taught according to business and industry standards. In addition to program industry certification, in order to certify that students are "highly skilled" in information technology, they may complete industry-recognized certification assessments. Students earning these certifications enter the world of work with credentials respected by employers. Possessing these credentials makes students more competitive and demonstrates they have technical skills that employers expect. One such certification-based program that states are embracing is the Microsoft IT academy program (Microsoft, n.d.).

Standards

Regardless of whether industry certification programs are used, the overall IT curriculum is designed around industry standards; national, state, and local needs; and the NBEA National Standards for Business Education. Many states use the NBEA standards as the foundation on which to develop the state curriculum and pathways. These standards are developed and updated about every five years by experts in the field. The standards for information technology address the following: (a) impact on society, (b) hardware, (c) operating systems and utilities, (d) input technologies, (e) productivity software, (f) interactive multimedia, (g) web development and design, (h) information retrieval and synthesis, (i) database management systems, (j) systems analysis and design, (k) programming and application development, (l) telecommunications and networking infrastructures, (m) IT planning and acquisition, (n) security, privacy, and risk management, (o) ethical and legal issues, (p) technical support and training, (q) IT and business functions, and (r) IT careers. Not only do the standards provide a content framework, they provide suggested academic levels at which IT content can and should be delivered: from kindergarten through postsecondary (K–14) (NBEA, 2007).

Whereas the NBEA standards outline IT standards for business education programs, ISTE (n.d.) has detailed IT skills for all students, teachers, and administrators, referred to as the NETS. The NETS for students identify six categories of skills that all students should possess to be successful in school and life. The NETS for teachers identify categories of skills that teachers should incorporate in their classrooms to enhance learning, promote digital citizenship, and encourage professional growth. The NETS for administrators provide a framework that can assist administrators in the development of technology-enhanced learning environments (ISTE, n.d.). All educators have the information they need to help them embrace the use of technology and integrate it into the courses they teach, either as a teaching tool, as the content of the course, or maybe as both.

Information Technology as a Tool

Information technology is a tool used to enhance instruction. Basic technologies used in classrooms today that support student learning include the SMART Board, tablet PCs, Skype, webinars, RSS feeds, blogging, wikis, podcasts, mobile learning, Webquests, Twitter, Facebook, LinkedIn, and iPads/e-readers (Kronowitz, 2012). Information technology is also a tool that students learn to use to complete tasks, such as a report or spreadsheet. In these examples, the technology is not the content; IT is the tool used to create a product. This use of technology demonstrates the interrelationship between IT and business functions as well as its integration with other academic areas (NBEA, 2007).

Information Technology as Content

When one of the purposes of a course is for students to learn to use information technology, IT is the content. For example, in a web design course students learn to use programs such as Microsoft Expression and Adobe Dreamweaver to develop quality websites, so technology is the course content. However, in a word-processing course, students learn to use programs such as Microsoft Word, WordPerfect, and OpenOffice Writer; students enrolled in a desktop publishing course may learn to use Adobe InDesign or Microsoft Publisher. In these cases, information technology is the content.

Junior High and Middle School Curriculum

The IT curriculum at the junior high / middle school level varies across the country. Several IT courses have similar content but different titles. For example, the "Computer Skills and Applications" course in North Carolina has content and skills development standards similar to courses titled "Business Technology" in Minnesota, "Information Technology Applications" in Nebraska, and "Computer Technology" in Arkansas. The junior high and middle school curriculum typically focuses on exploratory exposure to technology, with a moderate depth of skill development and advanced skills developed at the high school level.

High School Curriculum

High school IT programs of study and career pathways and majors are designed to teach students the knowledge and skills necessary for success in college and IT-related careers. For example, IT pathways available in Utah are business administrative support and business technology support (Utah State Office of Education, 2010). Georgia's IT pathways are administration/information support, computing, interactive media, and computer networking (Georgia Department of Education, 2011). In North Carolina, the career majors are information technology and office systems technology (North Carolina Department of Public Instruction, 2012). Examples of courses in the pathways/majors are Computer Technology I and II, Digital Business Applications, IT Essentials and IT Support, Multimedia and Web Design, Networking and Networking Administration, and Computer Programming I and II.

Postsecondary/College Curriculum

The postsecondary and college curriculum is defined by increased depth of content and integration of technology for problem solving and applications. Business applications of technology are examined and encouraged at the postsecondary level. This increased depth is reflected in the NBEA IT standards represented at level 4 in its standards document (NBEA, 2007). IT concepts that require advanced student preparation include advanced database systems, enterprise resource planning (ERP) systems, advanced programming, and advanced networking. At the college level, students are also able to specialize in a specific IT area and achieve advanced skill development in areas such as computer networking, web development, and programming.

Advanced courses and IT skills at the postsecondary/college level are typically included in technology programs such as computer science, computer information systems, and other IT areas. Some postsecondary and college programs require a basic computer course or proof of competency for all students, but many colleges now assume that students are entering these programs with basic technology skills.

Adult Learners

The adult learner market includes learners who require retraining or skills development to improve their current positions or to prepare for another career. Adults who already possess IT skills typically do well as they improve their skills to reach more advanced IT topics. Adults without an IT background, however, may find it more difficult and intimidating to work with a computer (Sivakumaran & Lux, 2011). Sivakumaran and Lux suggested a three-step process to alleviate computer anxiety for adult learners. Step one is to help the adult learner understand the purpose behind using the computer to help learners understand the importance of using the computer to meet their specific needs. Step two is to provide a positive environment that allows adult learners to work with the technology and receive assistance in a safe, bias-free learning environment. Step three is to provide ongoing support for the adult learner so they have a support structure to go to when they need assistance.

Industry Certifications

The goal of industry certification training is to verify independently an individual's competence in some application of computer technology. Employers use certifications as an indicator of skills competency. IT certifications can also result in increased pay, enhanced employee self-confidence, and improved employment opportunities. IT certifications are a preferred measure of the skills of potential employees that do not possess a preferred two-year or four-year IT degree (Wierschem, Zhang, & Johnston, 2010). These certifications may include hardware certifications such as the CompTIA A+ or Cisco Network Engineer, or software-based certifications such as Office Applications–Microsoft MOS certifications and network-server software applications such as Microsoft Certified IT Professional and Linux or Redhat certification. Individuals may also get web development certifications, such as the W3schools online certification or Adobe certifications. Database certifications in Oracle database administration and others are also available.

The IT curriculum should be constantly changing to remain current with the rapid changes in the industry. Although there is diversity in the skills and curricula that are taught and in the strategies used to introduce students to information technology, business educators are challenged to grow with the technology to be effective in the instructional environment. The next section will address specific strategies for delivering IT curriculum.

BASIC TEACHING STRATEGIES AND RESOURCES

Instruction generally progresses from teacher centered to student centered along a continuum that advances from passive to active student engagement. Instructional strategies along the continuum are lecture, demonstration, questioning, discussion, guided practice, independent practice, grouping, role playing, simulation, and reflective inquiry/thinking (Freiberg & Driscoll, 2005). Business educators practice these strategies. Business education students have the opportunity to work with their minds and their hands. Information technology, in particular, is an area that lends itself to more student-centered instructional practices. Because of the performance-driven nature of IT courses, students must be actively engaged in their learning experiences. Teachers must also keep in mind that the learners in their classroom have multiple intelligences and learning styles. For that reason, an effort must be made to differentiate instruction and make modifications for students with special needs.

Read, Reflect, Display, Do

The model, referred to as the Read, Reflect, Display, Do (R2D2) Model (Figure 1), can be effectively used to differentiate instruction and make learning activities more interactive. The R2D2 framework emphasizes reading and/or listening to information, reflecting on it, displaying what was learned, and doing something with that new knowledge (Bonk & Zhang, 2008). Each phase is designed to reach a different type of learner and uses technology-based resources and tools. Table 1 provides an example of resources and tools for each phase. In *Empowering Online Learning*, Bonk and Zhang (2008) shared and discussed more than 100 learning activities for reading, reflecting, displaying, and doing.

Figure 1: The Read, Reflect, Display, and Do Model (R2D2)

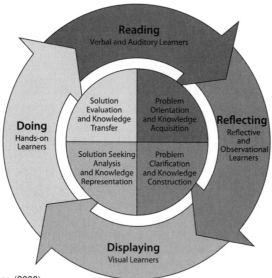

Source: Bonk & Zhang (2008).

Table 1. Sample R2D2 Uses, Resources, and Tools

Phase	Learner type	Uses, resources, and tools
1. Read	Auditory and verbal learners	Read/review materials before class using online articles, audio files, presentations, explorations, and podcasts.
2. Reflect	Reflective and observational learners	Reflect on information reviewed through use of blogs, chats, reflective writing, expert videos or performances, and self-check activities and examinations.
3. Display	Visual learners	Learn highlighted content through visual displays and activities, such as virtual tours, concept maps, timelines, animations, video blogs, and interactive media.
4. Do	Tactile and kines-thetic learners	Apply and display knowledge gained through hands-on activities—including gaming, simulations, scenarios, digital storytelling, and real-time cases—and role play and debate.

Note: Information for this table compiled from Bonk and Zhang (2008).

Career and Technical Student Organization Activities as Instructional Tools

"A CTSO [Career and Technical Student Organization] is a powerful instructional tool that works best when integrated into the CTE [Career and Technical Education] curriculum and classroom by an instructor who is committed to the total development of students" (Scott & Sarkees-Wircenski, 2008, p. 326). CTSO activities and events may be used to reinforce learning in information technology at the junior high and middle school, high school, and postsecondary levels. Future Business Leaders of America–Phi Beta Lambda (FBLA-PBL), Business Professionals of America, SkillsUSA, and the Technology Student Association have competitive events and award recognition activities related to information technology. At least 30 FBLA-PBL competitions are aligned with the NBEA standards for IT (Future Business Leaders of America–Phi Beta Lambda, 2011). The CTSO events and activities may be used as class projects, and students may also register to participate officially in activities and events via the CTSO.

Web-Based Teaching Resources

Often textbooks reference links to online teaching resources; however, teachers often teach without a textbook and must find their own resources. Web searches may yield results that are not helpful; however, some state departments of education and their affiliates have done an outstanding job providing resources for teachers. Colleges and universities also share helpful teacher resources. Other organizations work to provide teachers with resources that will help with curriculum development and instruction. Some resources that might be helpful for business educators can be found at the following URLs:

- Teach-ICT.com (http://www.teach-ict.com/index.html)

- The Texas Education Agency's CTE website (http://cte.unt.edu/it/curriculum)

- Virginia's CTE Resource Center (http://www.cteresource.org/verso/categories/information-technology)

- Wisconsin's Technology Web Resources website (http://bit.dpi.wi.gov/bit_websites)

- Utah State University's IT University Tutorials website (http://it.usu.edu/tutorials)

- Learners TV (http://www.learnerstv.com/computers.php)

- *MIT Technology Review* (http://www.technologyreview.com)

Digital Communication and Word Processing

Examples of digital communication media used today include e-mail, phone, voice mail, text messaging, instant messaging, web chats, and social media (Bovee & Thill, 2012). Computer applications can allow individuals to create electronic presentations and then share those presentations in web-based meetings and videoconferencing with people across a large geographic area. Digital communication also occurs via podcasting and online videos. Collaboration and digital communication are fostered through the use of shared workspaces, wikis (e.g., WikiSpaces and Wiggio), blogs (e.g., WordPress), microblogs (e.g., Twitter and Tumblr), and social networks (e.g., Facebook and

LinkedIn) (Bovee & Thill, 2012). When teaching about word processing and digital communication, the following strategies are recommended:

- Teach students to carefully plan, compose, and complete messages because all traditional and digital communications need to be thoroughly conceived and organized so they make sense to the audience when they are received (Bovee & Thill, 2012).

- Teach document formatting. Show students examples of exemplary communication products. Students should not rely on built-in templates.

- Have students prepare business-related documents: business plans/proposals, brochures, catalogs, contact lists, telephone scripts, news releases, newsletters, and product descriptions and reviews

- Chronicle class activities, lessons learned, helpful resources, and interviews of professionals in the field through student-produced class newsletters, websites, and blogs.

- Teach students to produce job search documents: letters of request for a recommendation, letters of application, resumés, responses to interview questions, and thank you notes

Spreadsheet Software

Spreadsheets are powerful mathematical tools that allow students to organize data into rows and columns, calculate, create charts and graphs, and analyze information. Spreadsheets are used for a number of business and personal tasks. In business, spreadsheets are often used for payrolls, inventories, price quotations, payment calculations, financial statements, sales reports, and schedules. Popular spreadsheet programs include Microsoft Excel, Corel Quattro Pro, OpenOffice Calc, and Apple Numbers. Microsoft Works and Google Docs also have spreadsheet programs. The Science Education Resource Center's (SERC's) Pedagogy in Action (http://serc.carleton.edu/sp/index.html) and K–12 Science portals for educators (http://serc.carleton.edu/k12/index.html) are valuable resources for spreadsheet lessons. Its "Teaching with Spreadsheets" (http://serc.carleton.edu/sp/library/spreadsheets/index.html) and "Teaching with Spreadsheets across the Curriculum" (http://serc.carleton.edu/sp/library/ssac/index.html) websites provide examples of teaching with spreadsheets, learning modules, and references and resources for spreadsheets in education. When teaching about spreadsheets, the following strategies are recommended:

- Stress "why" and "how" the technology is used by sharing real and relevant examples to give students an authentic view of what they will be learning to create.

- Guide students through the process of planning and producing a basic spreadsheet. Students must learn to think critically through the process of building a spreadsheet (Tort, 2010).

- Have students create spreadsheets "from scratch," given only a planning sheet, text for the first column and first row of the spreadsheet, and instructions written in word-problem format that inform them about the purpose/goal of the spreadsheet.

- Assign learning activities that are personal and relevant to students' lives. The following activities require students to research, plan, and create spreadsheets, and then make decisions based on results.

  - Recreate tax forms and schedules. Calculate the refund due or amount owed.

  - Comparison shop groceries/clothes (at least five items). Figure out differences in price and decide what is the best buy (at least two stores).

  - Calculate the cost of senior-class products. Determine payment schedules and savings goals. Then compute the number of hours necessary to work in order to pay for the products.

  - Plan a senior/spring-break trip (e.g., destination, method of travel [airplane/bus/ train or drive one's own or rental car], activities, lodging, food, and souvenirs).

  - Maintain a personal grade sheet for class. Use percentages from the syllabus to compute averages for grade categories and calculate the final course grade.

- Collaborate with math and science teachers on lessons and activities that reinforce concepts learned in those classes.

Database Management Software

Database software is typically included in some form in the K–12 and postsecondary education areas. The differences in the implementation of database software at different levels is designed to engage students from a beginning general knowledge and use of database applications to designing and using databases and information to solve business problems. The level of complexity of database software applications also typically increases as students reach higher academic levels. Students typically begin with flat-file databases (such as Microsoft Excel) to manipulate data into useful information, such as sorting a file or filtering data based on a set of criteria. Students then progress to relational databases such as Microsoft Access, Corel Paradox, or OpenOffice Base. These applications require students to build the database structures, determine and establish relationships, populate records, and query the database to obtain useful information. The highest level of database management software typically includes enterprise-level database applications such as Oracle and MySQL. These applications require not only the same development requirements of any relational database application but also that students understand and design large database structures, configure database servers, secure database servers, and create useful information through reporting and query functions using structured query language.

The following strategies for teaching database concepts are recommended:

- Begin database instruction by covering the key concepts and designs for databases, including types of databases, records, fields, tables, files, queries, forms, and reports. Have students use a database to understand why databases are important and how to use them to obtain useful information.

- Have students create simple flat-file databases that contain information of interest to them.

- Discuss and design relational databases that contain the same information in the flat file, but add relationships and additional data to demonstrate the difference and importance of relational database systems.

- Use Access to build advanced switchboard applications for a specific purpose: a student-advising database system, an inventory system, or a student organization (e.g., Future Business Leaders of America–Phi Beta Lambda and DECA) data management tool.

Graphics, Presentation, and Multimedia Software

Graphics, presentation, and multimedia software are well represented in business education classrooms. This category includes the manipulation and creation of graphics in all formats for numerous purposes, including desktop publishing and web development. Software in this category includes Adobe's Photoshop, Fireworks, and Illustrator; Corel's Draw and Paintshop Pro; as well as open-source applications such as GIMP (GNU Image Manipulation Program available at http://www.gimp.org), Inkscape (http://inkscape.org), and Paint.NET. Instruction in computer graphics should include the manipulation of existing images and the creation of original images and artwork. Digital cameras are also very useful tools in the computer graphics classroom for gathering original images for projects. Presentation software is used in almost all classrooms today, including at the elementary level. This software allows students to develop graphical and text-based presentations. Software in this category includes Microsoft PowerPoint, Corel Presentations, Prezi, and OpenOffice solutions such as OpenOffice Impress. Multimedia software can include a range of other development applications for multimedia; the most common is Adobe Flash. This category may also include 3-D development environments such as Maya (http://usa.autodesk.com/maya), Alice (http://www.alice.org), and Blender (http://www.blender.org). Students are drawn to courses that include these applications as it allows them to use their creativity and create amazing products. Because of the diverse range of applications and options, the teaching strategies also need to be diverse. The following strategies for teaching graphics, presentations, and multimedia concepts are recommended:

- Develop graphic designs for the school's sports programs, website, clubs, etc. Partner with these groups in the school to develop artwork for their programs.

- Partner students with local businesses to develop custom logos, presentation templates, and multimedia applications for those businesses.

- Create school presentation templates and assist school personnel and clubs with presentation development.

ADVANCED INFORMATION TECHNOLOGY STRATEGIES

The business education curriculum continues to evolve to include new advanced topics in information technology including electronic publishing, advanced web development, computer networking, ERPs, project management, mobile application development, and more. This section briefly describes typical learning objectives in each of these areas with recommendations for content coverage and teaching strategies.

Electronic/Desktop Publishing

Desktop publishing using standard tools and applications, such as Adobe InDesign, has been popular for developing publications for print media. Today, desktop publishers increasingly develop publications for web and other online delivery, including e-books. In fact, Apple just released a new product, iBooks Author, that facilitates the development of e-books for the Apple computer platform (Apple Inc., n.d.). Other publishers use the standard portable document format (PDF) and proprietary formats. These electronic formats include digital rights restrictions that limit the ability to duplicate and print these digital materials. Desktop publishing courses must address both print and electronic formats.

The following strategies for teaching electronic desktop publishing concepts are recommended:

- Cover core desktop publishing concepts such as good design, white space, typesetting, color, and separations.

- Partner with school personnel, clubs, athletics, theater, chorus, band, and any other groups that need publication assistance. Also, consider partnering with a marketing class. Together, develop marketing and promotion materials for these groups as a class or group project.

- Partner with local businesses and nonprofit organizations to design or redesign their business publications (e.g., menus, letterhead, brochures, flyers, or posters).

- Partner with English classes to develop books or e-books of class poetry or creative works.

Web Design, Development, and Programming

Although web development has been a core IT course in the business education curriculum for a number of years, this area continues to grow and develop to more advanced levels. The introductory level of web development should include good design and layout discussions and the use of tools to build cohesive and professional websites (not unintended, disjointed web pages). Once the basics have been covered, the course should evolve to include more advanced scripting (e.g., Javascript, VBscript, and anord XML) and begin to include web programming elements to build more dynamic websites (e.g., ASP and PHP). Database integration with websites should also be addressed with the programming elements. Students should also be exposed to web server hosting and the use of content management systems if possible.

The following strategies for teaching web development and programming concepts are recommended:

- The basics of good web design must be discussed throughout any web development course, including core graphics design elements to ensure correct use of graphics, spacing, white space, color, and other design elements. While teaching the design elements, introduce students to web development semantics and development tools, such as Microsoft Expression (http://www.microsoft.com/expression), Adobe Dreamweaver (http://www.adobe.com/ products/dreamweaver.html), or an open-source product such as Kompozer (http://kompozer.net). A working knowledge of basic coding (i.e., HTML or XHTML) should also be included in the curriculum.

- Students can create real websites for businesses and nonprofit organizations in their community or for school personnel, athletics, or clubs. Students could also partner with teachers to help them update and maintain their personal classroom web pages. These partnerships will serve to self-promote the quality of programs.

- Consider leaving development projects open ended, allowing students to self-select topics to encourage and foster diversity in the classroom. Make assignments authentic for the students.

- Obtain another computer from the school's IT personnel and resources to install Linux or Windows Server and work as a class to install and configure a web server. Discuss security, server layout, and design and functionality.

Computer Networking

Computer networking has tremendous potential for growth in business education programs. One restricting factor can be teachers who feel inadequately prepared to teach courses in computer networking. To address this issue, more teacher education programs and states need to provide coursework and training in computer networking to alleviate teacher apprehension about teaching computer networking. Computer networking areas include both hardware and software, although some states have correlated computer networking hardware courses (Cisco hardware coursework) with the technology education program area. Schools and school IT personnel need to embrace the use of virtualization tools, such as Virtual Box and Microsoft VirtualPC, that allow the newer standard computer lab machines to host multiple operating systems, including Microsoft and Linux server installations on one computer. Although computer networking courses are typically designed around specific software vendors, such as Microsoft and Linux, and their certification programs, it is vital that students be exposed to multivendor networking environments and develop projects that explore the integration of dissimilar systems. The following strategies for teaching computer networking concepts are recommended:

- Use newer computer systems (lab machines) with virtualization software (e.g., Virtual Box or Virtual PC) and allow students to begin network software courses with the installation process through initial configurations.

- Cover the networking core: users, groups, resources, shares, permissions, rights, services, applications, and configuration regardless of network operating systems used.

- Partner with or shadow networking personnel in the school, district, or local businesses.

- Explore business models and case studies to design effective and efficient network designs.

- Have students build server systems from installation to advanced service installation and configuration. Partner with other classes, such as the web development class, and build server solutions for them.

Trends: Project Management, ERP, Mobile Application Development

A number of new IT areas are beginning to appear in the business education curriculum as evidenced by state curriculum development and NBEA's new edition of *NBEA Standards for Business Education* (forthcoming in 2013). Some of these new areas include project management, ERPs, and mobile application development. Project management covers multiple curriculum classifications. For example, in North Carolina, project management courses appear under marketing education, family and consumer sciences, agricultural education, and technology education, in addition to business education.

The following strategies for teaching advanced topics (project management, ERP, and mobile application development) are recommended:

- Cover project management basics and the use of software applications (Microsoft Project or open-source software solutions) to organize and manage projects.

- Partner with other classes, individuals, and school officials who are working on projects. Have the project management students help organize and manage these projects.

- Use case studies or real-life partners and complete business analysis projects that identify business flow and business needs for an ERP solution.

- Partner with school officials or businesses to develop small mobile applications (e.g., a school calendar for Android and iOS).

Electronic Tools to Support Instruction

The IT curriculum area is large and diverse. To reach students at all learning levels and styles, educators need to use a variety of tools to engage and educate students. Many electronic tools are now available to assist instructors when teaching IT subjects. When teaching office suite applications, many textbook vendors provide modern electronic tools for instruction, reinforcement of concepts, testing, and remediation, including SAM, MyITlab, SimNET, and SNAP. These tools provide a complete software solution for training and testing skills development with the Microsoft Office software suite.

Online tools are also available—and many are free—that help instructors reach students; these include social media tools such as Ning (http://www.ning.com) and

Edmodo (http://www.edmodo.com), as well as content management systems such as Moodle (http://moodle.org). Teachers can also use blogs, wikis, and Web 2.0 tools such as Prezi (http://prezi.com) and others to engage students in new ways. Software costs can also be a concern; however, there are many open-source (free) software applications that mirror their commercial counterparts, and many have been noted in this chapter.

SUMMARY

The business education IT curriculum needs to continue to keep pace with the IT industry. This rapid curriculum change requires the national organization (NBEA) and state and local officials to review curriculum and revise offerings regularly and as rapidly as possible. Curriculum developers should also include industry partners, certifications, and standards to ensure that business education students are prepared for the workforce and ensure continuing education of careers in information technology. Instructional technologies offer new opportunities to design instruction that is authentic (real and relevant), engaging, and motivating to the students. The instructional process should also have flexible coursework that embraces and encourages the diversity within the student body. Service learning and partnerships should be explored by all business education programs. If done well, these partnerships are invaluable for the success and growth of business education programs in all schools. A successful website or portfolio of desktop publications for local businesses or organizations within your school will promote your program much more than "sending a flyer home to parents." The IT curriculum is an enormous portion of the overall business education curriculum and should be grown and developed to meet industry and student needs and expectations.

REFERENCES

Apple Inc. (n.d.). iBooks Author. Retrieved from http://www.apple.com/ibooks-author

Bonk, C. J., & Zhang, K. (2008). *Empowering online learning: 100+ activities for reading, reflecting, displaying, and doing.* San Francisco, CA: Jossey-Bass.

Bovee, C. L., & Thill, J. V. (2012). *Business communication today.* Upper Saddle River, NJ: Pearson.

Computer Science Teachers Association. (2012). Computer science k–8: Building a strong foundation. Retrieved from http://www.csta.acm.org/Curriculum/sub/CurrFiles/CS_K-8_Building_a_Foundation.pdf

Freiberg, H. J., & Driscoll, A. (2005). *Universal teaching strategies.* Boston, MA: Pearson.

Future Business Leaders of America–Phi Beta Lambda. (2011). Competitive events. Retrieved from http://www.fbla-pbl.org/data/files/docs/2011-12%20fbla%20competitive%20events.pdf

Georgia Department of Education. (2011). Business and computer science standards. Retrieved from https://www.georgiastandards.org/Standards/Pages/BrowseStandards/ctae-business.aspx

Gibbs, S., Steel, G., & Kuiper, A. (2011). Expectations of competency: The mismatch between employers' and graduates' views of end-user computing skills requirements in the workplace. *Journal of Information Technology Education, 10,* 371–382.

Grant, D. M., Malloy, A. D., & Murphy, M. C. (2009). A comparison of student perceptions of their computer skills to their actual abilities. *Journal of Information Technology Education, 8,* 141–160.

International Society for Technology in Education. (n.d.). NETS. Retrieved from http://www.iste.org/standards.aspx

Kronowitz, E. L. (2012). *The teacher's guide to success* (2nd ed.). Upper Saddle River, NJ: Pearson.

Microsoft. (n.d.). Microsoft IT Academy Program. Retrieved from http://www.microsoft.com/en-us/itacademy/default.aspx

National Business Education Association. (2007). *National standards for business education.* Reston, VA: Author.

North Carolina Department of Public Instruction. (2012). Business and information technology. Retrieved from http://www.dpi.state.nc.us/cte/program-areas/business

Pew Research Center. (2011). Global digital communication: Texting, social networking popular worldwide. Washington, DC: Pew Research Center. Retrieved from http://www.pewglobal.org/files/2011/12/Pew-Global-Attitudes-Technology-Report-FINAL-December-20-2011.pdf

Scott, J. L., & Sarkees-Wircenski, M. (2008). *Overview of career and technical education* (4th ed.). Orland Park, IL: American Technical Publishers.

Sivakumaran, T., & Lux, A. C. (2011). Overcoming computer anxiety: A three-step process for adult learners. *US-China Education Review B,* 154–160.

Utah State Office of Education. (2010). Business education. Retrieved from http://www.schools.utah.gov/cte/business.html

Wierschem, D., Zhang, G., & Johnston, C. (2010). Information technology certification value: An initial response from employers. *Journal of International Technology and Information Management, 19*(4), 89–108.

Business Communication

S. Ann Wilson
Marsha L. Bayless
Stephen F. Austin State University
Nacogdoches, TX

The authors, editor, and publisher acknowledge and express appreciation for the work done by Bobbye J. Davis and Clarice P. Brantley, authors of this chapter in the previous edition. Thank you for your contribution to this yearbook and to business education.

Communication plays an integral role in all areas of personal and professional interactions. Without excellent communication skills, students will not be equipped to compete in the global business economy. According to the National Association of Colleges and Employers website, employers are expecting job candidates to possess great team skills and strong verbal communication skills. Other desirable skills are decision making and problem solving; obtaining/processing information; planning, organizing, and prioritizing work; analyzing quantitative data; possessing job-related technical knowledge; demonstrating software proficiency; creating and/or editing written reports; and persuading others ("Job Outlook," 2011).

Technology has profoundly influenced business communication. Because technological competence is a requirement for career advancement, educators at all educational levels must study and integrate communication technologies into the curriculum. This chapter discusses the role of business communication in student success. Business Communication courses have usually been defined as Business English and/or Business Communication.

Definitions

Historically, Business English was a subject offered at the secondary level, whereas Business Communication, a course with a broader perspective, was offered at the postsecondary and university levels. Business English can be defined as the use of basic language mechanics that are developed into organized ideas presented orally or in writing, appropriately using precise language to ensure coherence, logical progression, and support for ideas in a business context. A high school Business English course is designed for students to enhance reading, writing, computing, communication, and reasoning skills and to help students apply them to the business environment (Texas Education Agency, 2011).

Business communication can be defined as the study of topics related to communication in the workplace. Those topics include oral communication, written communication (includes application of basic language mechanics), interpersonal and team communication, nonverbal communication, and technological communication. Some universities refer to the course as Managerial Communication, especially if it is offered at the graduate level. As more high schools and community colleges work together on advanced placement courses and articulated high school credit to community/junior colleges, Business Communication as a course title may be more frequently used at the secondary level. However, another course, Professional Communications, blends written, oral, and graphic communication in a career-based environment and is recommended for students in grades 9–12 by the Texas Education Agency (2011). Other states may or may not have similar requirements.

As rapid changes in technology have impacted society, future business leaders must learn to communicate effectively through e-mail, voice mail, text messaging, and instant messaging. Facebook and Twitter are increasingly used in the business world and demand skills from business graduates. Future business leaders also need a thorough understanding of cultural and ethical issues that impact the business communication field.

FRAMEWORK

The National Business Education Association's (NBEA, 2007) *National Standards for Business Education* provides standards as well as corresponding performance expectations for what America's students should know and be able to do in business. The standards address the areas of accounting, business law, career development, communication, computation, economics and personal finance, entrepreneurship, information technology, international business, management, and marketing. All students must master oral and written communication skills in order to be ready to enter the work world and interact effectively with fellow employees as well as all individuals in society.

IMPORTANCE OF COMMUNICATION SKILLS IN BUSINESS

Employers continually stress the importance of business communication skills for success in the workplace (Coyle, 2010; Holtzman & Kraft, 2010; Quible & Griffin, 2007). According to the Quintessential Career website: "By far, the one skill mentioned most often by employers is the ability to listen, write, and speak effectively. Successful communication is critical in business" (Hansen & Hansen, 2012).

In a report on business communication internships, industry supervisors rated students higher in attitude and interaction and lowest in written, professional, and spoken communication skills (Sapp & Zhang, 2009). Employers may also note that students who have taken business writing courses are not necessarily prepared to write in business settings. Writing in an academic setting often relies on responses to brief cases and may not fit as well in an actual business (Hollis-Turner & Scholtz, 2010).

Perhaps business communication teachers should use more of the assessment methods used by those in business, such as performance review, peer review, self-assessment, critical incident review, and casual review (Yu, 2010). Based on those workplace trends, Yu suggested the following applications for the classroom: longitudinal assessment, contextualized assessment, focus of assessment, and collaborative assessment.

BUSINESS COMMUNICATION STANDARDS AND INSTRUCTIONAL LEVELS

National Standards for Business Education (NBEA, 2007) defines the role of communication in the business education curriculum as the following: "encourages mastery of all communication skills essential for interacting effectively with people in the workplace and in society" (p. 40). Communication achievement standards are identified for communication foundations, societal communication, workplace communication, and technological uses for communication. Business communication foundation skills identified are listening, speaking, reading, and writing. Teaching these skills must be done in the context of application in both social and organizational settings. Specific objectives with two to four performance levels that align with elementary, junior high or middle school, secondary, and postsecondary instructional levels are listed.

Foundations of Communication

The achievement standard for the foundations of communication is to "communicate in a clear, complete, concise, correct, and courteous manner on personal and professional levels" (NBEA, 2007, p. 40). Performance expectation levels are provided for social and business listening, spoken communication, informational reading, and written communication.

Societal Communication

The achievement standard for societal communication is to "apply basic social communication skills in both personal and professional settings" (NBEA, 2007, p. 43). Performance expectation levels are provided for positive self-concept and image and human relations and interpersonal skills.

Workplace Communication

The achievement standard for workplace communication is to "incorporate appropriate leadership and supervision techniques, customer service strategies, and personal ethics standards to communicate effectively with various business constituencies" (NBEA, 2007, p. 45). Performance expectation levels are provided for customer relations, business relationships, leadership, supervisory communication, personal ethics, and employment communication.

Technological Communication

The achievement standard for technological communication is to "use technology to enhance the effectiveness of communication" (NBEA, 2007, p. 49). Technological communication performance expectations are provided for each developmental level, beginning with simple tasks through complex projects using different business communication technologies.

Teaching Strategies

Meeting the levels in the framework may be accomplished through a variety of teaching strategies. In order to prepare future business graduates, the following strategies are suggested for teaching writing, speaking, nonverbal communication, listening, and reading.

Writing Strategies

In a study of undergraduate business alumni and employers, Holtzman and Kraft (2010) reported that e-mail, business letters, and memos were the most frequently cited items that employees were required to write. Students in the academic Business Communication course are often expected to write a document based on a problem or case for which they have no additional company information, whereas in the workplace, communication is often in layers. For example, several e-mail messages might be the basis for a more formal document because company knowledge and research is important (Hollis-Turner & Scholtz, 2010). How can we prepare business students to interact effectively in the workplace?

Students should write, receive feedback, and edit their work as frequently as feasible in the Business Communication course. As grading student work is always a challenge, some assignments should be set up for peer review. Providing students the opportunity to edit other's work is a valuable skill that will be helpful to them as they work with colleagues in the workplace (Stowers & Barker, 2003).

It is critical that students understand the concept of audience. To whom are they writing the documents, and what are they trying to achieve? In the Business Communication course, they are trying to judge what the teacher wants. In the workplace, they will be trying to determine what a variety of clients or customers need (Coyle, 2010; Hollis-Turner & Scholtz, 2010).

Students should be asked to conduct research that will help them enhance the writing assignment. For example, a case letter might require students to do research. If a student were asked to write to a client about a cruise vacation, that student might be required to go online and research a specific cruise for details that could be included in the letter to the client. This exercise will help the student understand that when writing a business letter, research may be required before writing.

Business communication instructors should use activities and assignments that engage and are motivating to the students (Zumbrunn & Krause, 2012). For example, if the Business Communication class comprises 60% nonbusiness majors, do not pick a very technical business topic for the writing assignment, as the majority of students may not be able to identify with it. Instead, pick a topic such as green practices or charitable giving that will interest more students in the writing assignment.

The instructor should ask invited business speakers to address the value of writing in the workplace (Coyle, 2010). In one class, the invited speaker who was the head of the local community development agency asked the Business Communication class what they had been working on. One slightly disgruntled student said the class had been working on writing business letters. This prompted the speaker to say that he used his experience in writing letters in a Business Communication class every day and the students' attitudes toward writing letters definitely improved.

Students who arrive in the Business Communication class may be well grounded in writing using correct grammar but frequently still need assistance. Quible and Griffin (2007) propose exercises to help students combine thoughts and ideas by asking them to read several short sentences and combine them into one complex sentence. For example, "Deanne is my sister. She is the youngest child in the family of four siblings. She lives in Kansas City. She plans to visit me at the next holiday break." Any grammar errors made when combining the sentences should be corrected. Another idea to improve grammar and the correctness of writing is to allow five minutes of in-class editing time before an assignment is turned in. Students can review each other's work, use a team approach, or examine their own work. Any corrections or marks they put on the assignment will not count against them, encouraging the importance of a correct assignment (Smith, 2011).

Software is available that may assist students in an individualized approach to improving their grammar. Some software products come with supplementary textbooks. Their use may provide writing assistance to students outside the regular class approach (Sigmar & Cooper, 2011). Using personal, reflective writing exercises (Lawrence, 2007), such as blogs or personal mission statements, can also help business communication students express their thoughts effectively.

To evaluate a student's progress on the NBEA business communication standards (2007), a rubric such as shown in Figure 1 can be adapted to the specific level of writing. The scale for the rubric is that 5 indicates excellent; 4, above average; 3, average; 2, needs improvement; and 1, not acceptable.

Figure 1. Written Communication Rubric

Written Communication Rubric
(Based on National Business Education Association Communication Foundation Standards, 2007).

	5	4	3	2	1
Level 1 – Elementary (Grades K-6)					
Writes with correct spelling, grammar, word and number usage, punctuation, and formatting.	5	4	3	2	1
Writes logical, coherent phrases, sentences, and paragraphs incorporating correct spelling, grammar, and punctuation.	5	4	3	2	1
Composes simple requests for information, reports, and summaries.	5	4	3	2	1
Edits and revises written work.	5	4	3	2	1
Takes effective notes.	5	4	3	2	1
Composes digital communications such as e-mail, text, and instant messaging.	5	4	3	2	1
Level 2 – Middle School/Junior High (grades 6-9)					
Develops an outline to facilitate logical and understandable written documents.	5	4	3	2	1
Uses acceptable standards for grammar, punctuation, and word and number usage.	5	4	3	2	1
Distinguishes between paraphrasing, documentation, and plagiarism.	5	4	3	2	1
Documents properly both print and digital sources to avoid plagiarism.	5	4	3	2	1
Writes coherent business messages, instructions, descriptions, summaries, and reports using appropriate formats.	5	4	3	2	1
Proofreads documents to ensure correct grammar, spelling, and punctuation.	5	4	3	2	1
Demonstrates sensitivity to language bias (gender, race, age, religion, physically challenged, and sexual orientation).	5	4	3	2	1
Uses note-taking skills incorporating critical listening and reading techniques.	5	4	3	2	1
Level 3 – Secondary (grades 9-12)					
Identifies factors affecting the readability of text.	5	4	3	2	1
Uses acceptable steps in the writing process.	5	4	3	2	1
Uses language that is free of bias, such as bias related to gender, race, age, religion, physical challenges, and sexual orientation.	5	4	3	2	1
Applies a variety of specific proofreading techniques to identify and correct errors.	5	4	3	2	1
Compares drafts to final documents and makes editorial changes.	5	4	3	2	1
Proofreads business documents to ensure that they are clear, correct, concise, complete, consistent, and courteous.	5	4	3	2	1
Composes appropriate messages for specific audiences.	5	4	3	2	1
Uses a variety of references and resources (both printed and digital) when writing business documents.	5	4	3	2	1
Prepares formal and informal reports using suitable format and supplementing with appropriate graphics.	5	4	3	2	1
Uses the direct or indirect approach correctly in context.	5	4	3	2	1
Analyzes routine business problems both individually and collaboratively and responds in print and digital message form.	5	4	3	2	1
Prepares business communications that reflect cultural sensitivity.	5	4	3	2	1
Composes and produces a variety of business messages and reports using correct style, format, and content.	5	4	3	2	1
Organizes and promptly responds to digital messages such as e-mail, text, and instant messages.	5	4	3	2	1
Level 4 – Two-year postsecondary/community college or technical college					
Expresses empathy in messages written to individuals.	5	4	3	2	1
Incorporates information that has been gathered from other sources into written documents by the use of paraphrasing and citations.	5	4	3	2	1
Prepares industry-specific technical reports incorporating graphics.	5	4	3	2	1
Analyzes and responds to complex business case studies.	5	4	3	2	1
Researches, analyzes, and prepares collaboratively a spoken, written, and digital response to a complex business project.	5	4	3	2	1
Composes business documents that reflect cultural differences and incorporates current practice and protocol.	5	4	3	2	1
Edits business documents to improve content and effectiveness.	5	4	3	2	1
Composes and produces executive summaries.	5	4	3	2	1
Analyzes and responds to ethical decision-making case studies.	5	4	3	2	1

Source: Based on NBEA (2007) standards for business communication.

Speaking Strategies

Some employers are requesting improved oral presentation skills in applicants more frequently than written skills. Students also need more presentation skills, highlighting the ability to use software tools like PowerPoint (Stevens, 2005). How can we prepare students to meet employers' expectations for spoken communication? As with any skill, perfect practice makes perfect. In other words, the more opportunities students are appropriately guided to practice speaking informally or formally to different audiences, the more successful they will be when this skill is required in the workplace.

Role playing is another teaching method, but to be successful, the teacher should remember the following tips adapted from the National Capital Language Resource Center (NCLRC, 2007):

- Do not begin the role play until students thoroughly understand the process.
- Communicate the goal or outcome to the students.
- Assign "parts" to the students.
- Give students a chance to plan their role play before beginning.
- Make sure all students have a chance to participate.
- Act as the mediator and monitor for each group while they are preparing as well as when they are performing.
- Have students reflect on the experience.

Telling a story is another way that students can practice effective speaking. Almost any aspect of business can be turned into a relevant and interesting story, which will help to convey a message (Neal, 2010). Additional detailed information about structured output activities to build spoken communication skills may be found at the NCLRC (2007) website (http://www.nclrc.org/essentials/speaking/developspeak.htm).

Nonverbal Communication Strategies

Nonverbal communication includes all the gestures, expressions, and tones that accompany verbal communication and may include more than 90% of the weight of a typical communication (Morella, 2010). Nonverbal communication may include appearance, movements of the body, touching, eye behavior, proxemics, and paralanguage (Bayless, 2005).

Culture can also have an impact on nonverbal communication. Greene and Stewart (2011) contend that African-Americans have a specific nonverbal communication culture that conveys information that may not be understood by those of other cultures. In addition, in a study of the Arabian coffee-making ritual, Darweesh (2010) found that the nonverbal gestures were communicating specific cultural codes. In another study of college English classroom teachers conducted in China, nonverbal communication such as appearance, including the amount of makeup used by female teachers, conveyed cultural issues as a form of nonverbal communication; women faculty who used too much makeup and wore casual clothes for teaching were less likely to be viewed favorably by students or to get promotions (Peng, 2011).

Nonverbal communication extends beyond cultural differences and experiences to include gender issues. Women frequently outperform men in accurately assessing nonverbal behavior. This might be a result of women being taught to focus on emotional or nonverbal cues at a younger age than men (Schmid, Mast, Bombari, & Mast, 2011).

Conducting activities for students to become more aware of nonverbal communication could include such things as having a team of students study and report on a specific culture and focus on nonverbal communication. Another idea would be to turn down the sound on a television program and try to read the nonverbal communication. Role-playing exercises with students acting out different roles could also be helpful in enhancing nonverbal communication skills (Bayless, 2005).

Listening Strategies

Good listening is essential for effective communication. Students at every level must be made aware of their own listening skills through exercises that deal with listening and recall of facts. In a discussion about listening, Cronon (1998–1999) stated:

Educated people know how to pay attention—to others and to the world around them. They work hard to hear what other people say. They can follow an argument, trace logical reasoning, detect illogic, hear the emotions that lie behind both the logic and the illogic, and ultimately empathize with the person who is feeling those emotions (p. 3).

Thompson, Leintz, Nevers, & Witkowski (2004) provided a great resource for teachers to learn an integrative listening model as an approach to teaching and learning listening.

Students may find self-help tips for developing active listening skills on the MindTools website (http://www.mindtools.com). A practical exercise to reinforce active listening is for students to create podcasts to which other students listen and respond. Good listening exercises are information gap activities that may be found at the NCLRC (2007) website.

Reading Strategies

Teachers should focus on the reading process rather than the product. By using reading material that students will use in other contexts outside the classroom, students are able to develop reading strategies to maximize their comprehension of text, identify relevant and nonrelevant information, and tolerate less than word-by-word (stopping to look up every unknown vocabulary item) comprehension (NCLRC, 2007) website (http://www.nclrc.org/essentials/reading/stratread.htm).

Activities to help students develop reading skills include "pre-reading," "while reading," and "post-reading" (NCLRC, 2007) (see http://www.nclrc.org/essentials/reading/developread.htm).

- **Pre-reading** activities include teaching the student to use the titles, subtitles, and divisions within the text to predict content and organization or sequence of information, which will prepare, assess, clarify, and make students aware. Students should be encouraged to look at graphics and captions to infer meaning of the content.

- **While reading** activities could include techniques to skim the text for the main topic, students should look at vocabulary and watch for grammatical structures.

- **Post-reading** activities such as reading aloud, comprehension questions, and authentic assessment activities should check for comprehension and application. For additional reading strategies the instructor should refer to the NCLRC (2007) website (http://www.nclrc.org/essentials/reading/assessread.htm).

Integration of Business Communication in Other Courses

For students to be successful in business communication, they need to be able to reinforce these skills across the curriculum; other business courses should involve the key speaking and writing activities. Smith (2011) suggested several strategies, including emphasizing the importance of writing to each course in the syllabus, providing some time in class for writing activities, and using terminology and vocabulary that business students can follow. He also suggested using several forms of feedback, including in-class editing of documents before submission, a consistent grading rubric, marking errors by type of error instead of deducting points for the same type of error more than once, and grading the content and writing of the assignment separately.

An easy way to add writing or speaking to a business class is to add a related assignment when designing course modules or units (Coyle, 2010). Course modules will dictate what type of writing or speaking assignment is most effective. For example, an early module might include an e-mail or a short memo and more complicated writing might appear later in a course. Reflective blogs about the daily class might also be helpful for students to both grasp concepts and write.

Social Media

Social media, such as MySpace, Facebook, Twitter, and others is rapidly changing how we communicate. Not only have social media impacted personal communication, more businesses are using social media to connect with customers and employees.

Communicating with Media

Social media entered the business realm with sites like LinkedIn to connect business professionals who were seeking those with common business interests. With the rapid expansion of social media, businesses soon determined that having a Facebook page for a company or product was a fast way to contact and get feedback from interested customers. As customers tweeted about a bad customer experience at a business, companies found it in their best interests to follow tweets to solve problems quickly and effectively.

Originally, social media were primarily connected to a computer of some type. With the explosion of mobile media, including smartphones and tablets, social media are also increasingly mobile. Students like to send texts because they do not have to worry about conversations being overheard or being disruptive. Plus, it is more convenient to send just a few words. Students can check or post to Facebook from their phones.

Communication through social media has changed expectations for many people. The communication has to be faster and shorter. Some new to texting believe responses are rude. Those who have long texted one-word answers such as "yes," "no," or "duh" think a longer message is too much to read.

Information and communication technology is changing the way businesses conduct meetings. Many corporations are opting to provide their employees with communication technology such as video conferencing, smart phones, and tablet computers instead of paying for expensive travel for them to attend face-to-face meetings (Haynes, 2010.)

Tech Etiquette

Using technology ranging from text messages to e-mail to social media to cell phones and tablets does not stop at knowing how to work the various devices or use the different websites. In fact, knowing when and how to use technology can have a lasting impact on a business student's success in the workplace. Common sense would seem to dictate that driving a car and sending a text message at the same time is not a good idea. However, increases in automobile accidents that can be directly linked to texting have resulted in many states and municipalities setting standards resulting in regulations and penalties on texting while driving (Simpson, 2010). Students should be taught to be responsible.

In presenting ways to look at tech etiquette, Simpson (2010) offers four common-sense best practices. They relate to safety, security, privacy, and courtesy. Safety relates to issues such as texting while driving or walking into an intersection while talking on the phone. In terms of security, if you recite your private information such as social security number, credit card information, or birthdate on a phone when someone can hear you or the signal could be intercepted, that might be a security issue. Using free unsecured wi-fi could cause issues with hackers. As information is no longer self-contained and is open and accessible to others, students should be made aware of the need for information security ("The leaky corporation," 2011.) Privacy relates to how much an individual really wants to share with others. Increasingly, future employers refer to an applicant's Facebook page to see if they would be a good match for the company. Students who have shared party pictures that might be more suitable for friends than an employer to see may be surprised by a negative reaction from a current or future employer. Courtesy involves thinking of others when using the technology. Sending text messages when you are at a business dinner shows discourtesy to your companions. Answering or making cell phone calls at certain times and places may be considered rude. Even something as simple as placing your cell phone on the table may indicate to those around you that it has first priority.

An exercise to strengthen students' tech etiquette is to have them work in teams to list common-sense rules for using technology. The students should then interview individuals of different ages and ask for input about the lists. The instructor could then follow up the exercise with a discussion of any differences between the student lists and the interview results.

INTERNET RESOURCES

The Internet abounds with resources related to ideas about business communication. Table 1 presents a sampling of what can be found on the Internet.

Table 1. Useful Business Communication Websites

Purdue OWL http://owl.english.purdue.edu	This writing center provides handouts and information. It focuses on grades 7–12 as well as the collegiate level.
University of North Carolina at Chapel Hill, The Writing Center http://writingcenter.unc.edu/ resources/handouts-demos	This writing center has a series of handouts that can be used to cover areas such as comma use or other punctuation and grammar. Information on proofreading is also available.
UN World Food Program http://www.freerice.com	This website combines grammar and vocabulary practice with the opportunity to earn free rice for those in need. Other subject areas are also included.
http://www.syntaxis.com	This site is for business communication training for business professionals. A series of free grammar quizzes is available.
http://www.brainpop.com	This site offers some information about various secondary school subjects. Under writing, cartoon-style videos are available. One describes blogs and provides a quiz afterwards.
FLRT http://www.Mindplay.com	This is a reading fluency tool to increase reading comprehension. Pricing is based on the number of students using the system.
http://www.YouSeeU.com	This site allows an instructor to set up a class and students can post videos of their presentations and PowerPoint slides supporting the presentations, and sync the two together. The instructor can view videos and post comments. It is especially useful for online experiences. Fees are determined by the number of students and minutes used.
Google Blogger http://www.blogger.com	This site lets a user create a free blog. Blogs can be used to improve writing.
http://www.flatworldknowledge.com	This site provides access to free or low-cost college textbooks in a variety of business areas.
http://www.mindtools.com	This site showcases information on improving several business communication areas, including active listening.

SUMMARY

Business communication skills are critical for today's business graduates. Merely understanding how to operate a machine or software will not be sufficient in the year 2020. Students must understand that learning is a constant process requiring all of their communication skills: writing, speaking, nonverbal communication, listening, and reading. The Information Age continues as technology advances and social media and the Internet play an even more important part in the way we communicate. In addition to using new communication sources, the etiquette of new technology must be considered for successful business communication. Teachers should realize that the Internet may be their greatest resource for obtaining new ideas and techniques for improving student communication skills.

REFERENCES

Bayless, M. L. (2005). Nonverbal communication: The silent but important language. In J. C. Scott (Ed.). *Communication for a global society: NBEA 2005 yearbook* (No. 43, pp.146–157). Reston, VA: National Business Education Association.

Coyle, J. P. (2010). Teaching writing skills that enhance student success in future employment. *Collected Essays on Learning and Teaching, 3*, 195–200.

Cronon, W. (1998–1999, Winter). Only connect: The goals of a liberal education. *The Key Reporter, 64*(2), 3.

Darweesh, L. (2010). Nonverbal behavior as communication: The Arabian coffee making ritual. *International Journal of Interdisciplinary Social Sciences, 5*(7), 175–181.

Greene, D. M., & Stewart, F. R. (2011). African-American students' reactions to Benjamin Cooke's "Nonverbal communication among Afro-Americans: An initial classification." *Journal of Black Studies, 42*(389–401). doi:10.1177/0021934710376169

Hansen, R. S., & Hansen, K. (2012, February). What do employers really want? Top skills and values employers seek from job-seekers. Retrieved from http://www.quintcareers.com/job_skills_values.html

Haynes, P. (2010, November). Information and communication technology and international business travel: Mobility allies? *Mobilities, 5*(4), 547–564. doi:10.1080/17450101.2010.510337

Hollis-Turner, S., & Scholtz, D. (2010). Business writing in academic and workplace contexts. *Southern African Linguistics and Applied Language Studies 2010, 28*(3), 239–245. doi:10.2989/16073614.2010.545026

Holtzman, D. M., & Kraft, E. M. (2010). Skills required of business graduates: Evidence from undergraduate alumni and employers. *Business Education & Accreditation, 2*(1), 49–59.

Job outlook: The candidate skills/qualities employers want. (2011, October). National Association of Colleges and Employers. Retrieved from http://www.naceweb.org/printerFriendly.aspx?printpage=/s10262011/candidate_skills_employer_qualities

Lawrence, P. H. (2007). Personal reflective writing in business communication and management. (doctoral dissertation). Retrieved from http://scholarworks.umass.edu/dissertations/AAI3275795

Morella, M. (2010, December). Try talking for a change: Face time may beat e-mail. *U.S. News and World Report,* 48–49.

National Business Education Association. (2007). *National standards for business education: What America's students should know and be able to do in business* (3rd ed.). Reston, VA: Author.

National Capital Language Resource Center. (2007). The essentials of language teaching. Retrieved from http://www.nclrc.org/essentials/index

Neal, K. (2010, March/April). Stepping up to the plate: Developing an effective business communication strategy. *Information Management,* 38–41. ARMA International. Retrieved from http://www.arma.org

Peng, H. (2011). Effects of non-verbal communication on college English classroom teaching. *US-China Foreign Language, 9*(8), 505–516.

Quible, Z. K., & Griffin, F. (2007, September/October). Are writing deficiencies creating a lost generation of business writers? *Journal of Education for Business, 83,* 32–36.

Sapp, D. A., & Zhang, Q. (2009, August 11). Trends in industry supervisors' feedback on business communication internships. *Business Communication Quarterly, 72*(3), 274–288.

Schmid, P. C., Mast, M. S., Bombari, D., & Mast, F. W. (2011). Gender effects in information processing on a nonverbal decoding task. *Sex Roles, 65,* 102–107. doi:10.1007/s11199-011-9979-3

Sigmar, L. S., & Cooper, T. W. (2011). Incorporating web-assisted instruction into the business communication curriculum. *Academy of Educational Leadership Journal, 15* (Special Issue), 1–13.

Simpson, M. (2010, Spring). Tech etiquette is just common sense. *Common Ground Journal, 7*(2), 81–88.

Smith, W. (2011, March/April). The literate business student. *BizEd, 10*(2), 42–48.

Stevens, B. (2005). What communication skills do employers want? Silicon Valley recruiters respond. *Journal of Employment Counseling, 42*(1), 2–9.

Stowers, R. H., & Barker, R. T. (2003). Improved student writing in business communication classes: Strategies for teaching and evaluation. *Journal of Technical Writing and Communication, 33*(4), 337–348.

Texas Education Agency (2011, March 10). Career and technical education: Texas essential knowledge and skills, course crosswalks, and coherent sequences. Retrieved from http://www.tea.state.tx.us/index2.aspx?id=5415#Subchapter C

The leaky corporation. (2011). *Economist, 398*(8722), 75–77.

Thompson, K., Leintz, P., Nevers, B., & Witkowski, S. (2004, July). The integrative listening model: An approach to teaching and learning listening. *The Journal of General Education, 53*(3/4), 225–246.

Yu, H. (2010). Bring workplace assessment into business communication classrooms: A proposal to better prepare students for professional workplaces. *Business Communication Quarterly, 73*(1), 21–39. doi:10.1177/1080569909357783

Zumbrunn, S., & Krause, K. (2012). Conversations with leaders: Principles of effective writing instruction. *The Reading Teacher, 65*(5), 346–353. doi:10.1002/TRTR.01053

Accounting

Sharon Garvin
Wayne State College
Wayne, NE

The author, editor, and publisher acknowledge and express appreciation for the work done by Carol Blaszczynski and Patrick M. Borja, authors of this chapter in the previous edition. Thank you for your contribution to this yearbook and to business education.

It is indeed an exciting time to be involved in accounting education. Its focus has broadened, technological resources abound, and the vast variety of teaching/learning strategies available promotes higher levels of student engagement and enthusiasm. This chapter discusses accounting course content at introductory and intermediate levels and suggests resources that can be used to effectively teach that content.

CHANGES IN ACCOUNTING IN THE WORKPLACE

Accounting has changed. Technology advances have made financial information preparation and distribution quick, easy, and inexpensive. Anyone can record transactions in business without debits and credits by using software that requires only filling out forms on a screen. Report generation is easily done with a few clicks. Thus, the wages of those who perform such tasks are incredibly low. Store clerks or customers often enter sales information into the system when they scan items at checkout, and online sales order information, entered by customers, sets in motion the recording and filling of those orders with minimum human involvement. More individuals are preparing their own tax returns using question-asking software that is offered free or at very low cost.

All of this means that to acquire and maintain employment, accountants need to "add value" to their organizations. This can be visually demonstrated by the following accounting value-chain diagram, developed some years ago (as cited in Albrecht & Sack, 2000).

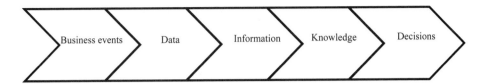

Thus, accountants will be less frequently involved in the lower stages of recording transactions and summarizing them into useful data (as has been the traditional focus of Accounting I and Accounting II courses). Instead they will spend more of their time manipulating data into meaningful information, converting that information into knowledge that supports decision making and using that knowledge to help their organizations create competitive advantages.

MASTERY OF CONTENT VERSUS DEVELOPMENT OF COMPETENCIES

Creation of a future workforce that is competitive in a global economy is at the forefront of objectives for business education professionals. A major shift toward inclusion of defined competencies that students should demonstrate now supersedes the former content mastery focus. More important than what students know is *what they can do with what they know*. Accounting teachers must include competency development into their curricula and conduct assessments to ensure that the profession's needs are being met (Foster & Bolt-Lee, 2002).

NBEA National Standards and the "Knowledge Worker"

The *National Standards for Business Education*, published by the National Business Education Association (NBEA, 2007), includes in its introduction a "call for a globally literate knowledge worker" (p. ix). Professionals prepared through business education must be able to create and use knowledge to help firms compete and succeed in an increasingly complex society. No longer are businesses looking for employees who simply follow directions.

As part of these national standards, those for accounting include traditional technical content and skills but also call on educators to address higher-stage competencies of conducting research, writing reports, making presentations, analyzing financial performance, evaluating accounting systems, considering internal controls to combat errors and fraud, planning strategies to minimize taxes, and making management or loan or investment decisions (NBEA, 2007).

Employer and Accounting Profession Expectations

As long ago as 1990, the Accounting Education Change Commission recommended accounting courses move away from memorization of rules. While rules change and content memorized for exams is often quickly lost, students' understanding of concepts will foster development of professional judgment that they will apply in the future. Students should cultivate learning processes so they can identify problems or opportunities, research for needed information, analyze the information, and reach reasonable conclusions (Accounting Education Change Commission, 1990).

By the year 2000, a visioning project, sponsored by the American Institute of Certified Public Accountants (AICPA, 1998–2000), involved numerous accounting professionals working thousands of hours in facilitated, one-day forums to identify challenges and opportunities the profession would face by the year 2011. The results of this project, combined with consideration of various frameworks, curriculum models, and research resulted in the online Core Competency Framework for Entry into the Accounting Profession, accessible through login at the AICPA's Educational Competency Assessment website. Among the 20 identified competencies within the framework are measurement, reporting, professional demeanor, problem solving and decision making, interaction, leadership, communication, and strategic/critical thinking (AICPA, n.d.).

The AICPA and American Accounting Association (AAA) sponsored the Pathways Commission to chart a national higher education strategy for the next generation of accountants. In the commission's 2012 report, it recommended closer connections among accounting teachers, students, and practitioners so those entering the profession are better prepared to meet employers' needs. It proposes new curricular models that include global issues, increase use of technology, connect learning to current practice, and provide opportunities to consider accounting problem areas critically (Pathways Commission, 2012). Accounting teachers should monitor the Pathways Commission home page (http://commons.aaahq.org/groups/2d690969a3/summary) for further developments.

Appropriate Levels of Competency Development

Performance expectations for accounting students are clearly defined by the NBEA national standards for both secondary students in grades 9–12 (designated as level 3) and two-year community/technical college students (designated as level 4). Such guidance can be used to evaluate or enhance business education programs (NBEA, 2007).

Guidance for college-credit courses is provided by the online Core Competency Framework for Entry into the Accounting Profession, mentioned above. The framework provides definitions for levels 1 through 4 of achievement. College/university faculty teaching introductory or intermediate accounting and seeking to evaluate/enhance their programs should focus on helping students achieve level 1 development using example learning objectives provided at this online site (AICPA, n.d.).

CONTENT COVERAGE GUIDANCE

If the focus on accounting education is shifting more toward competency development, some traditional content coverage will be lost. Today's students will become tomorrow's business professionals who will face business conditions and situations that are difficult to predict. It is therefore very important that business educators teach students how to find answers and how to learn independently.

Survey of Accounting

Most postsecondary students who take a one-semester overview accounting course (one course combination of Accounting I and II) are not business majors but will have jobs where they must work with accountants or use accounting reports to evaluate business situations. The criteria for content coverage should be what is "value added" for the particular individuals. Computer information systems majors, for example, need to understand the types of information captured in an accounting information system and the resulting internal and external reports to generate to serve decision makers. Future entrepreneurs need to be able to perform cost-volume-profit analysis, budgeting, performance evaluation, and financial statement analysis. Teachers can simplify (a) inventory valuation by only covering *first-in, first-out* (known as FIFO) omitting *last-in, first-out* (known as LIFO) and average methods, (b) depreciation by only covering the straight-line method (omitting declining balance and sum-of-the-years' digits), and (c) costs of manufacturing by only covering job order costing (omitting process costing). Some teachers omit debits, credits, and journal entries, choosing instead to do transaction analysis with plus and minus signs in accounting spreadsheet columns. Posting, closing, and trial balance generation are automated in most firms so teachers can briefly discuss these without assigning related exercises. Students still get the basic idea of the information generated by the accounting information system for decision making, which is a main objective of the course.

Accounting I

Content coverage in Accounting I is less clearly defined, especially when comparing secondary schools with postsecondary schools. The NBEA national standards for accounting provide some guidance on the dividing line separating topical coverage at the secondary level, indicating that certain standards should be restricted to the second high school course (NBEA, 2007). A major study in 2000 funded by the major players in accounting (AICPA, AAA, Institute of Management Accountants, and the "Big Five" accounting firms at the time) concluded that the primary focus of the Accounting I class should move away from financial statement preparation and more toward analysis (Albrecht & Sack, 2000). As the financial accounting focus of Accounting I strives to serve the needs of investors and creditors, activities involving loan or investment decisions should be emphasized.

Accounting I teachers traditionally covered accounting cycle procedures to preparation of financial statements to more specific accounting for cash, receivables, inventory, and property, plant, and equipment. They also covered some ethics and internal control and maybe some financial analysis considerations along the way. This approach has been labeled by some as a "bottom-up" approach.

To better address students' needs for answering the "why" questions related to accounting procedures, an alternative "top-down" approach to sequencing has been successfully implemented by many and will be seen more in the future. It starts by leading students to consider (a) what types of decisions investors and creditors and owners need to make, then (b) what financial reports will be needed to provide the information to make such decisions, and then (c) what type of accounting information system and related procedures will be needed to provide the necessary data to create those financial reports. Time spent on performing financial statement analysis is significant. The remaining time in class is then spent on an overview of accounting for general classes of assets and possibly light coverage of liabilities and equity. Publishers now provide textbooks with coverage more along this sequence (particularly at the postsecondary level).

The difference between the two approaches is not necessarily in the topics covered but in the teaching/learning methods used and depth of coverage. In the second approach, students do more homework on the computer or other devices outside of class, freeing up instructors for investor and creditor decision-making exercises and real-company financial analysis activities during class.

Accounting II

The 2000 Albrecht and Sack study emphasizes managerial decision making for the Accounting II course. For example, job order and process costing have been covered because they are required for reporting to investors and creditors under generally accepted accounting principles (GAAP) in the United States, but does such information help managers make good decisions? Assume the following:

Job order cost per unit:	
Direct materials	$10.00
Direct labor	8.00
Overhead (75% of direct labor)	6.00
Cost per unit	$24.00

Armed with this information alone and with a mandate from company leaders to reduce costs, a manager's options are limited. Common responses are to use cheaper materials, shortchange the customer by using less material, use cheaper labor (which may be less competent labor), use less labor by pressuring workers to work faster, or even replace workers with machines (because overhead in this case is assigned solely on the amount of labor). Although all of these options will reduce costs assigned to this manager, they are poor suggestions because they hurt the product's quality, disappoint customers, or undermine employee morale. Consider instead a manager's perspective when presented with this information for the same product:

<u>Activity-based cost per unit:</u>

Direct materials	$10.00
Direct labor	8.00
Overhead related to machine setups cost driver	1.00
Overhead related to machine hours cost driver	2.00
Overhead related to material receipts cost driver	1.00
Overhead related to product movements cost driver	1.00
Overhead related to quality inspections cost driver	<u>1.00</u>
	<u>$24.00</u>

Although the cost per unit is the same as before, managers now have many options to reduce costs. They may reduce the number of inspections or reduce the cost of performing each inspection. They may reduce the number of product moves through a more efficient plant layout or find a cheaper way to perform moves. They may reduce the number of raw material receipts (by having vendors deliver materials straight to the production area) or reduce the number of machine setups or find cheaper ways to perform these activities. Note that simply because costing information was provided in this costing format, managers can identify choices to help their firms cut costs and increase profitability without damaging the perceived quality of the product, the reputation of the company with customers, or the morale of employees. Both conventional and activity-based costing are still taught, but the emphasis in the course changes.

What is "value added" for Accounting II? Ultimately, managers need to make decisions concerning whether to go into business or expand their businesses (using activity-based costing information, cost behavior relative to cost drivers, and evaluation of alternatives under cost-volume-profit analysis). They need to plan for the future (budget) and compare actual results against the budget at period end (performance evaluation) to identify strengths and weaknesses and take corrective actions as needed. At the college level, teachers also often cover the effects of total quality management (cost of quality report), effects of just-in-time inventory systems, and the more comprehensive balanced scorecard performance evaluation.

Intermediate Accounting

Albrecht and Sack in their 2000 study recommended that if the goal is to teach students to be lifelong learners who can learn independently, the intermediate accounting teacher should provide an overview of selected topics such as structure of the accounting profession, conceptual framework, and financial statement areas (e.g., in-depth balance sheet, income statement, statement of cash flows, and earnings per share areas) after which students perform research of accounting standards to learn additional material on other topical areas. (Research would now include both United States GAAP and the International Financial Reporting Standards used by much of the rest of the world.) Intermediate accounting textbooks are enormous, with too much information to cover in classes for students to become effective "rule experts" anyway.

Again, the focus should be on developing competencies. Hurt (2007) recommends a focus on developing writing, professionalism, ethics, critical thinking, information technology, and research abilities early in the accounting major. In 2009 the online Financial Accounting Standards Board (FASB) Accounting Standards Codification (FASB, n.d.) became the profession's primary resource, defining all authoritative United States GAAP in one easy-to-access location. The codification is organized into 90 topics, which are easily updated. Codification search capabilities significantly reduce the time needed to determine proper treatment of complex accounting matters. Intermediate accounting cases and other assignments that require students to "learn by discovery" meet both content learning and competency development goals simultaneously (FASB, n.d.).

INTEGRATED COMPETENCY DEVELOPMENT AND ASSESSMENT STRATEGIES

To develop knowledge workers, accounting educators would do well to recall the Accounting Education Change Commission's monograph entitled *Intentional Learning: A Process for Learning to Learn in the Accounting Curriculum* (Francis, Mulder, & Stark, 1995). Still relevant, it recommends that accounting teachers use group learning, computerized tutorials, ethics seminars, and opportunities to meet with real practitioners and clients. Especially beneficial are the use of real company case studies in which students have to find and use information to address business problems. Through these activities, students not only learn technical knowledge but also how to work with others, communicate, negotiate, and lead. Technology is evolving, but the examples provided here do reflect the current state of available resources.

COMPUTERIZED/OTHER TECHNOLOGY INSTRUCTION

Many of today's accounting textbooks have an accompanying computer homework management system that allows students to complete textbook problems online. Students can have the software "check my work" to get immediate feedback before proceeding to the next exercise. A student can do the homework anytime and anywhere Internet access is available, with the student's choice of device. The instructor assigns specific exercises/problems in the system, sets the number of points, elects whether to provide hints, and sets the number of times the student can update answers and resubmit. To cut down on cheating, most systems allow the teacher to select algorithmic exercises (i.e., numbers in the exercises differ among students). The system grades the homework automatically and enters results in an online grade book. There is evidence that online homework systems motivate a number of students to exert greater effort (Peng, 2009). Popular choices for teachers to consider include Cengage Learning (South-Western), Connect (McGraw-Hill), WileyPLUS (John Wiley & Sons), and My Accounting Lab (Pearson). The system automatically gathers assessment information for review on achievement of learning outcomes, number of attempts, means, and high and low scores.

Some firms offer online, artificial intelligence software that focuses on covering the accounting cycle, and thus can be used with any number of Accounting I textbooks; some evidence exists that such software helps Accounting I students obtain higher financial accounting knowledge (Baxter & Thibodeau, 2011). Examples include ALEKS (http://aleks.com) and Quantum Tutors for Accounting (http://quantumtutors.com). Students who achieve mastery of content in an area (by correctly answering a significant number of exercises) move on to other modules, whereas those needing more assistance can click on "show answer" options with explanations to study before proceeding. In this way, instruction is self-paced.

Inkling.com has enhanced e-books specifically designed for use on Apple iPads that are now available for use on other devices. Common inclusions for accounting instruction are interactive multiple-choice questions, tap-to-review vocabulary words, online audio lectures accompanied by PowerPoint slides, real-business-example videos, tap-to-show-answer practice exercises, and even short (less than two minutes) demonstration videos for exercises similar to those at the end of each chapter. This is an exciting alternative for numerous students who no longer feel motivated to read traditional paper textbooks.

Some instructors create short screencast videos that capture the teacher's voice (via computer microphone) and whatever is showing on the teacher's computer screen during recording. Thus, teachers can record lectures with PowerPoint slides, demonstrate how to use software (e.g., Excel), or highlight sites on the Internet within videos for students to access outside of class for homework assistance or to help study for exams. Camtasia is a popular product for this purpose. Another option, Screencast-o-matic is free for videos of less than 15 minutes. After recording, the videos can be uploaded to the screencast software's site, to an instructor's website, to Google Docs, or to YouTube. One research study showed that providing short online tutorial videos (less than three minutes each) especially helped students who were intimidated in class or had low aptitude or motivation. Students using the tutorials were less likely to drop the class and had higher course grades (Sargent, Borthick, & Lederberg, 2011).

Teachers can create free online review flashcards for accounting students (or use sets of flashcards already created by others) using Quizlet (http://quizlet.com). Students can go to the site on their devices to use the decks or teachers can project the flashcards on a screen for an in-class review for all. (The author of this chapter creates review questions and answers in "A" and "B" columns in a free Google Docs spreadsheet, imports them into Quizlet and then has students download the sets onto iPads through a free app called Free Flashcards-Flashboard.)

Student response devices (also known as "clickers") allow teachers to make their presentations more interactive. True-false or multiple-choice questions are periodically projected on a screen or to students' hand-held devices, with each student responding with an answer choice. Immediate answer feedback can be provided to the class.

Students are more highly engaged; even those who do not like to speak up in class are able to participate while maintaining anonymity. To increase motivation, points can be assigned to the questions or student teams can be configured to provide a learning competition. Teachers gain insight into student comprehension of the subject matter. Results can be used as documented assessment data. Students' smart phones or iPads can also be used as clickers. (The author has used a free app called Nearpod for interactive presentations and a free app called Socrative for quizzes in an iPad Accounting I class.) Some research shows that students believe clickers motivate them to pay more attention in class; they also report enjoying using clickers to review course material (Eastman, Iyer, & Eastman, 2011; Premuroso, Tong, & Beed, 2011).

Remember that the purpose of the technology options mentioned above is to move more of the technical side of accounting instruction outside of class. This allows the teacher to spend more in-class time on decision-making or analysis activities.

Practice Sets

Teachers often want students to experience accounting software packages. Some textbooks include scaled-down versions of packages such as Peachtree or Quick Books. An online accounting software system from Wave (https://www.waveapps.com/accounting) runs on iPads or computers and is free and available on the Internet. Another option is Express Accounts' free accounting software that runs on Windows platforms. Preparing handouts to walk students through building a company's accounting system from scratch takes effort, but the opportunity for students to perform accounting procedures and generate reports through technology is very value added.

Formal practice sets are more commonly used at the secondary school level. Although the traditional, paper-based format for practice sets remains, a number of options have been developed for students to use accounting information system software (such as Peachtree) that might come with a textbook or be accessible online. The online versions can provide different students with different transactions to reduce students' ability to cheat and can grade electronic student submissions automatically for the teacher. Upon grading a portion of the practice set, a student can be led in correcting errors made before being allowed to proceed to subsequent parts of the practice set. Instructors can use Internet searches to seek out these online options.

Some colleges/universities assess effectiveness of accounting programs through portfolio evaluation of a series of comprehensive student projects at various stages of program completion. The author teaches at a college that assigns a "Knowledge of GAAP" project as part of Intermediate Accounting II. Given beginning-of-year financial statements for a unique business and various complex transactions from topics covered in the course, each student must research prescribed accounting under GAAP, exercise professional judgment in applying the standards, and communicate the effects on financial statements and disclosures to enhance decision making.

Decision-Making and Role-Play Activities

In financial accounting classes (Accounting I and intermediate accounting), decision-making activities should focus on loan and investment decisions for which students role play as bankers or stockholders. In the more managerial-like accounting classes (Accounting II and Survey of Accounting) decision-making activities should cast students as managers selecting among alternative strategies or performing evaluation of company subunits, such as product lines, geographic areas, or store departments. Many end-of-chapter exercises/cases in textbooks can be readily adapted to use as in-class decision-making or role-play activities.

Some examples of in-class activities presented at a recent NBEA annual convention can be found at http://academic.wsc.edu/faculty/shgarvi1, clicking on the NBEA handout. Young and Warren (2011) advocated for inclusion of decision-making or recommendation-to-management scenarios as an addition to traditional Accounting I exams and provided examples.

Group Research Assignments

The Internet can be a valuable tool to enhance learning in accounting. Public company financial statements are accessible from either company websites or through the Securities and Exchange Commission website (http://www.sec.gov) and using the "search for company filings" option. Once one has accessed the company's filings, limiting the search to 10-K reports (which is equivalent to an annual report in the Securities and Exchange Commission submission format) will bring up options to view the financial statements, often available through an "interactive data" option that allows for easy export to an Excel spreadsheet. Free industry average ratios to compare with company ratios calculated by students (to determine if the company measures are average, above average, or below average) are available at the MSN Money (http://money.msn.com/investing) and BizStats (http://www.bizstats.com) websites.

Intermediate accounting students should conduct accounting standards research through the online FASB Accounting Standards Codification system (see https://asc.fasb.org. choosing the academic access option). This option is available only to faculty and students of college/university accounting programs/departments that have paid an annual administrative fee of $150.00. Brenner & Watkins (2011) have provided training guidance as well as some practice research activities in an article referenced at the end of this chapter. Most intermediate accounting textbooks have codification research assignments as part of end-of-chapter materials. The author includes codification research situations on exams. Students must apply professional judgment on how a situation should be accounted for and include support from the codification by providing topic, subtopic, section, and paragraph number reference.

Real Company Financial Analysis Projects

Because financial analysis competencies have increased in importance, a number of schools have incorporated real company projects for groups of students to complete and professionally present. Analysis project ideas may be found in textbooks or are available to purchase separately from publishers. An example project written by the author is available by clicking on the NBEA Project at http://academic.wsc.edu/faculty/shgarvi1. Misch and Galantine (2009) also provide an example in an article referenced at the end of this chapter.

A note on business mathematics is warranted. When ratios and trend figures calculated from financial statements deviate from industry averages, accounting professionals label them as potential errors or frauds for investigation. Thus, having strong math skills to both perform calculations and to recognize when the "numbers don't look right" is very important in accounting. Teachers should provide numerous activities for students to practice these skills. Some research has shown that poor performance in math pre-tests can be used to identify at-risk students taking introductory accounting courses (Yunker, Yunker, & Krull, 2009). ALEKS, previously mentioned, offers artificial intelligence software to tutor students in mathematics.

Spreadsheet Analysis of Alternatives

Spreadsheets are vital for evaluating accounting information for making decisions. Some accounting textbooks provide a variety of spreadsheet templates for introducing students to the capabilities of spreadsheets. Others believe the real learning occurs when the students themselves program the spreadsheets to perform needed computations. Excel (Microsoft Office), Numbers (Apple iWork), Google Docs, or other spreadsheet software packages can be used by teachers to turn many textbook accounting homework assignments into "using technology assignments." The Accounting II course is particularly well suited for using spreadsheets, as the managerial accounting applications frequently require choosing among strategic alternatives or addressing "what if" sensitivity analysis issues. The website http://www.jaxworks.com/library.htm has numerous free templates that teachers can have their students use or that teachers can view to get ideas for spreadsheets to have students create.

Written and Oral Reports

This is where cases come into play, providing opportunities for students to think critically, apply prior learning, and communicate conclusions. Students giving presentations practice professionalism skills. Group presentations allow for development of interaction skills. Financial analysis projects work well if students are required to include a written report or presentation as part of the project. An idea used by the author involves taking several managerial accounting problems and adding written scenario descriptions so that the "case" involves students creating three analysis spreadsheets and writing memos to coworkers or orally presenting to the boss (i.e., the teacher) what the numbers show and making a recommendation on the course of action to take.

A number of textbooks now include short cases for each chapter. Otherwise, cases can be purchased from the Institute of Management Accountants, AAA, Harvard Business Educators, Massachusetts Institute of Technology, and European Case Clearing House. The Institute of Management Accountants and AAA cases are free for members. Solutions to all of these cases are available to teachers.

Ethics Cases

Integrity and professionalism are important attributes to enhance in students. To this end, Junior Achievement provides an online Excellence through Ethics Program at its "Classroom Activities: Business Ethics" web page (http://studentcenter.ja.org/Learn/ Ethics/Pages/ClassroomActivities.aspx).

OTHER RESOURCES

Resource	Sponsor	Location
"Great Ideas for Teaching Accounting"	Cengage Learning	http://www.cengagesites.com/ academic/?site=5384&SecID=5591
Improving teaching and learning webinars	Cengage Learning	http://www.cengage.com/teamup/ programs/webinars.html
Faculty network lecture series	Wiley	http://wfn.wiley.com/pg/event_ calendar/?type_filter=guest_lectures
Publications on curricula, standards, and teaching strategies	National Business Education Association	http://www.nbea.org
Information on curricula, standards, and shared teaching resources/strategies	State Departments of Education	Search for various Internet sites by state
"Start Here, Go Places" career information and class resources	AICPA	http://www.startheregoplaces.com
Educational competency assessment	AICPA	http://www.aicpa-eca.org
Locate accounting practitioners to visit classes	State Societies of CPAs	Search for various Internet sites by state
Online modules, lesson plans, handouts, assessment sheets, and solutions related to tax education	Internal Revenue Service	http://www.irs.gov/app/ understandingTaxes/teacher/index.jsp
Comprehensive site with accounting-academia-teaching section with accounting education resources	AccountantsWorld, LLC	http://www.taxsites.com

SUMMARY

This chapter noted current accounting practice in the workplace, discussed the move in emphasis from mastery of content toward development of competencies, provided content coverage guidance for introductory and intermediate accounting courses, and suggested a number of strategies and resources for use by accounting educators in response to the changing needs of businesses. Educators for introductory and intermediate accounting courses readily understand that accounting and bookkeeping are not the same; their job has evolved into doing so much more than covering journal entries. Instructors are encouraged to leverage technology to minimize time on manual accounting systems in order to free up more class time to spend in developing competencies that will serve students throughout their professional careers.

REFERENCES

Accounting Education Change Commission. (1990). Objectives of education for accountants: Position statement number one. *Issues in Accounting Education, 5,* 307–312.

Albrecht, S. W., & Sack, R. J. (2000). Accounting education: Charting the course through a perilous future. *Accounting Education Series, 16.* Sarasota, FL: American Accounting Association. Retrieved from http://aaahq.org/pubs/AESv16/toc.htm

American Institute of Certified Public Accountants (AICPA). (1998–2000). *CPA Vision Project: 2011 and beyond.* Retrieved from http://www.aicpa.org/research/cpahorizons2025/cpavisionproject/downloadabledocuments/cpavisionproject_finalreport.pdf

American Institute of Certified Public Accountants (AICPA). (n.d.). Welcome to the AICPA's educational competency assessment (ECA) website. Retrieved from http://www.aicpa-eca.org

Baxter, R., & Thibodeau, J. (2011). Does the use of intelligent learning and assessment software enhance the acquisition of financial accounting knowledge? *Issues in Accounting Education, 26*(4), 647–656.

Brenner, V., & Watkins, A. (2011). Introducing students to the FASB codification system. *The Accounting Educators' Journal, 21,* 63–82.

Eastman, J., Iyer, R., & Eastman, K. (2011). Business students' perceptions, attitudes, and satisfaction with interactive technology: An exploratory study. *Journal of Education for Business, 86*(1), 36–43.

Financial Accounting Standards Board (FASB), (n.d.). *FASB accounting standards codification.* Retrieved from https://asc.fasb.org

Foster, S., & Bolt-Lee, C. (2002). New competencies for accounting students. *The CPA Journal, New York State Society of CPAs, 72*(1), 68–71.

Francis, M., Mulder, T., & Stark, J. (1995). Intentional learning: A process for learning to learn in the accounting curriculum. *Accounting Education Series, 12.* Sarasota, FL: American Accounting Association.

Hurt, B. (2007). Teaching what matters: A new conception of accounting education. *Journal of Education for Business, 82*(5), 295–299.

Misch, M., & Galantine, C. (2009). A financial statement analysis project for introductory financial accounting. *Global Perspectives on Accounting Education, 6*, 83–96.

National Business Education Association (NBEA). (2007). *National standards for business education: What America's students should know and be able to do in business.* Reston, VA: Author.

Pathways Commission. (2012). The Pathways Commission: Charting a national strategy for the next generation of accountants. American Accounting Association and American Institute of CPAs. Retrieved from http://commons.aaahq.org/files/0b14318188/Pathways_Commission_Final_Report_Complete.pdf

Peng, J. (2009). Using an online homework system to submit accounting homework: Role of cognitive need, computer efficacy, and perception. *Journal of Education for Business, 84*(5), 263–268.

Premuroso, L., Tong, L., & Beed, T. (2011). Does using clickers in the classroom matter to student performance and satisfaction when taking the introductory financial accounting course? *Issues in Accounting Education, 26*(4), 701–723.

Sargent, C., Borthick, A., & Lederberg, A. (2011). Improving retention for principles of accounting students: Ultra-short online tutorials for motivating effort and improving performance. *Issues in Accounting Education, 26*(4), 657–679.

Young, M., & Warren, D. (2011). Encouraging the development of critical thinking skills in the introductory accounting courses using the challenge problem approach. *Issues in Accounting Education, 26*(4), 859–881.

Yunker, P., Yunker, J., & Krull, G. (2009). The influence of mathematics ability on performance in principles of accounting. *The Accounting Educators' Journal, 19*, 1–20.

Business Foundations and Management

Betty J. Brown

George Mundrake

Ball State University

Muncie, IN

The business education curriculum has long included courses *for* business (preparing students for business careers) and *about* business (preparing students with personal business literacy). Courses in the area of "about business" have evolved from traditional general business and business management courses. Introductory business and management courses ("basic business" courses) develop skills and knowledge for all students, for their personal lives and their careers. This chapter will discuss content and activities for introductory business and management courses at middle / junior high school, high school, postsecondary, and college levels.

The Role of Introductory Business and Management Courses

Secondary and college introductory business courses are often the first courses for students to learn about business. Various names identify this course in different educational systems, such as business concepts, business foundations, business fundamentals, business essentials, and introduction to business. All these courses have a role in providing conceptual knowledge about business. A secondary school course at a middle or high school prepares students to live in global economic societies and to gain skills and knowledge for managing their own personal finances. A course in both postsecondary and college/university programs builds on students' knowledge and often on their personal experiences in business. Management courses at all levels prepare students for business and for careers in management.

Introductory Business Courses

Introductory business courses are courses for students to survey business fields. These courses have two major focuses: personal financial literacy and economic education. A secondary introductory business course has one overall objective—economic understanding. All individuals must be able to handle their personal business affairs. They must understand economic systems, opportunities for consumers and business, and skills and knowledge for functioning effectively in an economic system. College introductory courses have two focuses: to promote economic understanding and to provide a base for advanced business study. Students learn about the role of individuals and businesses in an economic system, the interdependence of all types of economic systems, and their place in a global economy.

Management Courses

A high school management course provides a base for college study in business management and for employment after graduation. High school management courses often are part of career pathways for business. Career pathways for business have different programs in various states, but they all prepare students for business. Business management, entrepreneurship, and small business development are often a part of a state's career pathways. Students survey the structures and functions necessary for day-to-day operations of a business organization. The management course provides an overview of areas such as business organization, management, marketing, and finance. At the college level, students who plan a career in business usually complete a management course. Whether students plan to be corporate employees, small business owners, or entrepreneurs, they need tools for day-to-day management, human resource management, marketing, and strategic planning for the firm.

Introductory business and management courses fill several roles in high schools and colleges. These classes are foundation courses for students who will pursue further study in business.

Needed Skills and Knowledge for Business

Students who plan a career in business need to know how a business firm, large or small, operates. Because business is global, students see how local businesses—in their own community—participate in a world market. They can develop their decision-making and problem-solving skills with real-world cases and simulations. Business courses help students to develop valuable hard and soft skills for their careers. Business courses can help students to develop soft skills such as the ability to stay on task, relate well to others, accept responsibility, and work independently. What can students do in a business classroom to develop those skills? They can work together (teamwork), plan, accept responsibility for completing their work without prodding, present effectively, and critique others' work in a kind and suitable way. Managers try to motivate, inspire, and lead. For business, soft skills are the personal qualities that enable people in business to lead and inspire those with whom they work.

Decision Making

All individuals, companies, cities, states, and economic systems share a common problem: scarcity. Scarcity of resources for meeting needs and wants requires all individuals or groups to make choices. Introductory business and management courses deal with how individuals and groups make those choices. Students identify problems for various business firms, governments, and individuals and look for possible "real-world" solutions. Class activities can require students to think critically, to use problem-solving skills, and to arrive at solutions for problem situations.

Ethics in Business

Dunphy (2010) pointed out that in recent years ethical conduct in business has been a major concern. Consumers and businesses alike may act unethically. Sometimes people resist the idea of *teaching* about ethics, asserting that "by the time students are in high school, their values are defined." Although students form ethical beliefs and practices early in life, business educators can help them to identify ethical standards and conduct for business. Tiatorio (2011) described ethical behavior as finding the balance between self-interest and group responsibility and as largely learned behavior in opposition to instinct. Basic business and management courses are naturals for teaching strategies that emphasize ethical conduct and standards.

"Do the right thing"—the heart of ethics for business. Help students learn to use a process for ethical decision making. Can students examine issues from both sides, recognize their own biases and perspectives, and identify errors or defects in logic on both sides of the issue? Can they use the following process?

1. What are the facts in the situation?
2. Who are the stakeholders?
3. Who will be affected by my decision?
4. What ethical issues are involved?
5. What are different ways of looking at the problem?
6. What are the practical constraints?
7. What action should I take?
8. Is that action practical?

Help students to explore ethical and unethical behavior in a business setting. A good resource is a publication from Delta Pi Epsilon that includes 25 ethics cases with solutions for business classes (Meggison, 2010).

Social and Environmental Responsibility

Business firms have multiple social and environmental responsibilities. The goal of business is to make a profit, but profit-making activities must not result in harming others. Businesses should provide safe products, protect the environment, and contribute to the well-being of society. Powell (2010) stressed that all managers in all companies must have a sense of integrity. Students in basic business courses can consider the need for managers to meet their social and environmental responsibilities. If a manufacturing business dumps its waste into a nearby river, what are the effects on all who live downstream? What responsibility does a firm have to protect those who are affected? What is the responsibility of business to consumers, employees, and society? How can a business be more socially responsible? What can consumers do? Can they recycle? Can they buy products that are "friendly to the environment? Students can discuss the motto "we are all in this together," green initiatives in business, and social entrepreneurship. What individuals and businesses do affects others.

Technology Resources for Business

Teachers have increasing access to many technological resources for teaching their courses. The Internet offers an array of websites, simulations, and materials that are up to date and relevant (Glasgow & Hicks, 2009). Glasgow and Hicks reported that teachers often find that students interact more with content and engage with assignments if they use technology (p. 153). Sites such as EconEdLink (http://econedlink.org) from the Council for Economic Education offer interactive tools, lesson plans, and resources for teachers, students, and parents. Websites such as SlideShare (http://slideshare.net), PosterousSpaces (http://posterous.com), SchoolTube (http://schooltube.com), Wordle (http://wordle.net), as well as the popular YouTube (http://youtube.com) are worth exploring for materials for the classroom. For example, SlideShare permits a teacher to share presentations, documents, and videos in the classroom.

Students in introductory business and management classes gain the knowledge and skills they will need in business. They can apply their technology skills, value systems (ethics), and understanding of the social and environmental responsibilities of business. Experiences in the courses can help them to develop their decision-making skills for business decisions.

INTRODUCTORY BUSINESS COURSES

Standards for courses define expectations for students. For business teachers, the publication, *National Standards for Business Education* (National Business Education Association [NBEA], 2007) identifies standards and expectations for all business courses.

Performance Expectations

National Standards for Business Education provides expectations for students in high school and college introductory business and management courses. Standards for post-secondary/college courses require students to master advanced content and use more sophisticated decision-making and critical thinking skills. Textbooks for all levels include performance expectations matched to national and state standards. A standards movement, at all levels of education, mandates that course content must be matched to standards identified for the curriculum. Teachers can use the performance expectations used as a foundation for textbook content as a tool for achieving those standards.

Secondary and College Objectives

Middle schools and high schools offer introductory business courses. A goal of the course is to encourage students to think about the "real world." They explore business knowledge and skills they will need as consumers, employers, employees, and entrepreneurs and apply their knowledge to actual business situations. The course provides a foundation for business career pathways and knowledge and skills for various career choices.

Students in a college introductory business or management course have often not gained a business background during their high school years. Thus, a college course provides background knowledge for business. Students may plan a career in business, or they may want to acquire knowledge, skills, and good business judgment for any career they enter. In many communities, workers' skills and available jobs do not match, and workers need to prepare for different careers. Business and education may form partnerships to "pre-train" workers for high-demand positions in their community. Curricula emphasize concepts of business and economics that prepare workers for available jobs.

Strategies for Teaching Concepts

Activities are useful teaching tools for introductory business courses. Activities build on textbook content using individual, small-group, large-group, and Internet-based resources. Websites for textbooks connect students to simulations, puzzles, games, and supplemental content. For a teacher, technology resources can mean less use of books and more use of other resources of all types. Students can create documents, spreadsheets, presentations, and databases to summarize what they have learned. They can use the Internet to research business topics, find updated company information, and apply what they know in simulations. They can "connect" what they are learning about business to other academic areas by using their math, language arts/communication, science, social studies, and computer skills.

Provide students with choices among a variety of activities to demonstrate their knowledge and skills. If they can choose an activity that matches their individual learning styles, students enjoy their work and gain knowledge more readily. For example, students might interview someone, take a field trip to a business, use software to analyze business data, create diagrams, charts, posters, or collages, or complete online research and present their findings. Their choices help them to learn.

Archer & Hughes (2011) and others (Dunn & Honigsfeld, 2009; Glasgow & Hicks, 2009; Moore, 2009; Stone, 2004; and Tileston, 2004) emphasized the importance of activity-based strategies for individuals, small groups, and large groups. Innovative activities should engage students, consider student diversity, and use online resources effectively. Such activities can engage students in discovery learning, inquiry, and problem solving. The local business community can be a "laboratory" for learning—to help students connect what they learn with their own experiences. Various websites provide a "gold mine" of activities for teachers and students. Textbooks provide discussions and activities that help students to remember and apply what they learned. Cleveland (2011) and others (Dunn and Honigsfeld, 2009; Hanson and Carpenter, 2011; and Stone, 2004) advocated cooperative learning activities to allow students to collaborate. Students recognize that they learn by doing and that "three or four heads are better than one." Armstrong and Haskins (2011) recommended that students discuss not only what they have learned but how they know the information. Armstrong and Haskins' technique of "chunking" a lesson—dividing a lesson into "chunks"—can keep students' attention. For example, students listen for a few minutes (the first chunk) and then write (second chunk). In a third chunk, they talk to their partners about the information. They then summarize with an activity (fourth chunk), such as participating in a simulation or large-group discussion, preparing a poster, or creating charts. With "chunking," students think as they learn. The tasks and activities should involve both critical thinking and creative thinking. Tileston (2004) described graphic organizers to help students learn and remember. Graphic organizers cause students to think. Visual organizers such as concept maps, tables, flow charts, diagrams, or charts, in which students "fill in" information can set the stage for learning.

Activities for learning by doing can re-engage students who struggle with the classroom and content. Kame'enui, Carnine, Dixon, Simmons, & Coyne (2002) recommended that teachers help diverse learners by using strategies that make explicit the steps in learning. Visual maps or models, pictures, verbal directions, and full and clear explanations enable students to see the strategy they must apply to understand. These tools not only help students make connections between ideas but help them to connect familiar concepts with new, more complex concepts. In introduction to business, for example, students can apply what they know about their own business community to a larger economy.

The box on the following page lists activities to use with students in an introductory business course.

Authentic Assessments

Students in introductory business courses can benefit from frequent checks of their progress. They can use "quick and easy" diagnostic and formative assessments: checkpoints to measure their needs and progress. Assessment tools include simple techniques as well as comprehensive assessments that allow students to demonstrate mastery over time. Stitt-Gohdes (2011) discussed ways to select and use assessment tools appropriately.

If students in a course have had different experiences in business, an instructor can use diagnostic assessments such as pretests, self-assessment, or observations for planning course content. A pretest provides information about student knowledge and competencies related to course content. Students can assess their knowledge and competencies in a self-assessment survey. Even a simple checklist asking students for their opinions about their knowledge and competencies provides valuable information for a

Classroom Activities for Introductory Business Courses

Teachers can develop activities that ask students to think about their own environment—their community and local businesses. Here are some examples.

- Draw a map of a local shopping area with names of businesses and stores. Brainstorm about these points: Have we lost any businesses recently? Why? Have some businesses been replaced by similar businesses? By businesses offering different goods and services? What new businesses are needed? Where would you locate new businesses? Which businesses furnish goods or services for other firms? How do goods get to local businesses? By rail? By truck? Where do shoppers come from? How do they travel to businesses? How do businesses interact with each other?

- Develop a survey questionnaire about banking services. Examples: Do you use a checking account? Savings account? CDs for investments? Do you bank online? How often do you visit your bank or branch? Do you frequently use an ATM? For what purposes? Individually or with a partner, interview three persons with your questionnaire. Compile the results in class, and prepare a report or blog to post on your school website, if permitted.

- Team with two classmates and design a new candy bar to market. Create a name, logo, and slogan for your product; design a package to attract customers. Develop a marketing plan for your product; include plans for price, distribution methods, financing, and advertising/promotion strategies. Report on your product and exhibit your package to the class.

- Select a product to sell through TV advertising. Develop a 15-second commercial to present to your audience.

- You work in a local drive-in fast-food restaurant. The manager closes out each night and collects the receipts. One night the manager asks you to close up. One of your closest friends works with you and asks you to alter the records so the two of you can split some of the cash. What will you do?

- Assume you have $400 to spend. List on paper all items you will buy with the money. Now double the amount. List ways to spend $800. Double the amount again. Add items to your list of wants and needs. Continue doubling the amount until you have difficulty adding needs and wants. Classify all items on your list as needs or wants. What impact do individual values have on your spending decisions?

- Select several restaurants in your community. Collect information on products, prices, and services. Where do companies get their supplies?

- Using the Internet, research products produced in the United States. Which products of selected U.S. businesses are sold locally? Which products are marketing globally? Report your findings.

teacher. Particularly in a middle or high school course, a teacher can observe students engaged in an activity at the beginning of a unit of study. Those observations can guide planning for course content and activities.

COURSE CONTENT AND OBJECTIVES FOR MANAGEMENT COURSES

Management responsibilities in businesses are wide ranging and often complex. Business firms of all sizes operate in an international market, with all of its unique requirements. Students learn about the processes of management: how to use people, equipment, and money to achieve the goals of the business. All business firms face many decisions about the use of their resources.

Performance Expectations

Performance expectations for management courses from the *National Standards for Business Education* (NBEA, 2007) emphasize higher-level thinking skills. In today's climate of change, managers need these advanced skills to manage people and businesses. The standards recognize the importance of ethical and corporate responsibility and the global nature of business (p. 116).

Secondary and College Objectives

At the secondary level, management courses are often part of career pathways. Students have a foundation in business, and they prepare for a future as an entrepreneur, small business owner, employee, or manager in a large company. The management course can build on what students have learned in an introduction to business course. Because those students have a base of business knowledge, a management course can further develop their career preparation.

Business programs in secondary schools may include marketing as part of a career pathway, often using a school-based enterprise. Activities in the enterprise help students to develop competencies for owning and managing a business. Students work at an enterprise site (for example, a school store) and maintain complete and accurate records for the business. A management course includes knowledge and skills needed in marketing. If a school cannot offer a marketing program, a management course prepares students for further marketing or management education or workplace employment.

Students in college-level management courses have different goals. Some are preparing to start their own businesses; others want to advance further in the business careers they have now. Still others want the education needed for a new management career. A management course must meet all of these needs. At the college level, management students may be nontraditional students with a wealth of experience in business. Their collective experiences add realism to their studies. With their backgrounds and experiences, they can become active learners—learning while their instructors act as facilitators.

The traditional management functions—planning, organizing, staffing, leading and controlling—are the core of a management course. In addition, managers must manage interpersonal relationships within and outside the company, organize and manage information for the organization, and make decisions as representatives of their company (Rue and Byars, 2006, p. 14). As Rue and Byars commented, even managers of small businesses fill these roles. Lang (2009) reported that supervisors/managers often spend more than 18% of their time on employee conflict because of the growing complexity of organizations, the use of teams and group decision making, and globalization (p. 240). Managers/supervisors do not just manage a company. They "manage" people: customers, other managers, and representatives of regulatory agencies or government. Course activities prepare students to manage these multiple responsibilities in businesses of all types.

Strategies for Teaching Concepts

Teamwork is an important concept for managers. Discussions, brainstorming, project-based learning, simulations, and case problems from the local business community can help students develop teamwork skills. Project-based learning enables students to plan, organize, and complete tasks to meet their objectives. Simulations range from short group-based activities to simulations that require multiple class periods. Small groups of students can engage in activities such as "a nonverbal communication simulation." This in-class simulation uses toothpicks, sticks, sheets of paper, or other materials. In small groups, students build an object with those materials but are not to speak to each other. The goal is to build the product using nonverbal communication only. Students then analyze their ability to handle conflict, develop efficient and effective steps for the project, and produce a usable product in the simulation.

A "flipped classroom" enables an instructor to engage students and hold them more accountable for their work. Sams and Bergmann (2011) have used the process in their classrooms for several years. The technique requires students to gain knowledge outside the classroom and then "do the work" in the classroom. Outside of class, they read and view instructional videos, podcasts, Internet-based content, or materials on Blackboard or similar systems. In class, they work with interactive activities or complete problems. This concept can be applied to management courses. Students access content outside of class in multiple ways. The in-class activities focus on simulations, Internet research, team meetings, projects, research, fieldwork projects, or other group-based assignments.

Students can use tools such as WebQuests, video field trips, and business plan projects to build their competencies. With a WebQuest they discover a wealth of information from many sources. They can repeatedly view a video from a field trip in the local community to analyze management responsibilities. They can apply what they know about managing a business in their own video presentations. A person who wishes to start a new business must prepare a detailed business plan to be successful. Students can apply what they have learned by creating business plans—perhaps for businesses they plan to start themselves. "Active learning," applying all types of activities and strategies, is useful in management courses. For example, Mountjoy (2011) described an experiential learning project for students: "So You Think You Can Run a Business?" In this project, students play the role of small business owners, working in groups to form and run a business for a short time. The box below lists more ideas for teachers to try for active learning in a management course.

Classroom Activities for Management

Students can apply their knowledge of management responsibilities in case studies and activities such as these:

- Discuss the situation below and apply an ethical decision-making process: You work for a company as support staff entering data on your computer and assisting callers. Your company has a policy prohibiting personal use of company computers during working hours. Sometimes your work is slow and, as "no one knows," you keep yourself alert by accessing social websites, browsing the Internet, and playing games.

  What is your ethical responsibility in this case? If your employer discovers your activities, what action should be taken? If company policy says employees can be fired for personal use of company computers, what action do you expect your employer to take? What are different ways of assessing this dilemma?

- You are production manager for a company that produces picture frames. You employ 30 workers on an assembly line, where each employee completes one step in the manufacture of the product. You have high turnover and absenteeism. Quality control workers report they must reject an unacceptable number of products. Brainstorm about how to reduce the high turnover and absenteeism and improve the quality of the product. In a small group, prepare a report outlining your plans.

- You work for a vice president of a company that must downsize. Your order processing department has 58 employees: 50 order processors, 5 database specialists, 1 order proofreader, 1 clerk, and 1 supervisor. The department processes about 1,700 orders daily (online, phone, and mail). Each order requires about 10 minutes to process; about 10,000 records on orders and customers are stored each day (30 seconds per record). Hours are 8:30 a.m. to 4:30 p.m. with one hour for lunch and two 15-minute breaks. The vice president believes 20 percent fewer employees is reasonable. Determine which employees to retain. Share ideas about steps for downsizing and reorganizing the department.

- Your company has just invented a new miracle fabric that never wears out, is completely dirt resistant, and is about the same price and as attractive as conventional fabrics. Role play a labor union member, leading textile manufacturers, fashion designers, consumers, environmentalists, soap manufacturers, and dry cleaning companies. Prepare a paper on the long- and short-range effects of the new fabric. As a class, decide whether to produce and market the fabric, and how.

- Your firm manufactures baby cribs. You can install a less expensive crib pad that meets federal safety requirements for inflammability—but you believe the safety standards are not adequate. Or you can install a more expensive—and safer—crib pad. You will not be able to raise the price for the crib with a safer pad. What will you decide? Defend your decision.

- Select a foreign country that is a trading partner of the United States. Research the country on the web and collect information about exports and imports, particularly of consumer goods. Report to the class.

- List various sources of power (wind, solar, nuclear, fuel cells, biomass, battery, geothermal, steam, water, etc.). Then list various types of appliances, tools, and/or machinery. Use the two lists to brainstorm about new products, tools, and machinery and ways they can be powered in the future. For example, a cell phone powered by solar energy may be typical in the future.

- List major issues facing businesses, such as downsizing, offshoring, taxation, and competition. Identify steps or actions that business may take in each issue. List pros and cons for each action. Evaluate unintended consequences of each action that may occur.

- Use a Delphi probe with small groups. List items of information for different stakeholders in a payroll information system. Form groups representing managers, employees, payroll department staff, and executives or owners. Each group must reach a consensus about items they want. Each group reports their choices and discusses differences among the groups. Examples include the following: managers need productivity information and units produced. Workers want information about taxes, other deductions, gross pay, and net pay.

- In small groups, students select a product or service and develop a consumer satisfaction survey for that product or service. Report orally on the content and delivery methods possible. Compare groups by product or service to identify similarities and differences among survey items that measure satisfaction.

Authentic Assessment

Assessment in management courses can relate directly to a business community and activities within the classroom based on businesses. Students demonstrate their mastery of course content by projects, simulations, journaling, research, and problem-solving and critical-thinking assignments. Self-assessments can play a significant role in such activities. Mastery of course content is a major goal of the course, but students must also develop qualities for good managers. All types of individual and group assessments enable them to demonstrate those qualities. Chapter 4 includes authentic assessment tools for cognitive and affective goals that teachers and students can use in management courses.

Students often choose management courses because they intend to become managers, either of their own businesses or for other companies. The courses provide opportunities for all students to learn about business. Students with business experience often bring rich experiences and knowledge to a classroom. Class activities can build on their experiences to enrich the course for all students.

LEARNING RESOURCES

Many sources provide ideas and resources for teaching introductory business and management courses. For example, the U.S. Small Business Administration provides materials and resources for starting and managing a small business. For middle and high school courses, such sites give students an understanding of the processes of business. College courses can build on students' experience and background with experiential learning. Activities engage students, build their collaboration skills, and immerse them in learning experiences. The local business community can become a "laboratory" for assuring student learning. Projects can be instructor designed, drawing on community resources. Various sources provide a host of experiential learning materials. Table 1 lists a few of the many Internet sites that provide resources for classroom activities. Internet searches will locate many other resources that fit course content for courses.

Table 1: Internet Resources for Teachers and Students

Resources from Government	
http://www.census.com	**Business research data on companies and consumers:** U.S. census records and population statistics; census data and maps; local job information and online job search help
http://www.sba.gov	**U.S. Small Business Administration site:** Provides a wealth of resources on starting and managing a business, loans and grants for small businesses, how to find contracting opportunities, tax help for small businesses, counseling and training sources, and local resources for small businesses
http://www.ftc.gov	**U.S. Federal Trade Commission site:** Information about identity theft, credit and loans, consumer complaints, Internet fraud and safety, Do Not Call registry, etc.
http://www.federalreserve education.org/resources/search	**Federal Reserve site:** Search for lesson plans, publications, activities, and academic competitions, as well as economic data
Resources for Teachers/Classroom	
http://zunal.com	**WebQuest Maker:** Web-based software for creating WebQuests in a short time; includes WebQuests for business/economics that provide materials (such as student handouts), questions on the content, and structures for completing assignments. Examples include resources (WebQuest on use of resources in production of goods and services), corporate social responsibility and ethics, and creating a strengths, weaknesses, opportunities, and threats (SWOT) analysis.
http://www.Edmunds.com	**Online new and used car buyer's guide:** Ratings for new and used cars; guide to local car inventories; car buyer's guides; tips and advice for consumers.

http://www.miningco.com	**Selective listing of thousands of websites:** Includes business, finance/investment, entertainment, shopping, travel, careers/education, and news/issues.
http://www.bussim.info	**Example source for business simulations for all business management activities:** Includes web-based simulations (fees for semester access), MiniSims (free), and assessment modules.
http://www.jumpstart.org	**Coalition providing teacher and student resources:** Covers more than 100 partner companies and organizations with resources on personal financial literacy and news from business, including newsletters, brochures, and guides for parents and teachers.
http://www.themint.org	**Ideas for parents and teachers for teaching money management:** Provides access to activities for students and lesson plans for teachers developed by the Council for Economic Education, as well as information for kids, teens, parents, and teachers
http://www.lemonadestand.com http://www.omsi.edu/exhibits/moneyville http://www.prongo.com/lemon/game.html http://www.4webgames.com/lemonade http://codenautics.com/lemonade	**Sites for "Lemonade" games:** A popular tool for illustrating concepts of business management. Note: On OMSI site, choose "Lemonade Game" under "Online Activities."
Consumer Information	
http://www.bbb.org	**National Better Business Bureau site:** Access information from the local Better Business Bureau and materials from the national Better Business Bureau
www.consumer.ftc.gov	**Federal Trade Commission:** News, advice, and free resources for consumers
http://www.consumerworld.org	**Consumer World:** Links to more than 2,000 useful consumer sites, including consumer help sites, online store coupons, price comparisons, booklets, and product reviews

http://www.nfcc.org	**National Foundation for Credit Counseling:** Covers consumer services for handling credit problems, including calculators, budget worksheets, consumer tips, and videos
http://www.iii.org	**Insurance Information Institute:** Site with online consumer brochures on insurance issues; statistics about insurance-related events
http://www.standardandpoors.com	**Standard and Poor's site:** Provides information on U.S. companies; resource center includes answers to frequently asked questions about investments
http://www.business2.com	**Free online newsletter from CNN, Fortune, and Money magazine:** Covers general topics in business; links with companies and business leaders, e-commerce, and career sites
http://www.stretcher.com	**The Dollar Stretcher.com:** Tips for stretching consumer dollars; videos and newsletters for consumers; e-mail alerts; "how-to" guides
Publications and Business Resources	
http://www.levistrauss.com	**Levi Strauss:** News and financial data about this corporation (Levi's and Dockers)
http://www.mcdonalds.com	**McDonald's site:** Publishes quarterly financial data on the corporation, as well as information about policies on diversity, social responsibility, and franchising; online videos about McDonald's products
http://www.learning.blogs. nytimes.com	***New York Times:*** Provides lessons for subjects across the curriculum and blogs from students; Lesson Plan link contains resources and lesson plans related to articles in the New York Times
http://www.wsj.com	***Wall Street Journal:*** Subscription site with news items about business in the United States and worldwide

Table 2 lists websites with resources for teachers, particularly ideas for lesson plans. Many of the sites include downloadable materials for the classroom.

A variety of businesses and the Internet are rich sources of content and activities for teachers of introductory business and management courses. The tables presented here contain only a sample of ideas for teachers to supplement content and develop activities. In addition, students can use resources such as these to explore businesses for up-to-date information.

Table 2: Websites with Lesson Plan Resources for Teachers and the Classroom

Teaching Tools	
http://www.ae4rv.com/games	**ae4rv.com:** Downloadable simulation games, including Lemonade Stand
http://www.slideshare.net	**SlideShare:** An online community for sharing presentations; supports presentations, documents, PDFs, videos, and webinars
http://www.techsmith.com/jing	**Jing:** Offers free version or version to purchase; tool for capturing and sharing screen images
http://www.wordle.net	**Wordle:** Tool for eye-catching presentation of vocabulary
http://www.scholastic.com/teachers/teaching-strategies	**Teachers: Strategies & Ideas:** Includes graphic organizers, classroom organizing tips, and teacher resources
http://www.inspiration.com	**Inspiration Software Inc.:** Provides examples of graphic organizers, concept mapping, mind mapping, webbing, outlining, and plots and graphs to aid visual learning
Lesson Plan Sources	
http://www.teachnology.com/teachers/lesson_plans/vocational_ed	**Teachnology: Vocational Education Lesson Plans:** Includes lesson plans for all subject areas; good source for plans to emphasize soft skills (e.g., "Are You Ready for Work?" teaches skills required for seeking employment)
http://www.discovereducation.com/teachers/free-lesson-plans	**Discovereducation.com Free Lesson Plans:** Tools for creating puzzles, crosswords, word search puzzles, jigsaw puzzles, and fill-in puzzles to use online or to print out and share
http://www.councilforeconed.org	**Council on Economic Education:** Provides hundreds of online lesson plans sorted by title, grade, standard, concept, or type; online games; and online teacher training and offers print materials for purchase
http://www.lessonplans4teachers.com	**Teacher Planet Lesson Plans for Teachers:** Search for lesson plans from many sources; economics (business) lesson plans available from 10 sources
http://www.internet4classrooms.com/lesson.htm	**Internet4Classrooms Lesson Plans:** Resources include lesson plans, assessment tools, rubrics, and virtual field trips

http://www.google.com/apps/intl/en/edu/lesson_plans.html	**Google Apps for Education: Lesson Plans:** For using Google apps in class
http://www.lessonplansearch.com	**Lesson Plan Search:** Search database for multiple sources of lesson plans
http://lessonplans.btskinner.com	**Business Education Lesson Plans by Tonya Skinner:** Site for business teachers with bulletin board ideas, curriculum materials, lesson plans, online class tools, and freeware tools
http://www.teach-nology.com/teachers/lesson_plans/economics	**Teachnology: Economics, Business Lesson Plans:** Lesson plans, rubrics, and other resources for business
http://www.lessonplanet.com/lesson-plans/business-management	**Lesson Planet:** Business Management Teacher Resources: Lesson plans for business management and careers
http://www.internet4classrooms.com/ct-bus.htm	**Internet4 Classrooms:** Business Education: Compilation of dozens of sites with lesson plans and other resources for all areas of business, economics, and careers
http://www.educationworld.com/a_tsl/archives	**EducationWorld:** Lesson plans for starting and managing a business
http://www.econedlink.org	**Econedlink:** Includes lesson plans on starting and managing a business • All in Business • Business Ownership: How Sweet It Can Be!
http://inventors.about.com/od/businessplans/a/business_plan.htm	**About.com:** Inventors: How do I make a business plan? Four parts: description of the business, marketing plan, financial management plan, and management plan
http://www.lessonplanet.com/lesson-plans/starting-a-business	**Lesson Planet:** Starting a Business Teacher Resources: Lesson plans for starting a business, including worksheets; also has lesson plans for entrepreneurship
http://libguides.uwstout.edu/ed_marketing	**University of Wisconsin-Stout Library:** Guide to sites for business lesson plans
www.thirteen.org/edonline/lessons	**Thirteen EdOnline:** "Web-based activities that use the rich resources of Thirteen/WNET New York and the Internet"

SUMMARY

Introductory business and management courses provide economic understanding, knowledge, and skills for all persons, whether they will work in business or pursue other interests. At the middle and high school levels, the courses give students a background for career choices. At the college level, students often have already chosen a career path in business. Introductory courses in business and management prepare them for further study for their career choices. Materials and activities such as those described in this chapter can be used for active learning. As a result, students will develop needed knowledge and skills for their personal goals and future careers.

REFERENCES

Archer. A., & Hughes, C. (2011). *Explicit instruction: Effective and efficient teaching.* New York, NY: The Guilford Press.

Armstrong, S., & Haskins, S. (2011). *A practical guide to tiering instruction in the differentiated classroom: Classroom-tested strategies, management tools, assessment ideas, and more.* New York, NY: Scholastic Inc.

Cleveland, K. (2011). *Teaching boys who struggle in school: Strategies that turn underachievers into successful learners.* Alexandria, VA: ACSD.

Dunn, R., & Honigsfeld, A. (2009). *Differentiating instruction for at-risk students: What to do and how to do it.* Lanham, MD: Rowman & Littlefield Education.

Dunphy, S. (2010). Management goes to the movies (and takes business ethics as a "date"). *Journal of Business and Training Education, 19*(1), 47–55.

Glasgow, N., and Hicks, C. (2009). *What successful teachers do* (2nd ed.). Thousand Oaks, CA: Corwin Press.

Hanson, M., & Carpenter, D. (2011). Integrating cooperative learning into classroom testing. *Nursing Education Perspectives, 32*(4), 270–274.

Kame'enui, E., Carnine, D., Dixon, R., Simmons, D., & Coyne, M. (2002). *Effective teaching strategies that accommodate diverse learners* (2nd ed.). Upper Saddle River, NJ: Pearson Education, Inc.

Lang, M. (2009). Conflict management: A gap in business education curricula. *Journal of Education for Business.* 8(4), 240–245.

Meggison, P. (Ed.). (2010). *Case studies for computer ethics.* Little Rock, AR: Delta Pi Epsilon.

Moore, K. (2009). *Effective instructional strategies: From theory to practice.* Thousand Oaks, CA: Sage.

Mountjoy, K. (2011). So you think you can run a business: An experiential learning project. *Business Education Forum, 65*(4), 30–32.

National Business Education Association (NBEA). (2007). *National standards for business education: What America's students should know and be able to do in business* (3rd ed.). Reston, VA: Author.

Powell, C. (2010). *Colin Powell's leadership skills list for highly effective managers.* Retrieved from http://product-ivity.com/leadership-skills-list

Rue, L., and Byars, L. (2006). *Business management: Real-world applications and connections.* New York, NY: The McGraw-Hill Companies.

Sams, A., & Bergmann, J. (2011). Flipping the classroom. *Educational Horizons, 90*(1), 5–7.

Stitt-Gohdes, W. (2011). *The business education profession: Principles and practices* (2nd ed.). Little Rock, AR: Delta Pi Epsilon.

Stone, R. (2004). *Best teaching practices for reaching all learners: What award-winning classroom teachers do.* Thousand Oaks, CA: Corwin Press.

Tiatorio, A. (2011). Ethics in education. Retrieved from http://www.ethicsineducation.com

Tileston, D. (2004). *What every teacher should know about effective teaching strategies.* Thousand Oaks, CA: Corwin Press.

Economics and Personal Finance

Nancy G. Hite

Emporia State University

Emporia, KS

The author, editor, and publisher acknowledge and express appreciation for the work done by Roger Luft, author of this chapter in the previous edition. Thank you for your contribution to this yearbook and to business education.

Economic and financial decisions affect all aspects of life for every individual. Purchasing an automobile or flat-screen TV, selecting insurance, renting or purchasing a home, or choosing investments are all topics that consumers must consider. Additionally, students should understand student loan and credit card obligations. This chapter addresses the content of economics and personal finance education and discusses standards for curriculum development. The chapter also offers teaching suggestions and resources for business educators to help students understand and master concepts that are necessary for lifelong learning.

THE IMPORTANCE OF ECONOMICS AND PERSONAL FINANCE EDUCATION

Now is a great time to convince a high school or college to include a personal finance or economics course as a graduation requirement. Why? Because the recent recession has heightened awareness of the need for financial literacy for people of all ages! Almost every person, including school board members and politicians' families, knows of someone who has encountered a financial problem whether it was foreclosure on a home or car, credit card debt, or loss of a job. Therefore, it is easier to convince the groups in charge of setting policies or passing legislation that now is the time to implement such requirements rather than waiting until the economy improves.

Recent recessionary times have caused many national and global economic problems and many problems that affect individuals. The recession has raised awareness of the need to change saving and spending patterns, to have enough savings to cover one's living expenses for eight months (Orman, 2012) and to lower one's housing expectations, possibly from a house with 3,000 square feet of space to a house with 1,500 square feet. The importance of understanding and applying good personal finance practices is especially timely. In fact, the subprime mortgage meltdown may have been caused by a lack of financial literacy in addition to improper behavior by some lenders and borrowers (Campbell, 2006).

The recession appears to have increased the number of states requiring a personal finance or economics course. The number of states requiring a high school personal finance course (or personal finance content included in an economics course) has increased from 7 in 2007 to 13 in 2009 (Council for Economic Education, 2009). The number of states requiring students to take a high school economics course increased from 17 in 2007 to 21 in 2009. At a local level, in 2011 Wichita Public Schools implemented the requirement of a one-semester personal finance course before graduation for all high school students in the district, a requirement supported by politicians, parents, and teachers in the area.

Economics and personal finance are business education topics often shared by other curricular disciplines. Economics is commonly taught as a social studies course, and personal finance may be taught by either business or family and consumer science teachers. Both economics and personal finance have enjoyed a recent resurgence in the business education curriculum.

A national study commissioned by the Council for Economic Education to determine high school students' knowledge of economic concepts showed that they scored an average of 53% on the test (Markow & Bagnaschi, 2005). Adults taking the same test performed better with a 70% average. However, one area on this test where both students and adults needed improvement was personal finance. This research also found that almost all adults and high school students believed that Americans should have an understanding of economics.

The Jump$tart Coalition for Personal Financial Literacy (Jump$tart, 2007) reported that personal financial literacy test scores of high school seniors were lower than their 2006 peers, as measured by a national survey. High school seniors only answered 48% of the questions correctly in 2008 compared with 52% in 2006. The financial literacy scores among college students were much higher: 62 percent of the questions were answered correctly. Scores increased based on student classification; for example, college freshmen scored 59% on the test, whereas college seniors scored 65% on the questions.

Financial literacy is frequently taught in secondary schools, although one study reported that high school courses in personal finance may not improve students' financial literacy (Mandell & Klein, 2009). However, another study showed a positive relationship between students' financial literacy scores and an index showing self-benefitting financial practices (Hilgert, Hogarth, & Beverly, 2003).

The general lack of knowledge of economics and personal finance is reflected in the rate at which citizens save their incomes (Bureau of Economic Analysis, 2011). Although the savings rate is still low, the recession has caused some positive behavioral changes in terms of personal savings rates. In early 2007 U.S. citizens had a savings rate of just more than a negative 1%, indicating that Americans are spending more than their available personal disposable income; however, the personal savings rate went up to 3.5% of disposable income in November 2011 (Bureau of Economic Analysis, 2011).

Over the years, financial illiteracy has affected the individual bankruptcy rates in the United States. In 2010 the number of individual bankruptcy filings in the United States was 1,593,081, an increase of 849,319 since 2007 (American Bankruptcy Institute, 2009). The need for financial literacy at this time is quite evident.

COURSE CONTENT FOR ECONOMIC EDUCATION

Business educators can provide the needed expertise to assist in the battle against economic illiteracy. Most business teachers have completed course work in macro- and microeconomics, and some have also completed a course in personal or corporate finance. Today's business teachers need to present the basics of economics in ways that emphasize its importance to students' lives.

The Basics of Economics

Economics is typically described as the study of how a society attempts to solve the human problem of unlimited wants and the environmental dilemma of scarce resources (Luft, 2007). Economics courses focus on the economic problems of individuals, for example, why individuals decide to eat at a restaurant and go to a movie, rather than eating at home and watching the season's final episode of a television show. Basic to the content of economics is decision making relative to wants, needs, and scarcity. Human nature causes individuals to have wants, even though they do not need to own the desired good or service. Because human wants and needs are endless, scarcity of goods and services often occurs.

The factors of production include land, labor (human resources), capital, and entrepreneurship. From these four factors emerges the concept of specialization and answers to the following economic questions: What should be produced? How will production occur? How much should be produced? Who will be the recipients?

Economic systems around the world are linked more closely than ever before, and students should understand the interdependence among economies or how one system affects another. Students need to learn how different economic systems help determine standards of living, trade between countries, trade agreements, and embargoes. The reasons U.S. factories have moved to other countries are also important topics.

UNITS OF INSTRUCTION IN ECONOMICS

An economics course typically begins with a unit explaining why economics is important and that economic decisions are a part of everyone's life. The previous example of choosing to go out to dinner or staying home is a decision with economic consequences. Teachers can use a decision-making model to teach students to make wise choices. Three consumer decision-making models) are available from Richarme (2012).

Economic instruction typically includes units on supply and demand. Students should understand why shortages or surpluses occur and how prices are determined. Students also need to realize that profit is necessary for businesses to continue to operate, as well as understand the influence of competition and its role in economic decision making.

As consumers, students should understand how manufacturers make production decisions, as well as why products are imported and exported. Balance of payments and balance of trade are also important economic concepts. Students should be able to differentiate among arguments for increasing versus lifting trade embargoes against other countries.

Additional economics units examine labor and management relations and the reasons why some people earn more than others do. Students need to understand why and how governments influence economies. Topics such as taxes, governmental regulations, and public and private goods are also important issues. Some economics courses include units on personal finance also.

THE ECONOMICS CURRICULUM

Professional standards outline the elements for most business education curricula. This is certainly true for the economics curriculum.

NBEA Standards

The *National Standards for Business Education* by the National Business Education Association (NBEA, 2007) is an excellent framework from which to develop an economics curriculum. The NBEA standards address the general economic concepts of allocation of resources, economic systems, economic institutions and incentives, markets and prices, market structures, productivity, the role of government, international economic concepts, and aggregate supply and demand. Each standard includes performance expectations for each of four levels of instruction: elementary, middle / junior high school, secondary, and two-year postsecondary and community colleges.

Council for Economic Education Economic Content Standards

The Council for Economic Education (CEE, 2007) has also developed economic content standards. Each of its 20 standards is based on one or more important economic concepts and each standard includes a rationale, practical applications of the concepts, benchmarks to measure achievement, and assessment exercises for grades 4, 8, and 12. These standards serve as the basis for curriculum development and are available on the CEE website (see Table 1) or from CEE directly.

COURSE CONTENT FOR PERSONAL FINANCE EDUCATION

Personal finance concepts may be taught either as a separate course or as part of another course, such as introduction to business. Possibly because of the recent recession, personal finance courses appear to be increasing in popularity and many resources are readily available.

National Standards for Personal Finance

The *National Standards for Business Education* (NBEA, 2007) includes standards for personal finance in the following broad content areas: (a) personal decision making, (b) earning a living, (c) managing finances and budgeting, (d) saving and investing, (e) buying goods and services, (f) banking, (g) using credit, and (h) protecting against risk. NBEA specifies performance expectations for all four levels of instruction ranging from elementary through postsecondary/technical college education. In addition to those standards, the Council for Economic Education has economic education standards and student competencies for grades 4, 8, and 12 available on the Internet; some of those standards can be used in personal finance courses also.

The Jump$tart Coalition for Personal Financial Literacy published the third edition of *National Standards in K–12 Personal Finance Education* (2007). These standards offer a logical sequence of broad instructional areas to create units of instruction with standards, benchmarks, and assessment examples identified for grades 4, 8, and 12. The standards and other resources are available from the Jump$tart Coalition website (Table 1).

Personal Finance Units of Instruction

Units of instruction for personal finance can be based on those listed in three sets of national standards—those from NBEA, the Jump$tart Coalition, or CEE. Typical units include the following general content areas: (a) financial responsibility and decision making, (b) income and careers, (c) planning and money management, (d) credit and debt, (e) risk management and insurance, and (f) saving and investing (Jump$tart, 2007).

A variety of topics can be included within those instructional units. For example, topics within an "income and careers" unit could introduce students to economic conditions and structural shifts in the job market, such as away from manufacturing jobs. Other related topics may include the most-needed jobs in the current U.S. economy, educational levels needed to obtain those jobs, the cost to obtain the education (certifications or degrees) needed, and the potential yearly incomes for people in those occupations. The role of government in income taxation, social security, and benefits could also be included in the unit.

"Money management" units of instruction focus on the economic concepts of needs, wants and opportunity cost. Students should learn how to establish budgets and use computer software to assist them in planning and managing budgets. Additional topics include insurance, other ways to manage risk, and the importance of wills and other legal documents. A comparison of the cost of auto insurance for teenagers for various types of vehicles could be included. Within this unit, students should develop a basic financial plan for earning, spending, saving, and investing. Their financial plan could be based on potential income from their chosen careers with expenses based on all the consumer goods they want or they think they need. This financial plan could be created on a spreadsheet early in the course—a financial plan that could be added to and revised throughout the course after other units are covered.

A "spending and credit" unit should include consumer decision making and comparison shopping. A realistic activity is for students to "shop" for a new or used automobile. This unit should introduce students to websites that contain information on manufacturers' suggested retail price, dealer invoice prices, and specific information on the auto of their choice. A helpful website for this activity is Edmunds.com (http://www.edmunds.com), an excellent source for obtaining car pricing.

The annual consumer products buying guide published by Consumer Reports (Consumers Union, 2011) provides reviews of a wide variety of products, including a list of the best and worst cars and most prevalent repairs needed for various years, makes, and models. To get students actively involved, have them select four cars they would be interested in owning but restrict them to realistic choices. Then, have students search various websites and newspaper ads for the manufacturers' suggested retail prices, dealer invoice prices, and other prices, as well as ratings of the best and worst cars. Have students create a table or spreadsheet comparing the data gathered for the four cars. Furthermore, have them write a two- to three-page report describing why they chose one of the cars and have them present the report orally to the class. Additional follow-up topics include auto loans, down payments, interest rates, and cost of insurance.

Within the "spending" unit, students need to learn the consequences of failure to maintain adequate records of their spending. Teaching students to maintain the current balance in their checkbooks and to record any debit card transactions in their checkbooks can be valuable lessons, rather than relying on online banking. Coverage of the security risks of online banking should be included, as well as bankruptcy.

A "credit" unit should include consumer credit protection and what consumers should do if they encounter credit difficulties such as lost or stolen credit cards and identity theft. Given the huge credit card debt owed by many people, it is important to teach students to read and understand credit card policies and statements, including the impact of interest rates charged, of only paying the minimum balance, and of extra charges for not paying balances by the due dates. Because many students may take out a student loan at some point in their lives, student loan policies should also be covered, including the fact that student loans are seldom discharged through bankruptcy and the fact that student loan debt can follow one for the rest of one's life ("Debts that survive," n.d.).

A unit on "saving and investing" might include topics such as compound interest and the advantages of beginning a saving and investing plan early in life, using lessons from the CEE's (2007) EconEdLink website. Students should be introduced to methods for calculating interest; saving and investing in stocks, bonds, and mutual funds; importance of diversification; income-sheltering retirement plans such as 401(k), 403(b), and other employer-sponsored programs; and role of government in regulating the financial industry.

In past years, purchasing a home was often considered a topic in which teenagers would not be interested; but with more foreclosures of people's homes, the topic of home mortgages is an essential part of financial literacy. The topic could be covered in either an "investments" unit or a "spending" unit. Topics should include adjustable-rate and fixed-rate mortgages, closing costs, title insurance, property insurance, and inspection costs, as well as how large of a mortgage is affordable at various income levels. Guest speakers could include real estate agents and bankers. A real estate agent could show a house closing statement and address unrealistic expectations of first-time home buyers when it comes to location, cost, and the amenities they expect to have in their first home such as granite countertops, hardwood floors, and stainless steel appliances. Websites and iPad apps have calculators to figure monthly mortgage payments by inputting the down payment, amount of the loan, length of the loan, and interest rate. Spreadsheets can be used for the same calculations.

Even if textbooks do not include a ratio of yearly income to cost of a mortgage on a house, business teachers can still present rules of thumb, such as not buying a house that costs more than two and a half times one's yearly income (Why Realty, n.d.) or having monthly house payments of more than 33%–35% of one's take-home income (Bischoff, 2012). So, if one's yearly income is $40,000, an average starting salary even for college graduates in some parts of the country, the maximum amount that person should spend on a house loan is $100,000. Use various career scenarios in class and have students make those calculations; also, include examples of people with high student-loan debts and car payments.

Numerous curriculum resources are readily available to teach economics and personal financial literacy. A quick search of the Internet will produce hundreds of sites with lessons and resource materials. A popular resource for business educators is the Federal Reserve Board Education website, a source of excellent materials offered free or at nominal cost. Lesson plans, simulations, case studies, videos, and other vital resources for educators and students are available on various websites.

TEACHING STRATEGIES

No single method works best for teaching personal finance or economics because both areas are suitable for a myriad of instructional strategies. Educators should use methods and techniques that encourage and enhance decision-making skills in both disciplines. Active learning that involves students and encourages critical thinking is essential. Implementing a variety of teaching methods and materials to teach economics and personal finance can help all students to be successful.

Active Learning

One teaching strategy sometimes used in personal finance and economics courses is active learning, a strategy that involves students' active engagement in the learning process (Petress, 2008). Silberman (2006) pointed out something that all teachers have heard—that students learn best by doing—but not every teacher knows how to apply the concepts. Actively engaging students at all levels of instruction from early childhood through adult learners is important to keep students' interest but also provide deep learning. Active learning is the opposite of passive learning, such as listening to a lecture.

An example of an active learning activity on the topic of trade deficits could require students to either (a) identify the items in their backpacks and the countries they were manufactured in or (b) take an inventory of a room in their houses and identify the countries where each item was manufactured. Most items will have been manufactured in other countries. Then, have students identify a few businesses in the United States that manufacture similar products. The final class discussion should cover the pros and cons of global trade and of having trade deficits, as well as the concept of competitive advantage.

Another example of an active learning assignment related to international trade and scarcity of resources involves having students identify all the ingredients and products needed to make a Hershey Almond bar, including the wrapping paper, aluminum foil, and ink on the wrapper. List the ingredients on the board or in a spreadsheet. Have students locate and list all countries where those ingredients are produced by going to the library for resources or conducting Internet searches. Discuss why the United States does not have adequate supplies of some natural resources, such as bauxite, needed to make aluminum foil. Discuss the benefits of global trade not just to the United States but to other countries also.

An active learning activity related to wise shopping involves having students check the prices of a list of products—name brand and store brand products—at grocery stores, convenience stores, and large box stores. Then, have students combine the information they gathered onto one spreadsheet for everyone to view. The teacher can choose the products such as boxes of macaroni and cheese, paper towels, orange juice, and bananas. Furthermore, have a class discussion concerning where to shop to save money and how to save money by purchasing store brand products.

A related comparative shopping activity is a cola taste-test experiment to show not only the influence advertising has on consumer behavior but also the extra amount consumers are willing to pay for a brand name. Bring two name-brand colas and one store-brand cola to class with the labels concealed and identified only as Brand A, B, and C. Have students taste each one, identify the best-tasting cola, and guess the prices of them. Students often prefer the taste of the store brand cola—the cheaper cola. Relate this activity to other products young people often want, not because it is a better product but because the name brand has cachet. Rather than telling students the lesson to be learned, ask them what they have learned.

Many of the following teaching strategies involve active teaching. Economics and personal finance teachers should use the following strategies and examples to reinforce concepts:

Webquests. A Webquest is an inquiry-based activity in which most or all the information needed to complete it comes from the web. In a personal finance class, one could create a Webquest around the question "Does our state and federal government have strong enough laws to protect consumers?" After an initial discussion, have students use the web to answer specific questions related to different types of consumer protection/fraud, your own state's laws governing consumer protection/fraud, and federal laws that deal with consumer protection. Students should locate the answers using the Internet and then give class presentations on the data they have gathered. If enough students have smart phones in class, the teacher can have a competition between groups of students to determine which group can locate the answers first.

Collaborative learning. This form of learning is based on active sharing of knowledge or experiences within small groups (Gokhale, 1995). However, to be effective, students must have knowledge to share, and that means they must read the textbook or other materials. Collaborative activities can involve a multitude of elements: requiring students to (a) read and comprehend what they have read, (b) verbalize what they have read, (3) listen and remember information provided by other students, and (d) acquire the knowledge to answer questions posed by the teacher.

The following collaborative learning activity requires each student in class to read a different paragraph or paragraphs from the textbook, then close the textbook and be able to share two or three important points from the paragraph(s). Begin by numbering the students into groups of three, that is, all students number off 1, 2 and 3, but at first, stay with the students next to them with one of those numbers. Have each group of three students stand up and share two to three pieces of information from the paragraphs assigned; put a time limit of 30 seconds to 1 minute per student on this sharing activity and say "next" when the time is up. Then, have the students join groups of just 1s, 2s, or 3s, that is, a total of three groups. Have them share the same points they made about the paragraph they read plus the knowledge they learned from the other two students in their previous group. At the end of the discussion, pose questions to the whole class about the material.

Case analysis. Students can more readily understand the concepts that the teacher is presenting when they can relate these concepts to *case studies* that present real-life situations. Case problems can vary from short to long and simple to complex and are included in many textbooks. However, you can write your own cases based on people you know, have students create cases, or share cases from TV call-in shows that deal with personal finances. The cases can be described orally, in print, or on a computer screen. For example, a very simple case could deal with an individual who wants to go on a five-day snowboarding trip. Students would receive information about the person's income, savings, and debts; then, students would get to stamp the case "approved" or "not approved" to go on the trip. Numerous cases can be created for people of various ages, careers, and financial situations, as well as for businesses.

Questions. Proper questioning techniques lead to the discussion of important concepts, but many teachers ask low-cognitive level questions that can be answered with one or two words. Open-ended questions and follow-up questions are more effective. Teachers typically wait about one second for an answer before calling on another student (Wilen, Ishler, Hutchison, & Kindsvatter, 2000). That is seldom long enough for students to formulate an answer. Teachers should time themselves and see if they allow students at least 5 to 10 seconds to answer a question. But, what should a teacher do during the silence? You can walk to the back of the room or look down at lecture notes!

Games and simulations. Games and simulations are terms that are often used interchangeably. However, simulations may or may not include competition among students or have winners and losers. Games frequently involve competition, as in a classroom version of Jeopardy, a television game show that teachers may use to review for an exam. Games and simulations are very effective strategies for motivating students to participate and get involved. Although requiring a high degree of decision making, most games and simulations also motivate students to learn. Computer technology allows completion of games and simulations individually or as a group. Economics and personal finance have benefited greatly from computer simulations and games, and many of these resources are available on the Internet.

A simulation that has been popular for many years is The Stock Market Game developed by the Securities Industry and Financial Markets Association. This popular teaching tool combines a stock trading simulation with a classroom curriculum that teaches economics and personal finance while also building skills such as math and communication. Table 1 at the end of the chapter lists this activity, which is available both on the Internet and in paper format, as a resource. This simulation provides teacher support materials and is correlated with the economics standards. When combined with the *Wall Street Journal Classroom Edition* (http://www.wsjclassroomedition.com) (Table 1), the Stock Market Game simulation offers highly effective teaching/learning activities in both economics and personal finance courses. Besides that game, an Internet search will provide numerous other free stock-market simulations.

Role playing. As Vitt (2009) indicates, effective teaching within a personal finance course is more than simply providing basic knowledge at the lower cognitive levels; it must also include behavior management techniques. He recommends role playing and modeling rather than lectures to develop personal values such as social and financial values. For example, students could role play a situation in which a clerk in a shoe store is trying to sell a teenager and his/her parents an expensive pair of tennis shoes, even though the parents have budgeted only $50 for shoes. Have students play the roles of the clerk, teenager, and parents.

A higher-level cognitive activity could involve role playing trade negotiations dealing with tariffs charged by the United States on goods imported from another country such as South Korea or China. First, students would have to gather information on what tariffs are, why they are imposed by various countries, what the current tariff laws are in the United States, why other countries would not want the United States to impose a higher tariff and the potential consequences of doing so. Although only three to four students may do the role playing, all students could contribute background information.

Peer instruction. Peer instruction is an alternative partnership approach to teaching in which students serve as tutors, coaches, or models for other students. This strategy is particularly effective when the learning capacities of students vary widely. Students who have a difficult time grasping concepts can benefit from assistance from other students. Peer instruction helps develop social skills and self-esteem for students who are involved in the tutoring arrangement.

Traditional Instructional Methods and Strategies

Traditional instructional methods and strategies for teaching economics and personal finance include lectures, visual presentations, field trips, and interviews.

Lectures are an effective method to introduce new topics or ideas. Lectures must be carefully planned and organized. To maintain students' interest, lectures should be kept short and supplemented with dynamic visuals. Some slide presentations correlated with textbooks can be quite boring. However, by starting a lecture with an attention-getting story or graphic image, student interest in the topic can be aroused. For example, at the beginning of a lecture on insurance, you the teacher can show a picture of a car wrecked in an accident or a home burned by a fire or tell the story of someone the teacher has heard about who has had such an incident occur.

Another way to liven up a lecture is to bring *concrete objects* to class: objects related to the topic being covered such as a model of a car when the topic is car purchasing, a military aircraft model when discussing manufacturing in the United States, or a sack of wheat when discussing the price of wheat being determined by the "supply" of wheat in the United States and the "demand" for wheat here and overseas. Other concrete objects you can show in class include your own auto insurance policy or credit card policies, documents that you can project on a screen for everyone to see.

Field trips are very appropriate in many economic and personal finance units. Most of the 12 Federal Reserve Banks give tours, as well as many of the commodities exchanges located in Chicago, New York, Minneapolis, Memphis, Kansas City, and Atlanta. Imagine the excitement that could be created if students had an opportunity to visit a large trading room for an investment company. Follow up a field trip by having students write a report, give an oral report, or have a class discussion.

Speakers from businesses can provide expertise beyond the depth of knowledge of many business teachers. Speakers may include employees at credit bureaus; banks; real estate companies; auto, life, and home insurance companies; and tax accounting firms. Prepare students the day before a speaker comes to class so they have some pertinent questions to ask.

Classroom debates can involve two groups of three or more students, each of which presents different sides to an issue. For example, the groups might debate who caused the recent recession; one group might present evidence that investment bankers were the cause and another group might present evidence that consumers were the cause.

TEACHING RESOURCES

Numerous resource materials have been developed in recent years to support teaching and learning in economics and personal finance. Many of the printed resources are supported with computer software or online instructional materials. Some of the popular resources and websites are discussed and/or listed in this section, as well as identified in Table 1 later in this chapter.

Council for Economic Education

The mission of this organization is to help all students develop economic approaches to thinking and problem solving that they can use in their lives as consumers, savers, investors, members of the workforce, and responsible citizens. The CEE offers a vast array of services and materials to business educators. The organization has a network of state and regional councils for economic education with affiliated university-based centers for economic education that provide numerous instructional materials and classes for economics teachers.

Jump$tart Coalition for Personal Financial Literacy

Jump$tart is a national coalition of organizations dedicated to improving the financial literacy of kindergarten through college-age youth by providing advocacy, research, standards, and educational resources. Jump$tart strives to prepare youth for lifelong successful financial decision making.

Foundation for Investor Education

This foundation is affiliated with the Securities Industry and Financial Markets Association and was formed to promote public understanding of the stock market and the securities industry. One activity of the foundation is The Stock Market Game, which has been used by many teachers. The Stock Market Game program combines a 10-week stock trading simulation and an extensive classroom curriculum portfolio. This simulation correlates with standards in business education, economics, and mathematics.

Junior Achievement

Best known for its after-school entrepreneurial programs, Junior Achievement (JA) has been actively developing programs for elementary through secondary instruction. JA uses hands-on experiences to help young people understand the economics of life. Popular high school programs include JA Economics, JA Success Skills, and JA Titan (a business simulation). Many of the concepts and skills taught in the JA materials are correlated with the previously discussed standards.

The *Wall Street Journal* Classroom Edition

This online newspaper covers a wide variety of business and career-related topics and correlates with teacher guides. This student-targeted publication makes the study of economics and personal finance more timely and personal.

Federal Reserve Education

This website includes lesson plans and classroom activities designed to increase students' understanding of the banking system, economics, and financial education. All of the Federal Reserve's websites, curricula, booklets, and other resources are free. This site has many excellent links to interactive games and simulations. Information about tours and professional development training for teachers is also provided.

Websites

Table 1 presents a number of websites that can serve as valuable resources.

Table 1. Websites for Teaching Economics and Personal Finance

Web Address	Descriptions
http://www.councilforeconed.org/ea/standards or http://www.councilforeconed.org	The Council for Economic Education publishes economic resource materials and standards.
http://www.fte.org	The Foundation for Teaching Economics offers teacher seminars, lesson plans, and national economic contests.
http://www.jumpstart.org	The Jump$tart Coalition for Personal Financial Literacy is a clearinghouse with links to hundreds of instructional materials.

http://www.wsjclassroomedition.com	The *Wall Street Journal Classroom Edition* is an online publication designed for teachers and students.
http://www.stockmarketgame.org	The Stock Market Game sponsored by the Securities Industry and Financial Markets Association Foundation teaches about the securities industry through the use of a simulation.
http://www.ja.org	Junior Achievement has instruction on topics such as banking, ethics, personal finance, and economics.
http://www.irs.gov/app/understanding Taxes/student/index.jsp	This Internal Revenue Service site includes lessons, videos, and interactive exercises dealing with how federal, state, and local taxes work.
http://www.nyse.com	The New York Stock Exchange provides company information and real-time stock prices.
http://www.nasdaq.com	The NASDAQ over-the-counter market site includes stock quotes and company profiles.
http://www.federalreserveeducation.org http://www.federalreserve.gov	These two Federal Reserve sites include online resources, games, and publications related to the financial crisis, credit, consumer issues, and the Federal Reserve system.
http://www.practicalmoneyskills.com	The Practical Money Skills site has articles, lesson plans, games, videos, and teaching materials for personal finance courses.

SUMMARY

Economics and Personal Finance are courses that students will use throughout their lifetime. This chapter discusses the importance of economics and personal finance—topics included in the economics and personal finance curriculum, including critical standards for business education—and offers appropriate teaching strategies for both areas. Instructional strategies emphasize the need for active involvement by students in the learning process. These strategies include Webquests, role playing, collaborative learning, case analysis, and games. Traditional approaches for instruction include lectures, visual presentations, speakers, and field trips.

The use of a variety of teaching strategies and resources is recommended not only to teach important knowledge but also to teach valuable behaviors. A list and description of organizations that provide economics and personal finance standards, lesson plans, videos, and games for teaching economics and personal finance are included. These resources will help teachers bring active learning to the curriculum and at the same time challenge the student to learn about life situations.

REFERENCES

American Bankruptcy Institute. (2009). Annual business and non-business filings per year (1980–2009). Retrieved from http://www.abiworld.org/AM/AMTemplate.cfm?Section=Annual_U_S_Filings1&TEMPLATE=/CM/ContentDisplay.cfm&CONTENTID=63164

Bischoff, M. (2012). Coming to grips with your finances. Retrieved from http://www.cals.uidaho.edu/edcomm/pdf/MS/MS0112-1.pdf

Bureau of Economic Analysis. (2011, December 23). Personal income and outlays: November 2011 (news release). U.S. Department of Commerce. Retrieved from http://www.bea.gov/newsreleases/national/pi/2011/pi1111.htm

Campbell, J. (2006). Household finance. *The Journal of Finance, 61*(4), 1591.

Consumers Union. (2011). *Consumer Reports buying guide 2011*. Yonkers, NY: Author.

Council for Economic Education. (2007). EconEdLink online lessons. Retrieved from http://www.econedlink.org/lessons/index.cfm?page=teacher&lesson=EM37

Council for Economic Education. (2009) Survey of the states 2009: The state of economic, financial and entrepreneurship education in our nation's schools. Retrieved from http://www.councilforeconed.org/news-information/survey-of-the-states

Debts that survive Chapter 7 bankruptcy. (n.d.). Retrieved from http://www.thebankruptcysite.org/resources/bankruptcy/chapter-7/debts-that-survive-chapter-7-bankruptcy

Edmunds.com. (2011). Ask the car people. Retrieved from http://www.edmunds.com

Gokhale, A. (1995). Collaborative learning enhances critical thinking. *Journal of Technical Education. 7*(1).

Hilgert, M., Hogarth, J., & Beverly, S. (2003). Household financial management: The connection between knowledge and behavior. *Federal Reserve Bulletin, 309–322.*

Jump$tart Coalition for Personal Financial Literacy (Jump$tart). (2007). *National standards in k–12 personal finance education* (3rd ed.). Washington, DC: Author.

Luft, R. L. (2007). Economics. In B. Kaliski (Ed.), *Encyclopedia of business and finance.* Detroit, MI: Macmillan Reference USA/Thomson Gale.

Mandell, L., & Klein, L. (2009). The impact of financial literacy education on subsequent financial behavior. *Journal of Financial Counseling and Planning, 20*(1), 15–35.

Markow, D., & Bagnaschi, K. (2005, April 25). What American teens & adults know about economic education. Retrieved from http://www.vietnetlinks.com/thuvien/WhatAmericansKnowAboutEconomics_042605-3.pdf

National Business Education Association (NBEA). (2007). *National standards for business education: What America's students should know and be able to do in business* (3rd ed.). Reston, VA: Author.

Orman, S. (2010). Suze Orman's easy money to-do list. Retrieved from http://www.cnn.com/ 2010/LIVING/personal/01/06/o.orman.easy.money.list/index.html

Petress, K. (2008). What is meant by "active learning?" *Education? 128*(4), 566–569.

Richarme, M. (2012). Consumer decision-making models, strategies, and theories, oh my! Retrieved from http://www.decisionanalyst.com/publ_art/decisionmaking.dai

Silberman, M. (2006). *Teaching actively: Eight steps and 32 strategies to spark learning in any classroom.* Boston: Pearson Education, Inc.

Vitt, L. (2009, April). *Social and emotional links to our financial behavior* (presentation). Jump$tart Annual Partners Meeting. Washington, DC.

Why Realty. (n.d.). Determining your price range. Retrieved from http://www.why realty.com/determine-price-range.html

Wilen, W., Ishler, M., Hutchison, J., & Kindsvatter, R. (2000). *Dynamics of effective teaching* (6th ed.). Boston, MA: Allyn and Bacon.

Business Law

Paul Sukys
North Central State College
Mansfield, OH

Any study of business law must begin with an examination of the complex relationships that exist among three elements: the law, business, and ethics. To explain these relationships, the chapter begins by attempting to revise the inaccurate picture that some business students have about how the law works. The chapter then suggests some ideas for helping business students to develop a clearer understanding of the internal operation of the legal system and how it applies to the second element, business. Much of this learning involves helping business students see that the law, unlike most other social systems, uses an argumentative process to solve legal problems. The argumentative process, which is born from within the adversarial system, determines what the law is and how the law must be applied to a set of facts. All of this would be very confusing for judges, lawyers, and laypeople alike were it not for one constant factor: the law is based upon a third element, ethics. The chapter (a) explores the problems that arise when business people misunderstand the role of ethics in the law, (b) offers a solution to those problems, (c) investigates how to construct an effective course in business law, and (d) suggests several techniques for engaging students in the study of business law, ethics, and justice.

INTEGRATING THE LAW AND ETHICS

The law is a workshop in which paralegals toil next to associates; associates seek guidance from partners; partners read opinions by judges; and judges determine what the law is when real people stand before them and demand justice. Business students, and even some business instructors, may believe that the internal process of the law does not concern them. After all, they are interested primarily in business-related decisions, and they become concerned with the law only when they are entangled in a lawsuit. This attitude is understandable and correct as far as it goes. However, it misses several essential points. One point is that the process of the law sets down the rules for the operation of a business. The law establishes the parameters that dictate what business people may do and what they must avoid doing; most important, the law determines the consequences for ignoring or sidestepping the law (Morgan, Shedd, & Corley, 2010).

The Adversarial System

Despite this entanglement with business, the law works differently from all other aspects of the social system. This difference results because the law depends on an argumentative process (Dworkin, 1986). This argumentative process emerges from the fact that the American legal system is an adversarial system, rather than a fact-finding system as is true of courts on the European continent. The continental fact-finding process is aimed at uncovering the truth, whereas the American adversarial process is aimed at winning the case. In an adversarial system, each side has an advocate who promotes the interests of his or her client (Brown & Sukys, 2006).

Business students will be more comfortable with the law once they acknowledge that the pattern of the law is that there is no pattern, save the pattern of argument. The law is neither systematic nor asystematic but is, instead, an arena in which argumentative battles are waged every day to interpret what certain legal propositions really mean (Dworkin, 1986). Each side in a lawsuit has a champion who argues for the interpretation of the law that best helps his or her client (Brown & Sukys, 2006). What saves the law from total confusion is that each advocate promotes justice based on a universal ethical code. Moreover, what makes justice the preeminent ethical ideal is that it impacts several key jobs within the law. Those jobs include (a) supporting the welfare of the people (i.e., the distribution of goods, services, health, education, and so on), (b) protecting freedom of choice and action, and (c) encouraging virtuous behavior (Sandel, 2009). Ethical decisions are involved in all of these aspects of justice, and the law determines how to promote and preserve all three. It is important to remember, however, that justice is only one ethical ideal. Other ideals include but are not limited to honesty, self-restraint, courtesy, and benevolence (Morgan, Shedd, & Corley, 2010).

The Moral Minimum

Some laws are neutral in their ethical content. Such laws do not promote or restrict justice. No ethical principle declares, for example, what the proper speed limit might be for one stretch of highway as opposed to another. Nor is it possible, or even reasonable, for the legal system to integrate every ethical practice into the statute books. However, ethical considerations do influence many laws, regardless of their subject matter. This principle is referred to as the *moral minimum*. The moral minimum declares that, at the very least, every society follows a single ethical principle—citizens have a duty to obey the law. People who obey the law can be relatively certain that most (but not all) of their actions will be ethical (Clarkson, Miller, & Cross, 2012).

Still, even the moral minimum has limits. The moral minimum fades when the law itself is unethical or when it violates the ideal of justice. For example, majority voting blocs often pass laws that ignore minority rights and that sometimes even eliminate those rights (Ratzinger, 2006). The political and legal systems of various nations, such as Hitler's Germany and Saddam Hussein's Iraq, have institutionalized practices that are evil, such as genocide, ethnic cleansing, slavery, terrorism, and torture (Wolfe, 2011).

Practical Aspects of the Law

The law operates in many venues: in the legislature, in the executive mansion, and in the streets. However, the adversarial system and the argumentative process of the law are best seen in the courts. In the courts, people learn that the law operates differently from case to case, judge to judge, and place to place. This realization often shocks the layperson who assumes that all the players in the legal system follow a set of laws found in a codebook somewhere, listed as law #1, law #2, and so on (Dworkin, 1986). Standards do exist, but not in the patterned, systematic, and predictable way that most business students imagine. In practice, when a case reaches the court, an issue that seems straightforward to any layperson (the interpretation of the plain language of a statute, for instance) may become confusing as the layperson learns that two adversaries have opposing views on just what that "plain" language actually says (Dworkin, 1986).

An example of this difficulty can be seen in the case of *Kelo v. New London* (2005). In this case, the town of New London, Connecticut, confiscated the homes of a large number of its own citizens using the doctrine of *eminent domain*. Eminent domain is found in the Fifth Amendment of the U.S. Constitution and, in this case, in a Connecticut statute. Under both provisions, eminent domain permitted the government to take private land for public purposes (*Kelo v. New London*, 2005). Understandably, many homeowners opposed the sudden seizure of their homes. One of these homeowners, Susette Kelo, filed a lawsuit against the town to stop the confiscation of her land. Ms. Kelo's attorney argued that the town was not taking Ms. Kelo's home for public purposes but was, instead, confiscating the land for a private project, specifically the corporate development of an area of town that would be adjacent to the site of a new corporate research center (*Kelo v. New London*, 2005).

The case went to the Supreme Court, which eventually decided that the town did, in fact, have the authority to take the homeowner's land for private purposes as long as those private purposes led to a significant financial and economic benefit for the entire community (*Kelo v. New London*, 2005). This expansion of eminent domain troubled many people, especially private property owners, who saw it as a dangerous threat to individual property rights. In contrast, the decision was hailed as a victory by corporate developers who saw it as explicit approval for further projects along the lines of those in New London. The point here is not who won and who lost, but how easily two advocates can take one doctrine and interpret it in ways that are diametrically opposed to one another. None of this makes much sense to laypeople, unless they remember that both advocates are working within a common ethical framework.

Importance of Ethics to the Law

The legal system works because of its ethical foundation and the ideal of justice. As children we are taught, and rightly so, that there are such things as good and evil and that these concepts do not change even as the legal system evolves. Moreover, studies have demonstrated that all human beings, regardless of the culture in which they are raised, have an intuitive sense of right and wrong (Bloom, 2010). Murder is murder, for example, no matter what culture we consider (Holmes & Douglas, 2012). This remains true even as we develop new aggravating and mitigating circumstances to punish some and exonerate others. Moreover, cheating remains cheating, even if some people can rationalize their own dishonest activities (Lawton, 2012). This view can, of course, be challenged. We live, after all, in a multicultural world in which the Western view represents only one interpretation of ethics and justice.

Still the similarities are numerous enough that, in 1948, the global community implemented a Universal Declaration of Human Rights, a document that, in turn, inspired the creation of several mandatory agreements including the International Covenant on Civil and Political Rights and the International Covenant on Economic and Social Rights (Sands, 2005). The universal acceptance of these cross-cultural values has also led to the establishment of several international courts, such as the International Criminal Court and the International Court of Justice, that are presided over by judges from vastly different cultures (Brown & Sukys, 2013; Cheeseman, 2010).

Such judicial integration does not mean that the judges always agree. Nevertheless, when international justices do not agree, the disagreement is often based not on different ethical ideals but on different interpretations of those ideals—ideals such as justice. This is what happened in 1989, when the World Trade Organization tried to determine whether the United States could ban imports from certain Asian countries because those countries violated U.S. environmental laws. The original World Trade Organization panel ruled against the U.S. ban. The Appellate Division of the World Trade Organization reversed the panel's decision. Yet, the division also ruled that the United States could neither discriminate against the countries in the suit nor move forward without first exhausting diplomatic remedies. The case turned upon the question of whether it was fair for nations to select those laws they will obey and those they will ignore. The court ruled that such unilateral actions are inherently unjust. Again, the point is not who won but how the advocates on both sides focused on a common ethical ideal—the ideal of justice (Sands, 2005).

The mission of the business law instructor is to integrate ethics and justice into the study of the law so that students appreciate how the law and ethics impact business. Students must be made aware of the consequences of unethical conduct. Unethical conduct undermines the well-being of a business operation, threatens the security of the people associated with that operation, and endangers the entire social structure (Clarkson, Miller, & Cross, 2012). The instructor must help students appreciate that, even in the global context, ethics and the ideal of justice provide a foundation for the entire legal process.

PLANNING A COURSE IN BUSINESS LAW

The increased focus on the ethical foundation of the law does not mean that the instructor may abandon the legal concepts that stand as the bedrock of the course. On the contrary, these elements become even more important because they provide the students with a familiar context into which the ethical elements can be added seamlessly. One way to include ethics in the business law course is to begin with a unit devoted exclusively to ethics. This technique is effective because it focuses the student's attention on issues of justice and ethics and, in that way, emphasizes the importance of those concepts. The downside to this tactic is that it risks giving the student the idea that ethics and justice stand outside of the law. To prevent this misunderstanding, the instructor may, instead, integrate ethics and justice into each separate unit. This strategy unites ethics and justice with the law so that students see how these elements are intertwined with one another and with the business world.

Civil Procedure

A standard business law course will introduce the study of the law by defining the law, looking at the purposes of the law, and then distinguishing the law from ethics. However, a law course for business students will have to jump almost immediately into the concrete practical issues involved in the processes of the law. The first step is to help students see the difference between substantive law and procedural law. Substantive law establishes rights and duties, whereas procedural law determines how to enforce those rights and live up to those duties. The most effective way to begin any course in business law, then, is to examine civil procedure.

Procedural law is frequently involved in ethical disputes, many of which are related to justice. It is helpful for the instructor to demonstrate to business students that the U.S. Constitution is filled with safeguards that preserve the rights of people who are involved in legal disputes with one another or with the government. Chief among these safeguards are those found in the Bill of Rights, such as the right to an attorney, the right to a trial by jury in both civil and criminal actions, the right to a speedy trial, the right to be confronted by witnesses, and so on. The Bill of Rights includes protections against unreasonable searches and seizures, searches that are conducted without properly issued warrants, unreasonable fines, cruel and unusual punishment, and the seizure of private property by the government without just compensation.

Torts

An introductory level course in business law, whether at the secondary or postsecondary level, must include a unit on tort law. A tort is a public wrong that is committed by one person against another person, resulting in injury to the health, property, reputation, or business dealings of the innocent person. A person who commits a tort is known as a tortfeasor and the victim is known as the innocent party. Perhaps more than any other area of the law, tort law reveals the legal system's dependency on ethics. This fact is made clear when we consider that tort law is grounded within the concept of duty and the notion of duty is grounded within the concept of justice. Because each person has the right to be free from injury, to enjoy his or her property without unwarranted interference, to have a good reputation, and to be involved in business without undue intrusion, the rest of us have the duty not to violate those rights. These duties can be unjustly violated in one of three ways: intentionally, by accident (negligence), and under a doctrine known as strict liability. Students must be taught the various *intentional torts* starting with assault and battery and including at the very least false imprisonment, defamation, disparagement, invasion of privacy, and fraud; *accidental torts* committed through negligence; and *torts that result from ultra-hazardous activities* (strict liability) (Brown & Sukys, 2013).

Contracts

All business students benefit from a short introduction to the practical aspects of contract law because, for the rest of their adult lives, they will be involved in making contracts. All students should know that a contract is a legally binding agreement between parties (Gifis, 2003; Morgan, Shedd, & Corley, 2010). The law related to contracts is complicated and multifaceted, which makes it an especially challenging area of study for business students. Some of the initial resistance to this area of study can be alleviated if the instructor reminds students that, when people enter contracts, they take on duties that fit their individual needs. In exchange, they receive goods, services, or land. Because of the voluntary nature of all contracts and because all contracts are unique, the ethical ideal of justice requires that the law be flexible enough to deal with these contingencies.

Employment

Perhaps more than any other area of business law, the unit on employment will be immersed within questions of ethics and justice. These ethical issues emerge because the dominant doctrine in *employment law* in the country today remains *employment at will*. This doctrine means that an employee can be discharged by an employer without notice, at any time, for any reason (or no reason), as long as employment contracts, equal protection laws, and labor laws are not violated. Employment at will is based on the ideal of justice. The court argues that, because employees are free to work with and for whomever they please, it is only fair to allow employers to discharge employees whenever they please. Elements of change over time in this area include unjust dismissal exceptions to at-will employment and the passage of numerous equal protection laws (Siegel & Stephen, 2005).

Impact of Technology on Business Law

A study of the interrelationship between the law and electronic technology has become a vital component in all introductory business law courses. Two areas in which the law and technology intersect are civil procedure and employment. That part of civil procedure that has been affected the most by technology is the discovery process. Discovery is the search for evidence that can be used at trial. It is critical for the instructor to explain to students that the entire discovery process is driven by an ethical concern for the sharing of evidence so that cases are decided on their merits, not on the ability of one attorney to surprise or trick another. Recently, the Federal Rules of Civil Procedure were amended to include electronically stored information to prevent one attorney from taking an unfair advantage of a colleague simply because that colleague is unfamiliar with electronic discovery opportunities.

In employment, new problems have emerged in relation to social media. Business people communicate daily in their professional and personal lives using a variety of e-communication devices and techniques. For this reason, all business owners must write, communicate, and enforce individualized social media policies. A social media policy is a collection of principles developed by business owners informing their workers in a fair, open, and straightforward way what the employees can and cannot do in (and sometimes outside of) the workplace. Justice and ethics demand that, when employers write social media policies, they make certain that those policies are clear, uncomplicated, and communicated to their employees in a timely way. In addition, business owners must also reveal that they will be monitoring their employees' communications and will punish those who violate the policy (Rapp, 2011).

INTEGRATING BUSINESS LAW WITH OTHER SUBJECTS
Every level in the educational system from the elementary to secondary to post-secondary levels must include some of the elements of business law. Fortunately, the curriculum offers many opportunities for the law and ethics to be embedded within classroom studies beyond those courses that are dedicated only to the law. In the *National Standards for Business Education*, the National Business Education Association (NBEA, 2007) has established what young learners need to know in 12 areas of business education, including business law. The standards outline what students need to know in each business area at the completion of each level (NBEA, 2007). Although it is natural for business law instructors to prefer that students receive that instruction in a business law course, these topics can be added to courses in economics and accounting.

Business Law and Economics
Economics has its own team of dedicated professionals, those experts who work diligently to explain how markets work, why recessions occur, why inflation soars, and why unemployment rises (or falls). Moreover, these economic experts also develop strategies to prevent negative trends and to enhance positive ones. Of course, the experts do not always agree on what these strategies ought to be, which explains why the problems persist, year in and year out. Some experts, those who promote the free market such as Friedrich Hayek and Joseph Schumpeter (also known as "the Austrians"), tell us that the economy must be permitted to fluctuate naturally and, more important, to fall into periods of "creative destruction" (Cassidy, 2010; Hayek, 2007; Roubini & Mihm, 2010).

In contrast, other experts who promote governmental management, such as John Maynard Keyes, declare that the public sector must guide markets to reduce uncertainty, preserve stability, and promote a fair and equitable sharing of the wealth (Roubini & Mihm 2010; Skidelsky, 2010). Thus, it may be necessary for the teacher to show how economists identify grand patterns of active movement within the economy, while legal scholars have never been able to do so. Consequently, unifying economics with the law is often a matter of distinguishing the law from economics, rather than combining the two. However, when it comes to ethics and the ideal of justice, the study of economics provides fertile ground for a classroom discussion of the different views held by libertarians and egalitarians. Libertarians promote a free market in which people use their talents to make a profit openly and fairly, while egalitarians support a fair distribution of goods and services among us all (Sandel, 2009).

Business Law and Accounting

Accounting overlaps with the law, and the two of them together provide techniques for handling client problems, dealing with management issues, handling employee grievances, and compiling a client's accounting records. So, when budding accountants are taught to serve the client, they should also be taught the legal consequences of not doing the job or of doing the job poorly. This instruction would require acquainting students with the rules surrounding an accountant's duties to his or her clients and to third parties, including not only those that are actually and specifically foreseen but also those who are reasonably foreseeable. This might also include familiarizing budding accountants with the latest federal statutes, including both the Sarbanes-Oxley Act and the Dodd-Frank Act (Brown & Sukys, 2013).

TEACHING STRATEGIES FOR BUSINESS LAW

The lecture technique is a time-saving, popular, and effective way for an instructor to make certain that all indispensable legal concepts are covered properly. The risk of spending too much time lecturing is that students receive a superficial introduction to the topics but have no chance to examine any single topic in great detail. As an alternative, business law instructors can use a variety of additional teaching strategies to supplement the lecture technique. All three of these strategies are based on the notion that the classroom should be a place of active learning. Active learning occurs when students are involved in activities such as writing about issues, talking with one another about situations, analyzing and evaluating evidence, and working together in small teams (Caron & Gely, 2004). In the business law classroom, active learning strategies include, but are not limited to, mock trials, legal debates, and the technological enhancement of the classroom.

Mock Trials

One effective active learning strategy is the mock trial. The mock trial encourages learners to analyze a fact pattern, find the legal issues embedded within those facts, and then see how the law works to resolve the issues. Learners are taught how to use legal research, legal thinking, and legal writing techniques to solve the legal problems involved in the case. Consequently, learners become actively involved in the case as they learn how to analyze the facts, search for the law, and apply the law in ways that enable them to learn about the law as an argumentative process within the adversarial system. The development of a mock trial assignment starts with the creation (or discovery) of a scenario that highlights a legal concept that the instructor wants to emphasize. A scenario can be fabricated, fashioned from news stories, or taken from real cases. Business law textbooks and their electronic ancillaries often include cases that can be used for a mock trial or a mock hearing. Some textbooks or their electronic ancillaries contain entire mock trial exercises that are equipped with legal documents, possibly including complaints, answers, transcripts, interrogatories, affidavits, and so on.

Legal Debates

Like mock trials, legal debates can provide an energy-charged active learning environment in the classroom. Legal debates can revolve around a scenario that includes several legal issues. The scenario should be written to achieve two objectives, both of which give the students added insight into the adversarial system and the law as an argumentative process. The first objective is to show learners that legal issues are rarely clear-cut, and, in fact, can frequently be interpreted in several different ways. The second objective is to investigate the wisdom of retaining or removing the legal rule under examination. For instance, a scenario that explores the question of whether the National Football League should be considered a single entity or a conglomerate of competing teams could be used to examine the impact that a monopoly has on competition in a particular industry and to explore the legal measures that have been taken to protect or prevent such activities. Debates like this can make dry topics such as the Sherman Antitrust Act come alive for many students who might otherwise enter the business law classroom with a preconceived notion that the subject is not their cup of tea (*American Needle v. NFL*, 2010).

Technology in the Classroom

Another technique that encourages active learning is the addition of technology to the business law classroom. The modern secondary and postsecondary classroom is generally already equipped with a variety of computers, including at least one computer that has access to the Internet. Consequently, the problem today is not obtaining the technology but determining how to use it productively in the classroom setting. One effective application of technology is to have the students search the Internet for authoritative evidence as they prepare for their trials and debates. This type of research can be extremely helpful to students when the subject of the trial or debate involves unusual material not readily available in the school or public library (Kelly, 2012). For example, students involved in a trial or a debate based on allegations of corporate negligence in the meltdown of a nuclear reactor, may readily find information about such incidents on the Internet. Once the students have located hard-to-find information, they can develop detailed trial briefs or debate outlines that they can then use during classroom-planning sessions.

Beyond the use of the Internet for research, technology can also be used to enhance communication in the classroom and between classroom sessions. For example, students assigned to trials or debates that involve international law or the law of another country might use Skype to contact students on the other side of the planet for information about their legal systems (Ryder, 2010). Students can also use chat rooms to discuss class assignments with one another or with the instructor to continue team sessions after the end of class and to respond to exercises established by the teacher. Chat-room discussions may even be extended to include students located in other cities, states, and countries, thus giving classroom discussions a national and international flavor. Other social media networking tools that can be used in the classroom to enhance the educational process include but are not limited to blogging, instant messaging, and texting (Haley, 2012).

SUMMARY

The study of business law must help students see the complicated relationships that exist among three elements: the law, business, and ethics. Too often, the law is taught with little regard to its ethical foundation or to the ideal of justice. Although many schools and colleges have integrated ethics and justice into the study of business law, others have yet to do so. The law and ethics can be added to courses such as economics and accounting. Moreover, the business law teacher can use several strategies to engage learners when teaching business law, ethics, and justice, including mock trials, legal debates, and technological enhancements.

REFERENCES

American Needle, Inc. v. National Football League et al., 130 S. Ct. 2201 (2010). Retrieved from http://www.supremecourt.gov/opinions/09pdf/08-661.pdf

Bloom, P. (2010, May 9). The moral life of babies. *The New York Times Magazine*, pp. 44–49, 56, 62–63, 65.

Brown, G., & Sukys, P. (2006). *Business law with UCC applications*. New York, NY: McGraw-Hill/Irwin.

Brown, G., & Sukys, P. (2013). *Business law with UCC applications*. Chicago, IL: McGraw-Hill/Irwin.

Caron, P., & Gely, R. (2004). Taking back the law school classroom: Using technology to foster active learning. *Journal of Legal Education, 54*, 1–38.

Cassidy, J. (2010). *How markets fail: The logic of economic calamities*. New York, NY: Farrar, Straus, and Giroux.

Cheeseman, H. (2010). *Business law: Legal environment, online commerce, business ethics, and international issues*. Upper Saddle River, NJ: Pearson.

Clarkson, K., Miller, R., & Cross, F. (2012). *Business law*. Mason, OH: South-Western Cengage Learning.

Curtis, M. (Ed.). (1981). Section XI: Hobbes and Spinoza. *The great political theories: A comprehensive selection of the crucial ideas in political philosophy from the Greeks to the Enlightenment* (Vol. 1, pp. 326–356). New York, NY: Harper Perennial.

Dworkin, R. (1986) *Law's empire*. Cambridge, MA: Harvard University Press.

Gifis, S. H. (2003). *Law dictionary*. New York, NY: Barron's Educational Services.

Haley, C. (2012). Social media networking tools: Meeting our stakeholders in their world. *Trends & Issues in Business Education: 2012 NBEA yearbook* (No. 50, pp. 106–119). Reston, VA: National Business Education Association.

Hayek, F. A. (2007). *The road to serfdom: Text and documents*. Chicago, IL: University of Chicago Press.

Holmes, B., & Douglas, K. (2012, April 21). The nature of the beast. *New Scientist, 214*(2861), 38–43.

Kelly. M. (2012). Integrating technology into the classroom. Retrieved from http://712 educators.about.com/cs/technology/a/integratetech.htm

Kelo v. New London, 545 U.S. 469 (2005). Retrieved from http://www.supremecourt. gov/opinions/boundvolumes/545bv.pdf

Lawton, L. (2012, June 16). The cheating game. *New Scientist, 214*(2869), 30–31.

Morgan, J., Shedd, P., & Corley, R. (2010). *Business law*. Redding, CA: BVT Publishing.

National Business Education Association. (2007). *National standards for business education: What America's students should know and be able to do in business* (3rd ed.). Reston, VA: Author.

Rapp, A. (2011, May 6). *Labor and employment update: The responsible employer's social media policy*. Paper presented at the annual conference of the Ohio State Bar Association, Columbus, OH.

Ratzinger, J. (2006). That which holds the world together: The pre-political moral foundations of a free state. *The dialectics of secularization: On reason and religion*. San Francisco, CA: Ignatius.

Roubini, N., & Mihm, S. (2010). *Crisis economics*. New York, NY: Penguin Books.

Ryder, R. (2010, January 13). Using technology in the classroom. Retrieved from http://lawyerist.com/using-technology-in-the-classroom

Sands, P. (2005). *Lawless world: America and the making and breaking of global rules from FDR's Atlantic Charter to George W. Bush's illegal war*. New York, NY: Viking.

Sandel, M. J. (2009). *Justice: What's the right thing to do?* London, England: Penguin Books.

Siegel, B., & Stephen, J. (2005). *Ohio employment practices law: A practical guide for employers and their legal counsel*. Cleveland, OH: Thomson/West.

Skidelsky, R. (2010). *Keynes: The return of the master*. New York, NY: Public Affairs.

Wolfe, A. (2011). *Political evil: What it is and how to combat it*. New York, NY: Alfred A. Knopf.

Entrepreneurship

Karen Drage
Eastern Illinois University
Charleston, IL

Kathy Mountjoy
Illinois State University
Normal, IL

The authors, editor, and publisher acknowledge and express appreciation for the work done by C. Bruce Kavan, author of this chapter in the previous edition. Thank you for your contribution to this yearbook and to business education.

Nai Wang, an entrepreneur, advises anyone that has a great idea to just do it. He reported that in today's economic situation, entrepreneurs have the advantage because they have the ability to take a great idea and create a niche (Association of Career and Technical Education, 2011). The challenge for business educators is creating a learning environment that will cultivate the multifaceted knowledge, skills, and entrepreneurial spirit in students that will give them the tools to take that leap of faith, particularly when all economic indicators are pointing them in the other direction. This chapter discusses the role of entrepreneurship in the economy; risk aversion and risk management; entrepreneurial integrity and ethics; successful entrepreneurial ventures; entrepreneurship education curriculum, programs, standards, instructional strategies, and classroom activities; and resources for teaching entrepreneurship at all levels.

The importance of entrepreneurial activity for the economic growth of countries is well established. Donna Kelley, associate professor of entrepreneurship at Babson College in Massachusetts, reports that entrepreneurial activity is flourishing across the globe and that entrepreneurship, as an economic engine, is the best prospect for stimulating a weakened world economy (Coduras, Levie, Kelley, & Schott, 2010). Students find entrepreneurship both attractive and valuable partially due to the prospect of owning and operating a business, making money, and succeeding (Brown, 2003). Although entrepreneurship has connections to various content areas, it has the strongest, innate connection with business because it integrates the functional areas of business—accounting, economics, finance, marketing, and management.

ENTREPRENEURSHIP AND ECONOMIC DEVELOPMENT

Entrepreneurship is an important driver of economic development. Entrepreneurs create jobs, drive and shape innovation, and speed up structural changes in the economy. Competition contributes indirectly to productivity. Entrepreneurship is thus a catalyst for economic growth and national competitiveness (Mustafa-Topxhiu, 2012). An extensive study conducted by The Ewing Marion Kauffman Foundation (in partnership with Babson College, Ernst & Young, the London Business School, & researchers from dozens of developed countries) completed the *Global Entrepreneurship Monitor Report: 2000 Executive Report* (Camp & Autio, 2000). This study explored the relationship between economic growth and entrepreneurship in 21 of the world's leading industrial economies. The study found that the nations with high levels of entrepreneurial activity have above-average rates of economic growth. Only a few nations that have above-average rates of economic growth have low levels of entrepreneurship. The National Commission on Entrepreneurship expanded on the findings of the Global Entrepreneurship Monitor Report and explored the role that high-performing entrepreneurial companies play in the U.S. economy. The study found that about 4%–7% of all American businesses (generally small- to medium-sized entrepreneurial businesses) create two-thirds of all business growth and job creation and that well more than 50 percent of all business innovation comes from smaller entrepreneurial businesses (Buttress & Mackey, 2008).

This increased interest in the entrepreneur's role in the economy has led to a growing body of research attempting to identify the factors that promote entrepreneurship (Raposo & Paço, 2011). An important factor that determines if one has what it takes to be an entrepreneur is one's tolerance for risk. Whether a student chooses to become an entrepreneur or not, risk is inevitable and managing risk is a critical skill for everyday life.

RISK AVERSION, RISK TOLERANCE, AND RISK MANAGEMENT

Risk aversion, risk tolerance, and risk management are topics often disregarded in the entrepreneurial curriculum because the concepts are difficult to teach and resources are limited. But, it is very important to include them.

Risk Aversion

A risk-averse individual may prefer to have a career as a low-paid employee with apparent job security than as an entrepreneur with the opportunity to earn a large sum of money (Kolakowski, n.d.). If investors are risk averse, higher-risk investments will need to offer higher expected yields. Otherwise, the investment will not be competitive with the less risky investments (Scott, 2003). Entrepreneurs are often characterized as having a low level of risk aversion.

Risk aversion research can be categorized in two different types of entrepreneurship: (a) opportunistic entrepreneurship driven primarily by the recognition of opportunity arising from an innovative idea, and (b) necessity entrepreneurship driven primarily by the fact that other income opportunities are gone and that one's own business offers the likelihood of the highest advantage. Necessity entrepreneurs are expected to be less risk tolerant than opportunity entrepreneurs because necessity entrepreneurs have no other way to make a living. Opportunity entrepreneurs tend to have alternative employment and are therefore more risk tolerant (Block, Sandner, & Spiegel, 2010).

Research on necessity entrepreneurship has found that getting laid-off presents the opportunity to pursue business ideas that have long been considered but not followed up on due to the time commitment and the risk of leaving a job. Conversely, when there is a healthier economy, necessity entrepreneurships declines (Tozzi, 2010).

Risk Tolerance

Risk tolerance can be determined through decision questionnaires, social dilemma case studies, and self-reporting surveys. These risk tolerance tools should be used with caution, however, as at least one researcher contends that established measurement tools that accurately measure one's mind-set toward risk taking do not exist. Rohrmann (2005) reports that presumed risk attitude is not a one-dimensional generic personality feature. Instead, other personality characteristics are likely to influence one's risk attitudes—such as sensation seeking or impulsivity—but are not just a derivate of such factors. The questionnaires, social dilemma case studies, and self-reporting surveys can be used to generate awareness, discussion, and further research on the topic of risk tolerance.

Risk Management

Taking a leap of faith without doing one's homework is not only the opposite of risk aversion, it is bad business practice. Tools are available to assist entrepreneurs in assessing the market and determining if the venture fits the needs of the customer-driven market. Entrepreneur education should develop the ability within students to be able to investigate and locate resources to answer questions entrepreneurs may encounter, including how to manage risk. Having students conduct such an investigation will incorporate the Common Core Standards that emphasize career and college readiness skills, which will be discussed in further detail in the instructional strategy section.

When in doubt, consult the experts. Potential entrepreneurs can consult several sources to help them determine the level of risk involved in an entrepreneurial venture. Sprouter (http://www.sprouter.com) is an online platform that facilitates the exchange of knowledge between startups and business leaders. Sarah Prevette, the founder of Sprouter and a web entrepreneur, was named by *Inc.* as one of the top entrepreneurs in North America. Sprouter allows entrepreneurs to get answers to questions from people who are experts in the area of entrepreneurship. The Sprouter website has a carefully selected panel of experts who provide advice on a variety of topics, including law, marketing, and funding (Sprouter, n.d.).

Other sources of guidance include trade publications, industry associations, prospective customers, and the U.S. Small Business Association and organizations it sponsors. Sarah Prevette of Sprouter warns would-be entrepreneurs that "A lot of entrepreneurs tend to isolate and do things on their own, trusting their own opinions above all else. You need to get out there and realize there's a community that can help you find success" (Moran, 2011, p. 93).

ENTREPRENEURIAL INTEGRITY AND ETHICS

Unfortunately, not all entrepreneurial ventures are successful and, faced with the reality that the risk is too great to overcome, many entrepreneurs encounter grueling decisions. Teaching students how to handle failure gracefully is difficult, particularly when failure in many aspects of education and life have resulted in disgrace and often disciplinary action. However, students will instantly recognize numerous entrepreneurs, who having failed once, have gone on to be successful and can be used as examples. Therefore, entrepreneurial education should address issues such as maintaining integrity and making ethical and moral decisions, even in times of despair. Faced with the daunting reality that a venture may not be successful, an entrepreneur might be pressured to make choices that run counter to the creed of ethical and moral reasoning. According to Katz (2002), Marianne Hudson, manager of strategic alliances at the nationally acclaimed Ewing Marion Kauffman Center for Entrepreneurial Leadership, believes that in most cases entrepreneurs instinctively know the right thing to do; however, they will face times when the best decision does not seem obvious. Hudson (Katz, 2002) contends that, "Most successful entrepreneurs have developed a framework for decision making based on their personal values and the kind of culture they want to create in their companies" (p. 27).

ENTREPRENEURSHIP EDUCATION

National Standards for Business Education (NBEA, 2007) provides a framework and performance expectations for entrepreneurship education. An updated version of the National Standards for Business Education is set for release in 2013. According to these standards, the basics of entrepreneurship should be introduced at lower levels of education with more detailed, abstract concepts taught at higher educational levels.

Entrepreneurship can be taught as a stand-alone course or integrated in many elementary, secondary, and postsecondary courses. Several vital components of entrepreneurship education have already been identified in this chapter. Crews and Crews (2012) added communication, technology, management, and marketing to the list of basic components of an entrepreneurship course as well as entrepreneurial spirit, knowledge of laws that affect business, and insurance needs. Entrepreneurship lends itself to a plethora of content and instructional strategies.

Ashmore (n.d.) states that entrepreneurship education is more than teaching someone to run a business. It is also about encouraging creative thinking and promoting a strong sense of self-worth and empowerment. Entrepreneurs often provide needed innovations in all areas of industry when the larger companies cannot change quickly. Entrepreneurship education is a vehicle for teaching students to identify a need or a problem and create a solution. This section will discuss interdisciplinary instruction, centralized/experiential learning, and problem-based/challenge-based learning.

Interdisciplinary Instruction

Integrated-interdisciplinary instruction is an approach that allows educators to address simultaneously multiple content standards while helping their students to understand the interconnections among knowledge and skills from diverse disciplines (Commonwealth of Pennsylvania, 2009). Business teacher education programs should emphasize the importance of integrated-interdisciplinary instruction and require future business educators to demonstrate mastery of this approach. One example of integrative-interdisciplinary learning is to infuse the Common Core Standards with the National Standards for Business Education mentioned earlier in this chapter. The current entrepreneurship standards from the *National Standards for Business Education* (NBEA, 2007) cover basic entrepreneurial concepts—accounting, economics, finance, management, and marketing. The Common Core State Standards Initiative is designed to enforce real-world knowledge and skills needed for success in careers and college. English language arts and mathematics standards are currently available; science standards are expected to be released in 2013 (National Governors Association Center for Best Practices and the Council of Chief State School Officers, 2012). A second example of integrative-interdisciplinary learning is the incorporation of science, technology, engineering, and mathematics competencies with entrepreneurship education. The April 2012 edition of the *Business Education Forum* includes an article titled *Integrating STEM Competencies into Entrepreneurship Education*. In this article, McEwen & McEwen (2012) stated, "Introducing STEM into entrepreneurship courses—through materials that most students tend to find very interesting and motivating—is an excellent way to help students prepare for 21st century careers" (p. 33).

Contextualized Learning/Experiential Learning

Contextual learning and experiential learning require teachers and learners to become actively engaged in the learning process. The contextualized learning theory focuses on the multiple aspects of any learning environment, whether a classroom, a laboratory, a computer lab, a worksite, or a wheat field. It encourages educators to choose and/or design learning environments that incorporate as many different forms of experience as possible (social, cultural, physical, and psychological) in working toward the desired learning outcomes (Center for Occupational Research and Development, 2012).

Similar to contextual learning, experiential education is a philosophy and methodology in which educators purposefully engage with learners in direct experience and focused reflection in order to increase knowledge, develop skills, and clarify values (Association for Experiential Education, n.d.). Preservice and practicing business educators should incorporate contextualized learning and experiential education into the curriculum to not only make learning fun but to take learning to a higher level. By incorporating experiential learning into the entrepreneurship classroom, students are led to observe, interpret, analyze, make decisions, and consider consequences (Daly, 2001). For example, a web-based business project that groups students in teams directs them to choose a business to develop and devise a business plan, and instructs them to start up and run the business using information available through web resources such as the Small Business Administration's loan guidelines to obtaining funding. By participating in the project, students receive exposure to the resources on the web, develop an understanding of the various functional areas within a business and how these functions are interdependent, enhance electronic communication skills, and experience the entrepreneurial behavioral, affective, and cognitive attitudes that motivate individuals to succeed in small business endeavors (Kavan and O'Hara, 2003).

Virtual learning. Virtual learning is a form of experiential learning. Second Life is a virtual environment used by educators for learning projects at the secondary and post-secondary levels. Second Life is a 3D virtual world where people use avatars to explore and socialize with other people all over the world, not just the local community. Linden Labs, the creator of Second Life, has marketed its product to entrepreneurs in two important ways. First, Linden dollars, the Second Life currency, are easily traded for U.S. dollars at an official currency site. Second, Linden has taken the remarkable step of allowing players to retain the copyright for their in-game creations. It is these aspects of Second Life that attract entrepreneurs and entrepreneur educators. On the Second Life website, the company lists the businesses in the box below as some real examples of in-world enterprises run by residents:

Architect	Game developer	Real estate speculator
Automotive manufacturer	Jewelry maker	Tattooist
Custom avatar designer	Party and wedding planner	Tour guide
Fashion designer	Pet manufacturer	XML coder
Freelance scripter	Publicist	

Source: Tiffany (2007, p. 21)

By using Second Life as a platform for experiential learning, teachers are able to overcome challenges often experienced in the physical world. One issue the virtual world is able to address is the lack of resources. For example, in Second Life, the hypothetical fashion design student could open a store for a nearly trivial cost, while learning about marketing, resource management, and design in the process (Mason, 2007). Another obstacle in the physical world Second Life can overcome is exposing students to a global market. Students can also interact with other entrepreneurs in their areas of interest from all over the globe.

Second Life hosts a Second Life Education website. There is also a Second Life educators' listserv, and annual conference. Although Second Life is generally for adults 18 years and older, students who are 13 years or older can use Second Life with some restrictions.

Problem-Based and Challenge-Based Learning

In order to develop the soft skills necessary to be a successful entrepreneur, students should be presented with scenarios that test their ethical and moral decision making. These skills can be developed through problem-based and challenge-based learning opportunities. Through problem- and challenge-based learning, students are encouraged to work actively with materials and to seek advice, mentorship, and answers to specific problems from the teacher, instead of being a passive recipient of lectures. Students assume greater responsibility for their own learning. Problem- and challenge-based learning helps cultivate an entrepreneurial environment by encouraging students to apply the concepts from other experiences to solve a problem, in the same fashion as entrepreneurs develop new business opportunities.

There are barriers to the adoption of problem- and challenge-based learning for entrepreneurship education. Unfortunately, students are accustomed to highly structured textbook teaching and may feel lost. A key part of the learning experience is to have students cope with ambiguities and uncertainties. A second barrier is the amount of planning and preparation time needed to develop problem- and challenge-based projects. Both problem- and challenge-based learning require the development of a realistic problem and guidelines for pursuing a solution to the problem. Challenge-based learning has additional components not found in problem-based learning. The challenge-based learning process begins with a big idea and emerges with an essential question or a challenge guiding question. Students must then determine and articulate the solution, take action by implementing the solution, and then evaluate the results. The process also integrates important ongoing activities such as reflection, assessment, and documentation (Apple Pty Limited, 2012). Despite the barriers to problem- and challenge-based learning, the benefits of developing the critical thinking skills students rely on to become successful in life are worth the time and effort.

Teaching strategies should contextualize learning, provide students with opportunities to work and reflect for an extended period, emphasize self-reliance and flexibility, provide diverse ways of learning, deliver prompt feedback, and contain ongoing assessment. By engaging students in entrepreneurship projects, teachers serve as facilitators, allowing students to construct their own knowledge through learning, application, action, review, and reflection (Dwerryhouse, 2001).

ASSESSMENT STRATEGIES FOR ENTREPRENEURSHIP

Assessment should be conducted throughout the learning process. Using a variety of instructional approaches, incorporating multidisciplinary content, and enforcing those ever-important soft skills make assessment confusing and somewhat intimidating, particularly for preservice and new teachers. One major pitfall in assessing active learning is to focus only on the final product. In many cases, entrepreneur education requires formal and informal evaluation of both process and product. Self-reflection and peer evaluations can be used to assess the process aspects of entrepreneurial education. The topics presented through these assessment strategies can serve as a starting point for in-class and online discussions throughout the process. Teamwork is a soft skill that may be assessed during the process stage. Peterson (2004) states:

> Most students are initially puzzled about why they are being assessed on the team process. They have generally been put in groups, but the process that they use to produce the product has generally been ignored in the assessment process. The students have come to believe that the process is unimportant and that the only thing that is important is the finished project. If we do not assess the team process, then we create the very environment that draws complaints from both students and faculty regarding free riders, interpersonal conflict, and unclear direction (p. 58).

Other concepts and theories can be evaluated through responses to questions in case studies, research papers and reports, interviews, activities, and objective tests and quizzes. Presentations can be assessed by teacher and students using a rubric that has been developed with student input and shared with the students before the presentation. Websites such as rubistar.com can be used to develop rubrics that can be saved and edited.

Assessing a final product may be quicker and easier. However, just as a variety of instructional strategies should be used in entrepreneurial education to engage students in the process of developing a product, a variety of assessment strategies should be used to assess both the process and the product.

ENTREPRENEURSHIP RESOURCES AND ACTIVITIES

Entrepreneurs are not passive individuals; they are doers. Therefore, entrepreneurial education needs to take the student out of the spectator role and into the active participant role. Incorporating resources into entrepreneurial education can do this because these thought-provoking classroom activities intrigue and motivate students. Table 1 lists several resources that entrepreneurship teachers might find useful.

Table 1. Resources for Entrepreneurship

Resource	Description
Curriculum	
BizWorld http://www.bizworld.org/programs/index.php	This website helps students learn how the entrepreneurial cycle operates by using the friendship bracelet industry.
Online Games	
All Terrain Brain http://www.allterrainbrain.org	Animated music videos, interactive games, and a downloadable activity guide help teach entrepreneurship.

Coffee Tycoon http://www.coffeetycoon.net	In this simulation, students run their own coffee shop, coffee stand, and coffee empire.
Gazillionaire http://www.gazillionaire.com	Players run their own companies, trade exotic goods, get rich, and have an opportunity to expand their empires.
HotShot Business http://disney.go.com/hotshot/hsb3	Players can choose among a pet spa, a landscaping business, a candy factory, a comic shop, or a custom skateboard factory.
Lemonade Stand) http://www.lemonadegame.com	This online simulation gives students the opportunity to run a lemonade stand.

Organization

Junior Achievement http://www.ja.org	Free K-12 curriculum that fosters entrepreneurship.
SAGE http://www.sageglobal.org	SAGE provides teenage SAGE teams with an opportunity to complete a socially responsible business.
SIFE http://www.sife.org	Participating students form teams on their university campuses and apply business concepts to develop outreach projects.

Resources

Consortium for Entrepreneurship Education http://www.entre-ed.org	This web page is for people who help students of all ages find their own entrepreneurial opportunities. It includes the national content standards for entrepreneurship.
ENTERWeb http://www.enterweb.org/entrship.htm	This web page provides a guide to the best sites on entrepreneurship and entrepreneurship development.
Mini-Society http://www.councilforeconed.org/resources/lessons/classroom_minieconomy.pdf	This website provided by the Council for Economic Education details how to start a mini-economy in the classroom.
Network for Teaching Entrepreneurship http://www.nfte.com	This network provides e-learning workshops, professional development, a business plan competition, an experiential learning activity, etc. for teachers of entrepreneurship.
Sprouter http://www.sprouter.com	Sprouter contains resources to help with entrepreneurial startups.
Stanford University's Entrepreneurship Corner http://ecorner.stanford.edu	This entrepreneurship page from Stanford University offers 2,000 free videos and podcasts related to entrepreneurship.

Activities

The following can be used to help engage students in the entrepreneurship classroom.

- Exercises for innovation (students form groups and brainstorm about entrepreneurship ideas)

- Current event assignments related to entrepreneurship (students can search newspapers, business magazines, or the Internet for articles related to entrepreneurship topics)

- Personal assessment (free online quizzes to assess a student's affinity for entrepreneurship; e.g., "Are you an entrepreneur?")

- Panel discussions (local entrepreneurs or student entrepreneurs present/participate in panel discussions)

- Demographic analysis of the local community (students can use the demographics of the local community to assess and discuss which types of entrepreneurial businesses would most likely be successful)

- Marketing plans for entrepreneurial businesses (samples available online)

- Biographies of famous entrepreneurs (available online)

- Franchise analysis (students can use franchise information available on business websites to assess and discuss the pros and cons of franchising)

- Games (role playing and online simulations)

- Entrepreneurial case studies (students can analyze and discuss entrepreneurial cases)

- Entrepreneurial questions (students can form groups and discussion questions related to entrepreneurship)

- Business plans (students can create their own business plans; the teacher can provide a template or templates are available online)

- Entrepreneurship simulation (students can be divided into groups; each group can form a company, create a product, sell the product at school during a specific timeframe, liquidate the company, and analyze the experience)

- Operating an actual business (as a class, students can create a business that operates during the school year, such as a bakery, a sandwich shop, etc.)

SUMMARY

The number of people who want to own their own business is increasing; therefore, business educators should include entrepreneurship education in the curriculum. *National Standards for Business Education* (NBEA, 2007) guidelines can be used as a framework for entrepreneurship education at any grade level. Business education is a natural fit for entrepreneurship education because in the business education curriculum, students are exposed to a comprehensive view of how entrepreneurship and economic development are interrelated. Incorporating a variety of instructional strategies, such as experiential learning, problem-based learning, challenge-based learning, games, and simulations with course content based on these national standards creates a formula for success in entrepreneurship education.

REFERENCES

Apple Pty Limited. (2012). Take action and make a difference: Challenge-based learning, Terms of service. Retrieved from http://www.challengebasedlearning.org/help/terms

Ashmore, C. (n.d.). Entrepreneurship means change. *EntrepreNews & Views.* The Consortium for Entrepreneurship Education. Retrieved from http://www.entre-ed.org/_entre/change.htm

Association for Experiential Education. (n.d.). Association for Experiential Education: Frequently asked questions. Retrieved from http://www.aee.org/membership/background

Association of Career and Technical Education. (2011, February). An interview with CTE entrepreneur Nai Wang (electronic version). *Techniques, 86*(2).

Block, J. H., Sandner, P., & Spiegel, F. (2010, August). Do risk attitudes differ within the group of entrepreneurs? *Proceedings from Academy of Management Annual Meeting Proceedings,* 1–103. doi:10.5465/AMBPP.2010.54503711

Brown, B. (2003). The role of CTE in entrepreneurship. Eric Digest. ED482537. Retrieved from http://www.eric.ed.gov/ERICWebPortal/search/detailmini.jsp?_nfpb=true&_&ERICExtSearch_SearchValue_0=ED482537&ERICExtSearch_SearchType_0=no&accno=ED482537

Buttress, S., & Macke, D. (2008). Energizing entrepreneurs (electronic version). *Economic Development Journal, 7*(4), 20–25.

Camp, M., & Autio, E. (2000). *Global entrepreneurship monitor: 2000 executive report.* Kansas City, MO: Kauffman Center for Entrepreneurial Leadership.

Center for Occupational Research and Development. (2012). What is contextual learning? Retrieved from http://www.cord.org/contextual-learning-definition

Coduras, A., Levie, J., Kelley, D. J., & Schott, T. (2010). A global perspective on entrepreneurship education and training. *Global entrepreneurship monitor special report.* Retrieved from http://www.gemconsortium.org/docs/download/276

Commonwealth of Pennsylvania. (2009). Integration-interdisciplinary instruction. Retrieved from http://www.pa3e.ws/resources/governors-institute-workbook/17/40-integration-interdisciplinary-instruction.html

Crews, T., & Crews, M. (2012). Entrepreneurship and basic business skills. In W. Stitt-Gohdes, (Ed.). *Trends & issues in business education: NBEA 2012 yearbook* (No. 50, pp. 74–88). Reston, VA: National Business Education Association.

Daly, S. P. (2001, December). Student-operated Internet businesses: True experiential learning in entrepreneurship and retail management (electronic version). *Journal of Marketing Education, 23*(3), 204–215.

Dwerryhouse, R. (2001, May). Real work in the 16–19 curriculum: AVCE business and young enterprise. *Education + Training, 43*(3), 153–161.

Katz, M. (2002). How to keep your boardroom out of the courtroom (electronic version). *Women In Business, 54*(5), 27.

Kavan, C. B., and O'Hara, M. T. (2003, February). Stimulating entrepreneurship in the classroom. *Business Education Forum, 57*(3), 41–43.

Kolakowski, M. (n.d.). Risk aversion. Retrieved from http://financecareers.about.com/od/rz/g/Risk_Aversion.htm

Mason, H. (2007). Experiential learning in second life. *Proceedings from Second Life Education Workshop 2007, Chicago, Illinois,* 14–18. Retrieved from http://www.simteach.com/slccedu07proceedings.pdf

McEwen, T., & McEwen, B. (2012, April). Integrating STEM competencies into entrepreneurship education. *Business Education Forum, 66*(4), 32–36.

Moran, G. (2011, July). From paycheck to pay dirt. *Entrepreneur, 39*(7), 91–95.

Mustafa-Topxhiu, R. (2012). The role of entrepreneurship and enterprises for local economic development. *Academicus,* (5), 96–107.

National Business Education Association (NBEA). (2007). *National standards for business education: What America's students should know and be able to do in business* (3rd ed.). Reston, VA: Author.

National Governors Association Center for Best Practices and the Council of Chief State School Officers. (2012). *Common Core State Standards Initiative.* Retrieved from http://www.corestandards.org/the-standards

Peterson, T. O. (2004). Assessing performance in problem-based service-learning projects (electronic version). *New Directions for Teaching & Learning, 204*(100), 55–63.

Raposo, M., & Paço, A. (2011). Entrepreneurship education: Relationship between education and entrepreneurial activity. *Psicothema, 23*(3), 453–457.

Rohrmann, B. (2005, January). Risk attitude scales: Concepts, questionnaires, utilizations. Retrieved from http://www.rohrmannresearch.net

Scott, D. (2003). *Wall Street words: An A to Z guide to investment terms for today's investor.* Boston, MA: Houghton Mifflin Company.

Sprouter. (n.d.). About us. Retrieved from http://sprouter.com/about

Tiffany, L. (2007). Starting a second life business. *Entrepreneur.* Retrieved from http://www.entrepreneur.com/article/172768

Tozzi, J. (2010, March). Revisiting the face of "necessity entrepreneurship." *BusinessWeek.com.* Retrieved from http://www.businessweek.com/smallbiz/content/mar2010/sb2010039_995571.htm

International Business

Les R. Dlabay
Lake Forest College
Lake Forest, IL

In some areas of the world, you can see water buffalo tilling the land in the shadow of a modern office building. This disparity in emerging markets contrasts modern global business operations with traditional economic activities similar to hundreds of years ago. The need for international business education is evident in the diverse cultural interactions that occur daily, in the products used by consumers, and in the companies where people work. With economic interdependence continuing to expand, students must be equipped with knowledge and competencies to participate in global business activities. A survey of global leaders at Fortune 500 companies indicated a potentially widening gap between organizational needs and the topics emphasized in classes (Milhauser & Rahschulte, 2010). To address this situation, this chapter presents global trends and topics along with resources and instructional strategies for planning and implementing international business units and courses.

CHANGING GLOBAL BUSINESS ENVIRONMENTS

Globalization involves the process of expanding business activities in order to gain a worldwide perspective. Organizations attempt to use a standardized approach to business and marketing activities that extends across different cultures and levels of economic development, creating a global business challenge. Expanding globalization occurs in a context of change that includes evolving political environments, advancing technological applications, conflicting cultures, and growing importance of emerging markets.

The Politics of International Trade

Expanded political freedoms in various regions have set a new tone for global business relationships. As ideologies evolve and economies move from controlled settings to market economies, enhanced opportunities for foreign investment and entrepreneurial efforts are created. Although globalization is highly visible, regional economic integration is also evident. Trade agreements and organizations connect nations in close proximity. The North American Free Trade Agreement (NAFTA), European Union, Association of Southeast Asian Nations (ASEAN), and Mercosur in South America provide the foundation for this movement. More recently, emerging markets in Central America, the Caribbean, and Africa have created trading blocs to compete in the world economy (Hill, 2013).

Technology and Global Business Activities

Throughout history, innovations have enhanced the quantity and quality of international trade. Improved worldwide telecommunications systems, freight containerization, and overnight delivery services have expanded global activities. Today, e-commerce, wireless communication, and mobile technologies have opened up global opportunities previously restricted by geographic, financial, or political constraints.

Conflicting Cultural Diversity and Homogeneity

Expansion of global companies occurs in every region of the world. Cultural homogeneity can result as the Internet makes products and brands as easily available in Egypt and Thailand as in Houston and Miami. Global business expansion creates concern about the loss of a nation's cultural identity. Younger generations often prefer modern ideas, products, and activities at the expense of the more traditional aspects of their culture. However, nationalist groups may oppose the effect multinational companies have on a nation's customs and heritage.

Extensive cultural diversity also occurs within the borders of a country. With several hundred ethnic groups and languages spoken in New York City, and throughout the United States, students must be ready for global business interactions in their own neighborhoods. Because of this extensive cultural presence, Hagen and Berg (2012) encouraged international business knowledge for all students, even those who expect to work only in a domestic setting.

Emerging Markets and the "Base of the Pyramid"

More than two billion customers, with trillions of dollars of spending power, create an extensive potential market for the future of international business. Although BRIC (Brazil, Russia, India, China) countries receive the most emphasis, vast opportunities exist elsewhere. Those living on $2 or less a day, often referred to as the *base of the pyramid* (BOP), represent a market with many needs and strong business potential in Africa, Asia, and Latin America (Pralahad, 2009).

Paton, Harris-Boundy, and Melhus (2012) suggested that instructional inclusion of poverty-stricken markets can result in future economic growth for these areas as well as changed student perceptions and increased sensitivity. Companies must offer affordable products related to food, water, energy, health care, education, and financial services. However, BOP consumers and distributors live under very different conditions. Workers must be prepared to do business in open-air markets as well as traditional retail stores. Transport may be by oxcart and bicycle as well as truck and train. Examples of business activities in base-of-the-pyramid markets include Unilever in India developing an array of low-cost food, water, personal care, and home-care products and P&G (Proctor & Gamble) in Nigeria selling laundry detergent, soap, and diapers with plans to do business in more than 50 African countries.

INTERNATIONAL BUSINESS COURSE CONTENT

Education in global issues is a necessity for an organization to have a successful international presence. "Success in a global business environment requires knowledge and understanding of global components: economic systems, business practices, political and legal structures, and multicultural contexts" (Policies Commission for Business and Economic Education, 2004). This mandate creates the foundation for the international business curriculum. The *National Standards for Business Education* by the National Business Education Association (NBEA, 2007) outlines a comprehensive set of performance standards for teaching international business.

International Trade Foundations

Two economic principles form the foundation for international business transactions: absolute advantage and comparative advantage. *Absolute advantage* exists when a country can produce a good or service at a lower cost than most other countries. This situation often results from an abundance of natural resources or raw materials. A *comparative advantage* may occur when a country specializes in a certain good or service. The nation then becomes relatively more efficient than other nations involved in this industry.

A common measure of international business activity is *balance of trade*, which is the difference between the value of a country's exports and imports. Balance of trade does not include all international business transactions, just imports and exports. In contrast, *balance of payments* measures the total monetary inflows of a country minus the total outflows. This economic measurement includes exports, imports, investments, tourist spending, and financial assistance (Dlabay & Scott, 2011).

Global Business Environment

Geographic, economic, cultural, and political factors create the foundation for exporting and global business activities. Knowledge of location, climate, terrain, waterways, natural resources, and other geographic factors creates an understanding of international trade. Due to topography, products commonly transported by truck or train in some countries may require oxen or other traditional transportation modes in other countries.

Level of economic development reflects a country's ability to generate wealth and to participate in international trade. An *industrialized country* has an advanced level of production facilities with extensive technology, a highly educated population, and well-established infrastructure. A *less-developed country* has little economic wealth and an emphasis on agriculture or mining. Between these extremes are *developing countries*—nations characterized by improving educational systems, increasing technology, and expanding industries (Dlabay & Scott, 2011).

The *informal economy*, also known as unregistered businesses or the underground economy, which can account for 40 to 60 percent of a nation's business, includes pushcarts, street vendors, open-air markets, and home-based businesses. Although these informal business activities are most prevalent in the developing economies of Africa, Asia, Eastern Europe, and Latin America, industrialized nations also have many enterprises operating "off the books" with hundreds of millions of dollars of unreported sales revenue and unpaid taxes.

In addition to concerns about geography and economic development, culture (traditions, language, family relationships, education, and religion) must be considered when doing international business. Behaviors such as using an improper gesture, giving an inappropriate gift, or negotiating in an offensive manner can damage economic relationships.

Legal and political concerns also present global business challenges. Companies commonly face trade barriers such as tariffs, import quotas, and packaging regulations. Enforcement of intellectual property protection also creates difficulties when distributing products covered by brand names, copyrights, patents, and trademarks. The World Bank reports the status of business regulations in more than 180 countries at http://www.doingbusiness.org.

International Business Communication

Greeting methods, formal titles, nonverbal interactions, and negotiation styles vary when communicating across cultures. These intercultural situations range from managing work teams from various countries to business negotiations in exotic settings. To avoid potential obstacles, ongoing cross-cultural communication training is vital for international business organizations (Cardon, 2007).

Global Business Ethics and Social Responsibility

Culture and political environments can frequently influence business practices. Aggressive companies based in Europe and Asia have used payoffs to gain access to new markets. Although some countries may consider this payment a normal business expense, U.S. businesspeople are subject to the Foreign Corrupt Practices Act and may face fines or prison sentences when engaging in such practices.

Organizational Structures

Forms of business ownership and entrepreneurial opportunities differ widely in international settings. Global companies use modified approaches in various cultures (Dlabay & Scott, 2011). For example, breakfast cereals such as Cheerios, Lucky Charms, and Trix are sold under the "Nestle" brand, instead of "General Mills," in Latin America, Europe, Asia, and the Middle East. Cereal Partners Worldwide is a partnership combining the popular products of General Mills with the brand name and distribution system of Nestle. The most common forms of organizational strategies used for global business activities include the following:

- *Joint ventures*, also referred to as *strategic partnerships* or *strategic alliances*, involving agreements between two or more companies (often from different countries) to share a business project related to manufacturing and distribution

- *Turnkey projects* allow a company to enter a foreign market by creating a ready-to-use business facility, such as technology or a production plant

- *Management contracting* involves selling management skills and technical services by hotels, health-care companies, and information technology organizations

- *Contract manufacturing* occurs when a company in a foreign country produces an item for another company

- *Licensing* involves selling the right to use some intangible property (production process, trademark, or brand name) for a fee or royalty

- *Franchising* is the right to use a company name or business process in a specific way (Dlabay & Scott, 2011)

International Trade Relations

Strategic trade alliances, such as the North American Free Trade Agreement, which seek to promote free trade, create expanded business among countries. However, tariffs, quotas, various laws, and other formal trade barriers may restrict trade between countries (NBEA, 2007). In contrast, geography, culture, religion, and family relations create informal trade barriers, which also limit the free flow of goods, services, labor, and capital.

International Management

Managerial practices and leadership styles differ widely from one country to another. Human resource management issues include child labor practices and laws, compensation, benefits, labor-management practices, health and safety issues, environmental concerns, employee relocation, and career paths (NBEA, 2007).

International Marketing and Global Supply Chains

When a company does business in another country, it must decide whether to use a "standardized" or "customized" product strategy. Although some products such as cameras, cell phones, or computers can be sold in almost the same way throughout the world, others must be adapted. For example, McDonald's uses a revised menu in different countries based on tastes, customs, and religious beliefs. In the Philippines and other countries, Tide detergent is often sold in three forms—powder, liquid, and bar. The detergent bar is used for clothes washed by hand in areas without mechanical washing machines (Dlabay & Scott, 2011).

Globalization often involves sourcing from different regions of the world. Companies commonly have a supply chain involving raw materials, product designers, and assembly plants from several countries. When a company is directly involved in various stages of production and distribution, vertical integration occurs. An auto manufacturer with its own glass company or tire manufacturer is referred to as vertically integrated.

International Finance

Foreign exchange is the process of converting the currency of one country into the currency of another country. The *exchange rate* is the amount of currency of one country that can be traded for one unit of the currency of another country. Three main factors affect currency exchange rates among countries: a nation's balance of payments; economic conditions, such as inflation and interest rates; and political stability (Dlabay & Scott, 2011).

Countries may unite under a single currency; for example, the members of the European Monetary Union that use the euro as their official currency. The Central Bank of West African States issues a single monetary unit called the *franc* for the African Financial Community. This currency is used in eight countries—Benin, Burkina Faso, Guinea Bissau, Côte d'Ivoire, Mali, Niger, Senegal, and Togo.

Microfinance—also called *microlending* and *microcredit*—involves programs of small loans to poor people for self-employment projects. The business activities generate income to provide for life necessities and family needs (Dlabay & Burrow, 2008). In recent years, microfinance services have expanded beyond loans to include savings and insurance to better serve low-income clients without access to the formal banking system.

CURRICULUM IMPLEMENTATION PATTERNS

The international business curriculum may consist of integrated instructional units or specialized international courses. At the high school level, international business topics and units are often integrated into other business courses, such as introduction to business, marketing, keyboarding, computer applications, and cooperative office education. Many high schools offer a one-semester course in international business. At the two-year or four-year college level, international business concepts are included in courses such as management, marketing, and business communication. In most colleges and universities, specialized international courses are part of the business curriculum, which may also include a comprehensive international business program.

Integrated Instructional Units

Most people have either traveled to other countries or know someone who has traveled. Guest speakers, videos, sample global products, and social media exchanges with people in other countries can enhance the international context of a course.

In an accounting course, a starting point might be the study of record-keeping practices in other countries, along with a discussion of currency exchange rates. Online research as a source of information and a discussion of global stock exchanges would also be appropriate.

In a business communication course, students should develop an awareness of cultural differences in dress, greetings, and business hours around the world. For example, although shaking hands is appropriate in many countries, other types of greetings may include bowing or hugging. A business communication class might include a discussion of cross-cultural negotiation styles.

In a keyboarding or computer applications course, students should be introduced to differences in document formats used in other countries. When teaching students about spreadsheets, downloaded demographic and economic data from various nations can be used to analyze various trends. Foreign trade data may be obtained from the U.S. Census Bureau at http://www.census.gov/foreign-trade

In a marketing course, an analysis of consumer behavior differences in other cultures would be valuable. Students should be aware that collecting marketing research data in some countries might require observation and interviews rather than telephone or mail surveys due to poor infrastructure or a low literacy level.

Every business course should integrate international concepts and a global perspective into instruction. Students' awareness of varied cultures, global business practices, and international career opportunities create the foundation for their futures in the workplace and in the marketplace.

Specialized International Business Courses

An inclusive international business curriculum involves specialized courses and programs focusing on relevant internationalized content. These courses may include principles of international business, as well other courses such as economics, finance, marketing, management, and communication with an international emphasis.

Cross-Discipline Partnerships

Interaction among academic disciplines offers a more cohesive instructional approach. Collaborations and team-teaching activities involving business, foreign language, social studies, and other areas of instruction allow students to better understand the complexity of global business relationships.

COMPREHENSIVE INTERNATIONAL BUSINESS PROGRAMS

Many colleges and universities offer a specialized international business curriculum or academic major involving international courses and other academic experiences. Such curricula often include such components as a business core foundation, international electives, foreign language, and experiential learning.

Business Core Foundation

International business programs generally include foundational knowledge of business in the areas of accounting, finance, human resources, information systems, marketing, and management. In addition, a study of international trade, global marketing, comparative management, global marketing, and cross-cultural communication may be required.

International Electives

Global understanding among students can be enhanced with topics such as Middle Eastern religions, South African politics, Latin American music, Chinese art, French literature, Russian history, as well as the study of global cultures and geography. Establishing an interdisciplinary collaboration enhances the ability of students to better understand the cultures in which they will be conducting business (Loughrin-Sacco, 2000).

Foreign Language

Most areas of the world consider English the "language of business." However, studying a second or third language develops an understanding of a society's culture and business environment. Second-language skills also give job applicants an advantage in the process, both for domestic and international positions. The need for expanded language skills also increases as a growing number of Internet users do not have English as their native language.

Experiential Learning

Experiential learning includes field research projects, internships and work-study projects, foreign study programs, and service learning. Field research projects afford students with an opportunity to identify, research, and assess global organizations in a real-world setting (Aggarwal & Goodell, 2011). Internships and work-study programs are viewed favorably by employment recruiters. Students gain needed skills and insights by participating in these organizational experiences with international companies, embassies, trade associations, or government export agencies.

Foreign study programs present opportunities for international learning experiences. Information about study abroad and exchange programs may be obtained from the American Institute for Foreign Study (http://www.aifs.org), Institute for International Education (http://www.iie.org), Council on International Educational Exchange (http://www.ciie.org), StudyAbroad.com (http://www.studyabroad.com), and AFS Intercultural Programs (http://www.afs.org).

Involvement in international service learning projects such as planning and implementing a program to collect clothing, food, and other necessities allows students to serve recent immigrants and others in need. Volunteer activities may include assisting with office tasks, delivering supplies, completing repairs, tutoring, or other teaching to support international service organizations. Fundraising and public relation activities for global programs can also be the basis for an international service-learning experience. Information on various service learning models may be obtained at the National Service-Learning Clearinghouse (http://www.servicelearning.org).

INSTRUCTIONAL STRATEGIES FOR INTERNATIONAL BUSINESS

Effective learning activities and instructional methods from other business education settings are easily adapted to international courses. These techniques range from lectures and discussions to cultural role playing and team research cases. Innovative strategies enhance the effectiveness of student-teacher interactions.

Case Studies and Decision-Making Exercises

International case studies produce a strong foundation for student decision making and the development of critical thinking skills. Company situations and country scenarios create an understanding of financial, economic, cultural, and political factors affecting global business operations. Ramburuth and Daniel (2011) advocated the case method for international business instruction to facilitate learning and to engage students in virtual exchanges to develop intercultural competence.

Geographic and Cultural Environment Analysis

Maps, globes, and atlases are significant resources for international business instruction. The teacher should encourage students to learn about the location, major cities, waterways, climate, natural resources, and other geographic details for one or more countries. This information offers a better understanding of trade relations, economic development, and global distribution systems. Useful geography websites include http://www.geographic.org, http://www.worldatlas.com, and http://www.lib.utexas.edu/Libs/PCL/Map_collection/Map_collection.html.

Company and Country Research Reports

Research papers traditionally allowed students to develop in-depth knowledge of a topic. Today, online research enhances that experience. Topics for international business research reports might include studying the culture of another country, export opportunities for small businesses, stages of economic development, regional economic agreements, and joint ventures.

Information and financial data for multinational enterprises can be the basis for a research report. Company data may be obtained at Yahoo! Finance (http://finance.yahoo.com) and AnnualReports.com (http://www.annualreports.com) as well as on individual company websites. These online sources offer needed information when studying global company activities.

Country or regional research can be the starting point for an ongoing class activity. This project requires students to obtain geographic, economic, cultural, and political information for a nation. The resulting information may then be used to (a) prepare a profile of the foreign business environment and (b) identify potential business opportunities for companies considering this market. The findings from this research could also be used for other assignments during a course.

Useful websites with country information include the CIA's *The World Factbook* (https://www.cia.gov/library/publications/the-world-factbook), country background notes of the State Department (http://www.state.gov/r/pa/ei/bgn), the Library of Congress country studies (http://lcweb2.loc.gov/frd/cs/cshome.html), the World Bank (http://www.worldbank.org/countries), and NationMaster.com (http://www.nationmaster.com).

Cross-Cultural Experiences and Team Projects

Most employers value prospective workers with team experience. International business courses may include team projects describing unique cultural characteristics of a foreign market, presenting group oral reports, and creating videos or PowerPoint presentations to communicate proposed global business activities. The team concept can extend beyond the school setting. Virtual teams involving e-mail, websites, and social media interactions allow students in different geographic locations to collaborate on consulting projects and case problems. These cross-cultural exchanges involve online researching, sharing, discussing, integrating, and reporting information.

Creating an export plan provides students with a comprehensive team project involving several components. Elements for this assignment might include (a) identifying business opportunities in foreign markets, (b) developing a product concept adapted for the intended market, (c) planning funding sources, (d) planning human resource needs, (e) creating a distribution and promotional strategy, and (f) developing a flowchart time line.

Role Playing and Simulations

Interaction among students can enhance understanding of international business concepts, while developing an appreciation for other cultures. Suggested international role-playing scenarios may include simulated business negotiations among people from different cultures, debates about free trade, and demonstrations of different greetings, gestures, and other nonverbal communication.

Online teaching of international business expands along with other web-based delivery systems. A combination of face-to-face instruction and e-learning can result in an enhanced instructional environment with expanded opportunities for student interactions and team projects. These virtual learning environments can result in cross-cultural collaborations among students around the world.

The International Business Practice Firm Program involves creation of a simulated business in which students create and develop a company; technology processes the simulated business transactions with firms from other countries. This program also has regional and international trade fairs. Further information about this program is available at http://www.mccc.edu/ibpf/about.shtml.

Field Research and Experiential Learning

Field research methods provide direct knowledge of global business settings. Students can interview global workers, export assistance specialists, language interpreters, culture experts, and tourists to obtain insight into course topics. Interviews yield current information about international business activities and foreign markets.

When arranging an interview, students should be encouraged to make an appointment to meet or to talk by telephone. Help students develop four or five open-ended questions; avoid questions that can be answered in a few words. Instruct students to use follow-up questions based on the initial answers they receive.

Another field research technique is observational research. Ethnic communities and stores offer insight into cross-cultural consumer behavior patterns, international product offerings, and distribution methods. During foreign travel, students can observe shopping habits, interpersonal encounters, recreational activities, and business transactions.

Analyzing food packages, advertisements, and magazines from other countries can develop an understanding of culture, economic development, and government regulations. Clothing labels communicate information about the locations of global manufacturing facilities. Postage stamps, coins, and paper money from around the world can contribute to an understanding of business activities and culture. Sample bank notes reflecting the culture, geography, history, and business activities of various nations may be viewed at CollectPaperMoney.com (http://www.collectpapermoney.com), BankNoteWorld.com (http://www.banknoteworld.com), and BankNotes.com (http://www.banknotes.com). Using these and other items, students might create a visual journal, poster, display, or site to communicate various international business terms and concepts.

Online Research and Web Activities

Online interaction with students in other countries allows a cross-cultural collaboration for gaining cultural and economic knowledge. E-mail information requests to companies and international agencies can result in insights on international trade, global cultures, and exporting.

Searches related to "exporting," "foreign exchange rates," "global stock exchanges," and other international business topics can direct students to useful information sources. Students may use the Internet for answers to questions about course concepts, global companies, or countries. A variation of this activity might involve students locating unusual items online; for example, a country flag showing an animal, the map of a nation with no ocean seaports, or a country in which you cannot buy Coca-Cola.

Current values for various monetary units may be found at XE Currency Converter (http://www.xe.net/ucc) and X-RATES (http://www.x-rates.com). Students may use their findings to calculate the cost of various items in different currencies or explain possible reasons for the changing value of a nation's currency.

Electronic Portfolio

An electronic portfolio on a CD, DVD, website, social media website, or other electronic format media can serve as a culminating experience. Portfolio components might include completed class assignments, data collection results, PowerPoint presentations, student-created videos, website designs, proposed package designs and advertising messages, and a resumé.

GLOBAL BUSINESS RESOURCES

Extensive resources are available with basic information and current updates on global business topics. These resources include curriculum guides, online syllabi, journals and periodicals, reference books, multimedia and community contacts, and various international agencies.

Curriculum Guides and Syllabi

The *National Standards for Business Education* (NBEA, 2007) lists performance expectations for international business courses. The National Council on Economic Education (http://www.ncee.net) offers curriculum guides and teaching ideas related to foreign trade and international economics. Several states have also designed international business curriculum guides.

A web search for teaching strategies and learning activities can be useful. Searching "international business syllabus," "international business teaching ideas," and related topics will identify many relevant and innovative curriculum materials.

Journals and Periodicals

Articles about teaching international business appear regularly in the *Business Education Forum* published by NBEA. The *Journal of Teaching in International Business*, *Journal for Global Business Education*, *International Journal for Business Education*, and *Journal of International Education in Business* present research-based studies related to curriculum planning, faculty development, and instructional strategies.

The business and travel sections of newspaper websites offer an inexpensive source of current international business information. Periodicals such as *The Economist*, *Latin Trade*, *African Business*, and *Euromoney* report economic, political, and cultural news from around the world.

Reference Books and Websites

Numerous reference materials present current international business information. Recent books about global business culture include *Kiss, Bow or Shake Hands* (Morrison & Conaway, 2006), *Global Business Etiquette: A Guide to International Communication and Customs* (Martin & Chaney, 2012), and *Cultural Intelligence: Improving Your CQ to Engage Our Multicultural World* (Livermore, 2009). International business textbooks serve as resources for both teachers and students.

Travel websites offer information about a country's history, geography, culture, and business activities. Websites with resources for international business teachers include Global Edge (http://globaledge.msu.edu) and GlobaLens (http://www.globalens.com).

Multimedia and Community Contacts

Information about global business videos may be obtained at Films Media Group (http://www.films.com), Insight Media (http://www.insight-media.com), Bullfrog Films (http://www.bullfrogfilms.com), Public Broadcasting Service (http://www.pbs.org), and through online searches. Speakers from global companies and international agencies can enhance learning. Company representatives are often willing to share their international business and travel experiences in class settings.

Government and International Agencies

Several U.S. government agencies provide international business information, including the International Trade Administration (http://www.trade.gov), the U.S. Trade Center (http://www.export.gov), Office of International Trade in the Small Business Administration (http://www.sba.gov/oit), and the Foreign Agricultural Service of the U.S. Department of Agriculture (http://www.fas.usda.gov). In addition, state departments of economic development or state departments of commerce usually offer exporting and international trade information.

The World Trade Organization (http://www.wto.org), International Monetary Fund (http://www.imf.org), and World Bank (http://www.worldbank.org) encourage expanded international trade and global economic development. Embassies and consulates (http://www.embassy.org) are a vital economic link between the United States and other nations.

FACULTY DEVELOPMENT ACTIVITIES

Foreign travel and international study programs enhance global business knowledge and cultural awareness. Faculty internships with global companies, government agencies, and trade associations can provide international experiences.

International business organizations offer conferences, seminars, and professional development activities. The Academy for International Business (http://aib.msu.edu), International Society for Business Education (http://www.siecisbe.org), and National Association of Small Business International Trade Educators (http://www.nasbite.org)

offer information on curriculum and instructional strategies through conferences and publications. The International Faculty Development Seminars of the Council on International Educational Exchange (http://www.ciee.org/ifds) has foreign travel programs to enhance faculty knowledge of international issues and global topics.

Local and regional trade association programs provide updates on exporting and foreign business environments. Information may be obtained from the World Trade Centers Association (http://www.wtca.org), which has more than 200 affiliates in more than 100 countries. Information about other international trade organizations is available at the Federation of International Trade Associations (http://www.fita.org).

SUMMARY

The constantly changing global environment presents an ongoing challenge when selecting international topics and learning experiences for students. The fundamental knowledge of every business student should include international trade concepts, the global business environment, methods for conducting international business, global marketing activities, international finance, and global risks. Planning international business instruction based on appropriate content and student-centered activities will help ensure that every student will be a productive participant in the global economy.

REFERENCES

Aggarwal, R., & Goodell, J. (2011). Study abroad and experiential learning in international business. *Journal of Teaching in International Business, 22*(2), 71–72.

Cardon, P. W. (2007). The importance of teaching about globalization in business education. *Journal for Global Business Education, 7*, 1–20.

Dlabay. L. R., & Burrow, J. L. (2008). *Business finance.* Cincinnati, OH: Thomson/South-Western.

Dlabay, L. R., & Scott, J. C. (2011). *International business* (4th ed.). Mason, OH: Cengage South-Western Educational Publishing.

Hagen, J. M., & Berg, D. M. (2012). International business for domestic students. *Journal for Global Business Education, 12*, 47–59.

Hill, C. W. L. (2013). *International business: Competing in the global marketplace* (9th. ed.). New York, NY: McGraw-Hill/Irwin.

Livermore, D. A. (2009). *Cultural intelligence: Improving your CQ to engage our multicultural world.* Grand Rapids, MI: Baker Academic.

Loughrin-Sacco, S. J. (2000). Building a bridge to liberal arts. In R. F. Scherer, S. T. Beaton, M. F. Ainina, & J. F. Meyer (Eds.), *A field guide to internationalizing business education* (pp. 107–119). Austin, TX: Center for International Business Education and Research.

Martin, J. S., & Chaney, L. H. (2012). *Global business etiquette: A guide to international communication and customs* (2nd ed.), New York, NY: Praeger Publishers.

Milhauser, K. L., & Rahschulte, T. (2010). Meeting the needs of global companies through improved international business curriculum. *Journal of Teaching in International Business, 21*(2), 78–100.

Morrison, R., & Conaway, W. A. (2006). *Kiss, bow or shake hands: The bestselling guide to doing business in more than 60 countries* (2nd ed.). Holbrook, MA: Adams Publishing Group.

National Business Education Association (NBEA). (2007). *National standards for business education: What America's students should know and be able to do in business* (3rd ed.), Reston, VA: Author.

Paton, B., Harris-Boundy, J., & Melhus, P. (2012). Integrating global poverty into mainstream business classrooms. *Journal of Teaching in International Business, 23*(1), 4–23.

Policies Commission for Business and Economic Education. (2004). *This we believe about business education in a global environment: Policy statement 74.* Reston, VA: National Business Education Association.

Pralahad, C. K. (2009). *The fortune at the bottom of the pyramid: Eradicating poverty through profits.* Upper Saddle River, NJ: Pearson Prentice Hall.

Ramburuth, P., & Daniel, S. (2011). Integrating experiential learning and cases in international business, *Journal of Teaching in International Business, 22*(1), 38–50.

Marketing

William J. Wilhelm
Indiana State University
Terre Haute, IN

Judy Commers
Porter County Career and Technical Center
Valparaiso, IN

Marketing education programs offer students opportunities to develop career-related skills, civic responsibility, and leadership competencies by participating in a variety of activities. These activities include hands-on classroom exercises, cocurricular student organizations, school-based enterprises, and community service.

This chapter addresses the goals, methods of instruction, and resources for teaching marketing education. The chapter presents information regarding curriculum organization of marketing education programs, outlines national standards, identifies performance expectations, describes specific strategies for instruction, and suggests numerous resources.

MARKETING EDUCATION COURSES AND CURRICULUM STRUCTURE

Marketing education at the secondary level usually begins with a basic marketing course that introduces students to the foundations and functions of marketing and related business administration skills. An advanced marketing course, which explores these foundations, functions, and business-related skills in greater detail may follow the beginning course; this course prepares the student for entry-level marketing employment upon graduation or serves as a foundation to continue more specialized study of marketing at a community college or university.

Marketing programs at the community college level offer basic courses as well as specialized courses in marketing fields such as sales management, real-estate sales, industrial sales, and insurance. University-level marketing programs also introduce students to the basic concepts of marketing, but they explore the marketing function in more depth as it relates to overall business operations. University marketing programs allow students to explore both domestic and international marketing theories in greater detail. Many MBA programs offer opportunities to specialize in marketing at the graduate level.

Secondary-level marketing education curricular structures should consist of a broadly based business administration core, a marketing core, marketing pathways, and marketing specialties (MBA Research & Curriculum Center, 2013. The business administration core consists of content common to the four occupational groupings of business management and administration; finance; hospitality and tourism; and marketing, sales, and service. This core content is divided into 11 instructional areas: business law, communications skills, economics, emotional intelligence, financial analysis, human resource management, information management, marketing, operations, professional development, and strategic management. The next level of curriculum specificity, called marketing pathways, includes a variety of broadly based occupational opportunities: buying and merchandising, distribution and logistics, e-marketing, management and entrepreneurship, marketing information management / marketing research, marketing communications and promotion, and professional sales. The highest level of specificity, marketing specialties, contains curriculum content unique to a product or service. It addresses job opportunities associated with each pathway (MBA Research & Curriculum Center, 2013).

The marketing core at the high school level represents the skills and knowledge that are common to the employment clusters of marketing, business administration, finance, and hospitality and is based on six functions: distribution, marketing-information management, pricing, promotion, product/service management, and selling. The two core areas—business administration and marketing—constitute the content of most basic marketing and advanced marketing high school courses.

The performance indicators identified in the National Standards for Marketing Management, Entrepreneurship and Business Administration guide (MBA Research & Curriculum Center, 2013) are assigned to one of six curriculum-planning levels: prerequisite, career sustaining, specialist, supervisor, manager, and owner. These levels can also be used for developing instruction for articulation between high school and postsecondary marketing courses.

Depending on local economic bases for funding and community needs, many state-approved marketing programs include additional or analogous courses in marketing specializations, such as sports, recreation, and entertainment marketing; hospitality, travel, and tourism marketing; financial service marketing; and entrepreneurship. The third tier of the marketing education curriculum, marketing pathways, allows students to focus on content in a variety of broadly based occupational opportunities called pathways. Some examples include areas of study such as buying and merchandising, marketing information management / marketing research, distribution and logistics, marketing communications and promotion, E-marketing, professional sales, management, and entrepreneurship (MBA Research & Curriculum Center, 2013). These specializations are usually taught at the postsecondary level, although some school districts may offer some coursework at the secondary level.

CURRICULUM ORGANIZATION FOR TEACHING AT THE SECONDARY LEVEL

Educators preparing to teach marketing courses at the secondary level should become familiar with their state's marketing education course descriptions, content standards, and performance expectations before developing their lesson plans. Although various states may have similar course descriptions, content standards, and performance expectations, sequences of learning objectives and instructional activities may differ. In addition, school districts may vary the marketing education course offerings available to students. For example, one district may offer a marketing foundations course at the sophomore level, continue courses through the junior year, and culminate with an advanced marketing course in the senior year. Other districts may offer the marketing foundations course only at the junior level followed by advanced marketing at the senior level.

The basic two-year high school marketing curriculum aims to provide program completers with (a) a foundation of business knowledge grounded in free enterprise economics, (b) a comprehension of general business-management practices, and (c) a thorough understanding of core marketing functions applied to all levels of the distribution hierarchy. Figure 1 depicts the instructional flow of a typical two-year high school marketing education curriculum.

Figure 1. Marketing Education Program Curriculum Schema

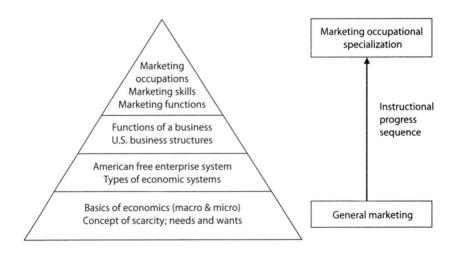

The curriculum model illustrated in Figure 1 presents a flow of instruction that emphasizes teaching marketing competencies and marketing specializations *after* teaching the basics of economic theory and the American free enterprise system. A beginning course in marketing usually is a high school student's first exposure to concepts of economic scarcity, micro- and macroeconomics, supply and demand theory, and the American free enterprise system. After introducing basic economic theory and the American free enterprise system, the teacher should present an overview of basic business concepts and the primary business functions, followed by focused instruction on marketing, its functional areas (see the marketing core in Figure 1), and their relationships to the success of a business venture. Only in this way will a student comprehend marketing as a functional part of the larger picture of a commercial enterprise and not as a scramble of abstract, unrelated business concepts.

Although not included as a specific component of the marketing education curriculum, electronic commerce has grown in scope, reach, and intensity since first discussed in this chapter in the *2003 NBEA Yearbook: Effective Methods of Teaching Business Education in the 21st Century* (Rader, 2003). *Scope* refers to the many new technologies (such as social networking, Quick Response or QR Codes, smartphone apps, podcasts, blogs, and advanced data-mining techniques used for web-based promotion) that are employed today as marketing tools for both businesses and consumers. *Reach* refers to the vastly larger number of businesses and consumers who now can be effectively targeted with various forms of electronic media and have accepted digital commerce as a way of transacting business. *Intensity* refers to the frequency of contact through the various forms of electronic media and the sheer quantity of information with which these media can communicate to customers. Figure 2 shows the increase in online retail sales based on fourth quarter comparisons from 2009 (actual) and 2010 (actual) through 2015 (forecast), the most recent data available (Indvik, 2011).

These data do not account for the business-to-business online sales volume, which has also grown at similar rates. Because of the broadening diversity of digital technologies used in marketing today and the steadily increasing scope, reach, and intensity of digital promotion, the authors of this chapter have devoted a separate section to the topic of digital promotion in the following section.

DIGITAL PROMOTION

Digital promotion is everywhere—electronic billboards, YouTube, digital coupons, search engines, and smartphone apps. Consumers are using all forms of digital promotion and beginning to expect it. Marketers like digital promotion because it can be updated very quickly and efficiently. Digital promotion is a great way to convey a brand and image to the customer and could also be used to convey or promote our programs to business/marketing students. For example, with smartphone apps, marketers can pull the technology by having customers actively go to mobile websites or scan published QR codes. Marketers can push digital promotion through social media, e-mail campaigns, or automatic text messaging. This section will present an array of digital

Figure 2. U.S. Online Retail Sales Forecast, 2009 to 2015

	2009	2010	2011	2012	2013	2014	2015
% change	11%	13%	12%	10%	10%	8%	8%
% of total retail	8%	8%	9%	10%	10%	11%	11%
% of total retail (excluding grocery)	11%	11%	12%	13%	14%	15%	15%

Source: Indvik (2011).

marketing techniques that are used today to promote goods and services throughout the world. Rest assured that this list of approaches to digital marketing will grow substantially shortly after the publication of this yearbook.

QR codes

QR codes are two-dimensional barcodes readable by a QR scanner, a smartphone, or a device with a camera and Internet connection. A QR contains thousands of bits of information that are similar to a barcode used by retailers. The difference is that a QR code can hold a lot more information. When a QR code is scanned using an iPhone, Android, or other camera-enabled smartphone, it is possible to view video, link to digital content on the web, activate other phone functions such as e-mail and Short Message Service or SMS, or connect the phone to a web browser.

Websites

Having a web presence is not just about having a website but having a link with current customers and an information link for prospective clients. When designing a website, one must decide what the objective is. Objectives might be to establish an online marketing presence to (a) sell goods and services, (b) promote the name and reputation of a company, or (c) offer support services and communication abilities with customers. Marketers need to be assured that visitors will reach their website and, to that end, usually hire in-house information technology personnel or outside companies to help them monitor online traffic to their websites. Additionally, marketers will often use a combination of other traditional and digital media such as e-mail campaigns, QR codes, and other techniques (discussed below) to get people to their websites.

Web advertising is a popular way for businesses to buy advertising space. Traditional advertising is in print, such as newspapers, magazines, or broadcast media, like radio and television. Web advertising is an approach through which advertisers promote their own web pages and/or buy space on other companies' web pages. Very similar to other forms of advertising, the ads are placed on websites that appeal to the target audience for the company's products or services. Web advertisements are usually described by how they appear on web pages. *Banner ads* are placed on a web page, typically in a box, and look similar to a print advertisement. *Floating ads* "float" across or around the screen and will disappear in seconds. *Pop-up ads* "pop up" when you go to a website. *YouTube videos* are an inexpensive way to advertise a company and its product mix.

Search Engines

When a person searches for information about a business or its products, in most cases, a search engine like Google or Yahoo is used. The product or business someone is searching for is typed in and immediately switches to a page of related businesses or products. All businesses that use digital marketing are concerned with *search engine optimization*: the process of improving the visibility of a website. Businesses want to make sure that links with their websites appear as close to the top of returned hits on a search engine listing so that more people will choose to visit their websites.

Social Media

Social media are Internet-based tools such as MySpace, Facebook, LinkedIn, Twitter, and Google+ that allow many users as well as marketers to share information within a specific friends' or customer group. Businesses can take advantage of social media sites to present products, suggestions, and other topics that would be of interest to the customer.

Marketers can choose from several social media options. Business blogs are popular and generally used to share information with customers or potential customers about products or the business. Professional networking sites, such as social media sites like LinkedIn, can be an effective way to promote a business as well as recruit employees to professional audiences. Social networking sites like Facebook provide opportunities for businesses to network with viewers, post target advertising, and post customer testimonials. Twitter is a vehicle to get instant access to your customers by sending short messages to subscribers to a company Twitter account. Location tools such as Foursquare and Yelp provide businesses the opportunity to find new customers looking for specific types of businesses. YouTube is a way for a business to offer videos or pictures of new products and serves to present news-related information. Each form of social media comes with its own rules and regulations. Some media are password protected, and a marketing specialist in the company typically oversees the site. Before launching a social media campaign, it is necessary to research the options and seek professional assistance.

Applications

Applications, more commonly known as "apps," have quickly gone from being a curiosity on smartphones and tablets to a necessity for businesses. Apps are software designed to help people perform an activity. The tricky part is to make money from the application. A business can make money from an app in several ways: charge a one-time fee for the app, charge a monthly subscription fee, or give the app away for free and generate advertising revenue from ads linked to the app. One additional popular new approach to apps is to give a basic model away for free that includes advertising and then offer a paid upgrade that removes the advertising or offers additional features. When a business has an app, it must share the revenue with Apple, Google, Microsoft, or Blackberry because these carriers charge anywhere from 10%–30% of the profits made and take a cut from any advertising on an app. Apps are big business. The sales of apps are expected to generate $58 billion in sales by 2014 (Gartner News, 2012) and the number of downloads are expected to reach $98 billion by the end of 2015 (Berg Insight, 2011). Apple leads the way and expects to make $7.3 billion from its App store in 2011.

E-mail

E-mail can be an effective way to reach customers and clients but it can also be a company's downfall. E-mail has been perceived as the "junk mail" you receive in your mailbox or the unsolicited phone calls you receive from telemarketers. Companies send e-mail directly to customers or clients that have interacted with them in some way—either through an order, asking a question, or responding through a different social media or website. E-mail can be very effective in providing highly targeted information, letting customers know about new products, announcing sales, and updating people about the company. The risk of having important messages intercepted by junk mail software or deleted by recipients is great. Most marketers who use e-mail as a communication media will ensure that their recipients are prescreened for receptivity to the e-mail and offer recipients the ability to easily unsubscribe to future communications if they so desire.

Blogs and Wikis

Blogs and *wikis* are also websites but serve different purposes. A *blog* is an online diary written in journal style. It can be personal or professional. Blogs can also include micro-blogs, such as Twitter, that only allow transmittal and/or posting of a limited number of characters with each action. The benefit of a blog is that the marketer can share information quickly and the blog allows for dialog between the writer and the reader.

A *wiki* is a website that allows others to add, delete, or change content on a particular topic and allows links with other sites. The benefit of wikis is that they are better for archiving information and gathering information from a group of people. The most familiar wiki is Wikipedia, the free online encyclopedia, but there are many others. Wikis that allow unlimited access to people to make postings can lead to problems in the accuracy of the information posted and how to control it.

Although this is a limited description of digital promotion, it is easy to see how rapid advances in digital technology has resulted in rapid growth of new and innovative approaches in advertising. Marketers often combine traditional forms of promotion with digital promotion. For example, a print brochure might be sent to a customer describing the features and benefits of a product. On the brochure, a QR code might be included for the customer to scan into his or her smartphone so they can be taken directly to the product page online. Several days later, the marketer may send a follow-up e-mail to see if the customer received the brochure. The e-mail can have a link to a YouTube product video. The customer may be offered a coupon or other discount to buy the product, or may be inclined to take some other action that would keep them engaged in consideration of the product.

Privacy

In today's laissez faire e-commerce marketing environment, the concern for privacy and protection of intellectual property has grown to paramount importance. The days of free and legally uncontested music downloading and file sharing are over. Students must be made aware of the rules that pertain to personal and business file sharing and downloading as laid out in the Digital Millennium Copyright Act (DMCA) of 1998, which criminalizes the production and dissemination of technology whose primary purpose is to circumvent measures taken to protect copyright. Although the DMCA gave copyright holders specific rights to control the use of copyrighted material and new protections that restrict access or copying, in the eight years since the DMCA's passage, piracy has not decreased (Von Lohmann & Seltzer, 2006). Students should also be taught that the fair-use doctrine allows copyrighted materials to be used without permission for a number of other purposes, including teaching under narrowly defined circumstances (Soronen, 2004).

INSTRUCTIONAL STRATEGIES FOR MARKETING EDUCATION

Instructional strategies may include traditional classroom instruction, a school-based enterprise, computer/technology applications, real and/or simulated occupational experiences or projects in the marketing functions, such as those available through the DECA program of activities. Content standards provide a solid basis for determining unit and lesson objectives. Carefully written performance objectives based on content-specific performance expectations serve as the targeted outcomes for which instructional activities are selected.

Because young people have been exposed to and have responded to marketing efforts from an early age, marketing topics are typically interesting, possibly familiar, and often exciting to them. The marketing education teacher is fortunate that most marketing students are enrolled in the class by choice, as marketing is an elective. In planning lessons, however, the teacher should ensure that he or she has developed an effective *anticipatory set* or *set induction*. These terms refer to what a teacher does at the outset of a lesson to get the students' undivided attention, to arouse their interest, and to establish a conceptual framework for the information that follows (Moore, 1999).

Lectures

A lecture by a marketing teacher or guest speaker from the business community is an excellent way of presenting background information when building a unit frame of reference or when introducing a unit, particularly dealing with abstract concepts with which students have had no empirical knowledge (Moore, 1999). Supplementary tools to support effective lecturing, such as Microsoft PowerPoint, Internet connections, and other presentation media software, are effective in capturing and maintaining student interest. Particular attention should be given to planning the related content into a meaningful framework and presenting it to students in a relatively short period. Following the lecture, a student-centered activity can help reinforce the learning.

Questioning Techniques

To check for understanding, a variety of questioning techniques may be used. These techniques may include focused or broad questions, convergent or divergent questions, probing questions, or redirecting (Moore, 1999). *Focused questions* usually ask only for factual recall or specific correct answers, whereas *broad questions* cannot be answered in simple one- or two-word responses. *Convergent questions* allow for only a few right responses, whereas *divergent questions* allow for many correct responses. *Probing questions* by the teacher should aim at correcting, improving, or expanding a student's initial response and compelling the student to think more thoroughly about their initial responses. *Redirecting* is useful for increasing the amount of student participation because it allows a teacher to draw students into a discussion by asking them to respond to a question in light of a previous response from another student.

The *Socratic method* is another very effective questioning technique that requires considerable practice before successful implementation. This method involves teaching by systematically asking questions and applying inductive reasoning that leads students to a logical conclusion and to discover contradictions. For example, in a discussion about comparative economic theories (e.g., capitalism, socialism, and communism), the teacher may ask questions about how students, acting as a society, would deal with extreme disparities of wealth, control of resources, and factors of production by only a few individuals. Most students grappling with this situation, when asked probing questions about economic inequality in a society, will discover the motivational factors and logical justifications for establishing economic systems based on socialistic and communistic concepts.

Demonstrations

Marketing teachers can use the demonstration method as an effective strategy for modeling presentation techniques, which students can employ effectively in classroom and DECA competitive role-play events. A *demonstration* is a technique of teaching by using materials and displays; the teacher or individual conducting the demonstration generally is the only person directly involved with the materials. However, an effective way to generate more interest is to involve one or more students in replicating or participating in the demonstration.

Many learning situations are appropriate for effective use of the demonstration method. The teacher should model all interpersonal performance outcomes, including selling, prospecting, or handling customer complaints, through demonstrations before requiring students to perform their own demonstrations.

Class Discussions

Class discussions are carefully planned interactions and exchanges of ideas among students directed toward a specific goal (Moore, 1999). Whole-class or group discussions are especially useful with issues that have no single correct answer but are derived from various attitudes, values, and behaviors. Variations of the discussion method include panel discussions and debates.

Acting more as a facilitator than a participant, the instructor should specify before the discussion begins that ground rules for discussions preclude unacceptable expressions of disapproval, domination by one or a few individuals, and include acceptance of everyone's right to express an opinion. Ethical issues such as promotional pricing techniques, warranties, collusion, and employee pilferage are just a few examples of the types of topics to which most students can relate. After learning about basic management theory and labor history, students can discuss philosophical differences between management and labor. Truth in advertising is another area that typically generates a broad range of opinions.

Problem-Based Learning

One of the most realistic and effective methods of teaching in a marketing education classroom is through the use of problem-based learning methods, also referred to as *discovery learning*. In a problem-based learning activity, the teacher presents a well-developed scenario to the students, who may work alone or in groups. For example, after the concepts of U.S. free enterprise, basic marketing principles, consumer behavior, advertising media, and media pricing are taught, a problem-based activity may involve students working in teams of four or five members in the role of an advertising agency. Their responsibilities could include analyzing a product of a fictional company, using a budget provided by the instructor, and formulating a detailed advertising strategy to market the product to consumers. In such a problem-based learning project, learning goals may include process-oriented outcomes such as explaining, describing, generalizing, paraphrasing, brainstorming, discussing, rating, ranking, constructing, designing, budgeting, comparing, contrasting, and justifying—all higher-order thinking skills of analyzing, synthesizing, evaluating, and creating (Anderson & Krathwohl, 2001; Bloom, Engelhart, Furst, Hill, & Krathwohl, 1956). The DECA competitive events provide many similar projects to engage students in actual problem solving.

Field Trips

To facilitate learning during a field trip, the instructor should give a specific assignment and review it with the students before the field trip experience. For example, during a trip to a new regional mall, the instructor could arrange for a presentation by the head of marketing operations for the facility and ask students to write a summary of the presentation. In visiting stores or behind-the-scenes operations, students can be assigned to record specific data about their experiences and write a report. Students could also be required to interview sales people during a field experience.

Simulations and Games

Students often find learning through simulations and games to be fun as well as educational. *Simulation* presents an artificial situation or event that represents real-life situations but removes the risk to individuals involved in the activity (Moore, 1999). Two basic types of simulations include human simulations, such as role-play events, and person-to-computer simulations. DECA provides opportunities for both these types of simulations. DECA competitive events include various role-playing components.

Games can make learning more enjoyable for beginning as well as advanced marketing students. The Monopoly game by Hasbro can serve as a familiar platform for beginning marketing students to "experience" the advantages and disadvantages of trading in different economic systems. Marketing educators can use several variations on the basic free enterprise structure of Monopoly to help students develop an appreciation of the freedoms of U.S. capitalism.

Service Learning

Service learning is a character-building educational strategy that links classroom learning with service to the community. Perhaps the greatest student benefit from participation in service-learning activities is addressing real community needs. Several states have service-learning projects funded by the Corporation for National & Community Service (http://www.cns.gov), which was created under the National Community Service Trust Act in 1993 (Otten, 2000). Service-learning projects for student groups or individual student placements should be designed to enhance the educational goals of the course and to serve the public good.

DECA has long been a student organization that has encouraged service learning and provided opportunities to its members through national, state, and regional projects. The purpose of the Community Service Project is for DECA chapter members to develop a better understanding of the role that civic activities play in society, to make a contribution to a community service or charity, and to learn and apply the principles of marketing management (DECA, 2013). The community service project provides an opportunity for participants to demonstrate the skills necessary to plan, organize, implement, and evaluate a civic-consciousness project.

School-Based Enterprises

School stores and other school-based enterprises have traditionally been a part of high school marketing education programs. Educational benefits include applying and extending knowledge acquired in the classroom, solving problems in the context of real social transactions, and working in teams. These activities provide many students their first work experience; for others, they provide an opportunity to build management, supervision, and leadership skills. Well-developed and well-managed school-based enterprises offer opportunities for students to learn skills and competencies in business management, including retail operations, inventory control, personnel operations, customer service, advertising and promotion, market research, bookkeeping and accounting, and interpersonal skills. Any school-based enterprise, whether housed on campus, off campus, or online, should be an actual learning laboratory and therefore tied directly to the marketing education curriculum.

School-to-Work Experiences

Customarily included as a component of a high school senior–level advanced marketing class, school-to-work experience gives students already grounded in basic marketing concepts an opportunity to apply these concepts as a part-time paid employee in an established business. Marketing field experience may be called by various names such as school-to-work, marketing internship, or job-shadowing experience. All of these opportunities may provide planned learning experiences structured by the advanced marketing instructor or work experience coordinator and the employer to ensure that the student receives exposure to a breadth of business operations in the course of the program, usually a full academic year.

Other Organizations

Toastmasters International is a nonprofit organization dedicated to helping people speak more effectively and has long supported marketing education programs. Local Toastmasters clubs offer programs for their members to conduct a series of planned public speaking meetings in the marketing classroom. At these meetings, students learn and practice the art of public speaking, an essential skill for success in marketing. Toastmasters' programs for schools enable students to have fun while overcoming fear and mastering public speaking. Educators can usually find a local phone listing for a Toastmasters International club in their area or contact the national organization at http://www.toastmasters.org.

Junior Achievement is a not-for-profit organization sponsored by corporate and individual contributors that "seeks to educate and inspire young people to value free enterprise, business, and economics to improve the quality of their lives" (Junior Achievement, n.d.). Junior Achievement volunteers bring to the high school classroom a range of different programs that teach concepts about business and economics in the sports, arts, and entertainment industries; business in our society; international trade; business concepts through math exercises; personal finance goals; interpersonal effectiveness; and problem solving. The volunteers are usually employees of local companies who bring real-life business experience and guidance into the classroom. Marketing educators should contact their local Junior Achievement office and ask to meet with a volunteer to discuss the range of educational programs available from the local organization.

Professional Associations

One of the best ways that a teacher can model leadership to students is by actively participating in professional marketing associations. Marketing associations offer a plethora of opportunities for the educator to learn and share new technologies and teaching strategies. Membership benefits extend beyond the cognitive benefits and include the rewards of serving as an officer in a leadership role and the personal reward of affiliating with like-minded professionals. The marketing educator should not only be an active member in DECA but also participate in his or her state's professional marketing and business education associations.

The **American Marketing Association** (http://www.ama.org) is a network of more than 40,000 marketing practitioners in industry and education. The association's academic division offers resources specifically for marketing educators; members can choose from a variety of special interest groups. The association's Academic Council consists of marketing academicians who are members of the association. The primary purpose of this group is to develop and improve its members' capabilities for instruction in marketing subjects.

The **National Marketing Education Association** is an organization of educators and business people committed to career development of youth and adults in marketing, management, and entrepreneurship (http://www.nationalmea.org).

The **National Business Education Association** is the nation's largest professional organization devoted exclusively to serving individuals and groups engaged in instruction, administration, research, and dissemination of information for and about business (http://www.nbea.org). Chapter 20 discusses this organization in more detail.

These organizations represent only a few of the many professional organizations available to marketing educators. New teachers should network with veteran marketing instructors to obtain their perspective on the benefits of various professional organizations that are active in their geographic area.

SUMMARY

The two-year high school marketing curriculum aims to provide program completers with a foundation of business knowledge grounded in free enterprise economics, a comprehension of general business management practices, and a thorough understanding of marketing functions applied to all levels of the distribution hierarchy. Students completing a marketing program have several options available to them. They are prepared for entry-level employment in many areas of the marketing function, they can build on their foundation skills by pursuing more specialized training in industry-specific marketing areas in community colleges, or they can thoroughly explore marketing theory in a four-year university in preparation for entry-level marketing management positions.

A range of instructional strategies are used in the marketing education classroom, including traditional methods such as lecture, directed questioning, demonstration, and class discussion, as well as student-centered activities such as problem-based learning, hands-on activities such as role plays and computer simulations, project construction, and participation in the DECA student organization. Outside the classroom, the various forms of school-to-work programs, service-learning projects in the community, and school-based enterprises such as school stores are also sound instruction methods.

The marketing educator has a wide range of resources to support his or her efforts in the educational process. By remaining active in discipline-related professional associations, marketing educators can stay abreast of these rapidly changing resources.

REFERENCES

Anderson, L. W., & Krathwohl, D. R. (Eds.). (2001). *A taxonomy for learning, teaching and assessing: A revision of Bloom's taxonomy of educational objectives* (Complete ed.). New York: Longman.

Berg Insight (2011). 98 billion mobile applications will be downloaded in 2015. Retrieved from http://news.cnet.com/8301-13506_3-20117256-17/98-billion-apps-to-be-downloaded-in-2015-study-says

Bloom, B. S., Engelhart, M. D., Furst, E. J., Hill, W. H., & Krathwohl, D. R. (1956). *Taxonomy of educational objectives* (Vol. 1: Cognitive domain). White Plains, NY: Longman Press.

DECA Community Service Project, 2013. (2013). Retrieved from http://www.deca.org/_docs/conferences-competitions/DECA_CSP_Guidelines.pdf

Gartner News (2012). Gartner says worldwide mobile application store revenue forecast to surpass $15 billion in 2011. Retrieved from http://www.gartner.com/it/page.jsp?id=1529214

Indvik, L. (2011). Forrester: E-commerce to reach nearly $300 billion in U.S. by 2015 [STATS], Mashable.com. Retrieved from http://mashable.com/2011/02/28/forrester-e-commerce

Junior Achievement. (n.d.). About JA: Who we are. Retrieved from http://www.ja.org/about/about_who_vision.shtml

MBA Research & Curriculum Center. (2013). *Marketing cluster report.* Columbus, OH: Author. Retrieved from http://www.mbaresearch.org/images/PDFs/MarketingCluster.pdf

Moore, K. D. (1999). *Middle and secondary school instructional methods* (2nd ed.). Boston: McGraw-Hill.

Otten, E. H. (2000). *Character education.* Bloomington, IN: ERIC Clearinghouse for Social Studies/Social Science (ERIC Document Reproduction Service No. ED444932).

Rader, M. (Ed.) (2003). *Effective methods of teaching business education in the 21st century: NBEA 2003 yearbook* (No.41) . Reston, VA: Author.

Soronen, L. E. (2004). Stealing music. *Principal Leadership, 5*(2), 57. Retrieved from http://www.nassp.org/portals/0/content/48612.pdf

Von Lohmann, F., & Seltzer, W. (2006). Death by DMCA. *IEEE Spectrum, 43*(6), 24. Retrieved from http://spectrum.ieee.org/computing/software/death-by-dmca

Work-Based Learning

Allen Truell

Ball State University

Muncie, IN

Quality business and marketing education programs include a work-based-learning (WBL) experience component, related class instruction, and a career and technical education student organization. This chapter provides an overview of the WBL components of business and marketing education programs. Specifically, the chapter presents the history and benefits of WBL programs, introduces several WBL options, outlines the roles of WBL teacher-coordinators, discusses legal issues related to work-based learning, explains the role of advisory committees, and describes related class content and student assessment methods.

HISTORY OF WORK-BASED LEARNING PROGRAMS

The first WBL program in the United States was established at the University of Cincinnati in 1906 (Sovilla, 1998). In that year Herman Schneider, a professor of engineering, proposed a new method of instruction, in which his college students studied both in classes and in paid work settings. Schneider believed that many concepts and skills could not be mastered without real work experience. In the first year, 27 students participated in this program. In the next year, more than 400 students applied to the program. Schneider's program was so successful that other institutions followed by developing their own versions of what became known as the "The Cincinnati Plan." Nearly 30 years after Schneider started his program, it was cited as the single most important development in engineering education (Sovilla, 1998).

By the 50th anniversary of Schneider's founding of this program at the University of Cincinnati, more than 60 colleges and universities had established similar opportunities for their students. The growth of these programs continued, and organizations such as the Thomas Alva Edison Foundation and The Ford Foundation's Fund for the Advancement of Education promoted and researched its value. The number of WBL opportunities continued to grow through the 1980s, when an estimated one-third of all U.S. colleges and universities reported offering similar programs (Sovilla, 1998).

Today, secondary schools also offer a variety of WBL programs. For many of the same reasons that Herman Schneider established a program at the University of Cincinnati in 1906, secondary opportunities combine related class instruction with that of practical WBL experience.

The *National Standards for Business Education* by the National Business Education Association (NBEA, 2007) notes the importance of career development. The standards addressed by the career-development component include career research, career strategy, lifelong learning, school-to-career transition, self-awareness, and workplace expectations. All of these concepts are addressed through WBL programs at the secondary level. Because WBL programs serve as a connection between related class instruction and practical work-based learning, they are an ideal setting for teaching career-development standards.

DESCRIPTION OF WORK-BASED LEARNING PROGRAMS
WBL experiences can be integrated into the education process in a variety of ways. Several approaches for integrating work-based learning into education include cooperative education, internships, job shadowing, and service learning.

Cooperative Education Programs
Cooperative education programs combine related classroom instruction and paid experiences at WBL training sites related to occupational areas of interest to students. WBL teacher-coordinators place students at WBL training sites that best develop the attitudes, knowledge, and skills needed in students' respective occupations and provide related class instruction. Signed training agreements and training plans prepared for each student formalize and guide the cooperative education process. These require that students be provided learning experiences at the WBL training site and WBL teacher-coordinator visits to solicit and provide feedback about their performance (Indiana Department of Education, 2008a; Virginia Department of Education, 2007).

Students earn academic credit based on the completion of required work hours and on their work performance (Indiana Department of Education, 2008a). Because policies for granting credit vary from state to state, WBL teacher-coordinators should contact appropriate state department of education personnel for specific requirements. Many states have their respective cooperative education / WBL manuals posted on education department websites to make them easily accessible to WBL teacher-coordinators. Some business teachers in schools that are too small to support separate business or marketing education cooperative education programs may coordinate interdisciplinary cooperative education programs, often referred to as *diversified cooperative education* programs (Husted, Mason, & Adams, 2003). *Interdisciplinary cooperative education* programs offer a wide variety of cooperative education experiences in business and nonbusiness occupations to enrich WBL opportunities for students (Indiana Department of Education, 2008a).

Internships

Students typically participate in internships at their selected WBL sites after or near the end of their academic programs. During internships, students apply the knowledge obtained in the classroom. Unlike cooperative education programs, internships usually have no concurrent, related class because interns have already mastered their occupations' content. Formal training agreements and training plans provide the framework internship experiences. Internships are most meaningful when learners plan additional study related to the occupational area (Indiana Department of Education, 2008b).

Job-Shadowing Experiences

Job-shadowing experiences are often completed as career exploration activities. Students typically shadow an employee for a few days to learn about a specific job. Because job-shadowing experiences are short-term, typically a day or two, students may explore a number of occupational areas. Students normally job shadow during their late middle school and/or early junior high school years. This introduction to work options in late middle school and/or early junior high school allows students to make better informed decisions when selecting tentative occupational courses to study in high school and to foster work readiness (Minnesota Department of Education, 2003).

Service-Learning Options

In *service learning*, students participate in volunteer work with nonprofit or public organizations. Students are usually placed in organizations that focus on fulfilling a community need. Careful planning and management of service-learning experiences are essential so that students learn from the experience. Students develop both a sense of community and the skills needed for work while participating in service learning. Assessment of learning is achieved through a student report or written description of the service-learning experience submitted to the classroom teacher/service-learning coordinator (Nebraska Department of Education, 2001).

BENEFITS OF WORK-BASED LEARNING PROGRAMS

WBL programs provide many benefits to stakeholders, including businesses, communities, schools, and students. By understanding the benefits of WBL programs, WBL teacher-coordinators can better position their respective programs to serve all stakeholders.

Business Benefits

Businesses and business personnel assist WBL programs by serving on advisory committees, providing student WBL training sites, assisting with work-based standards, and working with student organizations. For this service, businesses receive many benefits via WBL programs. Frequently noted benefits to businesses include reduced employee recruitment and training costs, improved employee retention, significant input in the employee training process, meaningful connections with related class content, and increased employer visibility in the local school system (Indiana Department of Education, 2008a; Office of Superintendent of Public Instruction, 2008; Virginia Department of Education, 2007).

Community Benefits

WBL programs provide numerous benefits to the local community. Advantages to the community include a closer school-community working relationship, a stronger link between school and work, a smoother transition from the classroom to the workplace for all concerned, a supply of well-prepared employees, and a stream of socially responsible citizens (Indiana Department of Education, 2008a; Virginia Department of Education, 2007).

School Benefits

Schools benefit from the positive relationships that are established by program successes in the community and the observation by students in work settings of the relevance of what they are learning. In addition, by placing students in community WBL sites, resources such as curriculum enrichment expertise, modern equipment, and facility variety that are not available at the school site become available for use in student learning (Indiana Department of Education, 2008a; Tennessee Department of Education, 2004; Virginia Department of Education, 2007).

Student Benefits

The benefits of WBL programs to students include fostering of positive safety and work attitudes, opportunity to apply what was learned in the related class at work, promotion of portfolio development, provision of opportunities to receive training in a selected occupation in the community, smoothing of the transition from school to career, development of safe work habits, and application of academic skills at the WBL site (Indiana Department of Education, 2008a; Tennessee Department of Education, 2004).

WORK-BASED-LEARNING TEACHER-COORDINATOR ROLES

WBL teacher-coordinators serve in many roles when completing their daily tasks. Among the roles described in this section are those of WBL teacher-coordinator, documenter, program promoter, instructor, and WBL training-site developer.

Work-based-learning teacher-coordinator

As coordinators, teachers are actively involved in the WBL method of instruction. WBL teacher-coordinator responsibilities include aligning related class curriculum with WBL experiences of students, assessing work performance of students, placing students at WBL training sites, and selecting and developing WBL training sites (Indiana Department of Education, 2008a; Virginia Department of Education, 2007).

Documenter

An essential responsibility of WBL teacher-coordinators is to maintain appropriate program and student documentation. Documentation is necessary to meet various federal, state, and local accountability, follow-up, and reporting requirements. Among the documents that WBL teacher-coordinators need to maintain are training agreements and training plans.

Training agreements establish the formal relationships among students, parents/guardians, and WBL training sponsors and teacher-coordinators (Virginia Department of Education, 2007). Training agreements outline the duties of all parties—parents/guardians, students, and WBL training sponsors and teacher-coordinators. In addition, to protect a student's civil rights, the training agreement should include a nondiscrimination statement (Indiana Department of Education, 2008a). Figure 1 presents a sample training agreement.

WBL teacher-coordinators develop training plans cooperatively with parents/guardians, students, and employers. These plans provide summaries of the competencies students are to develop in their selected occupational areas. Training plans should include specific safety-instruction objectives with instructional responsibility clearly defined and should be reviewed frequently to retain the focus of the students and WBL training sites. A safety checklist should be required for all WBL students. Topics on the safety checklist should be related to the type of job assignment (Indiana Department of Education, 2008a). A sample training plan is shown in Figure 2.

In addition to documenting and maintaining training agreements and training plans, WBL teacher-coordinators manage other documentation including pay stubs, permission and consent forms, proof of age, safety test results, student conference records, student work evaluations, student program applications, WBL training-site visit records, wage and hour forms, and work permits (Indiana Department of Education, 2008a). Because states vary on documentation policies, WBL teacher-coordinators should obtain their state handbook or policy for WBL programs for specific requirements.

Program Promotion

Promoting WBL programs is an essential task of WBL teacher-coordinators. A well-designed promotional program targets businesses, parents, school personnel, and students (Indiana Department of Education, 2008a; Virginia Department of Education, 2007). Each group is important to program success and must be included in any well-organized WBL teacher-coordinator's promotional effort. Without the support of businesses, WBL programs could not exist. Businesses provide service on advisory committees, support career and technical education student organizations, speak in the related class, assist with standards and curriculum, and offer WBL training sites. Promotional activities targeted to this group are very important, as the teacher must outline the value of and secure support for the program.

Figure 1. Sample Training Agreement

WORK-BASED LEARNING TRAINING AGREEMENT

Student name:_____

Home address:_____

Home phone:_____ Training site:_____

Address:_____

Training supervisor:_____ Phone number:_____

Student's career interests:_____

Student agrees to:

- Be regular in attendance, both in school and at work, and unless permission is granted, not to report for work on a day when absent from school.

- Perform the training station and classroom responsibilities to the best of his/her ability.

- Furnish the work-based-learning teacher-coordinator with necessary information about his/her training station and to complete all required reports promptly.

- Abide by the rules and regulations of the training station.

- Consult with the work-based-learning teacher-coordinator about any difficulties arising at the training station or related to the training program.

- Provide his/her own means of transportation to the training station.

- Refrain from terminating employment with the training agency without approval of the work-based-learning teacher-coordinator.

- Relinquish the job if he/she withdraws from school or from the cooperative education program.

Work-based-learning training sponsor agrees to:

- Provide a variety of work experiences for the student-learner that will give the student the opportunity to progress in competency achievement.

- Endeavor to schedule the student-learner for at least an average of 15 hours per week.

- Abide by all federal and state regulations regarding employment.

- Assist in the evaluation of the student-learner.

- Consult with the work-based-learning teacher-coordinator about any difficulties arising at the training station or related to the training station that involve the student-learner.

- Reinforce safety instructions and practices related to the job.

- Cancel this training agreement at any time provided due notice is given to all parties concerned.

- Refrain from discriminating in employment practices on the basis of gender, race, ethnicity, national origin, religion, age, disability, marital status, or veteran status.

(FOR HAZARDOUS OCCUPATIONS ONLY)

- The work of the student-learner in occupations declared hazardous shall be incidental to his/her training, shall be intermittent and for short periods, and shall be under the direct and close supervision of a qualified and experienced person.

- Safety instruction shall be given by the school and correlated by the employer with work-site training.

Parent/Guardian agrees to:

- Encourage the student learner to carry out effectively his/her duties and responsibilities both in the classroom and at work.

- Be responsible for the actions of the student learner where appropriate.

Work-based-learning teacher-coordinator agrees to:

- Provide related classroom instruction, including safety instruction for all occupations.

- Periodically observe the student-learner at work and to visit with the training supervisor in order to aid in the student-learner's development.

- Consult with the training supervisor in the evaluation of the student-learner.

Student:_____ Date:_____ Parent/Guardian:_____ Date:_____

Training Sponsor:_____ Date:_____ Teacher-Coordinator:_____ Date:_____

Figure 2. Sample Training Plan

WORK-BASED-LEARNING TRAINING PLAN

Student: _____   Date of hire: _____

Training sponsor: _____   Supervisor: _____

Degree of responsibility (place next to progress rating)

*Demonstrates in a timely fashion.   **Demonstrates with a positive attitude

Progress rating:

    1. Demonstrates without assistance.

    2. Demonstrates with minimal assistance.

    3. Demonstrates with assistance.

    4. Needs additional training to demonstrate.

    5. Not applicable at this time.

Competencies to be developed	Grading Period			
Specific occupational competencies to be developed at the training site:	1	2	3	4
Specific safety competencies to be developed at the training site:				

Comments/feedback: _____

Student signature: _____   Date: _____

Teacher/coordinator signature: _____   Date: _____

Training sponsor signature: _____   Date: _____

Parent/guardian: _____

WBL teacher-coordinators frequently place displays in local businesses that highlight student achievements, make presentations to civic and professional groups, provide certificates of appreciation to contributors to the program, and work with local media to foster public relations by writing feature stories about students in the program and their WBL training sites, as well as other activities. In addition, at least one employer appreciation event is generally held each year such as a breakfast, luncheon, or banquet where both students and employers receive recognition (Indiana Department of Education, 2008a; Virginia Department of Education, 2007).

Parents play an important role in making WBL programs successful, and promotional activities directed at keeping them informed are essential. One way to promote to this group is through direct mail, in which letters outlining the benefits of WBL programs are sent to parents of students taking one or more courses in an occupational area served by the program. Placing articles in school newsletters and local newspapers explaining the benefits of the program and supplying supporting statistics about program completers and their successes can inform parents of middle school and junior high school students about the program. Holding an open house for parents of prospective students is another option available to WBL teacher-coordinators (Indiana Department of Education, 2008a; Virginia Department of Education, 2007).

Positive relationships with school personnel at all levels, including administrators, counselors, faculty, and staff are important to the success of WBL programs. Administrators, counselors, and faculty are frequently invited to attend social functions such as coffee breaks or WBL training-site employer-appreciation events. Brochures explaining program goals and benefits can be distributed to all administrators, counselors, faculty, and staff. These promotional efforts are essential because many administrators, counselors, faculty, and staff are typically unfamiliar with the many benefits of WBL programs. Annual reports for administrators, counselors, faculty, and staff highlighting program accomplishments are another useful promotional device (Indiana Department of Education, 2008a; Virginia Department of Education, 2007).

Various promotional activities can be targeted toward students. English classes are often used as a setting for presentations, as all students take English. Student interest surveys are another effective promotional strategy. Students who identify a tentative career interest in occupational areas served by the program can be contacted directly. Bulletin board displays can be prepared in various locations in the school and at feeder schools. These promotional materials serve to raise awareness of the program and provide contact information for interested students. Other promotional activities include inviting junior high school students to visit the program, providing interest stories about student successes at work, holding an open house during appropriate times of the year, and submitting articles to the school newspaper (Indiana Department of Education, 2008a; Virginia Department of Education, 2007).

Instructor

WBL teacher-coordinators direct student learning in the related class. They foster learning environments in which students develop the attitudes, knowledge, and skills needed at work. Thus, WBL teacher-coordinators perform a variety of instructional tasks, such as aligning related class instruction with state and national standards, state-approved curriculum, and career and technical education student-organization activities; assisting students in developing their individual occupational competencies; and providing guidance as it relates to career, school, and work issues (Indiana Department of Education, 2008a).

Work-Based-Learning Training-Site Development

The development of WBL training sites includes finding appropriate job placements in the community for students and working closely with employers to achieve program goals. Students participate in WBL programs to develop occupation-specific competencies in a supervised environment. For WBL programs to function effectively, the WBL teacher-coordinator must familiarize all employers with program goals and strategies for achieving these goals. WBL teacher-coordinators provide the linkage between the WBL training site and school. They coordinate the WBL training site with classroom instruction, ensure supervision of students at the WBL training site, evaluate WBL training-site experiences, and prepare reports required by the state and the school district (Indiana Department of Education, 2008a).

WBL training sponsors have a variety of responsibilities, including orienting the student to the job; providing supervision and training for the student; providing the student with a variety of learning experiences that foster maximum learning; evaluating and providing feedback to the student; counseling the student on job-related matters, such as maintaining a good attitude and exhibiting a strong desirable and appropriate work ethic; communicating with the WBL teacher-coordinator regularly about job-related concerns; and following all state and federal laws related to the employment of WBL students (Indiana Department of Education, 2008a).

LEGAL ISSUES RELATED TO WORK-BASED LEARNING PROGRAMS

WBL teacher-coordinators are responsible for assuring that their programs comply with related federal, state, and local laws and regulations. Selected federal laws and regulations include the Americans with Disabilities Act, Title VII of the Civil Rights Act of 1964, Fair Labor Standards Act of 1938, Immigration Reform and Control Act, and Occupational Safety and Health Act.

Americans with Disabilities Act

The Americans with Disabilities Act (ADA) provides workers with protection from discriminatory hiring practices against individuals with disabilities. More specifically, the ADA provides civil rights protection to individuals with disabilities by guaranteeing equal opportunity in public accommodations, employment, transportation, government services, and telecommunications (Equal Employment Opportunity Commission [EEOC], 2001). The ADA was amended in 2008 to make it easier to establish disabilities for those seeking protection under this act (EEOC, n.d.). More information about ADA can be found at the ADA website (http://www.ada.gov/index.html).

Title VII of the Civil Rights Act of 1964

Title VII of the Civil Rights Act protects individuals from discriminatory workplace hiring practices (EEOC, n.d.). A statement indicating that the WBL training site does not discriminate based on race, religion, ethnicity, national origin, age, disability, marital status, or veteran status should be included on all program forms for WBL programs. Information on the provisions of Title VII of the Civil Rights Act of 1964 appears on the EEOC website (http://www.eeoc.gov).

Fair Labor Standards Act of 1938

The Fair Labor Standards Act of 1938 (FLSA) is enforced by the Wage and Hour Division of the U.S. Department of Labor (USDOL). The FLSA protects the educational opportunities and health and safety of youth workers by establishing working-hour standards and prohibiting employment in hazardous occupations. In addition to being well informed about working-hour regulations, WBL teacher-coordinators must be aware of hazardous occupations in which their students cannot be employed. For example, occupations that are generally prohibited for 16- and 17-year-olds include driving a motor vehicle (with certain exceptions for 17-year-olds) and operating power-driven hoisting equipment (USDOL, 2010). WBL teacher-coordinators must be knowledgeable of what their students can and cannot do at WBL training sites. Exceptions to some FLSA standards have been made for youth employed in agricultural occupations (USDOL, 2007).

Immigration Reform and Control Act

The Immigration Reform and Control Act (IRCA) of 1986 requires that only U.S. citizens or aliens lawfully authorized to work be employed in the United States. The documentation requirements necessary to work in the United States are the same for both adult and youth employees. A social security number and two forms of approved identification are needed to complete the required I-9 form, certifying that a person is eligible to work in the United States. The U.S. Department of Justice Immigration and Naturalization Service is responsible for enforcing the IRCA (U.S. Department of Justice, n.d.).

Occupational Safety and Health Act

The Occupational Safety and Health Act (OSHA), signed into law in 1970, was designed to prevent worker injuries and deaths by maintaining safe working environments. As such, WBL teacher-coordinators need to be knowledgeable on OSHA regulations when placing students at WBL training sites. Employers must comply with OSHA safety standards, correct safety standards, and offer workers protective equipment. Workers have a number of rights, including the rights to (a) experience conditions that pose little risk of serious injury, (b) receive information and training about hazards in the workplace and how to prevent injury, and (c) file complaints with OSHA when the workplace is unsafe (Occupational Safety and Health Administration, n.d.). More information about OSHA can be found on its website (http://www.osha.gov/about.html).

State Laws and Regulations

In addition to being knowledgeable of the various federal laws and regulations governing student workers, WBL teacher-coordinators must also be well informed about student work issues in their respective states. A list of state-level contacts and websites containing state youth employment information is available on the USDOL website (http://www.dol.gov/whd/contacts/state_of.htm).

ADVISORY COMMITTEES

Advisory committees are essential to the success of WBL programs. Advisory committees provide occupational standards updates, support for career and technical student organizations, WBL training-site recommendations, assistance or recommendations for marketing the program, and updates on workplace practices and expectations. Members of advisory committees usually represent businesses, current students, parents, program alumni, school professionals such as guidance counselors, and WBL training-site representatives. Advisory committees vary in size, depending on the tasks that need to be completed, but membership is normally 7 to 12 people serving staggered terms. Staggered terms provide the advisory committee with continuity from one school year to the next. Formal meetings are usually held about three times a year, with WBL teacher-coordinators meeting informally with advisory committee members on an individual basis throughout the school year (Husted, Mason, & Adams, 2003; Indiana Department of Education, 2008a).

RELATED CLASSES

Related classes are those in which instruction is tied to the attitudes, knowledge, and skills developed while at a WBL training site. Related class instruction seeks to develop the attitudes, knowledge, and necessary skills for all students, regardless of occupational area. Topics in the related class might include career planning, communication, computation, economics, employment, human relations, and life skills, as well as safety/wellness topics aligned with state and national content standards and performance expectations.

To make the related class most effective, the WBL teacher-coordinators must be well supplied with resources to make learning realistic. WBL teacher-coordinators have the advantage of working closely with WBL training sponsors and other community-based organizations that are rich sources of instructional information, materials, and assistance (Husted, Mason, & Adams, 2003; Indiana Department of Education, 2008a).

To make the connection between work-based learning and related class instruction the most meaningful one, rigorous assessment of student learning must occur. Assessment of related class and WBL experiences are tied to content standards and performance expectations. Examples of formal and informal assessment strategies include using in-class discussion, demonstrations, interviews, presentations, projects, and WBL teacher-coordinator observations. The use of formal and informal assessment strategies assists the WBL teacher-coordinator in providing meaningful feedback to students (Indiana Department of Education, 2008a).

SUMMARY

Valuable work experience can be provided to business and marketing students through WBL opportunities. WBL programs provide numerous benefits to students, businesses, schools, and communities. WBL teacher-coordinators serve many roles, including documenter, program promoter, instructor, and WBL training-site developer.

Essential documents include training agreements and training plans. Employers and schools must comply with various federal and state laws affecting WBL programs. Advisory committees provide assistance with WBL components. The related class provides instruction in essential academic concepts and skills that parallel the WBL component. The class also offers the opportunity to assess the WBL experience effectively.

REFERENCES

Equal Employment Opportunity Commission (EEOC). (2001). *The Americans with Disabilities Act: Questions and answers.* Civil Rights Division, U.S. Department of Justice. Washington, DC: U.S. Government Printing Office.

Equal Employment Opportunity Commission (EEOC). (n.d.). The Americans with Disabilities Act Amendments of 2008. Retrieved from http://www.eeoc.gov/laws/statutes/adaaa_info.cfm

Husted, S. W., Mason, R. E., & Adams, E. (2003). *Cooperative occupational education including internships, apprenticeships, and tech-prep.* Upper Saddle River, NJ: Prentice Hall.

Indiana Department of Education. (2008a, June). *Cooperative education: Guidelines and procedures manual.* Office of Career and Technical Education, Center for School Improvement and Performance. Indianapolis, IN: Author.

Indiana Department of Education. (2008b, November). *Internship manual: Guidelines and procedures for Indiana internship programs.* Office of Career and Technical Education, Center for School Improvement and Performance. Indianapolis, IN: Author.

Minnesota Department of Education. (2003). *Connecting youth to work-based learning: Blueprint for a quality program.* Department of Children, Families, & Learning. Roseville, MN: Author.

National Business Education Association. (2007). *National standards for business education: What America's students should know and be able to do in business* (3rd ed.). Reston: VA: Author.

Nebraska Department of Education. (2001). *Nebraska work-based learning manual: Planning and implementing guides for educators, employers, policymakers, and parents.* Lincoln, NE: Author.

Occupational Safety and Health Administration. (n.d.). At-a-glance: OSHA. Retrieved from http://www.osha.gov/Publications/3439at-a-glance.pdf

Office of Superintendent of Public Instruction, State of Washington. (2008). *Washington state worksite learning manual.* Olympia, WA: Author.

Sovilla, E. S. (1998). Co-op's 90-year odyssey. *ASEE Prism, 7,* 18–23.

Tennessee Department of Education. (2004). *Work-based learning: Policies, procedures, and resources.* Nashville, TN: Author.

U.S. Department of Justice. (n.d.). *The Immigration Reform and Control Act (IRCA) prohibits employment discrimination: What you should know.* Washington, DC: U.S. Government Printing Office.

U.S. Department of Labor. (2007). Child labor requirements in agricultural occupations under the Fair Labor Standards Act. *Child Labor Bulletin 102.* Retrieved from http://www.dol.gov/whd/regs/compliance/childlabor102.pdf

U.S. Department of Labor. (2010). Youth employment provisions for nonagricultural occupations under the Fair Labor Standards Act. *Child Labor Bulletin 101*. Retrieved from http://www.dol.gov/whd/regs/compliance/childlabor101.pdf

Virginia Department of Education. (2007). *Career and technical education cooperative education handbook.* Richmond, VA: Author.

Sponsoring Student Organizations

Kelly Scholl
North Dakota Department of Career and Technical Education
Bismarck, ND

Sandy Braathen
University of North Dakota
Grand Forks, ND

Jan Repnow
Minot State University
Minot, ND

The authors, editor, and publisher acknowledge and express appreciation for the work done by Robert Gryder, Janet M. Gandy, and Donna Green, authors of this chapter in the previous edition. Thank you for your contribution to this yearbook and to business education.

A number of business-related student organizations provide a wealth of opportunities for business students and business teachers at all levels of business and marketing education. This chapter will provide an overview of the background and history of student organizations, the benefits of student organizations, curriculum integration, general and legal responsibilities of the adviser, supervision of fund-raising activities, promotion of the organization, and description of some of the business student organizations.

Educators must note that some business-related student organizations are specifically defined as cocurricular associations that align with career and technical education courses. The U.S. Department of Education specifically recognizes career and technical student organizations (CTSOs), whose support is an allowable use of Carl Perkins funding. Throughout this chapter the term business student organizations (BSOs) refer to all business-related student organizations.

PURPOSE AND HISTORY OF STUDENT ORGANIZATIONS

The overarching purpose of business student organizations has been to provide additional learning opportunities and experiences for students in business- and marketing-related activities.

The start of CTSOs is credited to the Smith-Hughes Act of 1917 when funding was made available to support the organizations as part of career and technical education (then known as vocational education). Throughout the remainder of the 20th century and into the 21st century, CTSOs have continued to be supported in legislation providing funding for career and technical education. Some of this legislation includes the Vocational Education Act of 1963 and its amendments in 1968 and 1976; Public Law 81-740 from 1950; the George Acts of 1929, 1934, and 1936; the George-Barden Act of 1946; and the Carl D. Perkins Act and its revisions in 1984, 1990, 1998, and 2006 (Fiscus, 2008). Many of the business-related CTSOs were not formed until the 1930s and 1940s.

States and local education agencies currently have the responsibility for supporting CTSOs, and the U.S. Department of Education allows use of federal Carl D. Perkins funds to provide leadership and support for CTE student organizations. Additional support for CTSOs comes from the National Association of State Directors of Career Technical Education Consortium. This consortium recognizes the educational philosophies and programs embraced by CTSOs. It specifically lists Business Professionals of America, National DECA, and Future Business Leaders of America–Phi Beta Lambda (FBLA-PBL) among the organizations recognized as an integral part of career and technical education instructional programs (Fiscus, 2008).

BENEFITS OF STUDENT ORGANIZATIONS

Business student organizations provide opportunities for members and advisers in leadership development, professional development, competitive events, and community service. BSOs allow students to apply classroom learning, as well as offer programs and activities to help students reinforce what they learn in the classroom.

According to Browning, Gould, McFarland, Rinehart, and Ross (2002):

The specific benefits of membership in student organizations are numerous. Among those benefits are helping students foster professionalism, develop leadership abilities, and enhance communication skills. Additional benefits include learning to work in groups, setting and achieving goals, meeting deadlines, and networking (p. 51).

Participation in student organizations helps students develop many skills that prepare them for careers in business. Zeliff (2003) believed that "student leaders develop strong time management skills that enable them to juggle their academics, part-time work, student organization activities, and leadership responsibilities" (p. 48). In addition, "student leaders acclimate to the culture of business before it is a career must. They learn to dress professionally, practice business etiquette at social events, exercise appropriate protocol with introductions, and conduct business meetings using parliamentary procedure" (p. 48).

Corinne Alfeld and a group of other researchers (2007) conducted a study supported by the National Research Center for Career and Technical Education. Their study looked at whether and how high school students benefitted from participating in CTSOs. As a result of their literature reviews and discussions with national CTSO directors, the researchers determined that CTSOs provide four kinds of experiences for students who participate in them: leadership development, professional development, competitive events, and community service. They hypothesized that these "four organizational elements of CTSOs produce beneficial effects on students by (a) reinforcing the learning that takes place in the CTE course, and (b) providing an opportunity to put this learning into practice" (Alfeld et al., 2007, p. 3).

Leadership Development

"Within CTSOs there are many opportunities for students' leadership development, including becoming an officer at the local, regional, or national level" (Alfeld et al., 2007, p. 4). Students elect their peers to fill officer roles within the student organization. Officers learn the roles and responsibilities of their office and other techniques for effective chapter management.

Successful chapters ensure that all members share in the responsibilities of meeting chapter goals and objectives by including each of its members in committee and project work. Every student is encouraged to learn, gain self-confidence, and develop as a future leader. Chapter officers and members learn together through experience, conflict management, communication, teamwork, and resource management, as they plan and accomplish their chapter's goals.

Professional Development

It is generally assumed that both the content of CTE programs and the skills and experiences required in the CTSO contribute to professional development (the acquisition of knowledge and competencies that will be useful for future work in the profession) (Alfeld et al., 2007, p. 5).

CTSOs offer students opportunities to recruit members through networking, become involved in running a campaign, and run for an elected office. In addition, students gain an opportunity to develop social awareness, communication abilities, and organizational skills while learning time management and taking pride in their accomplishments. Students have the opportunity to develop business and social networks by attending conference sessions and interacting with presenters and other conference attendees.

Competitive Events

Competitive events serve to test both technical and non-technical job-related competencies. Many of these events integrate academic knowledge into industry-developed problem scenarios. Preparation for the competitive events provides hands-on experience in different trade, technical, and leadership fields; develops job-related technical skills and competencies; offers recognition to participants; and serves to ensure business and industry involvement in career and technical education programs (Alfeld et al., 2007, p. 4).

Student organizations also serve as a catalyst for recognizing student achievement at the individual, team, and chapter levels. As students meet and compete with other business and marketing students, they take pride in realizing that their studies have been relevant and meaningful.

Students develop proper attitudes toward competition through CTSO events. Learning how to compete successfully affords students an advantage in other competitive arenas such as applying for jobs, scholarships, or college admission. The competitive events are designed to align to standards and evaluate the skills learned in the classroom.

Community Service

Alfeld et al. (2007) noted, "most CTSOs engage in some form of community involvement, such as volunteering in community service activities" (p. 5).

Shrader (2006) further noted:

As leaders for career and technical student organizations, advisers understand that the local community provides a unique learning opportunity to enhance classroom instruction. Whether students are preparing for competitive events, developing curricular relationships, or simply learning some of life's valuable lessons, it is essential to make community connections. (p. 56)

Students quickly discover how classroom learning can be applied through community service projects and activities. Service opportunities permit students to become involved in real-world situations that cannot be replicated in a classroom. Students participate in community-service programs, linking them with the course curriculum, and opening opportunities for business and educational partnerships.

CURRICULUM INTEGRATION OF STUDENT ORGANIZATIONS

Integration of business student organization activities with business and marketing classroom instruction increases the effectiveness and relevance of instruction for student members. Integrated activities show correlation with curriculum standards and enrich classroom learning.

Making the Classroom Relevant: Cocurricular versus Extracurricular Approach

Although often categorized as extracurricular activities (outside of the regular curriculum), business student organizations serve a cocurricular purpose (related to the curriculum). It is the decision of local school districts to choose whether business and marketing teachers are able to apply a cocurricular or extracurricular approach to having a BSO. Even though a school district may determine that an extracurricular approach will apply, activities of BSOs should still support curriculum and classroom learning.

Taking a cocurricular approach to BSOs allows teachers/advisers to identify opportunities to involve students in diverse projects that can reach beyond the classroom. These educators develop unique lessons and activities to engage students by providing assignments that are authentic rather than simulated. Teaching such basic concepts as appropriate time management and taking pride in a finished product are more easily accomplished when the students know that their work is being used and has a real-life application.

Program of Work

Organizations are most effective when members plan and implement a realistic program of work. State and local chapters adopt projects and programs within the framework of the national organization with application to the local communities. The adviser must teach students how to plan effectively as they develop an annual program of work.

Smith and Edmunds (2010) suggested that a program of work should include professional, civic and service, social, and financial activities. They noted:

> In general, it is a good rule of thumb to have about half of the group's time spent on professional activities, with the remaining time divided between civic, social and fund-raising functions. Foremost consideration should be given to the educational value the project or activity will have for students. (p. 21)

Figure 1 illustrates a typical program of work, taking into consideration that each of the student organizations described in this chapter operates within its own rules and regulations with organization-specific timeframes and deadlines.

RESPONSIBILITIES OF THE ADVISER

Enthusiasm in student organizations is contagious. In many cases, this enthusiasm originates with the chapter adviser. The enthusiasm, along with a strong commitment to excellence, will make the involvement of chapter adviser a very rewarding assignment.

General Responsibilities

Advisers should model appropriate behavior. Students may listen to what an adviser says but more often will do what they see their adviser do. "Leadership is not about controlling the outcome of a group, but about enhancing the group process...A good leader establishes a clear direction and helps the team steer in that direction" (Neal & Woodbury, 2005, p. 47).

Figure 1. Typical Program of Work

September	<ul><li>Meet with officers before first general meeting.</li><li>Reserve rooms and meeting dates on school calendar.</li><li>Hold first general meeting.</li><li>Recruit and induct new members.</li><li>Collect local, state, and national dues.</li><li>Establish the program of work for year.</li><li>Develop a budget.</li><li>Establish committees and delegate responsibilities.</li><li>Hold parent/guardian information meeting.</li></ul>
October	<ul><li>Submit membership dues and other necessary paperwork to state and national offices.</li><li>Continue member recruitment.</li><li>Hold a fund-raising activity.</li><li>Participate in a school wide activity.</li><li>Review by-laws and make needed changes.</li><li>Attend fall leadership conference.</li></ul>
November	<ul><li>Conduct service activity associated with national and/or state goals.</li><li>Submit news release of chapter activities and awards.</li></ul>
December	<ul><li>Hold a social activity for members.</li><li>Evaluate progress to date and adjust program of work, if necessary.</li></ul>
January	<ul><li>Take members on a field trip.</li><li>Hold a fund-raising activity.</li><li>Begin work on state and national competitive events.</li></ul>
February	<ul><li>Conduct local community service project.</li><li>Promote Career and Technical Education Week.</li><li>Select competitors and officer candidates.</li></ul>
March	<ul><li>Prepare for competitive events.</li><li>Work on campaign materials.</li><li>Submit all necessary paperwork for state conferences and events.</li></ul>
April	<ul><li>Attend State Leadership Conference.</li><li>Host banquet for business partners and members.</li><li>Submit news releases of chapter activities and awards.</li></ul>
May	<ul><li>Elect officers for next school year.</li><li>Hold officer installation and awards banquet.</li><li>Hold a fund-raising activity.</li><li>Conduct officer training.</li><li>Complete all state and national reports.</li><li>Close out all accounting records.</li></ul>
June	<ul><li>Attend National Leadership Conference.</li><li>Make presentation to school board.</li><li>Evaluate year-end effectiveness of program of work.</li><li>Submit news release of chapter activities and awards.</li></ul>
July/August	<ul><li>Maintain student contact and enthusiasm with social gatherings and service work; also use this time to recruit new members.</li></ul>

Note: Adapted from NBEA (2008).

The adviser of a student organization has many responsibilities. This leader should possess knowledge of student organization–related policies/procedures and relay this knowledge to the student. This information can generally be found on the state/national website.

The adviser should help to build an effective officer team. The adviser should "identify characteristics and models of leaders, provide opportunities to demonstrate leadership abilities, and infuse leadership into the curriculum" (Gehrmann, 2011, p. 40). Advisers should aspire to develop a sense of responsibility in their students. Encouraging students to exercise initiative and delegate as much authority and responsibility as they are capable of accepting is valuable. By demonstrating faith in the students, the adviser will develop mutual confidence and respect and increase students' desire to accept greater responsibilities.

Student organization chapters should use parliamentary procedure using *Roberts Rules of Order, Newly Revised* at all chapter meetings. Public speaking activities should be incorporated into chapter activities for professional development. Advisers should infuse accounting and financial literacy activities into the organization's financial practices.

Advisers should encourage and prepare students to participate in competitive events. After reviewing the possible competitive events, the adviser and student should decide which event best suits the individual student. "The opportunity to build confidence through mock competitive events before the leadership conference can be a powerful learning experience" (Haltinner & Stanislawski, 2009, p. 36).

Legal Responsibilities

An important responsibility of the adviser is the compilation of legal and other required documentation. Each school district has requirements regarding student release forms, student dress code, travel and medical releases, insurance information, parent/guardian releases, and emergency contact information. All documentation must be properly signed, duplicated, and distributed. Medical forms and emergency contact information should be taken by the adviser to all functions.

Figure 2 is an example from the North Dakota Department of Career and Technical Education. It combines a member obligation and parent consent release form along with medical information and media permission.

Figure 3 is a code of conduct with dress code form used by North Dakota FBLA. Both the student and parent/guardian are required to sign the form.

Out-of-School Travel Responsibilities

Student members are involved in many activities that may involve out-of-school travel: regional/state/national conferences, competitions, fund-raising events, and

Figure 2. CTSO Consent and Medical Release

Career and Technical Student Organizations Consent and Medical Release
NORTH DAKOTA DEPARTMENT OF CAREER AND TECHNICAL EDUCATION
DECA•FBLA•FCCLA•FFA• SKILLSUSA-VICA •TSA

Participant's Name	Chapter
	Date of Birth
Name of Insurance Company	Policy Number
Known drug allergies	Last tetanus administration received

History of: (check if applicable) □ Heart Condition □ Diabetes □ Asthma □ Epilepsy □ Rheumatic Fever

□ Other (explain)

Medication currently being taken:

Any physical restrictions or other conditions?   □ No   □ Yes (explain)

In the event we are unable to reach you, please list name and telephone number of either nearest relative and/or family physician.

MEMBER OBLIGATION

While attending any Career and Technical Student Organization Function, I will make sure that my attitude, conduct and appearance will be such as to reflect credit to my chapter, school, community and our State Association.

_____
Signature of Participant

PARENT OBLIGATION

I, the parent/guardian of the above-named student do hereby grant permission for him/her to attend activities for the 2012-13 school year. I authorize adult advisors/chaperons to routinely check member's room to insure that students adhere to policies established by the local school district. In the event of an emergency, I do voluntarily authorize medical services to be administered and/or obtained for the above-named person as deemed necessary in medical judgment and in accordance with the above confidential information. I agree to indemnify and hold harmless the Career and Technical Student Organizations and/or assistants and designees for any and all claims, demands, actions, rights of action, or judgments by or on behalf of the above named person arising from or on account of said procedures or treatment rendered in good faith and according to accepted medical standards.

Home Phone:_____
Work Phone: _____   _____
                                    Signature of Parent/Guardian

MEDIA PERMISSION

We authorize Career and Technical Student Organizations to distribute for publication the above member's name and/or picture in any results for the 2012-13 school year (examples would include: printed publications, web pages, radio, etc.). (Note: At no time will addresses or phone numbers be published.)

_____   _____
Signature of Participant   Signature of Parent/Guardian

Subscribed and sworn to me this

_____ day of_____, 20 ____.

Notary Public in and for the State of

Residing in _____

_____
Notary's Signature

Source: Reprinted from North Dakota FBLA-PBL (2011).

service projects. Before each event, the adviser should discuss appropriate behavior and address all expectations with the students. The adviser should always accompany the students on these out-of-school travels.

Each school district has specific rules concerning out-of-school travel. Well in advance of an event, the adviser must communicate certain information to school officials: number of students attending the activity, details of the activity, and any transportation needs. Each school district will also determine the number of chaperones needed

Figure 3. Code of Conduct

North Dakota FBLA Code of Conduct
SFN 53432 (7/02)

Student Name (print/type) School (print/type)

☐ Fall Leadership Conference ☐ State Leadership Conference ☐ National Leadership Conference

Advisers: Have each delegate sign a copy. Signed copies must be turned in at registration.

FBLA-PBL Code of Conduct

FBLA-PBL members have an excellent reputation. Your conduct at every FBLA-PBL function should make a positive contribution to extending that reputation. Listed here are rules of conduct for the FBLA Leadership Conferences. All delegates will be expected to:

1. Behave in a courteous and respectful manner, refraining from language and actions that might bring discredit upon themselves, their school, other delegates, advisers, or upon FBLA-PBL.
2. Obey all local, state, and federal laws.
3. Avoid conduct not conducive to an educational conference. Such conduct includes, but is not limited to, actions disrupting the businesslike atmosphere, association with non-conference individuals, or activities that endanger self or others (running in the General Sessions, standing on chairs, using laser points during workshops, bodysurfing at dances, etc.)
4. Keep their advisers informed of their activities and whereabouts *at all times*. Accidents, injuries, and illnesses must be reported to the local or state advisers immediately.
5. Observe the curfews as listed in the conference program. Local and state advisers as well as security personnel will enforce curfews. Curfew is defined as being in your own assigned room by the designated hour.
6. Avoid alcoholic beverages and controlled or illegal substances of any form. These items must not be used or possessed at any time, or under any circumstances. Use or possession of such substances may subject the delegate to criminal prosecution.
7. Act as guests of the hotel and conference center. Delegates must obey the rules of these facilities. The facilities have the right to ask a delegate or delegates to leave. *Do not throw anything* out of windows or over balconies. Do not run down hallways. Noise should be kept at a reasonable volume, especially in the hotels. Remember there are other guests in the hotels who have rights as well. Trash (this includes pizza boxes, bottles, cans, etc.) must be placed in the proper receptacles and not left on guest room or meeting room floors. Individuals or chapters responsible for damages to any property or furnishings will be responsible for its repair or replacement.

Local advisers are responsible for the supervision of delegate conduct.

Disregarding or Violating the Code of Conduct

Delegates who disregard or violate this code will be subject to disciplinary action, including, but not limited to, forfeiture of privileges to attend further events, confinement to your hotel room, dismissal from the conference, and being sent home at your own expense. Parents and/or guardians will be notified and FBLA-PBL reserves the right to notify law enforcement.

I agree to abide by the Code of Conduct and the Dress Code.

Signed: _____

Parent Signature _____ Date _____

FBLA-PBL Dress Code

FBLA-PBL members and advisers should develop an awareness of the image one's appearance projects. The purpose of the dress code is to uphold the professional image of the association and its members and to prepare students for the business world. Appropriate attire is required for all attendees - advisers, members, and guests - at all general sessions, competitive events, regional meetings, workshops, and other activities unless otherwise stated in the conference program. Conference name badges are part of this dress code and must be worn for all conference functions. For safety reasons, do not wear name badges when touring.

Professional attire acceptable for official FBLA-PBL activities include:

Males
- Business suit with collared shirt and necktie
- Sport coat, dress slacks, collared shirt, and necktie
- Dress slacks, collared shirt, and necktie
- Business suit or sport coat with dress slacks and banded collar shirt
- Sweater or sweater vest, collared shirt with necktie, and dress slacks
- Dress socks and dress shoes
- Dress socks and dress Doc Marten style shoes (Not sandals, boots, or other shoes with heavy soles)

Females
- Business suit with blouse or sweater, sleeveless suit is appropriate
- Business pantsuit with blouse or sweater
- Skirt or dress slacks with buttoned-up blouse or sweater
- Business dress
- Capris or gauchos with coordinating jacket/suit, worn below the knee
- Dress shoes (closed or open toe)

Inappropriate attire, for both men and women, includes:
- Jewelry in visible body piercing, other than ears
- Hair dyed an unnatural color
- Cargo pocket or zip-off pants
- Jean-style khaki pants, capris, or skirt, or other pants or skirts with pockets sewn on the outside
- Denim, canvas, flannel, or chambray fabric
- Backless, see-through, tight-fitting, spaghetti strapped, strapless, or low-cut blouses/tops/dresses
- Dress t-shirts (Sweaters and blouses are only appropriate)
- Clothing that shows any midriff skin
- Skirts shorter than 2 inches above the knee
- T-shirts, spandex, tank tops, or bathing suits
- Blouses that are not buttoned appropriately
- Casual shoes – no sandals, athletic shoes, work shoes, hiking boots, over-the-knee-boots, flip-flop/thong sandals of any kind, or bare feet
- Athletic wear–including sneakers
- Hats
- Bolo ties
- Visible foundation garments

CLARIFICATION: Many women's two-piece suits are currently designed so that they do not require a blouse. Therefore, this will be accepted. In addition, sling-back shoes, open-toe shoes, and sleeveless dresses/suits are accepted.

Source: Reprinted from North Dakota FBLA-PBL (2011).

for the number of students attending the event. Specific guidelines may also be in place for the ratio of male/female students to male/female chaperones. Travel preparation may include requesting a substitute teacher to perform classroom duties, completing a requisition for bus/van transportation and driver, and securing financial resources for the trip from the school district or organization.

Advisers, along with school administration, must have additional guidelines in place for overnight trips. These guidelines and rules should address room assignments, curfews, and room checks. Chaperones should be advised concerning their specific duties.

Advisers should review with students the common courtesies and protocols involving travel (for example: tipping procedures, respecting hotel property and other guests, using proper table manners, elevator etiquette, or checking in luggage at the airport).

Before the event, both students and parents/guardians must be informed of the consequences that will result if a student fails to comply with stated rules. Many advisers plan a meeting with students, parents, chaperones, and school officials to discuss these rules and consequences.

Parent/Guardian Communication

Parents and guardians must be included in communications on all aspects of the student organization through newsletters, meetings/socials, websites, and electronic communication. Parents/guardians should be informed well in advance of activities and trips with dates, travel times, and location.

Many chapters use a social event to kick-off the year. The kick-off provides an opportunity to discuss the chapter's activities as well as securing chaperones and helpers.

SUPERVISION OF FUND-RAISING ACTIVITIES

Fund-raising should accomplish more than just raising money. The fund-raising project should be a team event with financial goals, marketing strategies, analysis of income and expenses generated, and analysis of project strengths and weaknesses.

School Policies and Procedures

Many school districts have specific guidelines for fund-raising activities. The adviser has a responsibility to seek out these guidelines and oversee the activities. School policy generally specifies records that must be completed and distributed appropriately for receipt and disbursement of funds. After reviewing the school district policy on fund-raising activities, the advisor should help the students find a project that can become a tradition in the school and that can *sell itself*, such as selling concessions at sporting events or producing a community calendar.

Community Regulations

The adviser should be aware of community regulations and legalities that may exist when pursuing fundraisers. Some fund-raising events such as raffles may require obtaining permits from the city government. Food handler permits may be required for off-campus food sales. Other regulations such as curfew ordinances may be an issue when student activities occur in the evening. Advisers should contact local government entities, including police and fire departments, and health inspectors in order to assure compliance with all regulations.

Social and Political Standards

The adviser should be aware of community norms and expectations on social and political standards, religious beliefs, and local customs before taking students into the community. All activities should be researched before investing time and energy into a project, to ensure that it will fit the social and political standards of that community.

PROMOTION OF THE ORGANIZATION

The adviser and the students are all responsible for promoting the organization. The many essential efforts of student recruitment, administrative support, and advertising are a constant challenge.

Student Recruitment

Recruitment is an ongoing endeavor. At the beginning of each academic year, activities should be undertaken to solicit new members. Common recruitment tools include classroom presentations, brochures, guest speakers, field trips, personal contacts, and information at career fairs and open houses.

Featuring chapter and individual projects as well as competition winners in student newspapers, local newspapers, or school websites not only publicizes the chapter but also can show the positive elements of belonging to the organization.

Administrative Support

Having a supportive school administration is important to the success of the student organization. The adviser should keep school officials informed about the importance of the organization and updated on the organization's activities. Administrators should be invited to events sponsored by the student organization and should receive chapter newsletters and promotional items.

Another group that is necessary for the success of the student organization is the support staff at the school. Custodians, administrative assistants, bus drivers, and others play a role in making activities run smoothly.

Advertising

A student organization will flourish if the adviser, officers, and all members persistently work to promote its activities. Visibility will enhance the reputation of the chapter in the eyes of community members, administration officials, and any prospective members.

Chapter advisers and students should routinely send news releases and pictures to local and school newspapers, and other community venues for publicity. Chapter websites should be maintained and updated on a regular basis. Radio features or spots on local television stations can be used. Presentations to local school boards, civic organizations, and community groups showcase the activities of the organization. The increasing use of social media, such as Facebook, Twitter, and LinkedIn, is also an excellent way to promote and advertise the activities of the chapter.

BUSINESS STUDENT ORGANIZATIONS

Some student organizations serve students in specific career paths. Several focus specifically on business and marketing students.

Business Professionals of America

Business Professionals of America (BPA) began in 1966 as the Office Education Association. The association changed its name to Business Professionals of America in 1988. BPA currently has members at the middle school, secondary, and postsecondary levels. BPA is a CTSO for students pursuing careers in business management, office administration, information technology, and other related career fields. It has more than 51,000 members in 23 states. "The mission of Business Professionals of America is to contribute to the preparation of a world-class workforce through the advancement of leadership, citizenship, academic, and technological skills" (Business Professionals of America, n.d.). BPA has been selected and approved as an official certifying organization for the President's Volunteer Service Award, created by the White House in 2003. More information about Business Professionals of America is available at its website (http://www.bpa.org).

DECA

DECA has been a student organization for more than 60 years, starting in 1946 as Distributive Education Clubs. In 1948 the organization changed its name to The Distributive Education Clubs of America (DECA). In 1991 the acronym DECA became its official name along with the words "An Association of Marketing Students." DECA currently has a high school and a collegiate division for members, and a professional, and alumni division. DECA has 185,000 high school members and 15,000 collegiate members from all 50 states as well as international members (DECA, n.d.; Louisiana DECA, n.d.).

The focus areas of DECA chapters include career and professional development, community service, and leadership skills (Fiscus, 2008). According to its website, DECA's mission is to prepare "emerging leaders and entrepreneurs for careers in marketing, finance, hospitality and management in high schools and colleges around the globe" (DECA, n.d.).

Future Business Leaders of America–Phi Beta Lambda

FBLA-PBL chartered its first high school chapter in 1942, its first collegiate chapter in 1958, and its professional division (which started as the alumni division) in 1979. In 1994 it added the middle-level division. The four divisions have a combined membership of more than 249,000. FBLA-PBL has chapters in 46 states plus international chapters (Fiscus, 2008).

The goals of FBLA-PBL focus on leadership skills, community service, preparation for careers, and business awareness. Its mission is "to bring business and education together in a positive working relationship through innovative leadership and career development programs" (FBLA-PBL, n.d., web page footer).

Future Educators Association

The Future Educators Association (FEA) has had several names and been sponsored by several organizations since its creation in 1937. The association started as the Future

Teachers of America. In the 1980s the association changed its name to Future Educators of America, and was given a permanent home with Phi Delta Kappa International in 1994. In 2005 the association changed its name to Future Educators Association.

Today, FEA high school and postsecondary members belong to 590 chapters in 46 states plus international chapters. The mission of FEA is to "foster the recruitment and development of prospective educators worldwide through the dissemination of innovative programming and relevant research" (Future Educators Association, n.d.).

Junior Achievement

Junior Achievement was founded in 1919. Initially, it was the Boys' and Girls' Bureau and was formed with the goal of raising funds to provide activities for boys and girls. In 1920 its name changed to the Junior Achievement Bureau. Today, Junior Achievement offers both in-school and after-school programs for elementary, middle, and high school students.

According to the website (Junior Achievement, n.d.-a), "Junior Achievement is the world's largest organization dedicated to educating students in grades K–12 about entrepreneurship, work readiness and financial literacy through experiential, hands-on programs" (para. 1).

Junior Achievement's curriculum is delivered through 167,000 volunteers who include businesspeople, college students, parents, and retirees. They deliver programs to more than four million students a year in 173,000 classrooms and after-school locations. Junior Achievement has more than 120 area offices across the nation in all 50 states (Junior Achievement, n.d.-b).

National Business Education Association Honor Society

The National Business Education Association (NBEA) started the National Business Honor Society in 2008. Any public or independent secondary school offering a business curriculum that reflects NBEA's *National Standards for Business Education* can apply for a local chapter charter. Once a local chapter is chartered, it can invite and induct members. Students eligible for membership are any high school junior or senior that has either completed or is currently enrolled in his/her third business course and has a 3.0/4.0 overall grade point average and a 3.5/4.0 business grade point average.

The purposes of the honor society are to:

- promote and recognize academic achievement in business education at the secondary level;

- foster and recognize leadership skills and character development;

- help members grow ethically and socially by promoting and encouraging an interest in business; and

- encourage member involvement in service learning initiatives. (NBEA, 2012, p. 7)

SUMMARY

Successful student organizations in business education significantly enhance today's challenging business curriculum. The background and history of each business student organization is unique. CTSOs began with the Smith-Hughes Act of 1917, which started the funding to support career and technical education, and support for CTE student organizations comes from state and local education agencies, as well as the U.S. Department of Education. Additional support comes from the National Association of State Directors of Career Technical Education Consortium.

Business student organizations have developed opportunities for students to enhance their knowledge of business subjects, develop their leadership and professional skills, and enhance their employability. These organizations are defined as cocurricular in nature.

Chapter advisers play an integral role in the success of student organizations. The adviser is responsible for helping to build an effective officer team, ensuring the use of parliamentary procedure, preparing students for competitive events, and incorporating leadership and responsibility into projects and community service events. The adviser is also responsible for observance of laws and school policies related to student travel, communication with parents/guardians, and supervision of fund-raising activities and must be knowledgeable of school and community procedures and regulations.

REFERENCES

Alfeld, C., Stone, J. R., III, Aragon, S. R., Hansen, D. M., Zirkle, C., Connors, J., & Woo, H. J. (2007). *Looking inside the black box: The value added by career and technical student organizations to students' high school experience.* St. Paul, MN: National Research Center for Career and Technical Education, University of Minnesota.

Awang, F. (2009, December). Achieving success through student organizations. *Business Education Forum, 64*(2), 45–46.

Browning, E., Gould, C., McFarland, J., Rinehart, M., & Ross, H. (2002, December). Business student organizations: Adviser tips and tricks. *Business Education Forum, 57*(2), 51–52.

Business Professionals of America. (n.d.). About BPA. Retrieved from http://bpa. org /about

DECA. (n.d.). About us. Retrieved from http://deca.org/about

Fiscus, L. (Ed.). (2008). *Career and technical student organizations: A reference guide* (3rd ed.). Alexandria, VA: Association for Career and Technical Education. Retrieved from http://www.tsaweb.org/sites/default/files/CTSO-Guide.pdf

Future Business Leaders of America–Phi Beta Lambda. (2011). Competitive events. *Future Business Leaders of America chapter management handbook.* Reston, VA: Author.

Future Business Leaders of America–Phi Beta Lambda. (n.d.). About FBLA-PBL. Retrieved from http://www.fbla-pbl.org/web/page/614/sectionid/614/pagelevel/1/main_interior.asp

Future Educators Association. (n.d.). Mission, vision, and tagline. Retrieved from http://www.futureeducators.org/about/mission.htm

Gehrmann, T. (2011, December). Expect excellence: Developing student leaders and mentors. *Business Education Forum, 66*(2), 40–48.

Haltinner, U., & Stanislawski, D. (2009, April). Preparing teacher candidates to effectively engage CTSOs in marketing education. *Business Education Forum 63*(4), 35–38.

Junior Achievement. (n.d.-a). About JA. Retrieved from http://www.ja.org/about/about.shtml

Junior Achievement. (n.d.-b). Newsroom: Fact sheet. Retrieved from http://www.ja.org/about/about_news_fact.shtml

Louisiana DECA. (n.d.). The history of national DECA. Retrieved from http://www.louisianadeca.com/id44.html

National Business Education Association. (2008). *Effective methods of teaching business education. NBEA 2008 yearbook* (No. 46). Reston, VA: Author.

National Business Education Association. (2012). *National Business Honor Society chapter start-up kit.* Reston, VA: Author. Retrieved from http://www.nbea.org/newsite/about/documents/NBHSStart-upKit_2012.pdf

Neal, W., & Woodbury, D. (2005, December). Excelling as the adviser of a student organization: Developing the leadership skills of students. *Business Education Forum 60*(2), 47–51.

North Dakota Future Business Leaders of America. (2011). *North Dakota FBLA chapter handbook.* Bismarck, ND: Author.

Shrader, K. (2006, December). Making community connections. *Business Education Forum, 61*(2), 56–58.

Smith, C. L., & Edmunds, N. A., (2010). *Career and technical educator's survival guide* (Rev. Ed.). Alexandria, VA: Association for Career and Technical Education.

Zeliff, N. (2003, December). Student leadership opportunities. *Business Education Forum, 58*(2), 48–50.

Investing in Professional Growth

Connie M. Forde
Mississippi State University
Mississippi State, MS

Kellie A. Shumack
Auburn University at Montgomery
Montgomery, AL

The authors, editor, and publisher acknowledge and express appreciation for the work done by James Calvert Scott, author of this chapter in the previous edition. Thank you for your contribution to this yearbook and to business education.

It has been said that "effectiveness in teaching is a journey, rather than a destination" (Killion & Hirsh, 2011, p. 12). Teachers never find themselves at the end of learning. Throughout the school year, in many ways, teachers focus on students: on their academic achievement and building them up and preparing them as individuals. There is a time, however, for a teacher to focus on professional growth. Without this investment, teachers are in danger of lessening their impact on what their students learn; missing out on innovative teaching methods that inspire, motivate, and empower students to achieve; and becoming outdated in their knowledge of the ever-changing technology.

WHY PROFESSIONAL DEVELOPMENT?

Research suggests that teachers who engage in concentrated, content-rich, and shared learning opportunities improve their own teaching and student learning in their classrooms (Darling-Hammond, 2009). The teacher who invests in professional growth is investing in student learning, innovative teaching methods, up-to-date technology, meeting state and district requirements, and potentially a greater salary.

Impact Student Learning

Research shows that that there is a direct link from teacher skill and content knowledge to student achievement (Berry, Johnson, & Montgomery, 2005; Buczynski

& Hansen, 2010; Hirsh, 2011). When teachers improve their practices, students have a higher probability of learning. Essentially, professional development opportunities shape, support, and provide the tools necessary for continual improvement of teaching practices, and "if teachers don't shape and own changes in practice, then frankly, they're not going to happen" (Hirsh, 2011, p. 19).

A teacher's self-assessment of his or her own ability to support student learning, known as teacher efficacy, is an important factor in professional development. Teachers with high efficacy levels are more likely to persist when the inevitable teaching challenges emerge (Bruce, Esmonde, Ross, Dookie, & Beatty, 2010).

Learn Innovative Teaching Methods

Investing in professional growth means investing in new ideas to help students understand the content of courses. It is an investment in being adaptable and progressing in teaching methods that engage and motivate learners.

Being innovative means knowing one's audience and understanding what motivates and engages each individual. Project-based learning, authentic activities, simulations, hands-on activities, open discussion, role playing, team activities, inclusive practices, and game-based learning are a few of the innovative methods and practices that may engage individuals of all generations and serve as a way to differentiate instruction to accommodate all learners (Moore, 2011).

Keep Abreast of Changing Technology

Between 2005 and 2009, the number of American 10- to 11-year-olds with cell phones grew almost 81% (Frommer & Angelova, 2010). Media tablets (such as the iPad) and smartphones bring the power of the laptop to the classroom with the added advantage of increased mobility. According to comScore (2012), it took seven years to reach the 40 million mark of individuals with a smartphone. It took only two years to reach that mark with media tablets. Teachers must change along with the technology, and that is possible through professional growth. Growing professionally means teachers meet the challenges of a tech savvy generation who also must be prepared to adjust to the technological changes of the workplace.

Meet School District Requirements

State graduation exams, and other tests that foster accountability, pressure teachers to use class time efficiently and effectively so that students reap everything possible academically and take tests as well-prepared students. District and state programs change and adapt to society's changes; therefore, it is natural to expect changes in programs, software, and regulations. Research shows that focusing professional development on training teachers to use state assessment tools targeting the specific needs of students is a key to improved instruction (Schmoker, 2002; Holloway, 2003).

Great teaching stems from a distinct vision for the classroom that is converted into a framework that specifies thorough outcomes for both student and teacher performance (Killion & Hirsh, 2011). The vision, the framework, and the rigorous outcomes are imperative, but without practical action in the classroom, they are just words. Teachers need professional learning to ensure theory and practice meet and both teacher and students improve performance.

Benefit from Increase in Salary Increments

Professional growth may involve certifications, recertifications, continuing education units, and additional degrees that could lead to an increased salary. Although personal initiative and the simple desire to be a better teacher motivates many to invest time and personal money into professional growth, some teachers also seek another degree to earn a pay increase.

Justifying an investment in professional growth is about change and being a lifelong learner. Obsolescence is not an option for the teacher who wishes to engage and excite each generation of students and prepare them for a future in an evolving society. Because learning kindles the desire to learn even more, the path of professional growth will most likely lead to diverse and exciting opportunities for continued professional development.

OPPORTUNITIES FOR PROFESSIONAL DEVELOPMENT

Establishing professional development plans is essential for the business educator, and the business teacher recognizes that professional development is not an option; it is essential. The next section of this chapter explores a number of opportunities for professional development.

College/University Coursework

Enrolling in college or university courses—either to fulfill requirements for renewal of the teaching license, add on other teaching certifications or endorsements, or pursue an advanced degree—is a common practice in professional development by business educators.

Renew license and add endorsements/certifications. In the past, teacher licensure or certification may have been granted for life, but now a business educator must provide continuing evidence of having updated knowledge, skills, and dispositions through additional education, training, and/or work experience to remain licensed or certified. Often completing credit hours at a college or university are choices for updating the license.

Advanced degrees. Enrolling in graduate courses and pursuing graduate degrees provide opportunities for academic and professional advancement, including professional development, better job opportunities, and sometimes, increased compensation. The graduate study may focus on increased understanding of business subject matter and/or improved business and general teaching methodology. Additionally, the courses may be delivered through traditional and/or electronic delivery modes of instruction (Scott, 2008).

In-Service and Individual Professional Development

Schools or school districts provide teachers some professional growth opportunities; each teacher should also individually seek out other professional development learning opportunities.

In-service development provided by schools. Schools across the nation provide professional growth opportunities for teachers, which are referred to in this chapter as in-service training. States and districts build in-service days into the school calendar and then set an agenda for training. Generally, school and/or school districts are required to submit local education agency plans for the comprehensive professional development training of all system employees to satisfy federal requirements for money spent on teacher training. In-service hours may be used to satisfy teacher recertification requirements, with more individual hours required depending on the state.

Individual professional development selected by teachers. Professional development chosen by an individual teacher may be tied to an annual evaluation plan. In some states, teachers are evaluated and areas for growth are identified so that teachers can formulate a plan to meet those identified goals.

Work Experience and Developmental Leave

Business teachers in secondary and higher education may seek to grow professionally through internships/externships with local businesses, working toward and obtaining industry and professional certifications, or taking sabbaticals to study an area of interest or need.

Internships/externships. Paid and nonpaid internships or externships exist in local businesses and are a valuable way to keep skills and knowledge current. These opportunities also assist in developing relationships with area businesses. These relationships can provide a network of professionals to provide guest speakers, serve as members of the business education advisory board, or contribute funds for special projects. Internships may also result in excellent locations for field trips or student internships in the future. Internships assist in developing authenticity that is important in academic activities because students want to make connections with the real world and see value in the hard work they invest in projects.

Industry and professional certifications. Aside from being certified to teach by a state department of education and maintaining that certificate, industry certifications may also increase the overall quality of instruction within certain content areas. Nationally, business education teachers teach a variety of subjects and may in many cases be training students to pursue industry certifications, such as the A+ certification. If teaching courses that involve certifications, teachers may wish to pursue the same certifications that their students are pursuing.

National board certification is a professional certification unique to the field of education. In some states or school systems, teachers gain monetarily through incentives or salary increases when the certification is granted (National Board for Professional Teaching Standards, 2012).

Sabbaticals. An individual chooses a sabbatical with a specific purpose in mind. For example, they may be pursuing an industry certification, writing a textbook, studying what other universities are doing in an academic area, studying abroad, doing post-doctoral work, completing research, or accepting a Fulbright Scholarship to teach in another country.

Professional Organizations

The Policies Commission on Business and Economic Education (2006) acknowledged the value and impact of business educators' active involvement in professional associations, as well as the impact of the business education profession, students, employers of educators, and business and community partners. For the individual member, the benefits are numerous and varied among professional associations; however, the primary goals of membership benefits are assisting members in staying up to date in the field, forming strong networks, and developing leadership and professional skills, all benefits related to professional development (Shumack & Forde, 2012). A business educator can make effective use of the benefits of membership in a wide variety of business education–related professional associations to foster lifelong professional development.

Six organizations that contribute extensively to lifelong professional development are briefly highlighted below. Become familiar with these organizations and consider the benefits for your own professional development.

National Business Education Association. The National Business Education Association (NBEA) is the largest U.S. organization devoted to those interested in education for and about business. The benefits of NBEA membership include the quarterly journal *Business Education Forum*, the quarterly newsletter *Keying In*, and the NBEA yearbook, which addresses a different educational theme each year. NBEA offers regional association membership, annual national and regional conferences, webinars on professional development topics, NBEAConnect, a professional learning network with more than 15 groups that represent a variety of interests, social networks (Facebook and Twitter), free and low-cost professional liability insurance, a group insurance plan, a professional awards program, linkage with the International Society for Business Education, legislative advocacy, and a credit card program. For additional information, visit NBEA's website (http://www.nbea.org) (NBEA, 2012).

In addition to the National Business Education Association, teachers may join their regional business education association and state business education associations. Regional and state associations offer professional development through conferences in local areas, publications, networking, and the opportunity to serve business education at the local and regional level.

National Association for Business Teacher Education. The National Association for Business Teacher Education (NABTE) is an institutional arm of NBEA, providing nationwide leadership and service to business teacher education institutions and business teacher educators in an effort to improve undergraduate and graduate business teacher education. NABTE members are colleges and universities that have state-approved business teacher education programs, as well as individuals interested in business teacher education (NABTE, 2012).

Membership benefits include its regular and special publications, the *Business Teacher Education Journal* (formerly *NABTE Review*) and *Business Teacher Education: Curriculum Guide and Program Standards*, a curriculum guide and program standards revised systematically to maintain high standards for business teacher certification. Additional benefits of NABTE include an annual research conference to stimulate research in business education, an annual business meeting held with the annual conference of NBEA, a model for alternative licensure/certification, and an award of merit program for outstanding undergraduate business teacher education graduates. For additional information, visit the NABTE website (http://www.nabte.org) (NABTE, 2012).

International Society for Business Education. The United States Chapter of the International Society for Business Education (ISBE or Societé Internationale pour l'Enseignement Commercial known overseas as SIEC-ISBE) is the international arm and linkage for NBEA to international aspects of business education. U.S. ISBE members are NBEA members who are particularly interested in promoting and strengthening business education around the world.

Membership benefits from SIEC-ISBE include the refereed *International Journal for Business Education* and other special publications throughout the year. SIEC-ISBE offers an annual international conference, annual U.S. chapter meeting, networking possibilities with business educators and trainers domestically and internationally, scholarships to a senior or graduate student attending a college or university seeking certification to teach business courses or a teacher of business education with 10 or fewer years of teaching, and various opportunities for the international exchange of business education information. For additional information, visit ISBE's website (http://www.siecisbe.org) (SIEC-ISBE, 2012).

The Association for Research in Business Education–Delta Pi Epsilon. The Association for Research in Business Education (ARBE)–Delta Pi Epsilon (DPE) formerly Delta Pi Epsilon (DPE), is a national honorary professional graduate society for professionals who are devoted to the improvement of business teaching through its members' engagement in scholarship, leadership, and service and is the research arm for NBEA. Members include business educators, administrators, researchers, and businesspeople, all of whom share a common interest in business education research. As of January 1, 2012, ARBE-DPE became an affiliate of NBEA and currently functions at the national level only (ARBE-DPE, 2012).

Membership benefits include ARBE-DPE's regular and special publications, including *The Delta Pi Epsilon Journal* and *Journal of Applied Research for Business Instruction*. DPE also sponsors an annual national research conference, conference research awards, national graduate and independent research awards, research grants funded by the Delta Pi Epsilon Research Foundation, Inc., and the DPE listserv. To add one's e-mail address to the listserv, send a message to dpe@ipa.net listing the e-mail address(es) to be added. For additional information, visit ARBE-DPE's website (http://www.dpe.org) (ARBE-DPE, 2012).

Pi Omega Pi. Pi Omega Pi is a business teacher education honor society whose purpose is to promote scholarship and service in business education. Its outstanding members include undergraduate and graduate business education majors ranking in the top 35% of their classes and people who meet the alumni, faculty, associate, and honorary membership requirements. Membership benefits include the newsletter *Here and There* (published quarterly), chapter meetings, an annual scholarship to a member during the student teaching semester, a biennial national convention held in conjunction with the annual conference of NBEA, annual chapter award competition (local, community, national service projects, and publication project), and a social network via Facebook. For additional information, visit Pi Omega Pi's website (http://piomega-pi.org) (Pi Omega Pi, 2012).

Association for Career and Technical Education. The Association for Career and Technical Education (ACTE), known as the American Vocational Association between 1926 and 1998, is a U.S. association that focuses on education and prepares people for careers within a competitive workforce (Hosler, 2003). ACTE members include students, educators, administrators, counselors, and local and state employees who represent 11 board divisions and 2 emerging divisions, including business education and marketing education, and five geographic regions (ACTE, 2012).

Membership benefits include its regular and special publications, *Techniques* and *Career Tech Update*, an annual convention and related trade show, a national policy seminar, regional workshops, webinars, online forums and social networks, an awards program, professional resources, a legislative action center, professional liability insurance, and a life insurance plan. For additional information, visit ACTE's website (http://www.acteonline.org) (ACTE, 2012).

Professional Literature
The professional literature forms the foundation of the profession by providing content information, policy statements, trends and issues, support for changes in the discipline, and current methodology and pedagogy in the field. It is important to note that professional associations play an important role in ensuring that the most up-to-date topics, issues, and research are investigated in their timely publications. Having immediate access to this vital information is a major reason to join key professional associations and maintain continuous memberships.

A business teacher who regularly reads business, business education, and general education literature acquires needed knowledge for staying current in the profession and fulfilling his or her own duties and responsibilities as an astute business educator. Real Simple Syndication (RSS) feeds, explained in the next section, can play a role in managing the professional literature read by business educators. It is the business educator's responsibility to identify the specific literature that should be read regularly.

In addition to reading the professional business education literature, a business teacher is also a valuable contributor to it. Valuable teaching strategies and methodologies can and should be shared with other business educators (Scott, 2008). Many publication avenues are available to business educators, beginning with school department newsletters and state and regional business education association newsletters.

Professional associations publish their calls for papers and manuscript requirements on their websites and in their professional publications. Scott (2008) wrote, "In the process of authoring a publication, a business educator refines thinking, research, writing, and teaching skills, contributing to professional development" (p. 281).

Personal Learning Networks

Personal learning networks (PLNs) are one way that teachers create unique opportunities to learn in order to grow professionally and contribute to the community of fellow teachers. PLNs provide a support structure for informal learning through interpersonal connections and resources. These connections may be face-to-face connections at meetings and conferences, whereas others may be formed in online communities such as *Classroom 2.0* (http://www.classroom20.com) and *The Educator's PLN* (http://edupln.ning.com) (Trust, 2012).

Peer relationships. Collaboration with peers takes place informally through periodic conversations about instruction and may include formal opportunities to collaborate through common planning or professional development activities. In a study completed by Lohman and Woolf (2001), teachers reported that knowledge exchange was the way knowledge and skills were developed, as they shared with other teachers about experiences and classroom application. Peer relationships are also notably important because they have the ability to strengthen morale, encourage the novice teacher, foster the sharing of information about new technologies or teaching strategies, and play a distinct part in success in the classroom (Carr, 2005; Scott, 2003).

Professional conferences. Professional conferences are where business educators form strong bonds with colleagues for a lifetime of collaboration. These relationships, both face-to-face and digital, strengthen morale, encourage the new teacher, and make meaningful collaboration a tool for new ideas and improved instruction in the classroom. State, regional, and national associations host annual conferences as an important forum for creating personal learning networks.

Web-based opportunities. The Policies Commission for Business and Economic Education (2010) held that virtual professional development is a necessity as a "component of ongoing, sustainable professional development" (p. 1). websites, nings, blogs, webinars, wikis, social media (Twitter, Facebook, etc.), virtual worlds (such as Second Life), and others provide for social interaction electronically. As teachers become learners in their PLN, they reciprocate by becoming "amplifiers" (Warlick, 2009, p. 15) by increasing their knowledge, connecting what they learned in the classroom, adding value from experience, and then sharing the information with others.

The following table provides links for professional and social networks, webinars, and podcasts for use in a PLN or as just-in-time training for business educators:

Table 1. Links for Business Educators

NBEA Ning	http://nbeaconnect.ning.com
NBEA Facebook page	http://www.facebook.com/nbeapage
ACTE Facebook page	http://www.facebook.com/actecareertech
Virtual Business Training	http://www.businessexpertwebinars.com
ISBE	http://www.iste.org/store/podcasts.aspx
Twitter with NBEA	https://twitter.com/#!/NBEA
The Educator's PLN	http://edupln.ning.com
Classroom 2.0	http://www.classroom20.com
Edmodo	http://www.edmodo.com/community/vocational-studies

The use of technology means the teacher's learning can be "both more individualized...and more collective" (Hirsh, 2011, p. 22). Teachers are in information overload as everyone's ideas can have a voice on the Internet. There are ways, however, to use technology to harness all this information and provide individualized learning to meet our specific needs. PLNs involve harnessing that information in a process called the "domestication of the information landscape" (Warlick, 2009, p. 13). Blog aggregators, such as Google Reader, tame the information overload coming from blogs.

Podcasts. Portable audio or video files that can be syndicated are called podcasts and are a helpful PLN tool due to the convenience of portability.

Blogs. Vast amounts of information about technology, teaching methods, business practices, changes in standards or regulations, available teaching tools, and resources can be aggregated using RSS feeds, which pull simplified information off a web page, such as text and images, but not the look or formatting. Google Reader is a popular web-based aggregator that uses RSS feeds to funnel information from chosen blogs and websites into one site controlled by the user.

To help build and manage a PLN using an aggregator like Google Reader, the teacher may consider setting the home page to Google Reader. Keep information manageable by only subscribing to two or three blogs.

Social bookmarking. Social bookmarking is another helpful PLN tool, primarily because users can search within a limited area. Social bookmarking sites let users share the links that interest them, so when a user searches a site, only the links that have been bookmarked about that topic result. Several popular social bookmarking sites include delicious.com and diigo.com.

Personal Development

Personal development or developing personally is also a valid way to grow professionally. Teachers who travel, read, are involved with civic or religious organizations, and find balance through hobbies directly and indirectly bring those experiences into the classroom.

Travel. Travel, specifically outside the United States, is broadening. The business practices and economy of the world take on different meaning because they have been experienced, and communication is valued differently because of the cultures and languages encountered.

Reading. Reading for pleasure not only improves reading ability but also increases general knowledge and improves understanding of different cultures, human nature, and how people make decisions (Clark & Rumbold, 2006). Teachers who place a high value on reading and also read for pleasure are more likely to employ instructional strategies that encourage students to read—such as allowing class time for silent reading and discussions or sharing personal insights or recommending books to students (McKool & Gespass, 2009). Reading helps people make sense of the world around them, and teachers who read for pleasure influence students to do the same.

Involvement in civic and religious organizations. Civic and religious organizations provide opportunities for teachers to give to the community, meet people outside of the school setting, serve in leadership positions, and plug into a cross-section of society that will give the teacher a better understanding of the diverse population that is served in the public school setting.

Hobbies: finding balance. Maintaining a balanced lifestyle helps teachers avoid burnout and sustain energy and excitement. Hobbies help develop moral and ethical values (Werner, 2002), keep people healthy, provide a sense of accomplishment (watching television is the exception), and provide "relief from the stress of acting under high pressure" (p. 210).

Teachers continue to learn by selecting one or more of the excellent professional growth activities described in this section.

THE PROFESSIONAL DEVELOPMENT PLAN

Setting short-term, intermediate, and long-term goals are essential activities required in plotting a successful career in business education. The profession needs enthusiastic and visionary leaders to take the profession into the future. A business educator's willingness to learn, stay up to date, and serve his/her profession is essential. Acquiring these skills requires a plan for professional development that leads to leadership opportunities. The professional development plan shown below is offered as one example of a professional development plan. Teachers are invited to revise the model to fit their needs and opportunities. Review the goals each year to determine progress and revise the long-term goals.

Sample Professional Development Plan

Short-term goals (years 1–2)

- Identify a mentor business education teacher and meet monthly.
- Join NBEA, read the publications, and attend at least one webinar per semester.
- Join the state business education association and attend the state conference to network.
- Set up your PLN and subscribe to two or three business or technology blogs.
- Read journals, newspapers, online publications, etc.
- Participate in school professional development activities and committees.
- Plan the activities required to renew your license and set deadlines for completion.

Intermediate-term goals (years 3–5)

- Continue participating in the items listed in the short-term list.
- Volunteer to serve on a committee in the state business education association and invite other business educators in your school and area to attend the convention with you.
- Write a presentation proposal and present it at your state business education association.
- Write an article about strategies you have used in the classroom to share with your peers.
- Attend the regional and/or national business education association conventions.
- Accept the role of committee chair in your school.
- Join other professional associations that provide needed benefits.
- Enroll in a master's degree to add credentials to the curriculum vitae you are building.
- Complete an internship/externship, industry or professional certification, or sabbatical.

Long-term goals (years 6–10)

- Continue participating in the items listed in the short-term and intermediate lists.
- Serve as an officer of your state/regional/national association.
- Write a presentation proposal and present at the convention or webinar.
- Write articles for national publications in the business education field.
- Assume leadership in your school as department head or other administrative role.
- Assume leadership in your community.
- Pursue advanced education to advance in your career.
- Mentor a business education teacher.
- Consider a sabbatical to focus on an area of development.

Setting professional goals and developing short-term, intermediate, and long-term goals is important, as you begin the rewarding career of a business educator. Begin today with a plan that fits you and your ambitions.

SUMMARY

Engaging in lifelong professional development is essential for the business educator. Professional development opportunities available to business educators include the following: (a) college coursework that leads to advanced degrees, license renewal, or additional certifications, (b) in-service and individual professional development, (c) work experience and developmental leave, (d) professional organizations, (e) professional literature, (f) personal learning networks, and (g) personal development. Business educators must plan for professional development by becoming aware of the many opportunities and developing short-term, intermediate, and long-term plans with the direction of a successful mentor.

REFERENCES

Association for Career and Technical Education. (2012). Association for Career and Technical Education. Retrieved from http://www.acteonline.org

Association for Research in Business Education–Delta Pi Epsilon. (2012). Delta Pi Epsilon. Retrieved from http://www.dpe.org

Berry, B., Johnson, D., & Montgomery, D. (2005). The power of teacher leadership. *Educational Leadership, 62*(5), 56–60.

Bruce, C. D., Esmonde, I., Ross, J., Dookie, L., & Beatty, R. (2010). The effects of sustained classroom-embedded teacher professional learning on teacher efficacy and related student achievement. *Teaching and Teacher Education, 26*, 1598–1608. doi:10.1016/j.tate.2010.06.011

Buczynski, S., & Hansen, C. B. (2010). Impact of professional development on teacher practice: Uncovering connections. *Teacher and Teacher Education, 26*, 599–607.

Carr, J. F. (2005). Peers add a potent perspective: Vermont teachers combine forces to create standards-based units. *Journal of Staff Development, 26*(1), 48–52.

Clark, C., & Rumbold, K. (2006). *Reading for pleasure: A research overview.* London, England: National Literacy Trust.

comScore (Producer). (2012). *U.S. digital future in focus* [Video]. Available from http://bcove.me/c0zaf7eh

Darling-Hammond, L. (2009). Teacher learning: What matters? *Educational Leadership, 66*(5), 46.

Frommer, D., & Angelova, K. (2010, January). Chart of the day: One third of U.S. 11-year-olds have cellphones. *Business Insider.* Retrieved from http://www.businessinsider.com/chart-of-the-day-us-children-who-own-mobile-phones-2010-1

Hirsh, S. (2011). What makes a good teacher? The Bill & Melinda Gates Foundation digs for answers with its Measures of Effective Teaching project. *Journal of Staff Development, 32*(6), 18–22.

Holloway, J. H. (2003). Linking professional development to student learning. *Educational Leadership, 62*(2), 85–87.

Hosler, M. M. (2003). The foundations of business education. In M. H. Rader (Ed.), *Effective methods of teaching business education in the 21st century: NBEA 2003 yearbook* (No. 43, pp. 1–16). Reston, VA: National Business Education Association.

International Society for Business Education (SIEC-ISBE). (2012). Societé Internationale pour l'Enseignement Commercial–International Society for Business Education. Retrieved from http://ww.siec-isbe.org

Killion, J., & Hirsh, S. (2011). The elements of effective teaching: Professional learning moves vision, framework, and performance standards into action. *Journal of Staff Development, 32*(6), 10–16.

Lohman, M. C., & Woolf, N. H. (2001). Self-initiated learning activities of experienced public school teachers: Methods, sources, and relevant organizational influences. *Teachers and Teaching: Theory and Practice, 7*(1), 59–74.

McKool, S. S., & Gespass, S. (2009). Does Johnny's reading teacher love to read? How teachers' personal reading habits affect instructional practices. *Literacy Research & Instruction, 48*(3), 264. doi:10.1080/19388070802443700

Moore, K. M. (2011). *Effective instructional strategies: From theory to practice* (3rd ed.). Los Angeles, CA: Sage.

National Association for Business Teacher Education. (2012). National Association for Business Teacher Education. Retrieved from http://www.nabte.org

National Board for Professional Teaching Standards (2012). State and local information. Retrieved from http://www.nbpts.org/state-local-information

National Business Education Association (NBEA). (2012). NBEAonline. Retrieved from http://www.nbea.org

Pi Omega Pi. (2012). Pi Omega Pi. Retrieved from http://www.piomegapi.org

Policies Commission for Business and Economic Education (2006). Policy statement 79: This we believe about the value of professional associations. Retrieved from http://www.nbea.org/newsite/curriculum/policy/no_79.pdf

Policies Commission for Business and Economic Education (2010). Policy Statement 87: This we believe about virtual professional development. Retrieved from http://www.nbea.org/newsite/curriculum/documents/PCBEEStatement87_000.pdf

Schmoker, M. (2002) Up and away. *Journal of the National Staff Development Council, 23*(4), 10–13.

Scott, J. C. (2008). Lifelong professional development. In M. H. Rader (Ed.), *Effective methods of teaching business education in the 21st century: NBEA 2008 yearbook* (No. 43, pp. 278–289). Reston, VA: National Business Education Association.

Shumack, K. A., & Forde, C. M. (2012). Professional association members: Extending the community of practice. In W. Stitte-Godhes (Ed.), *Trends & issues in business education: NBEA 2012 yearbook* (No. 50, pp. 174–187). Reston, VA: National Business Education Association.

Trust, T. (2012). Professional learning networks designed for teacher learning. *Journal of Digital Learning in Teacher Education, 28*(4), 133–138.

Warlick, D. (2009). Grow your personal learning network. *Learning and Leading, 36*(6), 12–16.

Werner, P. (2002). Teaching and avocations: An idle mind is the devil's workshop revisited. *Clearing House, 75*(4), 209–211.